Learning by Going: Transformative Learning through Long-term Independent Travel

Birgit Phillips

Learning by Going: Transformative Learning through Long-term Independent Travel

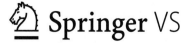

Birgit Phillips
Graz, Austria

Printed with the support of the Austrian Research Association.

This work received the Patricia Cranton Distinguished Dissertation Award for Outstanding Contribution to a Living Theory of Transformative Learning, presented at the XIII Transformative Learning Conference (2018) at Columbia University, New York.

ISBN 978-3-658-25772-9   ISBN 978-3-658-25773-6 (eBook)
https://doi.org/10.1007/978-3-658-25773-6

Library of Congress Control Number: 2019935539

Springer VS
© Springer Fachmedien Wiesbaden GmbH, part of Springer Nature 2019
This work is subject to copyright. All rights are reserved by the Publisher, whether the whole or part of the material is concerned, specifically the rights of translation, reprinting, reuse of illustrations, recitation, broadcasting, reproduction on microfilms or in any other physical way, and transmission or information storage and retrieval, electronic adaptation, computer software, or by similar or dissimilar methodology now known or hereafter developed.
The use of general descriptive names, registered names, trademarks, service marks, etc. in this publication does not imply, even in the absence of a specific statement, that such names are exempt from the relevant protective laws and regulations and therefore free for general use.
The publisher, the authors and the editors are safe to assume that the advice and information in this book are believed to be true and accurate at the date of publication. Neither the publisher nor the authors or the editors give a warranty, express or implied, with respect to the material contained herein or for any errors or omissions that may have been made. The publisher remains neutral with regard to jurisdictional claims in published maps and institutional affiliations.

This Springer VS imprint is published by the registered company Springer Fachmedien Wiesbaden GmbH part of Springer Nature
The registered company address is: Abraham-Lincoln-Str. 46, 65189 Wiesbaden, Germany

Acknowledgements

This book is the culmination of a long and challenging journey that started more than a decade ago. I would like to thank a number of people who guided me along the way and helped me complete this thesis successfully.

I would first like to thank my professors and colleagues in the Lifelong Learning Doctoral Program for their support and constructive ideas and suggestions that enhanced my scholarship. Most of all, I would like to express my gratitude to my supervisors, Prof. Lenz and Prof. Baumgartner, for their advice and guidance, as well as their patience throughout this long process.

I would also like to express my gratitude to my friends and family for their support and encouragement. To my adorable children, Mayalin and Sammy, for bringing joy and happiness to every day of my life, and to my husband Mike for standing by me through every step of this journey.

Finally, I owe a deep debt of gratitude to all of the travelers who gave so generously of their time and shared their many stories with me, which have been both an education and a continuing inspiration for me. I wish you all continued happy travels!

Table of Contents

1 **Setting the Scene** 1
    1.1 Introduction 1
    1.2 Guiding research questions 2
    1.3 Rationale for the study 2
    1.4 Situating the researcher 6
    1.5 Research approach 8
    1.6 Organization of the thesis 10

2 **Identity, Self and Transformation** 13
    2.1 Conceptualizing identity and self 13
    2.2 Identity in a postmodern context 15
    2.3 The narrative construction of self 20
    2.4 Transformation and learning 23
    2.5 Long-term independent travel as a form of lifelong learning 37
    2.6 Summary 41

3 **The Evolution of Long-term Independent Travel** 43
    3.1 A brief sketch of independent travel from ancient times to the late 20th century 43
    3.2 From drifters to flashpackers 47
    3.3 Introducing LITs 61
    3.4 Summary 66

4 **Transformative Travel** 67
    4.1 Before travel: Motivational dimensions 71
    4.2 During travel: Cross-cultural learning 87
    4.3 After travel: Reentry 95
    4.4 Summary 104

5 **Methodology** 105
    5.1 The research paradigm: An interpretive approach 105
    5.2 Data collection methods 109
    5.3 Participant demographics 121
    5.4 Interpreting the empirical data 126
    5.5 Validating the accuracy of findings 128
    5.6 Summary 130

6 **Findings** 131

7 **Reaching the Tipping Point** 133

7.1	Seed experiences	136
7.2	Lifestyle dissonance	141
7.3	Trigger experiences	148
7.4	Final obstacles – Preparing for the unexpected	156
7.5	Anticipated rewards	161
7.6	Summary	167

8 Experiences on the Road ... 169

8.1	Encounters with nature	170
8.2	Encounters with the self	179
8.3	Encounters with local cultures	191
8.4	Encounters with the traveler culture	226
8.5	Outcomes	266

9 Post-travel Experiences and Learning Outcomes ... 275

9.1	Pre-return expectations	275
9.2	Smooth sailing and the honeymoon phase	281
9.3	Facing the friends and family	284
9.4	Cultural value dissonance	310
9.5	From theory into practice	315
9.6	Striking a proper work-life balance	318

10 Final Learning Outcomes ... 327

10.1	Cultural and personal meaning-making	327
10.2	Who am I?	331
10.3	Communication Skills	333
10.4	On stories and storytellers	338
10.5	Summary of LITs' (transformative) learning outcomes	340

11 Conclusion ... 341

11.1	Answering research questions	341
11.2	Theoretical implications	345
11.3	Critical evaluation and future research directions	354
11.4	Practical implications	357

References ... 361

Appendices ... 385

List of Tables and Figures

List of Tables

Table 1. Phases of transformative learning 29
Table 2. Systems Theory of Intercultural Reentry 103
Table 3. Interviews and Questionnaires 121
Table 4. LIT's educational background... 123
Table 5. LIT's Key Characteristics.. 124

List of Figures

Figure 1. U-Curve: Adjustment to a new culture over time 89
Figure 2. W-Cure: Stages of transition shock 96
Figure 3: 1st round LITs' nationalities... 121
Figure 4: 2nd round LITs' Nationalities... 122
Figure 5: The transformative learning process in long-term independent travel.......... 132
Figure 6: Reaching the tipping point... 135

Abstract

In the last twenty years, academic interest in long-term independent travel has been on the rise. However, most researchers have focused primarily on motivations and travel behaviors, with little attention paid to the post-travel experience and long-term effects on traveler values and identities. In terms of the effects of the travel experience on the travelers themselves, this is a significant oversight, as it is the return to their home cultures which compels travelers to truly process the lessons they have learned on the road and figure out how to integrate these new ideas into their lives. Therefore, this paper is an attempt to fill this research gap by exploring the complete travel experience, from initial motivations all the way to post-travel reintegration and the long-term effects on the travelers' values and behaviors. Thus, the goal of this paper was to explore the potential of long-term independent travel to foster transformative learning and personal growth.

To this end, the overall travel experience was divided into three phases—pre-travel motivations, experiences on the road, and the post-travel phase, including a period up to thirteen years after the actual travel experience. For each phase, both the learning mechanisms and outcomes were investigated in an effort to identify typical patterns and themes both within and across the three phases. The paper is grounded in transformative learning theory, which focuses on how life experiences lead to significant changes in an individual's meaning structures, perspectives, and, ultimately, identity. It also draws on various theoretical perspectives on intercultural learning and adaptation. Furthermore, the paper is situated in the narrative identity paradigm, which conceptualizes identities as continuously evolving narratives into which individuals integrate new experiences with an ultimate goal of creating and maintaining a coherent sense of self.

In line with the focus on narrative, the travelers' own stories were deemed the most appropriate access point into the travelers' experiences and shifting meaning schemes. Therefore, empirical data was gathered primarily via two rounds of semi-structured interviews with travelers who had a minimum of six months of independent travel experience. In this context, "independent" was defined as moving from one location to the next with little or no fixed or pre-determined itinerary. The first round of interviews included 41 subjects, while the second round, which took place 6 to 13 years after the first interview, consisted of 23 follow-up interviews or tailored questionnaires. In addition, these interviews were supplemented by email correspondence, travel blog and social media research and several years of participant observation, which enabled the incorporation of autoethnographic research elements as well.

The results show that the complete process of long-term independent travel is replete with learning opportunities which have a powerful and enduring effect on those who engage in this form of travel. Through meaningful interaction with other cultures, travelers learn important lessons about themselves, their cultures, and the world as a whole that lead to dramatic alterations in personal value systems and identity constructs. In particular, the data indicates significant enhancements in critical thinking, self-awareness, self-efficacy, and adaptability. In addition, by expanding perspectives, long-term independent travelers seem to develop increased open-mindedness, empathy, tolerance and overall intercultural and interpersonal communication skills.

1 Setting the Scene

1.1 Introduction

Why do some people decide to leave everything behind, sacrifice long-term relationships and potential or established careers, in order to travel the world? And what are the outcomes – if any – of such a break, other than a "gaping hole" on the CV? The goal of this thesis is to explore the notion of transformative travel and shed light on the perceived identity transformations long-term independent travelers attribute to their travel experiences. More and more people today are engaging in long-term independent travel and seeing it as a vehicle for learning, self-discovery, self-awareness and an increased sense of self-determination (Goeldner & Ritchie, 2009; Hirschorn & Hefferon, 2013; McNamara & Prideaux, 2010). Long-term travel brings people into contact with new cultures and value systems and forces them to use their own resources to manage such situations. This often spurs travelers to question perspectives and values that they had previously taken for granted, which can in turn lead to transformed frames of reference or meaning perspectives. For many people, long-term travel represents a disruptive life event that fundamentally shifts perspectives and alters values, attitudes, behaviors and even life goals.

Despite the significant body of research on tourist motivations, modes of travel and cross-cultural encounters and an increasing prevalence of this type of travel, there is a remarkable gap in empirical research examining the transformative potential of long-term, independent travel. The present study helps close this gap by examining the elements and mechanisms that contribute to transformations and how identities evolve over time. In doing so, a strong emphasis is placed on the process of returning to one's native culture. This phase is crucial in identity renegotiation, as new values and perspectives are confronted with those that were characteristic before the travel experience. This thesis offers a broader philosophical understanding of the complex socio-cultural and individual processes involved in this identity negotiation by deploying a pluralistic, reflexive, interpretive research approach that foregrounds the personal lived experiences of the individual study participants and the meanings they attach to their travel experiences. Informed by personal field research and a review of relevant literature, this study analyzes travel narratives gathered through a series of recorded interviews.

© Springer Fachmedien Wiesbaden GmbH, part of Springer Nature 2019
B. Phillips, *Learning by Going: Transformative Learning through Long-term Independent Travel*, https://doi.org/10.1007/978-3-658-25773-6_1

1.2 Guiding research questions

This dissertation argues that long-term independent travel provides many opportunities for learning by placing travelers in situations that strongly challenge their attitudes, values and beliefs about both themselves and the world, which can result in a perspective transformation. The thesis explores the ways travelers construct meaning from significant experiences and how this process in turn helps shape their identities. To this end, the main research question is:

How does long-term independent travel transform the values and identities of travelers?

Thus, the study explores the ways in which long-term independent travel transforms consciousness and affects an individual's identity. It is specifically concerned with personal growth as an outcome of the long-term travel experience. A secondary goal of this thesis is to consider the long-term effects of travel on important life decisions. To this end, relevant sub-questions are:

- What are the critical motivating factors for extended travel?
- What different forms do (transformative) learning experiences take?
- How do long-term independent travel experiences influence travelers' values, lifestyles or life choices over the long term?

These questions are essential for understanding the complexity of long-term travelers' experiences and the meanings they assign to them, as they help situate these experiences within the broader socio-cultural context of the individuals' lives.

1.3 Rationale for the study

Broadly speaking, there are three primary rationales for this study: the growing interest in issues of the self in contemporary Western society, the importance of fostering awareness of one's own socio-cultural programming, and the need to explore these issues using new and innovative research paradigms. The following paragraphs explain these three aspects in greater detail.

Once considered too "unproblematic to be thematized" (Taylor, 1994a), issues of the *self* have permeated our late modern world in the 21st century. Globalization and the spread of free-market capitalism, coupled with increased global mobility, emerging technologies and the evolution of the post-industrial workforce have brought about profound changes in the

1.3 Rationale for the study

world order. These changes have altered traditional relations between people and places and transformed social hierarchies. This has brought a fluidity to self-identity, which is constantly being re-negotiated. The last few decades have thus seen an explosion of interest in issues of the self and identity.

For many people in affluent Western countries, the vast number of opportunities in today's world, coupled with unprecedented uncertainties about the future, can be simply overwhelming. Especially for young people facing a highly competitive marketplace, pressure to make decisions that have lasting ramifications on the rest of their lives can be unsettling. To meet this challenge, people have the capacity to engage in critical self-reflection, whereby they can evaluate the pros and cons of a decision in terms of its relationship to their beliefs and values and then take appropriate actions. Theoretically, the goal of educational systems should be to prepare people to deploy this skill in order to thrive in the changed world order of the 21st century.

However, by emphasizing rote learning and memorizing facts for short-term regurgitation, traditional education institutions often fail to equip people with the necessary skills to ask the right questions, reflect critically and question long-held assumptions (Hepner, 2015). In 2014, the International Association for the Evaluation of Educational Achievement (IEA) conducted a study of 8th-graders' computer literacy primarily in industrialized countries. Although 83% had basic computer knowledge, only 2% of the students were able to solve higher order tasks that required critical thinking when searching for information online. The tendency to neglect higher-order thinking in education seems to continue all the way through the tertiary level. Even though higher-order thinking is often included in university mission statements as a primary goal, the reality is quite different. This gap between real and idealized education goals is confirmed by former Harvard University President Derek Bok (2006) who maintained that, although various "nationwide polls have found that more than 90 percent of faculty members in the United States consider [critical thinking] the most important purpose of undergraduate education" (pp. 67-68), "many students graduate college today without being able to write well enough to satisfy their employers, reason clearly or perform competently in analyzing complex, non-technical problems" (p.3, cf. Hepner, 2015, p. 69). It seems that there is a need for alternative ways to fill this gap in traditional education.

While young people are more educated than ever, fewer people find well-paid jobs. Entry level jobs have been outsourced abroad, short-term work has replaced long-term careers, and unpaid internships have become the new entry-level positions (Jay, 2012). In light of these developments, it is hardly surprising that people are becoming increasingly dissatisfied with traditional life concepts and are seeking out alternative experiences.

Long-term independent travel is one such alternative trajectory that provides opportunities to imagine different versions of the self and engage in identity work. The link between travel and education is well-established (DeBotton, 2002) but until recently few academic studies have explored the factors that lead to transformation (Ross, 2010). Travel places people outside of their comfort zones by confronting them with aspects of the world and themselves that were previously beyond their consciousness. Travel experiences provide opportunities for travelers to engage in the critical questioning of long-held beliefs and assumptions, which may ultimately lead to transformed frames of reference and worldviews (Ross, 2010). As Pearce and Foster (2006) maintain, there is an implicit "University of Travel" that offers particular learning opportunities that formal educational institutions cannot provide.

While not all travel is transformative, this thesis is guided by the assumption that travel is rife with opportunities for self-reflection, personal growth and self-transformation. Transformations resulting from travel are sometimes taken for granted or assumed, and we tend to feel they require little or no explanation. However, the transformative processes involved in the context of contemporary long-term independent travel are far more complex and go beyond the physical travel experience. Traveling can be a catalyst for learning in that it can reveal to people how their socio-cultural contexts have shaped and constrained their perceptions of themselves and the world and then help them see beyond their ethnocentric biases.

These links between travel, self-transformation and personal growth are not new in academic scholarship or in popular fiction. In the latter, stories abound of people who embark on a journey to find themselves by leaving behind the familiar and entering the unknown. Likewise, a number of researchers from various disciplines (e.g. tourism studies, education, psychology, management studies) have investigated the connections between the self and travel. In his seminal work *The Tourist*, MacCannell (1976) argued that "self-discovery through a complex and sometimes arduous search for an Absolute Other is a basic theme of our civilization", which explains the enormous body of literature on the topic throughout history (p.5).

Although the transformative potential of travel has been discussed in academic scholarship, some critics have argued that most research is a "top-down" misinterpretation of tourist experiences, perhaps due to a lack of empirical research on what travel actually

1.3 Rationale for the study

means to the travelers (Desforges, 2000). In addition, researchers have tended to focus on isolated aspects, such as motivations, types of travelers, risk taking, host/guest relationships, planning, and destination choice, rather than pursuing a more holistic approach. Moreover, much of the research on the transformative potential of travel has focused rather exclusively on the journey itself, thereby excluding important aspects of the transformation that take place either before or after the journey. Such an approach, however, is rather narrow in scope, as it is limited by the temporal and spatial boundaries of the actual journey and fails to consider the dynamic nature of transformation and how it might evolve over time.

In contrast, this thesis attempts to consider more pluralistic epistemologies by examining the wider implications and contextual factors of transformative travel experiences. In order to gain a deeper understanding of the perceived self-transformations travelers undergo as a result of extended independent travel, this study examines how experiences and/or transformations that occur before embarking upon extended travel have some direct or indirect bearing on the actual travel experience, and how transformations triggered by physical travel develop over time and are affected by changing life situations after the travel experience. Although I argue that transformation is contingent on leaving the comfort zone, the "inward" transformational journey is perceived as an ongoing "story" of the self (Giddens, 1991) that includes the periods *before*, *during* and *after* the actual travel experience. By focusing on the entire trajectory, I explore both the factors that contribute to the transformation and the long-term outcomes.

This approach constitutes a holistic exploration of potential self-transformations through extended travel and answers the call to deploy more interpretive approaches in order to foreground the travelers' voices (Hampton, 2010; Urry, 2007) and to conduct more longitudinal studies (Hampton, 2010; Pearce & Foster, 2007; Richards & Wilson, 2004a; Ritchie, 2005). Cohen (2005), for example, called for more emic and reflexive approaches to studying travelers, which are "concerned with the manner in which they themselves construct, represent, and narrate their experiences" (p. 57). Moreover, this thesis positions long-term independent travel within the educational perspective of transformative learning and theories on cross-cultural transitions, including the culture shock/reverse culture shock framework. This paper draws upon Mezirow's theory of transformational learning (1981, 1990, 1991, 1994, 1998, 2000, 2012) to examine how travel experiences can contribute to learning about the self and others, personal growth and development, attitudes, values, worldviews and perspectives on life. By emphasizing the return phase as one of the most critical phases of the journey, this thesis also makes an important contribution to post-travel literature.

A qualitative, interpretative and emic research approach that emphasizes rich, descriptive data was deemed most appropriate for exploring how long-term travelers' perspectives change over time. Taking an emic approach involves finding out from the research participants "how they see the word, how they look at the setting, the other people in it and the value of their experiences" (Pearce, 2005, p. 3). In contrast to a positivistic research paradigm, which is normative in its nature and claims to reveal objective facts, qualitative, interpretive research does not focus on the presentation of an "objective" meaning. In fact, the interpretive paradigm is more suited to the post-constructivist position, which essentially denies the existence of an "objective" reality (see further details in section 5.1 of the methodology chapter).

Drawing on participant observation and empirical research material from interviews conducted in Latin America, Europe and India, this paper deploys a longitudinal approach to explore how transformation occurs over time. In addition, the majority of the research participants in this study traveled in parts of the world that are less frequented by backpackers, which sets this study apart from the majority of research conducted in typical backpacker enclaves in Australasia. Furthermore, unlike some other studies, which include various forms of intercultural experience (e.g. migration, volunteer travel, studying and working abroad), this study focuses exclusively on travelers whose main goal for their stay abroad was traveling (even if interrupted by short spans of work), as independent traveling provides travelers with different opportunities to leave their comfort zones than other forms of physical mobility.

Finally, it is important to note that, due to the interpretive nature of this research, it does not seek to develop definitions or typologies, or to uncover definitive truths relating to the transformation experienced by travelers. Instead, with a rich pool of data, the aim of the research is to focus on the travelers' descriptive accounts of their lived experiences and the meanings they attach to them and to highlight the complexity of the transformational processes at work.

1.4 Situating the researcher

As any research process is inherently influenced by the researcher's personal history, it is vital to acknowledge that "the personal-self becomes inseparable from the researcher-

1.4 Situating the researcher

self" (Creswell, 2003, p. 182). In fact, an increasing number of scholars are calling for greater levels of research transparency, with "researchers being more open about their personal biography and their experiences in the field" (Phillimore, 2004, p. 186), in order to clarify how the researcher's personal history may have influenced the research. For the researcher, this means developing a reflexive awareness of one's own identity and subjective position within the research project and making prior knowledge clear when examining the role of the researcher. For this reason, I would like to situate myself as a researcher within this project by discussing my motivations for embarking on this academic journey.

My fascination with "off-the-beaten-path" travel was sparked at an early age by my father. A banker by trade, but a hippy at heart, my father dragged the family all over Europe and northern Africa in a classic VW camper van for weeks at a time during our summer vacations. I can still remember the excitement of piling into that van in the wee hours of the morning and "hitting the road", wondering what adventures lay in store.

In our travels, I was always struck by how different the "world out there" was: the Mediterranean houses with "missing" roofs, Arab men wearing long dresses, holding hands and sporting long fingernails, the different ways people interacted with each other, and the different lifestyles in general. Although I reveled in these exotic experiences, these travels in the early to mid-80s were often fraught with adversity, including various illnesses contracted along the way, being robbed on more than one occasion, and even having a car crash in the middle of the Sahara desert, to name but a few. However, for a kid, this was all just part of the excitement, and it made for good stories when I returned back home.

When I returned home, I always had a new appreciation for the comfortable living standards in my small Austrian village and my middle class family. I was often happy to return home on some level, but even at that age, I already felt a sense of being different from my peers. The majority of my classmates had barely ventured beyond a 150 km radius, let alone left the country, and they could barely even conceive of the things I wanted to tell them about. As I got a bit older, I began to understand the signs of clashing worldviews among my peers and my parents' wider circle of friends and family. My father, while admired by some, was criticized and viewed with disdain by others, who thought his values were somehow "off" because he preferred to accumulate experiences rather than the traditional material trappings of a "successful" Austrian family man.

As soon as I was old enough, I started traveling on my own, which was a completely different experience. On my extended backpacking sojourns, I often left my comfort zone. I experienced situations for which my education had definitely *not* prepared me, and I often felt extremely vulnerable or even afraid about what might happen next. But I persevered, and in time I began to enjoy the feeling of not being 100% in control. I learned to let go of some of my pre-conditioned ways of thinking and enjoy the infinite differences between cultures. Furthermore, I learned to trust in myself and my instincts, and this gave me a new feeling of freedom and the confidence to push my personal boundaries and do things I never would have thought possible before I went traveling (e.g. hitchhiking 3,000 kilometers, sleeping in caves, diving with sharks, climbing a 6,000-meter mountain). All of these travel experiences have had a profound effect on my views about myself and the world in which I live.

In time, I found that I felt a greater feeling of discomfort not when I went to an unfamiliar place, but rather when I came back to my "familiar" home, which suddenly didn't seem so familiar anymore. I noticed that the longer I was away, the harder it was to "pick up where I left off" and get back to meeting the expectations imposed upon me by Austrian society (e.g. studying, working, starting a family, pursuing a career). I felt that while I had returned physically from my travels, emotionally I was still elsewhere, and traditional boundaries of home and away started to blur. I discovered that the lessons of travel were often most deeply learned and experienced when I returned home. The confrontation with my "old normal" sparked my awareness of the ways in which my travels had changed my values about so many aspects of life, including my professional and personal aspirations. Over the years, conversations and correspondence with fellow travelers confirmed my feeling that the returning stage of an extended travel experience is as vital, if not more vital, than the travel experience itself in terms of the transformative potential of travel, which is why I eventually decided to extend my research to embrace this stage, as explained in the next section.

1.5 Research approach

While living the lifestyle one is researching can bring valuable insight, it also presents a challenge in developing an appropriate research approach. In this paper, I have adopted some elements of autoethnography, in which researchers include some of their own experiences in their analysis (Ellis & Bochner, 2000; Denzin & Lincoln, 2005), as I feel that there is something important to be gained by incorporating aspects of the autoethnographic "mentality" into this project. In its extreme form, autoethnographic researchers

1.5 Research approach

place themselves and their experience at the *center* of their research (Denzin & Lincoln, 2005; Ellis & Bochner, 2000). While this is not the intention of the present study, it would be disingenuous to pretend that my personal experiences have not shaped this work. Clearly, this is not Levi-Strauss traveling to South America to study the indigenous myths of a foreign culture (Levi-Strauss, 1990). In my case, experience with the object of study (i.e. long-term independent traveler culture) actually preceded the intention to study that culture. And whereas Levi-Strauss never personally experienced the acculturation involved in growing up in a culture informed by the myths he studied, long-term independent travel very much affected the development of my own personal worldview long before I decided to investigate the process as a researcher.

In fact, as mentioned above, the research idea and design evolved gradually over the course of several years spent traveling in Latin America, during which time I was both conducting field research for this project and living the long-term traveler lifestyle, and then returning to my native culture and attempting to readjust to life within it. It is my belief that this experience has contributed greatly to the depth and insight of my research. As Jackson (1989) has argued, "our understanding of others can only proceed from within our own experience, and this experience involves our personalities and histories as much as our field research" (p. 17). Thus, I will attempt to show how my own experiences compare and contrast with those of my research participants to produce a more complete picture of the complexities of the topic at hand.

While I believe the researcher experience can contribute to the quality of the project's outcome, there is also clearly a danger of allowing one's own bias or personal views to monopolize the project. O'Reilly (2006) has asserted that it is not possible to start out without preconceived ideas and values. For example, as a person who has spent a significant portion of her life traveling, I have certainly felt the temptation to justify this time by emphasizing the potential benefits of this lifestyle. To combat these tendencies, personal values, biases and interests need to be identified explicitly, together with an evaluation of how one's personal biographical perspective shapes the relationships with research participants, the interpretation of the research data, and the form in which the research is presented (Elliott, 2005, p.155). As an example, the aforementioned tendency to rationalize and perhaps overvalue the traveler lifestyle is one of the themes I discuss in this paper: namely, that travelers, like most human beings, are prone to the dubious practice of using othering to re-affirm their own values and identities (as discussed in section 3.2.3).

In fact, to ensure that this paper did not become an autobiography or a political tract, I have made a conscious effort to observe, interview and interpret reports from many different types of long-term travelers. This practice helped me to adopt the "role of researcher as stranger and thus [to see] the familiar as strange" (Holliday, 2002, p. 93), thereby challenging or counter-balancing the meanings I might have personally assigned to certain experiences. It was highly valuable when an interviewee described a negative reaction to an experience that I myself may have found to be a positive experience. Such researcher experiences have helped me to see beyond my personal values by highlighting my own assumptions and providing me a deeper insight into the complex and multifaceted nature of human experience, as well as providing space for new themes to emerge in the course of the research. Thus, although my own experiences helped provide a starting point for the research, I have actively pursued and incorporated different voices and viewpoints in an attempt to present a well-rounded picture of the possible transformations that may result from long-term, independent travel.

1.6 Organization of the thesis

This thesis is organized in 10 chapters. This first chapter has provided a brief academic and personal context for this thesis and highlighted the gaps in academic scholarship in the area of transformation and travel. In addition to providing a rationale for a study on travel and transformation, this chapter also provided a glimpse into the research paradigm and the research questions that have guided this study.

To provide a theoretical framework for this thesis, the second chapter explores notions of self and identity and links them to transformative learning. First, the chapter defines the terms identity and self as they are understood in this thesis and puts them in the context of contemporary society. As this paper places traveler narratives at the center of the research, a particular focus is placed on the construction of narrative identity. The chapter then turns to Mezirow's transformative learning theory, with a particular emphasis on the notions of a disorienting dilemma and critical reflection for a perspective change. Finally, the chapter situates the present research in the context of the lifelong learning paradigm and highlights a few key controversial issues in this field for which this paper will provide some useful arguments.

Chapter three describes the subjects of the present research—long-term independent travelers. The chapter begins with a brief historical overview of different concepts of long-term independent travel and then focuses on contemporary travel and, in particular, backpacker culture, which is similar in many ways to the long-term independent travelers in this study. The chapter then critically examines the traditional tourist/traveler divide as an important aspect of the self-concept of long-term travelers before defining the term "long-term independent traveler" as used in this work.

Chapter four examines existing research and theory on the process of transformative travel, breaking it down into the three key stages of the pre-travel phase, the actual travel experience, and post-travel re-integration. For the pre-travel phase, the chapter provides an overview of the tourist motivation literature relevant to this research. Regarding the travel experience itself, I then offer some insight into cross-cultural learning theories and explore the work on culture shock and cross-cultural transition theories. Finally, the discussion of the post-travel phase examines literature on the reentry process and the factors that affect readjustment to one's home culture or to post-travel life.

Chapter five details the methodology used in this study. The chapter first describes the research paradigm and strategies deployed and outlines the data collection methods (field research, life-world interviews, questionnaires, email correspondence, and textual analysis of blogs and other forms of social media). The chapter then provides the demographic profile of the study participants and finally highlights the process of data analysis and validation.

Chapters six to nine discuss the research findings. Chapter six looks at traveler motivations in the pre-travel phase, breaking them down into three categories of seed experiences, lifestyle dissonance and trigger events. It then examines the final obstacles, both internal and external, that travelers must overcome and concludes with an explanation of the travelers' anticipated rewards.

Chapter seven elucidates the experiences on the road. It is oriented around disorienting experiences springing from four primary sources: encounters with nature, encounters with the self, encounters with local cultures, and encounters with the traveler culture. A final section summarizes the learning outcomes of the actual travel experience.

Chapter eight examines the post-travel re-integration process. The chapter starts by highlighting pre-return expectations. After describing the initial reentry stage, the chapter then explores the value differences travelers face in their native cultures and the wide variety of strategies and techniques they deploy to create a meaningful fulfilling post-travel existence by fostering new or enhanced relationships striking a proper work-life balance.

Chapter nine, the final chapter in the results section, outlines the final outcomes of the overall long-term independent travel experience, with a particular focus on the meanings, identities and competences developed by travelers through the transformative learning process.

By way of a conclusion, chapter ten first answers the research questions and then highlights the main theoretical implications of the present research. This is followed by a critical evaluation of the research, which also highlights some potential avenues for future research. Finally, the paper concludes by addressing the debates surrounding lifelong learning with regard to long-term independent travel and then offering some thoughts on the potential practical benefits of this form of learning through travel for the individual, the community and the global society as a whole.

2 Identity, Self and Transformation

The "postmodern" complexity of social life has given rise to a burgeoning interest in issues of self and identity in many disciplines, including psychology, sociology, anthropology, philosophy, and cultural studies (Ashmore & Jussim, 1997; Côté & Levine, 2002; Leary & Tangney, 2012; Oyserman, Elmore, Smith, 2012). While it would far exceed the scope of this research to decipher the multiple concepts of self and identity found in the various disciplines, the following section will provide a theoretical context for the discussion of the transformation of self in long-term independent travelers within this thesis. In addition, this chapter highlights the importance of narrative in the construction of identity for long-term independent travelers. Finally, in order to provide a theoretical framework for the current investigation into how people make sense of their experiences, thoughts, feelings and behaviors in relation to their travels and integrate them into their sense of self, this section will introduce Mezirow's transformative learning theory.

2.1 Conceptualizing identity and self

Discussions of the self have been traced all the way back to Plato (c. 428-347 BC) and essentially revolve around the fundamental human questions of "Who am I and how do I fit into this world?" To answer these questions, philosophers have grappled with the essential tension between the concepts of human autonomy/agency vs. external control by various forces (e.g. god(s), society, biology). While certainly not the first philosopher to explore this issue, William James (1890) was perhaps the first to highlight the importance of the self for understanding human behavior (Leary & Tangney, 2012). James adopted linguistic terminology to highlight the tension between agency and social control when he distinguished between the self as subject ("I") and the self as object ("me"). The self as subject is also called the "self as knower" (I) and is responsible for self-awareness and self-knowledge, which differs from the self as object, or the "self as known" (me). However, James argued that these were two deeply intertwined aspects of the self which were both heavily influenced by social interactions. In this way, James was an early proponent for using the concept of "self" to examine and understand human behavior (Leary & Tangney, 2012).

James's ideas were picked up and expanded many years later by the developmental psychologist Erik Erikson, who has been credited with being the first to emphasize the concept of identity development and the related link between self and society in some of his famous works, such as *Identity and the Life Cycle* (1959), *Childhood and Society* (1963), *Identity: Youth and Crises* (1968) and *The Life Cycle Completed* (1982). Rooted in a highly interdisciplinary approach, Erikson's broad conceptualization of identity development remains highly influential and relevant today and has been further advanced and revised by numerous neo-Eriksonian theorists (e.g. Marcia, 1966, 1980; McLean & Syed 2016; Schwarz, 2001; Syed, 2012). While a complete discussion of Erikson's theory of identity is beyond the scope of this thesis, I will highlight the aspects that are relevant for this thesis.

Erikson conceptualized identity development as a life-long process, with the ultimate goal of achieving *ego identity*. This means figuring out who you are and how you fit in with the rest of the world. Thus, the individual must develop a unified self-image that features coherent values and beliefs that the person finds meaningful. An important corollary thereby is that these values and beliefs must be in harmony with the various roles one is called on to play in society. Here, Erikson stressed that an individual's psychology cannot be understood separately from his or her social context, as the identity structure is constructed via a continuous interaction between individual and environment.

The word "continuous" here emphasizes that the individual must struggle to maintain a sense of sameness and continuity across time. To this end, Erikson (1963) constructed a model that consisted of eight developmental stages that a healthy individual should pass through between birth and adulthood. While a detailed look at these eight stages is beyond the scope of this discussion, it is important to mention Erikson's concept of an "identity crisis". This term describes a period when the individual's previous identity is no longer perceived as suitable, but a new identity has not yet been established. While such crises can occur during any transition between stages, Erikson focused on adolescence, a crucial stage in the development of adult identity which is often accompanied by instability and confusion about important life choices. Erikson (1968) argued that experiencing an identity crisis at this stage is a normal part of the transition between childhood and adulthood that can potentially serve as "a turning point, a crucial period of increased vulnerability and heightened potential" (Erikson, 1968, p. 96).

As part of resolving this crisis, Erikson (1980) introduced another term that is relevant for the present discussion: the *psychosocial moratorium*. The main idea of a psychological moratorium is that life is suspended, and the individual has the freedom to experiment with different roles in an effort to answer the key questions "Who am I?" and "What is my place in this world?" Erikson posited that psychological moratoria can take the form of travel, service (military or voluntary), schooling or simply "dropping out" for a while (Erikson, 1968, p. 157). In the context of the present paper, it is interesting to point out that Erikson himself spent some time right after his high school graduation wandering around Europe, sleeping under bridges and occasionally working as an artist, a period which he considered a valuable delay of adult commitments that allowed time for identity exploration (Boeree, 1997). Thus, it is clear that Erikson recognized the potential value of travel for furthering identity formation.

Ultimately, for Erikson, the degree to which an individual successfully resolves identity crises determines whether or not a person will effectively complete one developmental stage and then transition into the next stage. Success, according to Erikson (1968), leads to "identity synthesis", in which the individual achieves coherence between values, beliefs and social roles, while failure can lead to "identity confusion", which involves a feeling of dissonance between these crucial aspects of identity. Indeed, various researchers, inspired by Erikson's work, have shown a link between a clear and coherent sense of identity and an increased positive self-image, stable and enjoyable relationships, confidence and decision-making ability, as well as reduced psychological distress and engagement in destructive behavior towards oneself and others (Beyers & Seiffge-Krenke, 2010; Luyckx, Goosens & Soenens, Beyers, Vansteenkiste, 2005; Luyckx & Zamboanga, 2012; Schwartz, 2007; Schwarz et al. 2011).

While many researchers have demonstrated the continued applicability of Erikson's concepts, others have pointed out the need to adapt this model to account for important changes that have occurred in the postmodern era. Since these changes have clear relevance for the topic of contemporary long-term travel, it is important to examine these further. To this end, the following sections will explore some of the main characteristics that have been ascribed to the postmodern world order and their effect on concepts of identity, in particular.

2.2 Identity in a postmodern context

While scholars have continued to embrace Erikson's key concepts related to identity development (i.e. the importance of social context, the catalyst of identity crises, and the potential function of a moratorium), some scholars have suggested that his theories need to be adapted if they are to be relevant for the postmodern era. In particular, they have called into question two key aspects of Erikson's work: the timeline that he assigned to the identity formation process and the presumed goal of the process. These two important criticisms are discussed in the following sections.

2.2.1 The changing timetable of identity development

In terms of Erikson's timeline for identity development, he argued that a coherent identity is supposed to unfold epigenetically, according to and from within an innate timetable (Schachter, 2005b, p. 379). According to his model, an individual's final identity is "fixed at the end of adolescence" (Erikson, 1968, p. 161). In other words, once young adults have successfully mastered the adolescent identity crisis and given up earlier identifications, they achieve a sense of stable and coherent identity.

Many theorists (e.g. Kroger, 2007; Loevinger, 1996; Kegan, 1994) have criticized this focus on adolescence and early adulthood. Their criticisms stem largely from the sociocultural changes that have occurred in developed countries since the end of World War II. The relative prosperity and stability that emerged in America and, eventually, in Western Europe after the war led to a gradual shift in the definitions of social roles. As women started to make headway in their battle against the paternalistic hegemony that defined them as child-bearers and housekeepers, the average age at which people got married and began having children increased, leaving individuals more time to focus on developing their identities.

As a result of shifting role definitions, psychologist Jeffrey Arnett (2000b, 2004, 2012) pointed out that more young people are postponing adulthood by attending college and therefore entering the workforce later. To capture this new reality, Arnett (2012) proposed a period of identity exploration between adolescence and "true" adulthood, which he called "emerging adulthood". Arnett defined this period as "an age when people explore various possibilities in love and work as they move towards making enduring choices. Through trying out these different possibilities they develop a more definite identity, including an understanding of who they are, what their capabilities and limitations are, what their beliefs and values are, and how they fit into the society around them" (p. 12).

Similarly, as early as 1976, Gail Sheehy's bestselling "pop" psychology book *Passages* offered a new timetable for identity development. Her "passage" was essentially a different term for Erikson's identity crisis. Thus, she defined these passages as crucial turning points that force people to re-define their conceptions of themselves (p. 12). Although they are frequently uncomfortable and difficult to manage, Sheehy argues that such critical events change us from within and result either in stagnation or act as a catalyst to move on to the next developmental stage and ultimately result in personal growth.

While Sheehy's mechanisms for identity development are essentially the same as Erikson's, her timetable is decidedly different. Thus, similar to Arnett's "emerging adulthood", Sheehy (2011) conceptualized the 20s as a *provisional adulthood*, during which individuals are still sorting out fundamental identity issues. While she acknowledged the importance of this stage, in later works, Sheehy (2011) expanded the timetable of identity development even further by emphasizing that "adulthood continues to proceed by stages of development throughout the life cycle. Unlike childhood stages, the stages of adult life are characterized not by physical growth but by steps in psychological and social growth" (p.10). Sheehy argues that people today experience predictable crises in adulthood that lead to further identity exploration in midlife or later. She maintains that the longevity revolution that is prolonging our lives by twenty to thirty years makes possible many *new passages* earlier in adult life, which many people today are no longer willing to wait until retirement to experience. Sheehy (2011) thus proposed a *Second Adulthood*, which "takes us beyond the preoccupation with self. We are compelled to search for greater significance in the engagement of our selves in the world" (p. 149). She refers to second adulthood as the "meaning crisis" and argues that it is a period which is mainly preoccupied with a universal search for meaning.

In essence, for all of the aforementioned theorists, there is a common recognition that socio-cultural changes in the last 50-60 years have shifted the identity development process to later life stages and opened up the possibility for lifelong evolution of one's identity. Of course, the concept of evolution suggests an ongoing improvement, which leads us to the second challenge that post-modernism presents for the Eriksonian model.

2.2.2 Stable identities in postmodernity

One of the core aspects of Erikson's identity theory (1968) was an "invigorating sense of sameness and continuity" (p. 19). Erikson argues that this stability is essential for psychological well-being. However, in the postmodern world, two factors work against the establishment of a stable identity: the pace of socio-cultural change and the variety of socio-cultural contexts in which a single individual can be situated simultaneously.

To take the former challenge first, as mentioned above, expectations surrounding roles assigned to particular genders and life stages have been evolving rapidly. Where before role definitions might shift from one generation to the next (i.e. one generation's roles would be different than those of their parents' generation), these shifts now occur within an individual's lifetime and career. The rapid acceleration of technological evolution has certainly played a role in this process, as advances in computers and robotics have eliminated many jobs in developed countries and radically altered the jobs that have survived. As a consequence of this rapidly changing environment, an identity relevant in one moment may no longer be relevant in another (Schachter 2005a, p.141).

The second challenge of postmodernity is that individuals are now routinely embedded in multiple socio-cultural contexts simultaneously, each of which may involve different demands and role definitions. As Schachter (2005a) points out, "if one is embedded in multiple contexts, each with a different set of norms, role models and modes of interaction, then cultural contradiction may result in inner confusion" (p. 141). As a result, in postmodernity it is difficult to establish and maintain a coherent and stable identity "because of a bombardment of external influences that erodes the very sense that there is an authentic core" (Côté & Levine, 2002, p. 41).

In a related note, Schachter (2005a) also points out that Erikson's concept of a stable, healthy identity also presupposes a "confidence that one's inner sense of sameness and continuity are matched by the sameness and continuity of one's meaning for others" (p. 141). Of course, many postmodern theorists (e.g. Derrida, Foucault, Lacan, Lyotard) have suggested that such an objective yet shared meaning construct is virtually impossible. Baudrillard (1994) even suggested that the rapid advances of communication technologies (in particular the internet) have transformed the world into a set of simulations, where the boundaries between the real and the unreal have been blurred.

In a similar vein, Kenneth Gergen (1991) discussed the problematic issues of self in our media-saturated environment in his book "*The Saturated Self: Dilemmas of Identity in Contemporary Life*":

> Emerging technologies saturate us with the voices of humankind – both harmonious and alien. As we absorb their various rhymes and reasons, they become part of us and we of them. Social saturation furnishes us with a multiplicity of incoherent and unrelated languages of the self. For everything we 'know to be true' about ourselves, other voices within respond with doubt and even derision. This fragmentation of self-conceptions corresponds to a multiplicity of incoherent and disconnected relationships. These relationships pull us in myriad directions, inviting us to play such a variety of roles that the very concept of an 'authentic self' with knowable characteristics recedes from view. The fully saturated self becomes no self at all (pp. 6-7).

2.2 Identity in a postmodern context

Here, Gergen asserts that the self is a mosaic of stories, experiences and social relationships with others, which are based on the messages mediated by our environment.

Bearing in mind the abovementioned aspects of rapid social change and multiple conflicting contexts, maintaining a coherent and stable sense of identity is difficult, if not impossible. As early as 1978, Kohut & Wolf described a form of psychoanalytic self-psychology that featured the concepts of the "fragmented" or "uncohesive" self to highlight the challenge of developing and maintaining a stable identity in postmodernity. Similarly, Schachter (2005a) suggests that the postmodern world may produce "men and women alienated, anxious, emasculated, and solitary, stripped of vitality, fearing to ask Erikson's questions of "Who am I?" and "How do I fit into an adult world?" (p.141). Schachter (2005a) summarizes six possible features affecting identity formation in the postmodern context: juxtaposed multiple contexts, constant change, lack of direction and skepticism toward the hope for progress, extreme individualization, an atmosphere of reality, and a sense of frail reality (p.143). With all of these postmodern obstacles, if one accepts Erikson's proposition that a stable identity is necessary for psychological health, one must agree with Schachter's diagnosis that "the postmodern condition fails to support psychological well-being" (Schachter 2005a, p.143). This concept has been further supported by Hammack (2008), who argues that psychosocial identity insecurity is a symptom of the postmodern context, and Kinvall (2004), who has suggested that people whose identity lacks coherence perceive this as existential uncertainty and thus turn to insular social systems, such as religious extremism, to find personal coherence.

While this paints a bleak picture for healthy identity constructs in the postmodern era, others have taken the exact opposite stance. While acknowledging the instability of identity in postmodernity, they reject Erikson's claim that a stable identity is necessary for psychological well-being. If one sets aside this mandate, the postmodern condition can be seen as liberated from the restraints of a fixed identity. Thus, psychologists Lifton (1993) and Gergen (1991) emphasize two major points:

> (a) individuals can and are adapting to the multiplicity and fluidity of the postmodern context by creating a different structure of identity; and (b) stable identities can be depicted not as a psychological asset within such a context, but rather as a barrier to freedom, self-actualization, and personal well-being (cf. Schachter, 2005a, p. 144).

The idea that stability and consistency limit an individual's personal freedom and require the repression of other identity elements implies that the problem is not postmodernity, but rather a rigid concept of identity that defines a fluid and flexible self as an unhealthy self.

One psychologist who has embraced the potential freedom of the postmodern, fluid self is Kenneth Gergen (1991). He conceived of a relational self that represents a more radical view of social constructionism and emphasizes the self as constructed "in relation" (McLean & Syed, 2016). Gergen (1991) agrees that the technological advances of the late 20th century have led to social saturation and the erosion of the self, as individuals are more and more exposed to the opinions, values and lifestyles of others (p. 49). This leads to a multiplicity of investitures or fragmented selves, which Gergen labels "multiphrenia". Yet, the state of multiphrenia is not necessarily to be viewed as negative or pathological. On the contrary, Gergen (1991) postulates that it opens up a new sense of expansiveness, adventure and exploration. He suggests that, although the multiphrenic condition and lack of a unified view of the self may be initially destabilizing, with time, this radically different postmodern consciousness may become normal.

Although the idea of replacing the goal of a stable inner core with that of developing a postmodern relational self may be attractive, some have argued that a functional fragmented/fluid self is a difficult if not impossible aim. For example, McAdams (1997, 2006), one of Gergen's strongest critics, holds that multiple identity would mean "no identity". However, this does not mean that he advocates a fully coherent and stable identity. Indeed, he recognizes that few people realize a coherent, unified identity in contemporary Western society, but he argues that people nevertheless strive for some sense of unity and purpose as they progress through adulthood. He suggests that individuals seek to impose some form of structure that brings the various events and phases of their lives into some coherent, meaningful whole. To understand this process of constructing a whole out of many parts, McAdams relies on the concept of narrative identity, which is explained in greater detail in the following section.

2.3 The narrative construction of self

"Life is not what one lived, but what one remembers and how one remembers it in order to recount it."

Gabriel García Márquez

One way to understand the identity formation process that has garnered significant attention in identity scholarship is the narrative epistemological paradigm (e.g. Clandinin & Connelly, 2000; Hammack, 2008; McAdams, Josselson, & Lieblich, 2006; McLean, Pasupathi, & Pals, 2007; Nelson & Fivush, 2004; Reese, Yan, Jack, & Hayne, 2010). The main

2.3 The narrative construction of self

assumption underlying the narrative model is that human development is essentially an interpretive process that is mainly concerned with making meaning in context (Hammack, 2016). Thus, as Márquez suggests in the quote above, individuals make meaning of the world around them (e.g. Bruner, 1986, 2002; Riessman, 2008) by creating personal narratives or life stories (McLean, Pasupathi, & Pals, 2007) which emphasize the retrospective and subjective interpretation of how their life stories unfold (Rossiter, 1999). In other words, narrative approaches to identity formation manifest themselves through the subjectively experienced life story, taking into account the various dimensions of social and cultural engagement.

In a similar vein, Jerome Bruner (1986) differentiated between two different ways of knowing. He labeled one mode of thought *paradigmatic*, which relies on reasoned analysis and logical proof as a way to predict and control reality and to generate an objective and unambiguous truth about reality that can be proven or disproved. In contrast, *narrative* modes of thought draw on stories of lived experiences and the meanings created as they are interpreted. According to Bruner, the narrative paradigm helps make sense of the complexity and ambiguity of human lives, and identity is negotiated as life stories unfold. He (2002) later argued that people are continuously engaged in constructing "self-making narratives" (p. 66).

This concept has been reinforced by several researchers. Ricoeur (1987) views narrative identity as a central form of self-interpretation, and Charles Taylor (1989) considers it as "a basic condition of making sense of ourselves" (p. 47). Kenneth Gergen (1998) eventually conceived of identity as a "discursive achievement" and pointed to the creation of stories of oneself which give meaning and stability to a person's identity (p. 188). Building very much on Erikson, McAdams (e.g. 1985, 1988, 1997, 2006a, 2006b, 2011), put forward his own theory of narrative identity, and he (2006a) went on to emphasize the ideal of maintaining a coherent identity by synthesizing and integrating stories of self into a narrative identity:

> People construct stories to make sense of their lives; [...] lives become meaningful and coherent (or not) amidst the welter of social constructions and discourses that comprise contemporary postmodern life. It follows, furthermore, that story construction – at the level of the individual, group, and even culture – moves (ideally) in the direction of coherence (p. 110).

Thus, McAdams (2011) suggested that "narrative identity is an especially compelling construction – a psychosocial first among equals – in that it conveys how the author-self constructs a self-defining story that serves to integrate many other features of the Me in order to provide a life in full with some degree of unity, purpose, and meaning in culture and in time" (p. 103-4).

In a similar vein, Habermas and Bluck (2000) elaborated on the ability to create a coherent account of one's past to foster self-understanding and make connections between the self and one's environment. They argue that the ability to create a life story, or what they call a sense of *autobiographical coherence,* develops in adolescence. This autobiographical coherence is part of the larger global coherence that defines the life story and analogous representations of the lives of significant others (Haberms & Bluck, 2000 p. 749). Habermas and Bluck argued that "only life narratives that are causally and thematically coherent will be recognized as good or real life narratives" (p. 750). They highlighted the importance of establishing *causal coherence*, which "is used not only to link the episodes within a life phase and to relate life phases but also to explain changes in the narrator's values or personality as a result of events over time" (Habermas & Bluck, 2000, p. 751). Establishing causal coherence within one's narrative life story is critical, and failure to achieve this would mean that life appears to be meaningless.

In addition to causal coherence, Habermas & Bluck (2000) also highlighted the importance of establishing *thematic coherence*; that is, generating thematic similarities between various life events and integrating them into a larger narrative. Thematic coherence can be explicitly established by recognizing and even stating that a specific episode is typical of many others, or implicitly established by relying more on abstract terms that suggest trajectories, such as being "born under a lucky star". In both types of coherence, the person telling the story comes to a conclusion about the self.

Charles Taylor (1989) also pointed to implicit and explicit levels of identity and emphasized that the explicit level depends on the implicit orientations in life. In other words, human beings can make explicit (i.e. narrate or articulate) their implicit values and self-interpretations to themselves and others. As Rossiter (1999) pointed out, "the process of telling one's story externalizes it so that one can reflect on it, become aware of its trajectory and the themes within it, and make choices about how one wishes to continue" (p. 69).

This final point highlights the importance of the narrative concept for the present research. As outlined below in sections six to nine, this paper places traveler narratives at the center of the research and uses these stories as indications of the identity that travelers are constructing for themselves and others (i.e. the researcher). To this end, a few central themes can be drawn from the aforementioned researchers that are of importance. First, an individual's identity is a fluid construct which is constantly negotiated via narrative construction in discussions with both the self and others. Second, although the degree of stability required or desired may vary, when constructing life stories most individuals seek some kind of coherence between different aspects of their lives at a given moment and between different temporal phases of their lives. While postmodernity has certainly complicated this search for coherence, the need for some level of coherence has seemingly endured. In the end, even one who explicitly rejects the need for stability in life is stating a philosophical value that can help provide coherence to a sequence of events over a lifetime (i.e. the stated need/desire for variety assigns a higher and positive meaning to a seemingly random series of events). Finally, it is important to recognize that this whole process differs widely from one individual to the next, not just in terms of the associated values and goals, but in terms of the degree of conscious attention with which these stories are constructed (i.e. implicit vs. explicit). Vignoles, Schwartz, Luyckx (2011) captured this complexity admirably when they suggested that

> identity is simultaneously a personal, relational, and collective phenomenon; it is stable in some ways and fluid in others; and identity is formed and revised throughout the lifespans of individuals and the histories of social groups and categories, through an interplay of processes of self-discovery, personal construction, and social construction, some of which are relatively deliberate and explicit, whereas others are more automatic and implicit (p. 8)

Despite this complexity, one key theme that emerges from this discussion is the importance of change and transformation. To examine the mechanisms of these transformations, one final theory of learning is needed to explain how this ongoing identity evolution occurs.

2.4 Transformation and learning

Most people would agree that learning does not end in the classroom, but is rather a lifelong endeavor that constantly reshapes people. While a considerable amount of learning occurs in adulthood, most learning is additive in that when we learn new things, we add them to things that we already know or things we can do. This type of learning can be as simple as memorizing facts or learning to use a new tablet or smartphone. Although such learning may occur during long-term travel, the focus here is on highly individualized, complex and multifaceted learning that has the potential to be transformative.

When I started doing research for the theoretical framework of this study, I was quite overwhelmed by the large number of learning theories that the academic literature had to offer. Even though I could not put a name on the theory I was looking for, I knew that it had to describe how long-term travelers learn and also why they learn in that way. I was looking for a learning theory that would describe a different type of learning that is much less common, but more complex and significant. I was looking for a learning theory that involves a fundamental change in the way we see ourselves and the world in which we live, a theory that would account for how learning shapes people and constitutes a transformation in their personalities and worldviews; a developmental learning theory that ultimately deals with identity transformation.

Another point clear to me was that this learning theory had to be based on *experience* and *self-reflection*, two key points that I had realized through my own travel experience. When leaving our comfort zone, we are suddenly confronted with a reality that is completely different from our own. In our own culture, we often accept the way life is, without giving it too much second thought. Leaving the comforts of home and moving between different cultural environments can be a highly transformational experience for many people because deeply embedded cultural patterns of which they are often completely unaware suddenly become visible. Reflecting on these experiences of strangeness often leads to a transformation in that the strange gradually becomes familiar, which can lead to a perspective change.

Transformative learning theory, as postulated by Jack Mezirow, is based on experience and critical reflection and provides an ideal conceptual framework for this study. The following sections will discuss the transformative learning experience, including its evolution, phases, characteristics and principles, as well as criticisms of the theory.

2.4.1 Transformative learning theory

The American professor of adult and continuing education Jack Mezirow was probably the most prolific thinker on the topic of transformation. He introduced transformative learning theory (TLT) to educational research and explained that it "is a theory where learning is understood as the process of using a prior interpretation to construe a new or revised interpretation of the meaning of one's experience in order to guide future action" (Mezirow, 1996, p.162). In studying older women's experiences of returning to school or the workplace after an extended time away, he formulated his theory on perspective transformation and explained the process through which transformation occurs in adults' meaning structures.

2.4 Transformation and learning

Mezirow's initial theory was influenced by Freire's (1970) theory of conscientization and Habermas' (1971) domains of learning. Paulo Freire (1970), a Brazilian educational theorist, was very critical of traditional education and argued that traditional education scenarios are problematic because students are dependent upon the teacher for knowledge and are thus not able to think for themselves. This is because traditional educational institutions focus on teaching *what* to think instead of *how* to think, and they are therefore not suitable for developing critical consciousness. Teaching *how* to think can only be achieved through critical reflection and rational discourse. Thus, for education to be transformative, it has to stimulate consciousness and raise awareness of one's own perspective. Moreover, Freire (1970) believed that education is not confined to the classroom but can happen anywhere and anytime.

Mezirow (1991a) also adopted some of the ideas of the German philosopher and sociologist Jürgen Habermas, particularly his view on emancipatory learning. Habermas (1971) devised three generic domains of learning: technical, practical (renamed "communicative" by Mezirow in 1991a) and emancipatory. Technical learning, which is grounded in the world of work, is governed by rules and is specific to a particular task. Memorizing the periodic table of elements would be technical learning. Communicative learning is governed by social knowledge and interaction within agreed upon norms. For example, learning how to interact effectively with people from another culture would be considered communicative learning. And finally, emancipatory learning is governed by self-reflection or self-knowledge. For example, critically reflecting on a mistake made and coming to understand why and how that error occurred in order to take action and correct it would be emancipatory learning.

Mezirow's (1991a) analysis of the three domains resulted in his definition of perspective transformation, also known as transformative learning, which he identified as "the process of becoming critically aware of how and why our assumptions have come to constrain the way we perceive, understand, and feel about our world; changing these structures of habitual expectation to make possible a more inclusive, discriminating, and integrative perspective; and, finally, making choices or otherwise acting upon these new understandings" (p. 167). Mezirow (1981) situated transformative learning between the domains of emancipatory and communicative learning and held that transformative learning can only be achieved if one is capable of understanding one's underlying assumptions and is willing to critically examine them.

2.4.2 The importance of meaning-making

The cardinal goal of transformative learning is to make meaning. Making meaning means making sense of and interpreting an experience (Mezirow, 1990). This may involve revising or making a new interpretation of the meaning of an experience. Mezirow (1991a) argues that meaning-making is

> central to what learning is all about. The learning process may be understood as the extension of our ability to make explicit, schematize (make an association within a frame of reference), appropriate (accept an interpretation as our own), remember (call upon an earlier interpretation), validate (establish the truth, justification, appropriateness, or authenticity of what is asserted), and act upon (decide, change an attitude toward, modify a perspective on, or perform) some aspect of our engagement with the environment, other persons, ourselves (p. 11).

At the center of TLT are meaning structures that affect a wide range of aspects in life, including an individual's concept of good and bad, readiness to learn, how a person reacts to a cheating spouse, and how a person thinks about euthanasia, gun control or any other topic of interest to the person. In order for transformative learning and a perspective change to occur, Mezirow (1991a) postulated that people need to be mature enough to question their *meaning structures* (or *frames of reference*), as well as being willing and able to do so. The meaning structures are shaped by two constructs: meaning perspectives and meaning schemes (Mezirow, 1991a).

A *meaning perspective* (or *habit of mind*) refers to "the structure of cultural assumptions within which new experience is assimilated to – and transformed by – one's past experience" (Mezirow, 1978, p. 101). It is the large-scale frame of reference that shapes the individual's worldview, which acts as a filter through which experiences are viewed and interpreted. Meaning perspectives are socio-culturally constructed through the process of socialization, are constantly reinforced throughout an individual's daily life, and "govern the activities of perceiving, comprehending and remembering" (Mezirow, 1991a, p. 4). Mezirow (1991a) identified three different types of meaning perspectives: epistemic, which relates to what we know and how we use this knowledge; sociolinguistic, which comprises our learned social, cultural and communicative structures; and psychological, which refers to our self-concept, personality, character and attitudes.

In contrast, *meaning schemes* (or *points of view*) are small-scale structures that are "made up of specific knowledge, beliefs, value judgments and feelings that constitute interpretations of experience" (Mezirow, 1991a, p. 5-6). While a person's meaning perspective is difficult to alter, meaning schemes are more easily influenced and constantly challenged during an individual's day-to-day life. That is, a person's worldview (i.e. meaning

2.4 Transformation and learning

perspective) is not typically changed by a single event, but is rather influenced by a number of aspects that challenge the meaning schemes. Simply put, an individual's meaning perspective is a frame of reference composed of a number of specific meaning schemes. Learning becomes transformative when meaning schemes are changed or new ones are created when old ones can no longer be applied.

Mezirow (1991a) pointed out, however, that not all learning is transformative and leads to a perspective change. He identified four forms of learning. The first one is *learning through existing meaning schemes*, whereby we simply interpret new experience with the meaning schemes we acquired in the past. The second form, *learning new meaning schemes*, involves expanding the scope of a previously acquired meaning scheme when interpreting a new experience. In the third form, *learning through the transformation of meaning schemes*, new experiences cannot be interpreted through old meaning schemes, and these meaning schemes must therefore be transformed. And finally, the fourth and most profound form is learning through perspective transformation, which involves "a structural change in the way we see ourselves and our relationships" and allows us to "move toward perspectives which are more inclusive, discriminating and integrative of experience (Mezirow, 1978, p. 100).

2.4.3 Phases of transformation

Mezirow (1991a) described transformative learning as a conscious and intentional process and laid out 10 phases of transformation (see table 1) that depict the entire process of how a person attaches meaning to a new experience and integrates it into a transformed perspective. However, the transformative learning process comprises four main aspects: experience, critical reflection, reflective discourse, and action (Merriam, Caffarella, & Baumgartner, 2007) (see section 2.4.4 for a more in-depth discussion of critical reflection and reflective discourse). The process begins with a disorienting dilemma, which acts as a catalyst for transformative learning. A disorienting dilemma is an incongruent life event that creates a state of disequilibrium or internal dilemma and encourages someone to make changes in her life. This may be a life crisis, the death of a loved one, loss of a job, an accident or illness, separation or divorce, graduation from school or university, or retirement – in short, situations that are common in adult lives.

These disorienting dilemmas cannot be resolved by deploying usual problem-solving strategies and coping skills, such as learning more about the problem or learning how to cope with it effectively (Mezirow, 1978, p. 101). In other words, one's frame of reference or meaning perspective can no longer explain or manage the new disorienting situation.

Mezirow (1991a) further argued that disorienting dilemmas can be either incremental or epochal. Transformation that is triggered by incremental dilemmas is characterized by a series of gradual transitions or through sudden insight (Mezirow, 2000). Incremental dilemmas are therefore a number of smaller events that accumulate over time and may result in a shift of perspective. Epochal dilemmas, which are more dramatic, less common and often more painful, include abrupt life crises, such as the death of a loved one or the loss of a job.

After experiencing some type of disorienting dilemma (phase 1), the person must engage in self-examination (phase 2) – a process that is often accompanied by anxiety, pressure or other undesirable emotions, such as guilt or shame – and this eventually leads to a critical assessment of one's underlying assumptions of the present situation (phase 3). Mezirow (1991a) called this process *critical reflection*, which is one of the cornerstones of his theory. He theorizes that "resolution of these dilemmas and transforming our meaning perspectives require that we become critically aware of the fact that we are caught in our own history and are reliving it and of the cultural and psychological assumptions which structure the way we see ourselves and others (Mezirow, 1978, p. 109).

After a period of self-examination and critical reflection, the individual realizes that others have undergone a similar process (phase 4), begins to explore new options, roles and relationships (phase 5), and finally devises a plan of action (phase 6). This plan of action is implemented by acquiring knowledge and skills (phase 7), trying out new roles (phase 8), and thereby building competence and self-confidence in these new roles and relationships (phase 9). Mezirow (1991a) holds that building competence and self-confidence is a critical final step before the perspective change is complete and the new attitudes, beliefs and behaviors are fully incorporated into the person's life and meaning structure (phase 10).

Although Mezirow (1991a) initially conceived of his theory as linear and sequential, Taylor (1994b, 1997) conducted a critical evaluation of TLT studies and found that many had shown that the phases were nonsequential and that not all individuals who experience perspective transformation undergo all 10 phases.

2.4 Transformation and learning

Table 1. Phases of transformative learning (Mezirow, 1991a, pp. 168-169)

Phase 1	A disorienting dilemma
Phase 2	Self-examination with feelings of guilt or shame
Phase 3	A critical assessment of epistemic, sociocultural, or psychic assumptions
Phase 4	Recognition that one's discontent and the process of transformation are shared and that others have negotiated a similar change
Phase 5	Exploration of options for new roles, relationships, and actions
Phase 6	Planning a course of action
Phase 7	Acquisition of knowledge and skills for implementing one's plans
Phase 8	Provisional trying of new roles
Phase 9	Building of competence and self-confidence in new roles and relationships
Phase 10	A reintegration into one's life on the basis of conditions dictated by one's new perspective

2.4.4 The importance of critical reflection and rational discourse

Critical reflection and rational discourse are two integral components of Mezirow's TLT. Our complex late modern world is characterized by "contradictions generated by rapid, dramatic change and a diversity of beliefs, values and social practices", and adults today "face an urgent need to keep from being overwhelmed by change" (Mezirow, 1991a, p. 2-3). Previously accepted sources of authority and learning obtained through schooling and socialization are no longer enough (Mezirow, 1991a). In order to be able to get a better understanding of constantly changing events and to reclaim control over one's lives, it is important to be able and willing to question and challenge one's underlying assumptions and presuppositions, to critically reflect on them in order to open up new ways of thinking and new perspectives on oneself and the world. Mezirow (1991a) argues that too many people passively accept approved and preconceived ways of doing and seeing things, which limits our future learning. He laments the failure of adult learning theories to acknowledge the importance of the individual's frame of reference, through which all learning takes place. Mezirow (1998) maintains that "learning to think for oneself involves becoming critically reflective of assumptions and participating in discourse to validate beliefs, intentions, values and feelings (p. 198). Mezirow (1990) further laments that educational institutions today fail to facilitate critical reflection and maintains that "the transformation of these uncritically assimilated habits of perceiving, thinking, remembering, problem solving, and feeling affords the most significant opportunities for learning, creativity, self-realization, and social action in adulthood" (p. xiv).

When discussing the broader field of reflection, Mezirow (1990) differentiates between three different types: reflection, critical reflection and critical self-reflection. *Reflection* is defined as the "examination of the justification for one's beliefs, primarily to guide action and to reassess the efficacy of the strategies and procedures used in problem solving" (p. xvi), whereas *critical reflection* involves the "assessment of the validity of the *presuppositions* of one's meaning perspectives, and examination of their sources and consequences (p. xvi, highlight in original). Finally, Mezirow (1990) suggests that *critical self-reflection* involves the "assessment of the way one has posed problems and of one's own meaning perspectives" (p. xvi). Transformative learning is learning through critical self-reflection by critically reassessing what is already known in order to enable a more discriminating, integrative and inclusive understanding of one's experience.

Mezirow (1991a) identified three different forms of reflection on experience: content, process and premise reflection. Content reflection is reflecting on what happened and about any available data on the problem or experience. Process reflection involves thinking about how to deal with the problem or experience and devising an adequate plan of action. And the most radical form, premise reflection, involves reflecting on one's underlying premises, assumptions, beliefs and values concerning the problem or experience. Essentially, it involves "becoming aware of why we perceive, think and feel or act as we do" (Mezirow, 1991a, p. 108). It is this form of reflection that enables transformative learning.

Another cornerstone of Mezirow's transformative learning theory is communication, or more specifically, the ability to engage in rational discourse. In this context, Mezirow drew on the work of Habermas (1984) and distinguished between instrumental and communicative learning, each with its own logic and standards of validity. The instrumental learning domain is about controlling and manipulating the external environment, for example to obtain food or shelter or to perform a specific task, whereas communicative learning is "learning what others mean when others communicate with one another in the service of sensemaking" Mezirow, 2000). Thus, communicative learning involves understanding what someone means when they communicate with you and includes apprehending someone's intentions, assumptions and qualifications (Mezirow, 2003, p, 59). By communicating with others, we are able to look beyond ourselves, connect with others, create meaning and reach a mutual understanding (Mezirow, 1978, 1991, 2000). Communicative learning also acknowledges the importance of relationships. Mezirow (1991a) explained that "personal meanings that we attribute to our experiences are acquired and validated through human interaction" (1991a, p. XIV). Moreover, human interaction and negotiating new relationships are critical factors for developing openness and self-confidence.

2.4 Transformation and learning

In the context of transformative learning, Mezirow (2003) termed this communicative learning "critical-dialectical discourse". He maintains that learners who can participate fully and freely in critical-dialectical discourse are capable of being critically reflective and exercising reflective judgment. This means changing perspectives, assessing alternative points of view and not shying away from questioning or even abandoning one's strongly held beliefs and assumptions. Moreover, critical-dialectical discourse requires skills, insights and sensitivities, such as the ability to listen empathetically, maintain an open mind, seek common ground and bracket premature judgment (Mezirow, 2003). Such engagement in critical-dialectical discourse leads to more developed and autonomous thinking.

While Merriam (2004) agrees that transformative learning appears to result in a more mature and autonomous level of thinking, she asked what level of maturity was necessary for such transformation to occur. Mezirow (1991a) himself suggested that advanced-level transformation of meaning perspectives does not tend to occur before the age of 30 because most people do not develop the tools to engage in such higher-order thinking at an earlier age. He also pointed out that, in addition to a certain level of maturity, other preconditions (e.g. safety, health, education, economic security, emotional intelligence) also affect the ability to engage in rational discourse (Mezirow, 2000). Belenky and Stanton (2000) affirmed this viewpoint and concluded that "Most adults simply have not developed their capacities for articulating and criticizing the underlying assumptions of their own thinking, nor do they analyze the thinking of others in these ways. Furthermore, many have never had experience with the kinds of reflective discourse that Mezirow prescribes" (p. 73, cf. Merriam, 2004).

Merriam (2004) concludes that a certain level of cognitive development is a prerequisite for transformative learning to occur. Having an experience, whether positive or negative does not suffice to effect transformation. She argues that "mature cognitive development is foundational to engaging in critical reflection and rational discourse necessary for transformational learning" (p. 65).

2.4.5 Principles of transformation

Michael Poutiatine (2008) put forward a list of nine fundamental principles that are critical to understanding the process of transformation, which are also pertinent to this study. Poutiatine (2008) considered these principles macro concepts that apply equally to individuals, organizations and societies. Moreover, they also serve to highlight the differences between ordinary change and transformational change. Following is a brief synopsis of his principles.

1. *Transformation is not synonymous with change.* Although many researchers have devised their own frameworks for transformative learning (e.g. Anderson & Anderson, 2001; Dirkx, 2006; Dirkx, Mezirow, & Cranton, 2006; Kovan & Dirkx, 2003; O'Sullivan, 1999; Quinn, 1996), they all agree to conceive of transformation as being different from change (Taylor, 1997). Transformation is a very particular type of change that happens far less frequently in life than change. Typical change tends to be limited in scope, is reversible (Quinn, 1996), and does not "challenge existing, taken-for-granted assumptions, notions and meaning of what learning is about" (Dirkx et al., 2006, p. 4).

2. *Transformation requires assent to change.* This means that transformation is a voluntary process, and no one can be forced to transform their perspective. Hence, it has to start as an internal process, which can be driven cognitively, emotionally, affectively or even through aspects of the unconscious (Cranton, 1994; Dirkx, 2001, 2006; Kovan & Dirkx, 2003).

3. *Transformation requires a 'second order change'.* Here, second order change is "a multidimensional, multi-level, qualitative, discontinuous, radical organizational change involving a paradigm shift" (Levy & Mary, 1986, p.5). The paradigm shift can be equated with Mezirow's perspective change.

4. *Transformation always involves all aspects of an individual's life.* It has been argued that transformative change always involves many, if not all dimensions of an individual (Strickland, 1998). Thus, "transformative learning is best facilitated through engaging multiple dimensions of being, including rational, affective, spiritual, imaginative, somatic and socio-cultural domains through relative content and experiences" (Tolliver & Tisdell, 2006, p. 38).

5. *Transformational change is irreversible.* This is one of the most significant aspects of transformational change. This means that once an individual has gone through a paradigmatic shift, it is impossible for them to go back to "not knowing" (Quinn, 1996). Quinn (1996), who called this irreversible change "deep change", is in line with other scholars (Cranton, 1994; Levy & Mary, 1986; Mezirow, 1991a) who hold that once the entire paradigmatic worldview has been enlarged and an individual has *seen* the

larger picture, it is impossible to *unsee* that which the individual now knows and to regress to levels of less understanding. Reaching this point of full understanding and commitment can be extremely difficult, however, and many people do regress before they reach this point (p. 152). Mezirow (1991a) explained that if a learner becomes overwhelmed by an insight that has transformed a meaning scheme, he or she may be unable to act upon this new insight and may therefore regress to an earlier stage of learning, thus impeding full perspective transformation. He pointed out that this regression, which he termed "backsliding", is a common occurrence in TLT. This stands in stark contrast to change, as change is surely reversible.

6. *Transformational change involves letting go of the myth of control.* Quinn (1996) notes that to experience deep change, one needs to surrender control because "deep change effort distorts existing patterns of action and involves taking risks" (p. 3). Embracing transformational change is thus a risky endeavor, full of uncertainty and ambiguity that involves questioning things that were once taken for granted.

7. *Transformational change always involves some aspect of loss and letting go.* If transformational change results (at least in part) in a paradigm shift or perspective change (i.e. a new worldview), it stands to reason that transformation therefore involves loss, or as Anderson & Anderson (2001) put it, a "death of the old worldview". Loss and letting go are commonly associated with grieving, fear and anxiety. Cranton (1994) writes that "learners will often cling stubbornly to their opinions, values or beliefs. To change is frightening and threatening" (pp. 84-85) and "grieving is integral to transformation" (Scott, 1997). This process of letting go of old worldviews and belief structures that no longer fit with the new one takes place within the process of critical reflection and relies on the assistance of trusted allies, such as friends, family, teachers, colleagues or even mental health professionals (Cranton, 1994; Mezirow, 1991a).

8. *Transformational change always involves a broadening of the scope of worldview.* Transformation requires individuals to increase their awareness and skills and to expand their worldview (Anderson & Anderson, 2001). It forces them to revise their meaning perspectives (Cranton, 1994; Mezirow, 1991a) and to see the world differently and more effectively (Quinn, 1996), and it creates a more expansive understanding of the world and one's self (Cranton, 1994) without fully forgetting the previously held worldview (Cranton, 1994; Mezirow, 1991a). Therefore, the transformative

process requires critical reflection about one's current operating assumptions and the willingness and ability to evaluate what is no longer useful or necessary for the new meaning perspective (Cranton, 1994, 113-120).

9. *Transformation is always a movement toward a greater integrity of identity – a movement toward wholeness.* One of the central characteristics of the transformational processes is that it always embodies a movement towards wholeness or growth (Dirkx, 2006; Dirkx et al., 2006; Palmer, 2004). Growth, in this sense, is similar to Maslow's (1970) concept of self-actualization (being at peace with oneself) and Palmer's (2004) conception of integrity (wholeness). The transformative process must therefore work on both internal and external levels in order to create a better sense of alignment or harmony between one's true self (identity) and how that self manifests itself in the world (integrity) (Palmer, 2004).

As Poutiatine (2008) argues, these nine principles are by no means exhaustive, but rather aim to help understand the nature of transformation and delineate it from ordinary change. Ideally, the outcome of transformative learning is a change in perspective that leads to more mature, autonomous people who are also more developed in their thinking.

2.4.6 Criticisms of transformative learning theory

While Mezirow's TLT has been tested, critiqued and revised by researchers in many disciplines, it is still considered a robust theory of adult learning (Cranton, 2006; Cranton & King, 2003; Kitchenham, 2008; Taylor, 1997, 2007; Whitelaw, Sears & Campbell, 2004). There is consensus among researchers on the three tenets necessary for transformation to occur, albeit with varying degrees of importance: experience (e.g. disorienting dilemma), critical reflection and (rational) discourse.

Over the years, a number or scholars have added their own perspectives to Mezirow's transformative learning theory. Taylor (2007), who examined 41 peer-reviewed studies involving transformative learning, concluded that Mezirow's framework on TLT was generally supported by academics "through its stability over time, its relationship to expanding the self and pursuit of autonomy, and the applicability for informing classroom practice" (p. 185), but noted that a number of questions remain to be addressed.

For one, Taylor (2007) pointed out that previous studies failed to accurately capture critical reflection in that they generally assumed that study participants were capable of critical reflection and articulation of critical reflective thought. It is a common but false assumption that once people reach physical maturity, their cognitive development is complete (Kegan, 1994). In fact, different individuals may process and interpret an event completely differently, depending on their cognitive capacity (Merriam, 2004). Merriam also pointed out that the question of how cognitively developed a person must be in order to have a transformative learning experience is still open for debate.

Mezirow's theory has also been criticized for its strong focus on rationality, and it has been pointed out that rationality, as well as autonomy and individuality, are concepts prevalent in Western society (Hanson, 1996). Some cultures, in contrast, favor collectivist thinking approaches as opposed to an individualized focus on critical autonomy. Hanson noted that "critical self-reflection is not always beneficial, as self-awareness and criticism are often the characteristics of seriously depressed people. Self-reflection and critical thinking may be reputed to be universal 'goods', but we need to be aware of their cultural specificity and power" (p. 105). From my point of view, this criticism is not tenable, as the main point of TLT is that disturbing experiences force you to become aware of your value system and meaning structures, which are naturally shaped by one's culture. Readjusting one's worldview and changing one's perspective is the ideal outcome, irrespective of whether one's cultural roots are collectivist or individualist.

Moreover, Taylor (2007) pointed out that the emphasis on the rational nature of TLT ignores the fact that transformative learning strongly depends upon social interactions, support, friendship, empathy and even intimacy (Taylor, 2007, p. 187). A number of researchers have thus refined Mezirow's theory to include a more holistic viewpoint that not only considers transformation as a rational but also an intuitive and emotional process. Lyon (2001), for example, emphasizes the importance of relationships in transformative learning, as they can be both a source for a disorienting dilemma as well as a means for negotiating disorienting dilemmas. Taylor & Cranton (2013) contend that more focus should be placed on the role of empathy in TLT, as it is empathy that "provides the learner with the ability to identify with the perspectives of others; lessens the likelihood of prejudgment; increases the opportunity for identifying shared understanding; and facilitates critical reflection through the emotive valence of assumptions" (pp. 37-38). They suggest that a possible major outcome of a perspective transformation may be an increase in empathy towards others, and call for more in-depth research to understand the significance of empathy in transformative learning.

Another criticism related to rationality is that some researchers have questioned the role of critical self-reflection in the transformation process, asking whether it is truly the key component or even a necessary component of transformation. Robert Boyd (1991) addressed this concern by modifying Mezirow's theory to emphasize the process of *discernment* rather than *reflection* as the core process in transformation. In his view, the discernment process allows the exploration of both cognitive (rational) and affective (non-rational) aspects of transformation, as it also depends on non-rational sources such as images, symbols and archetypes to assist in the meaning-making process. Similar to Mezirow's disorienting dilemma, in Boyd's (1991) model grieving is the most important phase in the discernment process, when the individual realizes that old meaning schemes and ways of doing things no longer apply. In a similar vein, Dirkx (1997, 2001, 2008) suggested that transformative learning is an emotional, spiritual and intuitive process, and Merriam (2004) suggested incorporating more affective, connected and intuitive dimensions (i.e. extra-rational dimensions) to Mezirow's TLT and putting them on equal footing with rational and cognitive components. Mezirow (2000) himself acknowledged that "transformations may be [...] mindless assimilation – as in moving to a different culture and uncritically assimilating its canon, norms, and ways of thinking" (p. 21), and over time, there has been an emerging consensus that the rational and extra-rational dimensions of transformative learning are complimentary rather than contradictory (Dirkx, Mezirow & Cranton, 2006).

Another line of criticism involves the neglect of context in TLT. Clark and Wilson (1991), for example, argue that Mezirow's seminal research on women returning to school largely ignored the historical, cultural and social context that shaped the women's experiences. They argue that learning "is always an interpretation from a contextually defined perspective" (p. 85). Mezirow (1991b) responded to Clark & Wilson (1991) in the same year by clarifying the apparent misunderstanding and pointed out that he had always acknowledged the importance of context, yet possibly failed to communicate it effectively. In response to his critics, he writes "meaning is always an interpretation from a contextually defined perspective [...] but our culture provides us with consensually established criteria to differentiate perspectives which are more or less adequate, functional or distorting and criteria for judging claims based upon them" (p.191).

Taylor (2007) concludes his critical review of empirical research on transformative learning by lamenting the fact that research has almost exclusively confined itself to formal settings, such as universities and workshops, and called for more research in contexts that are less controlled by the instructor and therefore more susceptible to external influences (e.g. natural environment, public) (Taylor, 2007, p. 186).

The present study is an answer to Taylor's (2007) call, as it examines the travel context, which is highly informal and uncontrolled and provides countless opportunities for disorienting dilemmas that are conducive to questioning existing frames of references, which may lead to a perspective transformation. Cranton, Stuckey & Taylor (2012) found that living outside one's culture is among the most common life-changing events (in addition to death of a loved one or loved ones, divorce or separation, life threatening illness, and loss of a job). Transformative learning theory is useful for studying the long-term effects long-term travel has on an individual's perception of the self as it "is not so much what happens to people but how they interpret and explain what happens to them that determines their actions their hopes, their contentment and emotional well-being, and their performance" (Mezirow, 2000, p, xiii). Where Mezirow (1978) has argued that adult education "can be used to precipitate, facilitate and reinforce perspective transformation as well as to implement resulting action plans", I argue that long-term, independent travel can do just the same (p. 109).

2.5 Long-term independent travel as a form of lifelong learning

Transformative learning's essential focus on altering broad meaning perspectives and modes of thinking and relating to one's environment places it squarely within the wider domain of lifelong learning. Of course, one of the challenges of dealing with lifelong learning is that the domain can be seen as rather too wide. That is, the term itself has been a topic of debate since its inception, as various parties have struggled to define what exactly the term means or should mean. In fact, one could say that the defining characteristic of "lifelong learning" is its seemingly inherent non-definability. Although a full review of the history of this debate is well beyond the scope of this thesis, here I would like to highlight some of the key areas of that debate, as many of these arguments have direct bearing on the concept of long-term, independent travel as a form of learning, and then clarify the vision of the concept embraced in this paper.

As a useful starting point, we can take the European Commission's definition of lifelong learning, which they released in 2001: "All learning activity undertaken throughout life, with the aim of improving knowledge, skills and competences within a personal, civic, social and/or employment-related perspective" (European Commission, 2001, p. 9). This is obviously an extremely broad definition that encompasses a wide range of both objectives and methods for learning, and indeed, these are the two areas where controversy has emerged. To cover the latter issue first, I will cite a different passage of the same document where they expanded on the phrase "all learning", stipulating that lifelong learning "should encompass the <u>whole spectrum of formal, non-formal and informal learning</u>" (p. 3, emphasis in original). In fact, delineating these three categories has itself proven problematic, but to provide the reader with a general sense of the difference between them, we can take the following summary from Boeren (2016):

> In general, formal learning refers to those learning activities that take place in formalized settings, comparable to the initial schooling system; they are characterized by the possibility of obtaining a recognized certificate, diploma, degree or other qualification. Non-formal learning differs from formal learning insofar as an officially recognized qualification will not be granted upon completion of a non-formal learning activity. While a certificate might be provided, it does not have any civic or legal value. Informal learning is usually defined as learning that takes place in a non-intended and accidental way, such as learning through undertaking activities with family or friends. The European Commission defines informal learning as learning that takes place outside formalized settings, whether it has been the intention of the adult to learn something new or otherwise. (p. 10)

In this scheme, long-term independent travel clearly fits into the informal category. However, this is only true if one takes the EC definition, for as we will see, many travelers embark on their journeys with a clear intention of learning something about the world or themselves. Thus, Boeren's first definition of informal learning, which includes "non-intended and accidental" as defining criteria would exclude many travelers who are consciously seeking learning, whereas the EC definition simply focuses on the format "outside formalized settings" and excludes the learner's conscious intention. Here already, the reader can see the danger of terminology and definitions when trying to classify a learning activity that falls beyond the realm of traditional educational settings.

Returning to the objections to these non-traditional forms of learning, they stem basically from a concern that recognizing these alternative forms of formal education might undermine the prestige or the resources traditionally allotted to the formal education system. While the former complaint can be seen as simple territorialism and insecurity, the latter is perhaps more worthy of examination. As a representative example, one might take the criticism of Boshier (1998), who favored lifelong education but resisted lifelong learning. Boshier worried that embracing an idea of lifelong learning would lead to a decrease in public investment in education as a whole, as governments would assume that individuals could, and perhaps even should, get their learning someplace else:

2.5 Long-term independent travel as a form of lifelong learning

> Lifelong learning is a way of abdicating responsibility of avoiding hard choices by putting learning on the open market. If the learner as consumer doesn't decide to take advantage of available opportunities, then it is his or her fault. It is easier to blame the victim than overcome structural or psycho-cultural barriers to participation. (p. 9)

Boshier is right to be wary of anything that would decrease public investment in education, and his concern is valid. However, the opposing danger is that the term "education" is too strongly linked in the popular consciousness with structured, formal forms of learning to truly embrace non-formal, and especially informal learning, which would lead to a situation where public investment for these forms of education, or even a basic acknowledgement of their potential value as tools of learning, may be harder to come by. Thus, in the context of long-term independent travel, which currently has very little public acceptance as a form of learning (as we will see in this paper), the use of the term "lifelong learning" is far more desirable, as it can be used as a tool to build public awareness of the value of non-traditional learning activities. In addition, it is important to point out that neither I nor any other supporter of long-term independent travel, nor even the travelers themselves (as we will see) have argued that travel should replace formal education. Rather, the focus should be on finding synergies between the two forms of learning, and I will have more to say about this topic at the end of this paper.

The second area of disagreement about lifelong learning is the question of how its objectives should be defined. In his insightful review of the history of lifelong learning for the *Oxford Handbook of Lifelong Learning*, Paul Hager (2011) traces the modern roots of the concept to the early 70s and the UNESCO concept of "lifelong education." Hager points out that the vision behind this concept was to create a society that would offer meaningful learning opportunities for its members throughout their lifetimes (p. 13). Although competing definitions and arguments sprung up even then, Hager then identifies a turning point in the 1990s, what he calls the "second wave" of lifelong learning, focusing on the European Union's official launch of its initiative of the same name. Hager highlights an important difference in this second wave: while the first wave was at least partially informed by "a utopian optimistic philosophy leading to a scientific humanist learning society" (p. 16), the second wave grew out of an anxiety about maintaining Europe's place as a dominant power in the globalized marketplace. As Hager (2011) explains:

> It was widely perceived that there was a crisis of economic competitiveness as globalizing trends fueled increased mobility of capital and industry. As western economies gradually lost their previous advantages over emerging economies, a new focus on creation of knowledge and its application was widely mooted as the means to maintain competitive advantage (p. 15).

The difference between the humanistic perspective and the economic perspective of the second wave is at the heart of the debate about the proper purpose of lifelong learning. While many supporters of lifelong learning embrace a wider humanistic agenda, the anxiety of global economic competition has created a strong pull towards the more "practical", career-oriented vision. In fact, when the European Commission received feedback from the member states about their original proposal, they noted that there were "concerns that the employment and labor market dimensions of lifelong learning were too dominant within the definition", and they therefore redefined the mission statement to embrace "four broad and mutually supporting objectives: <u>personal fulfilment</u>, <u>active citizenship</u>, <u>social inclusion</u> and <u>employability/adaptability</u>" (European Commission, 2001, p. 9, emphasis in original). Without wading too much deeper into this debate, here it is important to mention that the vision of lifelong learning embraced in this paper is a far more inclusive one that highlights the first three criteria listed above. That is, I will show that long-term independent travel has the potential to produce human beings with greater self-awareness and self-esteem, which in turn gives them the knowledge they need to become more active citizens and the security they need to be more accepting and even embracing of difference (i.e. more socially inclusive). However, I will also show that this activity can lead to potential career benefits as well. In fact, the ECs elusion of "employability" and "adaptability" into one compound term will be a key aspect of that argument, as we will see in the end.

In the end, the vision of lifelong learning embraced herein is essentially the one put forward by Peter Jarvis (2009), which closely parallels Mezirow's transformative learning theory. Jarvis (2009) builds his theory around the idea of disjunction, which he defines as:

> ...the gap that occurs between our experience of a situation and our biography, which provides us with the knowledge and skill that enable us to act meaningfully... The ambiguity of disjuncture is that it is when we know that we do not know that we are in a position to start learning, and, in order to cope with the disjunctural situation, we have to learn something new. (p. 10)

Based on this concept, which is closely related to if not the same as Mezirow's concept of a disorienting experience, Jarvis (2006) arrives at the following definition of lifelong learning:

> The combination of processes throughout a life-time whereby the whole person – body (genetic, physical and bio-logical) and mind (knowledge, skills, attitudes, values, emotions, meaning, beliefs and senses) – experiences natural and social situations, the content of which is then transformed cognitively, emotively or practically (or through any combination) and integrated into the individual person's biography resulting in a continually changing (or more experienced) person. (p. 25)

In the course of this paper, I will show how independent long-term travel is, in fact, a highly effective form of this type of transformative lifelong learning, which yields benefits for the individual, the community, the economy, and even, I will argue, the planet.

2.6 Summary

This chapter has offered an outline of the theoretical concepts of identity and transformation upon which this paper is grounded. This began with a concept of identity rooted in Eriksonian theory, which posits an ongoing negotiation between individuals and the demands placed upon them by the cultural setting in which they live. In this process, individuals are called upon to play certain roles, and a major challenge therein is trying to establish and maintain a coherence both in the moment (i.e. between the various roles that an individual might have to balance at any particular point in her life) and across time (i.e. between the roles that the individual will play over the course of her lifetime). In developing this identity, the individual passes through several phases, and these transitions between phases are often marked by periods of turmoil (e.g. Erikson's "identity crises" or Sheehy's "passages"), in which the individual struggles to adapt the identity construct to the demands of a new life stage.

This chapter also highlighted the conditions of postmodernism that can increase both the number of these crises and, potentially, their intensity, pointing out in particular the changing timeline of life stages as well as the barrage of information and overlapping cultural influences to which the individual is subjected. The chapter then went on to discuss the concept of narrative identity as a way of understanding the human effort to maintain identity coherence in these turbulent times by organizing the events of a particular life into a narrative that makes some kind of meaningful, cohesive sense. This concept also offers a window into the process of identity evolution for a researcher who can gain access to the stories individuals tell themselves and others in order to construct and maintain their identities. Finally, the chapter covered the concept of transformative learning, which offers a model for the process by which identities change over time by confronting crises (i.e. Mezirow's "disorienting dilemmas") and then finding ways to resolve these crises by transforming meaning structures and identity concepts.

To tie this back to Erikson, it is important to mention one final concept: the psychosocial moratorium. This is a "break" from the "normal" process of identity development prescribed by society, during which the individual can explore other possible meanings and identities and use the time to adapt their identities to the cultural demands and to their own personal desires. The premise of this paper is that long-term independent travel, which can function as such a moratorium, offers a wealth of potential for identity transformation and development because it presents individuals with a series of disorienting dilemmas, which they are then compelled to resolve. Before looking at the nature of these challenges (covered in chapter 4), one final task remains: a clarification of what exactly constitutes a long-term independent traveler. The following chapter will address this task by first providing a brief history of independent travel to show where LITs came from and then going on to describe the specific characteristics which define the participants in this study.

3 The Evolution of Long-term Independent Travel

The trope of corporal travel as a life-changing transformative experience which broadens the mind and acts as an agent of change is as old as the earliest recorded literature on traveling (Leed 1991). In the course of history, traveling has taken many forms, some of which are precursors to tourism in general, and others to modern-day, long-term independent travel in particular. While academic scholarship on the relationship between personal transformation and long-term independent travel is still in its early stages, the topic has gained traction for a number of reasons, including the increasing popularity of long-term travel among people of all age groups, recent societal changes (e.g. globalization, the recent global recession), the emergence of new tourist spaces, and technological advances.

Different conceptions of the meaning of travel have evolved over time, which have implications for transformative travel today. To understand current views on the transformative potential of travel, it is helpful to briefly examine the wider history of tourism and, in particular, the evolution of modern-day, long-term independent travel. There are significant differences between ancient and contemporary notions of the meaning of travel (Leed, 1991, 2001). Each period in world history has had its own types of travelers, and travel has had very different meanings for different people, depending on their motivations, gender, social status, race and ethnicity (Robertson, 2002). In the following sections, I will highlight some of the key factors across history that contributed to the evolution of independent travel. The contemporary academic literature on long-term independent travel is then discussed, in order to provide the reader with a deeper understanding of the independent travel culture, which is necessary to understand the present study and its results.

3.1 A brief sketch of independent travel from ancient times to the late 20th century

The heroic journeys of ancient times were neither undertaken for pleasure nor conceived of as entirely voluntary acts; rather, they were typically viewed as penance and suffering endured to enlighten and purify the mind (Leed, 2001). Traveling, which involved significant difficulty, was either seen as human fate or something which must be done out of necessity. This conception of the meaning of travel permeates ancient travel epics, such as *The Odyssey* and *The Epic of Gilgamesh*, where travels were decreed by God(s) or fate (Leed, 1991). Nevertheless, it is important to recognize that stories of these "involuntary travels" already emphasized the transformational value for the protagonists, who returned home wiser and stronger.

In the Middle Ages, in contrast, pilgrims embarked on journeys in pursuit of enlightenment and, in some cases, to visit sacred places to worship deities, while wandering European scholars traveled for several years on a "peregrinatio academia" (Leed, 1991) or study trip in search of experiential education. Such travelers left behind the material comforts of home and traveled light, taking only what they could carry on their shoulders and seeking education and enlightenment by practicing a simpler life (Kottler, 1997). Goeldner and Ritchie (2006) pointed out that the legacy of pilgrims is quite significant for understanding modern travel motivation in that it defines travel as a vital life activity and also suggests that certain key sites are of permanent spiritual benefit to the traveler.

During Renaissance times, the discovery of the New World and ongoing colonial exploration/exploitation opened up new possibilities for travel. In this age, travelers ventured into new areas to seek out scientific knowledge and experience the unknown (Leed, 1991). These long-term travelers were adventure-seekers who traveled as traders, amateur anthropologists, cartographers, botanists and above all, explorers (Riley, 1988). Although such travelers have often been portrayed (sometimes by themselves) as "heroes" traveling the world in search of knowledge, many were in fact unscrupulous mercenaries out to conquer and colonize new lands (Riley, 1988). In fact, the imperialist attitudes of such individuals are evident in many pre-modern travel accounts (particularly those before 1500), which are full of stereotypes about the indigenous cultures, which are depicted as not only exotic and strange, but inherently inferior to the traveler's cultures (Gosch & Stearns, 2008). In the context of the present research, one could say that the acquisitional motives of these travelers seems to have largely shielded them from the transformative process. That is, their store of knowledge about the world may have increased, but in many cases it seems that their cultural biases and fundamental beliefs about themselves and the world were not significantly transformed.

At the beginning of the 17th century, the socio-cultural environment fostered by the spirit of Renaissance Humanism led to the emergence of the Grand Tour, which lasted an average of three years. The Grand Tour was primarily undertaken by the young aristocracy or members of the highest social classes. This primarily involved white males who traveled for an extended period with a guide/tutor in order to increase their worldliness, sophistication and social awareness and to observe the manners of upper class people from other countries (Loker-Murphy & Pearce 1995; Galani-Moutafi, 2000). The typical Grand Tour itinerary spanned the European cultural centers of the time, including Paris, Florence and Rome (Goeldner & Ritchie, 2006). This kind of "tourism" was not understood as taking time off work, since those involved did not have to work. In addition, it is important to recognize that many of these travels were not "independent", due to the aforementioned guide (who sorted out most of the details of travel) and the financial resources available to most Grand Tour participants. Furthermore, education was an essential aspect of the tour (Urry, 1990, p. 154). In fact, some tourism researchers (Adler, 1985; Loker-Murphy & Pearce 1995; O'Reilly, 2006; Towner, 1985; Ivanovic, 2008) view this as the starting point for theories about modern day travelers, primarily due to the stated goals of education and self-improvement. In addition, the tour offered invaluable opportunities for networking with the European aristocracy (Weaver & Lawton, 2006) and engaging in behaviors considered deviant in their home societies such as "drinking each other under the table" (Feifer, 1985, p. 102). The Grand Tour was a marker of status and considered a rite of passage designed to supplement the formative cognitive education of the upper class.

One oft-cited example of the Grand Tour from the German-speaking world is the famous writer and statesman Johann Wolfgang von Goethe (1749-1832). In the midst of a full-blown mid-life crisis and dissatisfied with his political life, Goethe set off on a journey to the Mediterranean that lasted almost two years, where he experienced what he called a 'rebirth', living a life 'exactly like a youthful dream' (1816/17). His writing illustrates a strong desire to find himself while traveling. "My purpose in making this wonderful journey is not to delude myself but to discover myself in the objects I see" (Goethe 1816/17, p. 57). Traveling gave him the opportunity to reflect and see himself in a new and foreign context. "Nothing, above all, is comparable to the new life that a reflective person experiences when he observes a new country. Though I am still always myself, I believe I have been changed to the very marrow of my bones" (Goethe 1816/17, p. 147). This excerpt clearly exemplifies the transformative potential of traveling, as he was deeply affected by his journey.

The 19th century saw the emergence of a new class of travelers in Europe called tramps tramping brothers or journeymen (*Wandergesellen* in Germany or *compagnons* in France). The European tramping phenomenon emerged around 1870 and lasted until the First World War (Adler, 1985; Creswell, 2000). Tramps were primarily young, working-class males who wandered the world in search of employment, enjoyment and transformative experiences (Adler, 1985). They were itinerant tradesmen who were required to travel for several years in order to be certified as masters in their craft. A typical tramp trip would cover a thousand miles or more, including the Continent, the British isles, and even North America, and the German *Wanderpflicht* (travel duty) or the French *Tour de France* could last as long as 5 years.

Judith Adler (1985), who studied the tramping phenomenon in pre-modern Western society, considers the tramp a formative model for the contemporary long-term traveler. Similarly, Ateljevic & Doorne (2004) have called tramping the Grand Tour of the lower classes, as it gave young working class males the opportunity to experience some of the values of the upper class (Adler, 1985). Unlike the aristocratic Grand Tour, the journeyman's tramping system emerged out of economic necessity, as many tramps would not have had the funds to travel without engaging in work along the way. Despite their material differences, the functions of the tramping system and the Grand Tour were quite similar, as tramping also "served as a ritual aid in accomplishing the separation from home and family required by Western styles of adulthood, while offering young men an opportunity for sightseeing, adventure and education" (Adler, 1985, p. 337).

For example, Bayard Taylor (1846), the most prolific travel writer of the 19th century, started his career with the publication of *Views Afoot: Europe seen with Knapsack and Staff*, which tells the story of a tramp trip he undertook at the age of 20. He introduced his book as a "guide for those who would study in the college of the world" and explained his desire to "try the world with little dependence on worldly means." (cf. Adler, 1985, p. 348). For him, as for many other nineteenth-century novelists, tramping was the ultimate source of inspiration and a superb educational experience. The desire to see the world was the main motivation to engage in tramping. Similarly, English novelist and self-proclaimed tramp Bart Kennedy once wrote *"I listen to the tramp, tramp of my feet, and wonder where I was going, and why I was going."* (Kennedy, 1900, p. 161). Tramp travel was a good way to experience a different kind of reality, and even when tramp travel waned as a labor-related institution, novelists continued to romanticize it as a sublime educational experience (Adler, 1985).

The tramping system became highly institutionalized in several countries, and young tramps stayed in small inns established by their trade societies, which also paid them small travel allowances (Adler, 1985). This institutionalization can be explained by the fact that the privilege to move freely from place to place was historically reserved for the upper class, and traveling common people were viewed as vagrants. For this reason, efforts were made to officially control them. For example, German *Wandergesellen* (journeymen) were required to keep a *Wanderbuch* (travel diary), and French journeyman had to keep a *livret*. Failure to provide such documentation during a police inspection resulted in an arrest for vagrancy. However, due to this institutionalization, the dominant classes had a relatively favorable view of tramping. I was seen as a kind of education and often romanticized as the workingman's way to experience some of the values of the aristocracy.

In the time leading up to the First World War, the tramping system declined. This was due to the decline of formally organized craft associations resulting from increased industrialization, which concentrated labor in urban areas. Moreover, the extension of railways also contributed greatly to the decline of the tramping system by allowing tramps to bypass country roads and small towns on their way from one large employer to the next. Tramps would no longer spend years on the road, but rather visit only a few major cities.

Despite these developments, many working-class males continued the tramping lifestyle without the legitimization of craft associations. They soon came to be considered a social problem, as society began to see them as roving, unskilled vagrants viewed as juvenile delinquents who were motivated by a pathological "Wanderlust" (Adler 1985). Thus, when European tramping declined in Europe in the 1930s and became an informally structured road culture, the larger western society came to view this practice with skepticism and as marginal or even deviant behavior (Adler, 1985; Riley, 1988). In essence, the word "tramp" began to take on the derogatory meaning it has in American English, where it is synonymous with hobos, vagrants, beggars, vagabonds, or bums, and is used to connote a homeless person or vagrant wandering about on foot without a permanent home, living by begging or doing casual work.

3.2 From drifters to flashpackers

While many parallels can be drawn between historical long-term travel, the Grand Tour and the tramping phenomenon, modern-day, long-term, independent travel is of course dependent upon the specific characteristics of modern society. Although leisure tourism has become widespread in Europe and North America in the past century and a half (Urry, 1990), it wasn't until the 1960s that the age of global tourism was heralded, and "the tourist" emerged on the radar of academics. By the mid-1960s, travel had become internationalized, and greatly improved transportation made even the most distant and exotic places accessible to mass tourism (Urry, 1990).

This era was viewed as the democratized expansion of historically aristocratic or upper-class travel (Boorstin, 1964, p.77), which slowly grew to include the post-war middle classes in Western societies. The democratization and commercialization of tourism was made possible by numerous interdependent factors, including higher amounts of disposable income, increased standards of living, longer paid vacations, better work-life balance, advanced tourist infrastructure and increased motivation to travel (O'Reilly, 2006; Scheuch 1981; Young, 1973). In terms of motivation, the dominant emerging discourse of travel was based on the premise of escape, and holidays were considered culturally sanctioned periodic escapes from the everyday routine to "recharge one's batteries", i.e. to restore physical and mental health. Holiday-making became "almost a marker of citizenship, a right to pleasure" to which everyone was entitled (Urry & Larsen, 2011, p. 43). Travel became a routine event, and the tourist was the norm, rather than the exception.

The first scholarly conceptualizations of the tourist (e.g. Boorstin, 1964; Turner, 1973) presented a rather homogenous picture and neglected their pluralistic character, as well as the multiplicity of tourist experiences and motivations. The stereotypical picture of a tourist that emerged in the early 1960s was that of a middle-class, presumably western male (either single or as head of a family), a "wealthy, free-spending individual without taste or agency – literally deep pockets to be exploited" (Graburn & Barthel-Bouchier, 2001, p. 148). The tourism industry that had developed was "geared to dealing with people *en masse* and had become highly efficient and organized at attracting and coping with armies of working people from the cities" (Walvin, 1978, p.107, cf. Urry 2002, p.26).

In the 60s and 70s, two opposing viewpoints emerged among tourism scholars, On one side was Daniel Boorstin (1964), one of the first critics of mass tourism, who contended that "real travel", as performed in the golden era of individual travelers, was no longer possible because the development of mass transportation has made travel more pleasurable, affordable and accessible. He lamented that tourism had become a mindless, hedonistic, commodified activity whereby tourists prefer to stay in antiseptic "environmental bubbles" with all the comforts of home. In his view, tourist activities revolved around thoroughly inauthentic, staged attractions and contrived pseudo-events, rather than what he considered "authentic" experiences, where tourists seek to engage with the host society.

This view was in stark contrast to the American sociologist Dean MacCannell (1973), who pointed to the deeper structural significance of tourism and argued that many tourists are "secular pilgrims" in quest of authenticity, and that the modern tourist's quest for authenticity is similar to the "concern for the sacred in primitive society" (MacCannell, 1973, p.590). He equated the authentic with the pristine, the natural and the primitive, which had not yet been altered by modernity (MacCannell, 1976). MacCannell's quest for authentici-

3.2 From drifters to flashpackers

ty rests on the assumption that tourists need more than "'pseudo-events" because many of them feel alienated from their own society and are in search of authenticity, which they hoped to find outside of their home.

Indeed, at this time, many young people felt at odds with the materialistic values of their parents and the predominant socio-political context (Welk, 2004). The mid-1960s saw a worldwide upswing in student and youth revolution in response to global issues, such as the Vietnam War and specific national, environmental and political issues, all of which contributed greatly to the feeling of alienation from society and a desire to pursue alternative and countercultural lifestyles (Oliver, 2014). Israeli sociologist Erik Cohen (2003) traces the traveler's desire to adopt a nomadic lifestyle back to the widespread alienation among young people from their Western societies of origin, particularly the United States and Western Europe. This early differentiation in research between a mass tourist who experiences contrived pseudo-events and the traveler who seeks more authentic experiences marked the beginning of an ongoing debate on the tourist/traveler dichotomy, which is discussed further in section 3.2.3.

3.2.1 The drifter

Acknowledging the complexity of the debate, Cohen (1972) attempted to reconcile these two oppositional viewpoints by proposing a typology of four tourist roles. Cohen (1972) differentiated between two "institutionalized" and two "noninstitutionalized" tourist roles and positioned them along a continuum of novelty and the degree of familiarity/strangeness sought. The institutionalized group was divided into *organized mass tourists* and *individual mass tourists* depending on whether they traveled in large groups or alone. The group tourists take fully planned trips and have little say in daily decisions, as they are confined to tourist institutions established exclusively for tourists. Although the individual tourists pre-purchase only parts of their trips (e.g. airfare, accommodation, tours) and therefore had some level of flexibility in their itinerary, they are essentially the same as the group tourists, as both seek low-risk, familiar situations, and individual decision-making responsibility is almost completely eliminated.

In contrast, the two non-institutionalized roles—the *explorer* and the *drifter*— share values such as novelty, independence, risk, spontaneity and the ability to venture 'off the beaten track' (Cohen, 1972; Vogt, 1976). However, Cohen identified some key differences in the two roles. Although *explorers* try to avoid mass tourist paths, they still seek to maintain comfortable accommodations and reliable means of transportation, as well as some of the home comforts. They may try to engage with the local population, but they do not fully immerse themselves in the host society (Cohen, 1972). In contrast, *drifters* travel outside the tourism infrastructure altogether. They avoid typical tourist comforts and institutionalized accommodation and seek maximum engagement with their host communities. Cohen (1972) considered the drifter more of a risk-taker than the three other types (Riley, 1988). He defined drifters as a type of international tourist who:

> ...ventures furthest away from the beaten track and from the accustomed ways of life of his home country. He shuns any kind of connection with the tourist establishment, and considers the ordinary tourist experience phoney. He tries to live the way the people he visits lives, and to share their shelter, foods, and habits, keeping only the most basic and essential elements of his old customs. The drifter has no fixed itinerary or timetable and no well-defined goals of travel. He is almost wholly immersed in his host culture (Cohen, 1972, p.168).

In addition to the limited budget and absence of a fixed itinerary, the drifter also embodies a countercultural being who is alienated from society, often unpatriotic, hedonistic and anarchistic and emerging from a middle- or upper-class background (Cohen, 1973, p. 91-92). The drifter is thus "the true rebel of the tourist establishment and the complete opposite of the mass tourist" (Cohen, 2004, pp. 44-45). Moreover, Cohen (1973) suggested links between drifters and the drug culture, although he cautioned that not all drifters view drugs as the main motive for traveling. However, this connection was confirmed later by other researchers (e.g. Belhassen, Santos, & Uriely, 2007; Scheyvens, 2002; Uriely & Belhassen, 2005), who argued that drug-taking is a common recreational activity among backpackers and indicative of the adherence to countercultural ideals and the abandonment of accepted norms. In her study of Israeli backpackers in India, Maoz (2006) found that one of the main motivations for Israelis to travel to India was to experience drugs, and many travelers "arranged their days, and sometimes their entire trip, around drugs" (p. 129).

Cohen's drifter type seems to capture the stereotypical hedonistic hippie traveler of the 60s and 70s. It depicts Western youths as alienated from their mainstream societies of origin, drifting the world and attempting to create alternative lifestyles that would replace their home societies (Cohen, 2003). The 'hippie overland trail', which was traveled by hundreds of thousands of Westerners in the early 1960s, stretched from London to Istanbul, ran through Iran, Afghanistan, Pakistan and India, and ended in Nepal or further east to South-East Asian and Oceanic countries (MacLean, 2006). The travelers themselves, carrying nothing but steel or aluminum-framed backpacks, considered the travel lifestyle as a more meaningful or authentic way of existence (Ateljevic & Doorne, 2004), a form of

3.2 From drifters to flashpackers

rebellion against their home societies, and even a way to change and revolutionize them (Welk, 2004). Many hippies were also inspired by beat generation writers such as Jack Kerouac and Allan Ginsberg, with their strong countercultural stance and openness to Eastern religions (Oliver, 2014). However, drifter travel began to decline with the end of the hippie era, when Cold War hostilities and conflicts in many countries along the hippie trail made overland travel on these routes too dangerous.

During the late 70s, 80s and 90s, international, long-term budget travel began to grow, and inexpensive regions such as Southeast Asia became increasingly popular (O'Reilly, 2006). This was also reflected in increased academic interest, with some researchers seeking to re-define Cohen's derogatory image of drifters and remove their hedonistic stigma. Thus, in academic literature, Cohen's drifter has also been referred to as wanderers (Vogt, 1976), hitchhikers (Mukerji, 1978), tramping youth (Adler 1985), long-term budget travelers (Riley 1988), backpackers (Loker-Murphy & Pearce 1995; Richards & Wilson, 2004), and more recently flashpackers (i.e. upscale backpackers, see for example Jarvis & Peel, 2010), or lifestyle travelers (Cohen, 2011).

Jay Vogt (1976), for example, agreed in principle with Cohen's differentiation between institutionalized and noninstitutionalized tourists. He suggested that the travel style of the group that he labeled "wanderers" was a product of and reaction to affluent society. However, he cast a more positive light on his wanderers. Rather than citing alienation and rebellion against society as their main motivation, Vogt asserted that their goal was personal growth and learning, including developing an understanding of themselves, other people and other cultures (Vogt, 1976).

Similarly, Pamela Riley's (1988) study on "international long-term budget travelers" provides valuable insights into this travel style and the psychology behind it. She describes the long-term budget traveler as a form of the non-institutionalized role that shares characteristics of both the explorer and the drifter. Due to the lack of a fixed itinerary and the low budget, Riley's type of traveler is closest so Cohen's (1972) early description of the drifter. However, she argues that the derogatory label "drifter" is misleading in that it suggests deviant behavior (Riley 1988, p. 327) undertaken by social dropouts (O'Reilly, 2006). She posits that long-term budget travelers are neither deviants nor heroes, and thus the earlier characterization of them as anarchistic or hedonistic drifters is no longer accurate, as today's travelers are not generally alienated from society.

Broadly speaking, Riley (1988) argued, "the average traveler prefers to travel alone, is educated, European, middle class, single, obsessively concerned with budgeting his/her money, and at a juncture in life" (p. 313). Riley (1988) builds on Nelson Graburn's (1983) rite-of-passage tourism, which Graburn associated with major changes in one's biography, such as adulthood, career breaks, divorce (p.12). Riley (1988) depicts her long-term budget travelers as rite-of-passage travelers and compares them to the tramp travelers of former times. Rite-of-passage travel is a type of liminal experience (Turner 1974) that allows a kind of self-testing (more on rite of passage in section 4.1.4). Moreover, in contrast to Cohen and Vogt, who both focused on young travelers, Riley (1988) does not restrict long-term budget traveling to any age limit and shows that all age groups engage in this travel style. The terms "long-term" and "budget" are useful in this definition in that they describe the individuals' desire to extend the trip beyond a cyclical holiday in order to gain flexibility in their itinerary, but they are still subject to the constraints of limited financial resources (Riley, 1988).

3.2.2 Backpacker culture

Philipp Pearce (1990), who introduced the term "backpacker" to academic scholarship, also supported Riley's assertions. The term "backpacker", which has now largely replaced the more derogatory term "drifter", is commonly used to define a wide range of independent travelers, including Vogt's "wanderer" and Riley's "international long-term budget traveler". Pearce (1990) asserts that "backpacking is best defined socially rather than in economic or demographic terms. Being a backpacker is an approach to travel and holiday taking rather than a categorization based on dollars spent or one's age" (p.1). He delineates backpackers as usually young, primarily white and middle-class Westerners, who pursue longer holidays with a flexible and independently organized itinerary and have a preference for budget accommodation (Pearce, 1990; Pearce & Foster, 2007). In terms of the activities that are characteristic of backpackers, research suggests that they prefer more informal and participatory activities, while also pursuing formal activities such as visiting historical monuments, museums and other cultural sites (Richards & Wilson, 2004b).

Pearce's (1990) definition of backpackers corresponds largely with that of other researchers who assert that backpackers constitute a distinct category of tourists that differs from institutionalized mass tourists (Loker-Murphy & Pearce, 1995; Pearce, 1990; Richards & Wilson, 2004b; Uriely, Yonay & Simchai, 2002). They range from "gappers" or "gap year travelers" (i.e. young people taking a year off between school and university, during or after university) to people in their 20s and early 30s seeking to experience the adventure of a lifetime (O'Reilly, 2006; Jarvis & Peel, 2010). However, since the 1990s, the backpacker market has grown from a marginal segment into a global industry at the margins of mainstream tourism and is now recognized as an important market by policy makers and the tourism industry alike (Cohen, 2003; Hampton, 1998; Richards & Wilson, 2004a; Scheyvens, 2002).

However, despite the growing popularity of backpacking, the bulk of the existing literature on international tourism focuses on the two institutionalized roles of mass tourism, and until recently, academic scholarship paid little attention to backpacker activities. The scant research on backpackers may be because of their limited economic impact and because they are commonly viewed as impecunious and even undesirable drifters or hippies (Cohen, 2003; Hampton, 1998; Jarvis & Peel, 2010; Richards & Wilson, 2004a). Like drifters, backpackers have been criticized for their appearance, stinginess, conduct (e.g. sexual freedom and use of drugs) and seclusion in backpacker enclaves (Cohen, 2003). Moreover, backpackers are a diverse tourist type and harder to pin down and investigate than more institutionalized travelers.

3.2.2.1 The institutionalization of backpacker tourism

The backpacker enclaves, in particular, have contributed greatly to the institutionalization of backpacker tourism and growing academic interest. With the first enclaves created along the hippie overland trail in the 1960s (e.g. Istanbul, Kandahar, Kabul, Goa), certain well-trodden circuits most favored by backpackers (primarily in South-East Asia and Australia) have experienced a "massification" (Hampton, 2010); that is, more and more Europeans and Australasians traveled to these regions and stayed in backpacker enclaves. These enclaves are functional spaces that were created specifically for backpackers, which offer many home comforts, such as familiar and inexpensive food, cafes, internet access, laundry services, second-hand bookshops, visa services and travel agencies. Many private transportation networks comfortably link well-developed destinations along backpacker trails, which makes it possible for backpackers to never really leave the well-trodden path and engage mostly with other backpackers rather than the local population. Thus, enclaves are concentrated spaces in which the backpacker community is reinforced, rejuvenated and maintained (Richards & Wilson, 2004).

Within academic literature, these enclaves have received different names, ranging from "gathering places" (Vogt, 1976), "safe havens" (Hottola, 2005), "spaces of suspension" (Wilson & Richards, 2008), "metaworlds" (Hottola, 2004), "a cultural home away from home" (Westerhausen, 2002), or more derogatively, "ghettos" (Krippendorf, 1987) and "backpacker bubbles" (Llyod, 2003). Moreover, they provide recreational and psychological benefits for travelers via opportunities for networking and in-group socialization and restore a sense of control they may have surrendered during their travels when navigating complex cultural environs (Hottola, 2008). Many backpackers settle down in these enclaves for varying periods of time to recharge their batteries before returning to the road again, while for others – more institutionalized backpackers – these enclaves are the final travel destination point that offers opportunities for hedonistic mass consumption.

Backpacker enclaves also contributed greatly to the negative image associated with backpacker tourism. It has been argued that the enclaves create a temporary social world that enables a "surrogate cultural experience of difference which is more akin to the home culture of the traveler" (Wilson & Richards, 2008, p. 191). For many backpackers, these enclaves represent liminal zones with suspended social strictures that allow hedonistic and culturally insensitive behaviors, such as drug-taking, drunkenness or casual sexual activity that both their home and host cultures consider unacceptable. Such "casually imperialistic" behavior may negatively impact local cultures and stir up hostile sentiments among the local population. In Thailand, for example, until recently a "No hippies welcome" sign greeted people upon arrival at the airport (Pearce, 2005, p. 30). In the worst case, it may even result in events such as the 2002 bombings of two night clubs in the backpacker enclave Kuta Bali, which killed hundreds of backpackers (Coward, 2002). In the end, these enclaves, which represent a socially unrestricted environment, have contributed to the institutionalization of backpacker tourism and reinforced the negative image of backpackers, especially along the popular backpacker routes in Australia and South-East Asia (O'Reilly, 2006).

As early as 1973, Cohen had already highlighted the emergence of such enclaves and pointed out the link between these institutions and two types of drifters: outward- and inward-oriented. While the former sought far-away locations and engagement with locals, the latter were more interested in remaining in the enclaves and engaging with their fellow drifters. In 2003, Cohen introduced the term *Vermassung* (i.e. massification) to describe a change in the nature of backpacking in late modernity that caused a growing rift between the ideology and the actual practice of backpacking. He argued that backpacking today is more akin to mass tourism than genuine travel and maintained that traveler enclaves had created the very institutionalization of tourism infrastructure that drifters had initially rejected. Although they claim to idolize the concept of drifting, many backpackers travel on itineraries that are parallel to those of organized mass tourism (Elsrud, 2001). Cohen has identified a new group of "contemporary drifters", who strive to distinguish themselves from mass backpackers just as mass backpackers seek to set themselves apart from mass tourists (2003 p. 97).

In the context of backpacker research, it is important to point out that these enclaves also make very convenient data sources for researchers, and indeed, much of the backpacker research has been conducted along well-developed backpacker trails (i.e. South-East Asia and Australasia). Some researchers have even pointed out the need for backpacker research conducted beyond these routes. This study helps fulfil this need to some degree, as much of my field research was conducted in Latin America, which offers a different kind of backpacker experience, which I have witnessed first-hand. My initial backpacker travels within the Southeast Asia circuit included obligatory stops in places such as Bangkok's Khao San Road, the full moon party in Koh Phangan (southern Thailand), and the backpacker retreats in Kuta Bali or Ubud (Indonesia), where the motivations of most backpackers were routed firmly in relaxation and partying. Latin America offered a less institutionalized backpacker experience. While certainly not devoid of backpacker infrastructure, it is far less developed than the Southeast Asian backpacker circuit, and thus presents different challenges.

In fact, many of the travelers I met in Latin America had gained their first experiences on the South-East Asian or Australasian circuit. They had then decided to head to Latin America because they wanted to get away from the beaten backpacker trail in South-East Asia and Australasia. As Glen (26, England) explains:

> It's the kind of British normal thing about just going to do the [*Australian*] East Coast... like going to Ibiza... It's a party place. It was a good place to go first. At that age I would have been too scared to go to South America, it would have been too much of the unknown, at that time." And Australia was more safe.

This was true for me as well, and I would not have had the courage to venture alone to Latin America without having gained confidence traveling in South-East Asia first. I noticed that the balance between outward- and inward-oriented backpackers was tilted more in favor of the latter in Latin America (with the possible exception of the Brazilian coast, where the beach scene and well-developed tourist infrastructure tended to draw more outward-oriented backpackers). Thanks to this diversity of locations, I have been able to compare these mentalities in my research, as discussed later in the paper.

3.2.2.2 Heterogeneity of backpacker culture

With the steady growth in backpacking and the concomitant increase in research activities, this tourist style moved out of the periphery of academic interest. Until recently, backpacking was viewed largely as an undifferentiated phenomenon and as a sub-segment of tourism studies, neglecting important factors such as the social forces at play in the traveler's societies of origin that may have triggered their desire to travel (Cohen 2003). Recently, more and more academics have cautioned against this homogenization of backpackers (Ateljevic & Doorne, 2000a; Cohen 2004; Nash, 2001; Sørensen, 2003; Uriely et al. 2002) due to the growing size and scope of the community. Cohen (2004), for example, argues that the emergence of the large-scale contemporary backpacking phenomenon is a result of a number of distinctive traits of modern Western societies and has called for research into the diversity and fragmentation of the phenomenon, particularly with regard to age, gender, nationality and subcultures. However, Richards & Wilson (2004b) suggest that it is important not to define backpackers solely on the basis of external characteristics, which may differ greatly from the experience of the travelers themselves (p.19). In the same vein, O'Reilly (2006) asserts that while it is certainly true that backpacking has become more mainstream, which may have caused some to question the validity of experiences, it cannot be assumed that the experiences are any less valuable from the point of view of the backpackers.

In responding to the call for more differentiated research that highlights the heterogeneity within the backpacker culture, a number of recent studies examined the culture of backpacking (Binder, 2005; Muzaini, 2006; Murphy, 2001; Sørensen, 2003; Westerhausen, 2002), backpacker enclaves (Ateljevic & Doorne, 2005; Howard, 2005, 2007; O'Regan, 2010; Wilson & Richards, 2008), destination development (Hampton, 1998; Scheyvens, 2002) backpacking experiences (Uriely, et al., 2002;) gender (Maoz, 2007, 2008; Muzaini, 2006) age (Cave, Thyne & Ryan, 2007; Hecht & Martin, 2006; Thyne, Davies, & Nash, 2004), nationality (Noy & Cohen, 2005), social interactions (Huxley, 2005; Murphy, 2001; Ryan & Mohsin, 2001) and themes such as risk-taking and adventure (Anderskov, 2002; Elsrud, 2001; Lepp & Gibson, 2003; Noy, 2004; Ryan, 2003), drug-taking (Belhassen, et al., 2007; Uriely & Belhassen, 2005), postcolonialism (Teo & Leong, 2006), backpacker learning (Pearce & Foster, 2007), motivations (Maoz, 2007; Murphy, 2001; Richards & Wilson, 2004b). Some studies have looked specifically at different ethnic groups, particularly from certain Asia-Pacific countries (Chen, Bao, & Huang, 2014; Teo & Leong, 2006) and Israel (Hottola, 2005; Maoz, 2008; Reichel, Fuchs, Uriely, 2005).

In addition to studying the social construction of backpacker tourism this travel style also feeds into other types of tourism such as "OE" (overseas experience) travelers (e.g. Bell, 2002; Wilson, Fisher, & Moore, 2009), volunteers (e.g. Wearing, 2001b; Brown & Lehto, 2005; Zahra & McIntosh, 2007; Ingram, 2011; Simpson, 2005), missionaries (e.g. Walling,

3.2 From drifters to flashpackers

Eriksson, Meese, Ciovica, Gorton, & Foy, 2006), exchange students/sojourners (e.g. Gaw, 2000; Brown, 2009; Milstein, 2005) and expatriates on work assignments (e.g. Hurn, 1999). There is now an ever-growing list of new forms of tourism that are considered alternatives to conventional mass tourism, trying to "bring back the true spirit of the traveler" and moving holidays "beyond sheer relaxation towards the opportunity to "study", "learn", and "experience" the world (Singh, 2004, p. 4, emphasis in original) and tourism scholars have come up with a multitude of terms to describe types of tourism that differ from mainstream mass tourism, such as alternative tourism, authentic tourism, green tourism, responsible tourism, integrated tourism, adventure tourism, ecotourism, nature-based tourism (Singh 2004, p. 4) and even psytrance tourism in Goa (D'Andrea, 2010).

As evidenced in the research activities outlined above, the backpacker market is becoming increasingly fragmented, and new forms of backpacking have emerged over the last few years. Thus, some researchers have proposed further sub-dividing backpackers into specific sub-types (e.g. Binder, 2004, Cohen, 2011; Maoz & Welk, 2004; Sørensen, 2003; Uriely, et al. 2002). In the last decade, new types of backpackers have been identified, starting with Cohen's distinction between outward- and inward oriented backpackers (as described above) or the "backpacker plus" (Cochrane, 2005), who may still travel with a backpack but takes shorter trips (i.e. weeks rather than months) and may stay in slightly more expensive accommodations (Hampton 2010).

The most recent literature on backpacking has produced several subtypes, the most prominent of them being the lifestyle traveler (Cohen, 2011) and flashpackers (Jarvis & Peel, 2010). Lifestyle travelers constitute a niche segment within the backpacker market for whom travel is not a cyclical break or a once in a lifetime transition to another life stage. Instead, for lifestyle travelers, traveling ceases to be a transitional experience and has morphed into a way of life which they may pursue indefinitely (Cohen, 2010). Another sub-segment of backpacker tourism that emerged recently is flashpackers, who are considered "upmarket backpackers" (Jarvis & Peel, 2010). They are defined as older backpackers (late twenty to forties), often on a career break, with more disposable income and not afraid to 'splash out' during their travels. Many of them had backpacked when they were younger and are now returning to the backpacker travel style but with more money. They tend to travel with technology (e.g. laptop, mobile phone, flashdrive) but engage with mainstream backpacker culture (Hannam & Diekmann, 2010, p. 2). Flashpackers have been considered one of the key constituents of modern travel manifested by the changing demographics and motivations in Western societies (Hannam & Diekmann, 2010).

3.2.3   Tourist/traveler dichotomy

A discussion on situating long-term independent travelers within this study would not be complete without examining the difference between the notions of "tourist" and "traveler", as they cannot be used synonymously. As Singh (2015) pointed out, "all tourists include some travel, but not all travel is tourism" (p. 4). Academics have debated this seemingly simple distinction for years, and research has shown that the traveler's identity is primarily constructed in opposition to what it avoids being – the tourist (Boorstin 1964; Cohen, 2003, 2011; Dann 1999; Galani-Moutafi 2000; Jacobsen, 2000; Spreitzhofer, 1998; Welk, 2004). Thus, the tourist-traveler dialectic is closely linked to the question of identity and self-definition, and many travelers themselves take great pains to distinguish themselves from the masses of tourists, whom they often detest. The distinction between traveler and tourist has been underpinned by the rhetoric of moral superiority (MacCannell 1976). In line with Fussell (1980), who spoke of *tourist angst*, I propose the term *touristophobia* for this phenomenon.

The proliferation of tourist typologies trying to classify tourist practices and behaviors, such as Cohen's (1972) distinction between institutionalized tourists and non-institutionalized travelers, and Gray's (1970) basic distinction between tourists who are motivated by *sunlust* (i.e. the desire for a single destination, stay put vacation) and travelers who are motivated by *wanderlust* (i.e. leave familiar things and seeking to explore new places and cultures), fueled the battle waged between the classificatory distinction of tourist and traveler.

A common argument is that travelers set themselves apart from tourists by actively searching for the authentic "Other" with whom they envision meaningful encounters, while at the same time wanting to overcome a superficial "Other", as represented by mass tourism (Huxley 2005). This quest for authenticity was first conceptualized by Dean MacCannell (1976), who contended that alienated people from Western society are unable to be satisfied in their own societies and thus look for it elsewhere, in places that they think of as more authentic and original. Such places are often "the pristine, the primitive, the natural, that which is as yet untouched by modernity" (Cohen, 1988, p. 374). The quest for otherness and authenticity is simultaneously associated with a desire to disassociate oneself from mass tourism (Munt, 1994). This is in line with Savener (2016), who argues that travelers search for the primitive in remote regions of the world "in order to quell the mundanity of everyday life and incorporate unusual experiences as part of a deliberate construction of identity (p. 139). Indeed, it has been argued that unusual travel experiences fulfill the promise of adventure and physical as well as intellectual challenge, which many people cannot find in the (late) modern world, and which are reflected in the personal narratives and self-representations which result from gazing into the Other (Galani-Moutafi, 2000). Thus, unusual, authentic travel experiences hold the potential to reveal the authentic self (Steiner & Reisinger, 2006).

Drawing on Kierkegaard, MacCannell's (1976) concept of authenticity was expanded further by other scholars into the human attribute of being true to one's essential nature (Steiner & Reisinger, 2006, Wang 1999). Existential authenticity is intrinsic to the search for meaning and to the search for one's inner self and living in accordance with one's sense of self. This authentic self can be realized much more easily outside the limits of ordinary life and the constrictions of socially prescribed roles (Kim & Jamal, 2007; Wang, 1999).

> The role of long-term travel in providing 'authentic' experiences of the other and of the self consists of a series of opportunities for escaping the restrictions of previous identities and providing experiential material for the reconstruction of self-identity. Travel experiences are thus drawn upon to re-imagine and redefine the self. (Wearing, Stevenson, Young, 2010, p. 48)

Thus, it has been argued that travel facilitates existential authenticity (Reisinger, 2013; Wang, 1999), personal growth and self-development:

> Travel is seen as pursuing the ageless aristocratic principle of broadening the mind. [...] Travel experience is presented as a resource in the task of self-making. Travel is required to yield an intensified, heightened experience of oneself. It shakes you up in order to make you a more mature, complete person (Rojek, 1993, p. 175).

The themes of searching for authenticity and countercultural attitudes, including a rejection of mass tourism, have been explored by many other travel writers as well (e.g. Paul Theroux, Bill Bryson, Ernest Hemingway, Jack Kerouac), and are resonant in the long-term travel culture as well. Paul Theroux, for example, was quite outspoken about his disdain for tourists and sought to set himself apart by stressing the solitary nature of his travels and expressing the sense of freedom and novelty of this kind of travel. He also recognized that traveling not only engaged his visual senses, but all of his other senses as well, as travel triggered a variety of feelings within him (Galani-Moutafi, 2000, p. 218). Similarly, in his posthumously published collection of essays "Anatomy of Restlessness", the inveterate traveler Bruce Chatwin (1996) mused at great length about the virtues of the nomadic lifestyle and noted that it is an emotional, rather than a rational impulse that lets people "abandon civilization and seek a simpler life, a life in harmony with "nature", unhampered with possessions, free from the grinding bonds of technology, sinless, promiscuous, anarchic, and sometimes vegetarian" (p. 85).

Many travelers agree with Chatwin's (1996) deliberations on travel as a way to reveal the authentic self and reject the mindless consumption commonly associated with mainstream tourism by incorporating social responsibility and personal growth into their travel practices and motives. They subscribe to this anti-tourist stance by stressing the individuality that separates them from the tourist masses. Cohen (2003) noted that this tourist-traveler dichotomy does not seem to be of concern to ordinary (mass) tourists, and suggests that backpacking is more "ideologically 'loaded', and hence necessitates some express mechanisms which may help to maintain the identity of the backpackers in face of the discrepancy between their ideology and practice" (p. 100).

This has been confirmed by various studies (e.g. O'Reilly, 2006; Spreitzhofer, 1998; Welk, 2004). Just as many backpackers are keen to distinguish themselves from tourists, many travelers now distinguish themselves from mainstream backpackers, particularly the party backpackers (Welk, 2004). Richards and Wilson's (2004b) study on backpacker behavior included a question about whether the respondents considered themselves travelers, backpackers or tourists. Interestingly, less than 20% identified with the 'tourist' label, while more than half considered themselves 'travelers' and about a third 'backpackers'. The self-defined backpackers in the study tended to be young and traveling in areas with a significant backpacker infrastructure and enclaves, such as in Australasia and Southeast Asia, whereas the self-defined travelers tended to be older and had previous travel experience.

According to Ateljevic and Doorne (2000b), long-term travelers now often strive to distinguish themselves from mainstream backpackers because their travel ideology and purposes are different from those of mainstream backpackers. White & White (2004) found that older long-term travelers in the Australian outback self-identified as travelers rather than backpackers or tourists because the concept of travel more accurately reflects the meaning these trips had for the people undertaking them (p. 202). Many travelers associate mainstream backpackers with the practices of partying and having fun (hedonistic principles) rather than engaging with the host community and immersing oneself in new cultures. In this way, the backpacker scene has experienced a further subdivision and a new wave of "anti-backpackers" has emerged, who self-identify as (long-term) travelers and aim to follow less institutionalized backpacker trails (Welk, 2004).

3.3 Introducing LITs

As we have seen, the nature of travel is quite heterogeneous and encompasses a wide range of motives, travel styles and time frames, and it would be rather superficial to classify travelers as members of a unified group (Elsrud, 1998). And while this thesis does not strive to pigeonhole long-term independent travelers into a specific tourist typology, it is important to delineate the concept of traveler deployed in this study, in order to better understand their transformative experiences and the meanings they attach to their travel experiences. It is therefore useful to define the terms *long-term, independent* and *traveler* because the length of time immersed in another culture and the travel style impact the type of experiences and thus the potential for transformation. In addition, for reasons of readability, throughout the term *long-term independent traveler* will be shortened to LIT throughout this paper.

3.3.1 Long-term

Long-term refers to the powerful notion of time within the context of travel, as the temporal aspect is critical with respect to the transformative potential that long-term travel entails. Long-term travelers enact journeys that are distinct from other types of mobilities in that long-term travel affords individuals the opportunity to slow down their pace of life (Krippendorf, 1987) and to become "makers of time" (Elsrud, 1998). It allows travelers to take a break from the fast pace of life at home and exert self-determination by structuring their personal lives according to their own free will. In light of the constant struggle for work-life-balance and modern life practices determined and constricted by the industrial imperatives of productivity and consumerism, long-term travel provides a space that is free from social expectations and from what Parkins & Craig (2009) have termed the "late modern malaise of hurry sickness" (p. 1). It thus provides an insight into other ways of experiencing, appreciating, seeing, feeling, hearing, tasting, and knowing the here and now.

Moreover, temporal and spatial dislocation from one's home culture facilitates the accumulation of varied experiences and the longer and more engaging (enjoyable) experiences last, the more value they create (Pine & Gilmore, 2011). Being in control over one's own life and the pace of one's journey is, in itself, a truly rewarding experience for some people. For many, slowing down "creates time and space to experience and appreciate the journey – to engage with and enjoy other people and places, to immerse themselves in nature and self, to pursue special interests, to share their experiences with like-minded travelers" (Tiyce & Wilson, 2012, p. 118). The existing literature on international sojourns has shown that longer programs impacted participants more strongly than shorter programs (Kehl & Morris, 2008), and Ateljevic & Doorne (2000b) have shown that longer tourist experiences provide more time for self-reflection, which they linked to personal growth and self-discovery.

For the purpose of this study, a minimum duration of six months of travel was selected as the pertinent criterion for defining "long-term". As illustrated in section 5.3 in the methodology chapter, participants in this study traveled between six months to 8 years before returning home or settling down elsewhere. When selecting research participants for the (first) interview, it was important that travelers had traveled for at least six months without interruption or returning home. Travelers who indicated that they had an accumulated six months of travel over multiple trips (e.g. three trips of two months each) were not included in this study.

A minimum of six months was considered an adequate time frame to enact a travel style that is distinct from other tourist mobilities, in that such travelers can engage with time and space in different ways and may consciously decide to travel slowly (Tiyce & Wilson, 2012), as well as experiencing identity conflicts and potential readjustment difficulties upon their return. Anecdotal evidence from countless conversations with fellow travelers during the participant observation part of this research led to the assumption that that the longer one is away from one's home culture, the more challenging the return was perceived, and this assumption underpins this thesis. This time frame is also long enough to allow for a flexible itinerary and distinguishes long-term traveling from a typical holiday break, as discussed in the following section.

3.3.2 Independent

The travel industry considers all tourists who are not package tourists (i.e. purchase their air travel and accommodation package with a travel retailer) independent travelers (Hyde & Lawson, 2003). Broadly speaking, this is also *one* of the defining characteristics of the LITs in this study, as they distinguish themselves from other "tourists" by actively avoiding mainstream and mass tourism and formalized tourism infrastructure. Independent travelers tend to make their own travel arrangements (e.g. accommodation & transportation), often with little or no prior planning. They travel with a flexible, rough itinerary in mind or with no itinerary at all and often rely on word-of-mouth recommendations from other travelers, which allows them to change locations frequently or stay in a place for as long as they wish. This also demonstrates their competence in navigating through other cultures (Sorenson, 2003) without relying on external assistance. While they may join a tour group for a short period to access certain destinations, the ideology of autonomy, independence and free will lies at the very core of their travel agenda.

However, independence, as it is framed in this thesis, does not simply refer to the lack of pre-booked travel arrangements and flexible itineraries. Independence also refers to the individual's perceived sense of freedom and self-determination that is not normally available in everyday life (Krippendorf, 1987). It highlights the significance of the liberation from institutional and social structures and the ability to exercise unconstrained independence, with its inherent benefits and challenges. Independent travel provides a space where the individual is removed from the dictates of mainstream values, such as status competition and the accumulation of material wealth commonly imposed by contemporary Western society.

Naturally, the notion of independence as a state of being free from any confinement, influence or subjection to dominant institutional control and commercialism is problematic. To a certain extent, travelers' independence is always confined by general aspects, such as the temporal, local, cultural, social and environmental conditions of a place, as well as individual aspects, such as budget constraints, personal state of health, and language ability – many of which are beyond the traveler's sphere of influence. In this context, however, independence must not be understood in this literal sense, but rather in how these travelers construct an "independent" sense of self through the performance of traveling. Independent travel can thus be understood as an identity project, and may even be one of the key motivations for LITs. The theme of travel and self-development will be elaborated on in section 4.1.5 of this thesis.

3.3.3 Travel

The term travel in this context refers to a specific kind of mobility that sets itself apart from other types of cross-cultural mobilities, such as working, studying or volunteering abroad. Some researchers have grouped these different types of mobility under the travel label, which makes perfect sense if the focus of the research is, for example, on cross-cultural adaptation or general engagement with another culture. However, while the benefits derived from volunteering, working and studying abroad have been studied widely, they are inextricably linked to an institutionalized context that limits the freedom of choice that many LITs seek out in the first place. These other types of mobility represent a considerable reconceptualization of the meaning and purpose of travel by blurring the lines between the demarcations of leisure/labor, freedom/discipline, novelty/routine, and agency/structure. Thus, travelers who travel abroad for the *sole* purpose of studying, paid or unpaid work or expatriation have been excluded from this study.

That being said, I did not exclude travelers who interrupted their travels for short spells of work, especially since many LITs traveling for months or even years need to replenish their funds periodically or want to linger in a place for a while to volunteer or study the language. Ateljevic & Hannam, (2008) have argued that travel should not be viewed as distinct from everyday life, as lifestyles in general are becoming increasingly mobile in the late modern world, often blurring the lines between leisure and labor. Indeed, the combination of work and travel is becoming increasingly common and is even actively promoted by some countries that receive large numbers of independent travelers. New Zealand and Australia, for example, have developed working holiday systems by offering extended visa programs for people to interrupt their travels and take on odd jobs. Similarly, the WWOOF movement (which stands for either World Wide Opportunities on Organic Farms, or Willing Workers on Organic Farms, depending on the source) is a network of organizations that work to match volunteers with organic farms around the world (Deville & Wearing, 2013). Although these positions are not paid, the food and accommodation provided afford volunteers the opportunity to experience a different culture first-hand, and some travelers incorporate such experiences into their journeys in order to prolong their time abroad and deepen their involvement with another culture.

Such work experiences connect modern-day travelers to 19th-century tramps, and indeed, some of the LITs in the present study took on various jobs in the course of their travels. This was true for myself as well. In my extended Latin America trip, I stopped several times to pick up work when the opportunity arose, both to supplement the travel fund and to expand the scope of experiences abroad. In Honduras, for example, I worked as a scuba divemaster for several months; in Costa Rica I taught English to adults for two months; and in Bolivia I worked as a jungle guide with a small ecotourism company for three months in a large cloud forest, guiding fellow travelers on single to multi-day trips through the jungle. Although none of these jobs were particularly lucrative, they served the important functions of taking a break from being constantly on the move and providing the opportunity to experience the local culture more deeply. Nevertheless, it is important to emphasize that this study focused on people who spent the majority of their time abroad "on the road", where they could make autonomous choices and pursue interests according to their own free will.

Finally, related to the concept of free will, it is important to mention that LITs are not to be confused with migrants or refugees, who have become displaced or "homeless" for economic, religious, political or environmental reasons. Long-term independent travelers in this study are conceived of as leisure travelers who engage in a wholly voluntary kind of mobility, and while some may settle down elsewhere after their travels, the majority of travelers intend to return home at one point.

3.3.4 Delineating LITs from other types of alternative tourism

Due to the similarities, many researchers have categorized long-term independently organized travel under the header of "backpacking" (e.g. Kontogeorgopoulos, 2003; Richards and Wilson, 2004b; Sørensen, 2003; Spreitzhofer, 2002). Although backpacker research and other sub-types such as lifestyle travel provide useful reference points and are similar in many ways, they also differ from this paper's conceptualization of LITs in a number of ways.

LITs are a diverse group of individuals, ranging from so called "Gap-year" travelers" (i.e. young travelers taking a year off before study or work), to people in their 20s and 30s all the way to the 60s and possibly older taking the opportunity to travel independently and for an extended period, i.e. for a minimum of six months. Many see in their first long trip a one-off adventure or trip of a lifetime, while others may return to this or shorter types of travel regularly. In fact, research (e.g. Richard and Wilson, 2003) and personal experience has shown that once the "travel bug" bites, a travel career that spans an entire lifetime may be the result of a long-term travel experience. In this context, Cohen's (2011) lifestyle traveler, who periodically returns to extended travel, forms a small subset of LITs.

As with other tourist types, the demographics (age, socio-economic, educational and cultural backgrounds), motivations, attitudes, budgets and travel styles of LITs vary significantly. However, it should be noted that LITs most often belong to a privileged elite who have access to a variety of financial, social, technological and cultural capital that allows them to leave their home cultures for an extended period and to immerse themselves into different cultures (including the travel culture) on their own terms. The majority of LITs in this study are primarily (though not exclusively) middle class and come from northern to central Europe, North America, Australia, New Zealand, South Africa, Israel. Hence, they are people from more affluent Western societies who have increased options and resources to participate in long-term independent traveling. The recent years, however, have seen a sharp rise in backpackers and long-term travelers from the emerging industrial countries in Latin America and Asia, which opens up a new and rich vein of future research.

3.4 Summary

This chapter provided the broader historical context from which contemporary LITs emerged, from ancient pilgrims to modern hippie drifters. It also offered a glimpse into the heterogeneity of present-day traveler culture. In this context, we have seen some of the tensions between different factions of this community, as both the travelers themselves and the scholars who study them have sought to define different factions based on factors such as motivations, travel styles, behaviors, or budgets. Recognizing this diversity, the chapter nevertheless concluded with a functional definition of the target group of the present research – long-term independent travelers. In essence, they are people who travel for at least six months with very limited pre-planning of their itineraries and a general tendency to move from one location to the next. Finally, it is important to point out that many of the participants in this study did not travel for the sake of mobility alone, but as a means to stimulate transformation and personal growth. These are people who viewed their travel experience as a mission with a particular purpose. To understand the nature of this mission, the next chapter explores the transformative potential of long-term independent travel.

4 Transformative Travel

The previous section attempted to provide a historical context for the emergence of the contemporary LIT, as proposed in this thesis. We have seen that the alienation felt by many people in the 1960s as a result of socio-political events served as a driving force for many to create alternative lifestyles and participate in modern-day long-term travel. While some researchers argue that towards the end of the 20th century this alienation from society faded due to the changing social, economic and cultural environment (Cohen, 2003), I believe that the prevailing economic, socio-political and cultural environment stimulates many people today to seek fulfilling experiences outside their comfort zone.

Since Cohen's drifters in the 1960s, life in contemporary Western society has changed dramatically, and our comfort zones have changed as well. Some have even argued that travel today offers fewer possibilities for exploration, adventure and novelty than in the past (Boorstin, 1964) and therefore less opportunity for personal growth and transformation. This view, however, is rather limited, as the processes of globalization and increased mobility do not produce cultural uniformity but rather make us aware of new levels of diversity (Featherstone 1995, pp.13-14). Moreover, the increasingly mobile world does not reduce or limit the potential for transformation through travel, but rather makes it a far more multifaceted, complex and intricate phenomenon to explore. The richness of the travel experience is embodied by "sensual performances that take place, the unique psychological and physiological reactions triggered by physical, carnal encounter, the altered performances that travel away from familiarity seems to permit and the effects of the plethora of random happenings that may unfold – varying degrees of encounter with mobile, fluid and transforming spaces, places, landscapes, people/s and objects at unique moments in time" (Lean, Staiff, Waterton, 2014, p.12).

The term *transformation* is context-dependent and can mean different things in different contexts. A generic description of transformation is "a complete change in the appearance or character of something or someone, especially so that that thing or person is improved" and associated with terms such as change, metamorphosis, paradigm shift, transition, transfiguration and perspective change (Cambridge Dictionary, 2017). By this definition, transformation has to result in an improvement. While I challenge the notion that all transformation results in improvement, this implication has certainly held true for the vast majority of the travel and tourism discourse. Travel experiences in foreign cultures are commonly associated with transformative processes, as they may affect or influence an individual's sense of self and cultural identity (Sussman, 2000). The psychologist Jeffrey A. Kottler (1997), who coined the term "transformative travel" and introduced it to academic discourse (Ross, 2010), agrees:

> Travel offers you more opportunities to change your life than almost any other human endeavor. People who structure their journeys in particular ways consistently report dramatic gains in self-esteem, confidence, poise, and self-sufficiency. They enjoy greater intimacy as a result of bonds that were forged under magical and sometimes adverse circumstances. They become more fearless risk takers, better problem solvers, and far more adaptable to ever-changing circumstances. They become more knowledgeable about the world, its fascinating customs, and its diverse people. Finally, travel teaches you most about yourself – about what you miss when you are gone and what you don't, about what you are capable of doing in strange circumstances, about what you really want that you don't yet have. Regardless of what exactly you are looking for, and where you hope to find it, travel may change your life for the better. (Kottler, 1997, p.xi).

A staunch advocate of the transformative potential of travel, Kottler considers physical travel a panacea that acts as an agent of change and offers a myriad of opportunities for self-exploration, personal growth and transformation that may lead to a better life (Brown, 2013) and have enduring implications on attitude and behavior (Kottler, 1997, 2014; Lean, 2009, Ross, 2010).

Kottler (1998), compared successful transformation through travel with the successful outcome of therapy in that the individual integrates the lessons learned while traveling into the new self when back home. In contrast to therapy sessions, however, Kottler (1998) argues that travel places the individual in a novel context that forces him or her to develop new resources and respond creatively to challenging situations, which ultimately leads to faster and better learning (p. 25) and a greater potential for transformation.

In a similar vein, Reisinger (2013) advocates transformative travel and argues that human survivability is inextricably linked to our ability to transform our attitude, values and behavior and to become better citizens of the world.

> In order to make a change, and consequently, reach the next stage of human growth, we need to follow a transformation path. We need to transform ourselves – our values, life priorities, lifestyle and the way we use resources and spend time and money. We must move towards a world in which we learn about the purpose and meaning of our life, a world that gives way to new values of ecological awareness, empathy for others, non-violence, human rights and equality (Reisinger, 2013, p. xii).

Reisinger (2013) argues that travel can do just that – it can transform a person into an improved self; it holds the potential to transform our taken-for-granted perspective, behavior, lifestyle and relationship with the world. It can turn us into "responsible thinkers" (Mezirow, 1991a) who have acquired more inclusive, tolerant and self-reflective ways of thinking.

While the nexus between personal transformation and travel is well-established and has been written about extensively, academic interest in the transformative potential of travel is still in its infancy and has only slowly gained traction since Kottler's introduction of transformative travel in the late 1990s. The last decade, in particular, has seen increased interest in transformative travel and even led to an academic paradigm shift towards the emerging perspective of *hopeful tourism* (Pritchard & Morgan& Ateljevic, 2011). Hopeful tourism scholarship seeks to transform tourism enquiry, education and practice by engaging emancipatory and democratic learning agendas, by emphasizing critical thinking, action and education for a sustainable and just world (Pritchard, Morgan & Ateljevic, 2012 p.7). Pritchard et al. (2011) believe that through tourism we can "re-discover contemplative life, but only if we have the philosophical ambition and intellectual courage to do so" (p. 958).

The World Tourism Organization (UNWTO) propagates this new tourism mindset and dedicated its 2016 report to transformative travel. The introduction statement of the report "*The Transformative Power of Tourism – a paradigm shift towards a more responsible traveler*" (2016) states: "Tourism is much more than a leisure activity; tourism holds an immense potential to set new paradigms of thinking, to encourage social and cultural changes and to inspire a more sustainable behavior" (p. 8).

This raises the question of how this paradigm shift towards transformative travel came about. Ateljevic et al. (2016) provide an answer by referring to the inception of the "21st century era of consequences and responsibility", largely precipitated by the dominant socio-economic model of continuous mindless consumption and limitless growth (p. 12). In a world dominated by post-9/11 terrorism fear and political populism, economic and social insecurity, threats posed by climate change and resource depletion (Pritchard et al., 2011), many of the so-called "cultural creatives" in contemporary western society feel disillusioned by the paradigms of success and consumerism imposed by society (Ateljevic et al. 2016). They have long realized that the socially imposed ideals of accumulating material wealth and gaining status may only bring temporal fulfillment, but ultimately bring emptiness (Layard, 2005). Another reason may be found in the increased disposable income and access to travel, particularly in the Western World. Despite significant challenges in the recent past (e.g. financial crises and the global threat of terrorism), international tourism has experienced a steady growth since the 1960s. With international tourist arrivals of 1.24 million in 2016, it is one of the fastest growing industries in the world, surpassing that of food, oil or automobiles. (UNWTO, 2017).

Transformative tourism embraces socially and environmentally conscientious travel practices that are underpinned by the "silent revolution" which is spearheaded by a growing number of so called "cultural creatives". The concept of cultural creatives was put forward in 2000 by the sociologists Paul Ray and Sherry Anderson (2000) and they are defined as individuals who acquire "new ways of looking at, and new ways of being in the world" (Ateljevic et al., 2016, p. 12). Cultural creatives are inner-directed, embrace globalism, positive human values and relationships, spirituality and authentic experiences, altruism and social activism and adopt lifestyles that are reflective of these values (Ateljevic et al., 2016; Ray & Anderson, 2000). In line with cultural creatives, Ateljevic et al. (2016) defined transformative travelers as individuals who

> travel in order to re-invent themselves and the world; they travel in order to volunteer and make a difference; they value what is small and simple and aim for self-reliance; they are connected and communicative; they seek meaningful experiences which help them develop personally and collectively. In sum, they use travel to reflect upon their lives and get the courage to make crucial life changes upon their return back home, not only in terms of their lifestyle, but also the type of work they do (Ateljevic et al., 2016, p. 17).

Thus, cultural creatives are transformative travelers or new conscious consumers (Ateljevic et al., 2016), who consider travel a powerful medium to reinvent themselves and search for new ways of living and new worldviews.

With their study on transformative travelers and visitors to the south Indian township of Auroville, Ateljevic et al. (2016) contributed to the scarce amount of empirical research on the travel characteristics of cultural creatives and their desire for transformative tourism. The empirical survey results showed that the majority of transformative travelers are mostly young to middle-aged, highly educated, well-traveled and prefer to travel independently. Their research also confirmed their assertions that transformative travelers demonstrated a strong commitment to social and environmental justice and valued the learning aspect of the travel experience (pp. 12-34).

While addressing many aspects of the travel characteristics of transformative travelers, the study, however, provides only limited insight into the multidimensional nature of transformative learning. Specifically, it fails to address crucial elements of transformative travel, such as why and how some experiences are transformative and others are not, as well as contextual factors, and transformational triggers. In addition, it does not specifically say in what way their travel contributed to this socially and environmentally responsible worldview, or whether they had adopted this worldview prior to their travels. It also does not explain how the actual transformative processes occur within the individuals and if the transformational changes are permanent.

In this thesis, I have adopted a "fluid" view of transformation, as travel does not occur in a vacuum but is embedded in the social context of the individual. I argue that many different aspects of an individual may be subject to transformation, including one's knowledge, behaviors, values, attitudes and beliefs, roles in society, relations with others and personal narratives, to name but a few. These aspects are interrelated and fluid in that they can change over time and in different contexts and at different rates, and transforming any of these will have a different effect on the individual, depending on the importance assigned to it. I believe that one of the main reasons why travel has such high transformative potential is because it offers numerous opportunities for experiencing disorienting dilemmas, where old habits of thinking and acting no longer work, and the meaning perspective cannot filter new experiences using preexisting meaning schemes. These disorienting events often precipitate the decision to travel, occur while traveling and sometimes again upon returning home. The navigation of disorienting dilemmas, where a dissonance between frames of references occurs, is also at the core of cross-cultural transition theories. For this reason, this chapter explores the stages before, during and after the actual travel experience.

4.1 Before travel: Motivational dimensions

The theme of tourist motivations, which seeks to answer the seemingly simple question of *why* people travel, has been a central focus of academic scholarship since the 1960s (Hsu & Songshan, 2008) when tourism became a topic of interest in various disciplines. With the onset of mass tourism in the 1960s, travel motivation was commonly perceived as a means of hedonic pleasure and relaxation (Carr, 2002; Dann & Cohen, 1991; Shields, 1990). However, while enjoyment and relaxation may be the main motivating factors for some tourist types, the view of travel as a means to satisfy hedonistic desires is a rather simplistic one that ignores many other facets of this complex human behavior.

The commodification of leisure travel coupled with the changed world order in the late 20th century order brought about a proliferation of highly specialized tourism products (e.g eco-tourism, spiritual tourism, heritage tourism, adventure tourism, volunteer tourism) (Gibson & Yiannakis, 2002) and concomitant research activities into tourist motivations have illustrated that travel motivations are far more diverse than initially conceived. This is certainly true for the LITs in this study, who at one point in their life decided to replace the creature comforts of home with a transient way of life, at least for a certain period of time. From a strictly financial point of view, each of the travelers in this study could have chosen a shorter and infinitely more comfortable and luxurious vacation, but instead they opted for an extended "time out". Understanding the triggering factors and motivations underlying the decision to engage in long-term independent travel is crucial for understanding the potential transformations during or after the journey. Thus, this section seeks to first provide a theoretical foundation of the main travel motivation theories and then discuss some of the existing research on the travel motives of long-term travelers and backpackers.

4.1.1 Conceptual approaches to travel motivation

Conceptual approaches to tourist motivation are primarily rooted in sociology and psychology. Tourist motivation has been linked to the satisfaction of psychological needs, and several models and frameworks have been developed over the past few decades that try to classify tourists based on their motivations and travel styles. A review of the literature on tourist motivation has shown that there is no universally accepted conceptualization on why tourists set out to travel, but researchers have identified a number of (often interrelated) factors. The most basic distinction was probably the one proposed by Gray (1970), who identified two main travel motives, contrasting between *sunlust* (i.e. the desire for a single-destination, stay-put vacation) and *wanderlust* (leaving familiar things and seeking to explore new places and cultures).

One of the most widely adopted conceptualizations of travel motivation is the *push/pull* model initially advocated by Dann (1977, 1981) and Crompton (1979). The sociopsychological push factors refer to intrinsic or intangible travel motives that stimulate people to seek travel activities that satisfy their needs, whereas pull factors refer to external destination attributes that trigger people's desire to travel.

In his sociological approach to tourist motivation, Dann (1977), focused on push factors and argued that they are often an antecedent to pull factors (Hsu & Songshan, 2008). He proposed *anomie* and *ego-enhancement* as important push factors within travelers. In his theory, the sociological term "anomie" refers to situations where "norms governing interaction have lost their integrative force and where lawlessness and meaningless prevail" (p. 186). In other words, anomie is representative of an alienated individual's desire to "transcend the feeling of isolation obtained in everyday life" and to simply "get away from it all" (p. 187). Dann's (1977) second factor, ego-enhancement, derives from the social need for recognition and status. He suggested that travel provides one way for individuals to feel superior, which ultimately results in an ego-boost. Pearce (1982) pointed out that Dann's anomie echoes Maslow's need for love and belonging while ego-enhancement is similar to Maslow's self-esteem need, but lamented that these two factors only provide a limited insight into the multidimensional motivations for travel.

Crompton (1979) sought to make up for this limitation and identified seven socio-psychological push motives (*escape, self-exploration, relaxation, prestige, regression, kinship-enhancement,* and *social interaction*) and two cultural or pull motives (*novelty* and *education*). He argued that the push factors have a certain degree of influence on the destination choice, which in turn influences the travel behavior and travel style. Crompton's decision to classify novelty as a pull factor may be questioned, and it can be argued that novelty, which in motivation theory has been used synonymously with curiosity, appears to be more like a push factor (Hsu & Songshan, 2008). Curiosity has commonly been described as a driving and motivational force that stimulates learning. Freud (1915), for example defined curiosity as a "thirst for knowledge" (p. 153) and Maslow (1970) viewed it as an important intrinsic determinant for acquiring knowledge.

The push/pull framework has been widely adopted in tourist motivation research (e.g. Hsu & Lam, 2003; Turnbull & Uysal, 1995; Yoon & Uysal, 2005), but opinions diverge on whether push and pull factors are equally relevant for studying tourist motivations. Although some researchers consider both push and pull factors equally important motivators (Yoon & Uysal, 2005), others do not consider pull factors as relevant for studying tourist motivations (Kim & Lee, 2002; Klenosky, 2002; Nicolau & Mas, 2006) and have even suggested eliminating them from tourist motivation studies (e.g. Kim & Lee, 2002; Klenosky, 2002; Pizam, Neumann & Reichel, 1979). While push and pull factors may refer to different stages in decision-making (Hsu & Songshan, 2008), it has been argued that they are interrelated and "two sides of the same motivational coin" (Goossens, 2000, p. 302). For example, travelers may be pushed to leave by internal forces, for example, by the desire to quench their thirst for novelty, and simultaneously pulled towards a destination because it offers certain attractions that may satisfy this need.

Another model commonly referred to in travel motivation literature which builds on the push-pull model is the two-dimensional *escape/seeking* framework proposed by Iso-Ahola (1982) and Mannell & Iso-Ahola (1987). They theorized that travel motivation is triggered by two motivational forces which influence tourist behavior: (1) the desire to escape everyday environments (e.g. routine and stressful environments) and (2) the desire to seek intrinsic rewards (e.g. stimulation through novel experiences, feelings of mastery and competence). These two primary motivational forces can be further subdivided into personal and interpersonal factors. Intrinsic personal rewards include relaxation and learning about other cultures, while interpersonal rewards include meeting and socializing with other people. Escaping the personal world means getting away from personal problems or failures while escaping the interpersonal world means getting away from family, friends and acquaintances (Iso-Ahola, 1982).

The main idea underpinning their dialectical framework is that individuals are internally motivated to travel because they hope to obtain certain intrinsic rewards in a contrasting environment while simultaneously avoiding something (Iso-Ahola, 1982; Mannell & Iso-Ahola, 1987). Iso-Ahola's escape-seeking model is similar to the push-pull motivational forces, but offers an important refinement to the latter in that it does not simply view the seeking (pull) forces in terms of destination attractions, but rather stresses the intrinsic benefits derived from travel. Although commonly perceived as conceptually useful, Iso-Ahola's model fails to explain why people want to escape from their social worlds, which will be discussed further below in section 4.1.3.

It has also been proposed that traveler's motivational patterns change over their life and with accumulated travel experience. Following Maslow's (1954) hierarchy of needs theory of motivation, the social psychologist Philip Pearce (e.g. 1988, 1993, 2005, 2009) developed the travel career ladder (TCL) approach, which identified five different levels of tourist motivation which are arranged on a hierarchy or ladder towards higher-level needs. At the lowest level are relaxation needs, followed by safety/security needs, relationship needs, self-esteem and development needs, and finally self-actualization and fulfilment needs at the very top of the ladder (2005). Pearce postulated that people progress upward on the travel career ladder as they accumulate travel experience and seek satisfaction of higher-level needs later in life.

Although frequently cited in tourist motivation literature, the model's practical application and underlying assumption that travel motivations follow a linear manner could not be confirmed empirically (Ryan, 1998). In fact, in a later study that sought to further confirm and expand the original TLC theory, Pearce and his colleagues (Lee & Pearce, 2002, 2003; Pearce 2005; Pearce & Lee, 2005) found an important contradiction to the original study, and proposed the travel career pattern (TCP) as a further development of the TCL.

They found that those travelers with less travel experience actually rated the motives of self-actualization and self-development as more important, whereas the more experienced travelers emphasized host-site involvement as the driving forces for travel (Pearce, 2005, p. 67). The model also suggests that people's motivation changes across their life stages and emphasized patterns rather than a hierarchy of motivations.

Pearce's TLP theory is a multi-motive approach suggesting that "all travelers, regardless of their travel career levels, are influenced by the most important and central travel motives (such as novelty, escape/relax, and relationship) as well as by less important motives (such as isolation, nostalgia, and social status)" (Pearce, 2005, p. 79). While the validity of the model requires further empirical testing, the proposition that travelers tend to be affected by multiple motivators rather than a single one has been put forward by other researchers as well (e.g. Hsu & Songshan, 2008; Kim & Lee, 2002; Swarbrooke & Horner, 2007).

Although the aforementioned motivational models and frameworks offer insight into the general reasons why people travel, it is unclear whether they help explain the travel motivations of those individuals who set out to travel independently for a longer period of time. However, it is crucial to understand the triggering factors or trigger events that motivate someone to leave as these triggers often impact all events involved in travel (Parrinello, 1993). Motivation literature on long-term travel is very limited and the majority of studies have a strong focus on young backpackers, which include, but are not limited to long-term travelers. Nonetheless, a review of the literature on the motivations of long-term travelers/backpackers yields four main motivational triggers based on patterns and combinations and include novelty-seeking, escapism, freedom and self-development.

4.1.2 Novelty-seeking

> I can't think of anything that excites a greater sense of childlike wonder than to be in a country where you are ignorant of almost everything. Suddenly you are five years old again. You can't read anything, you have only the most rudimentary sense of how things work, you can't even reliably cross a street without endangering your life. Your whole existence becomes a series of interesting guesses.
>
> Bill Bryson (1991, p. 44)

Novelty-seeking is considered one of the key motivators for travel. Cohen (1972) first introduced novelty-seeking to the tourism literature by placing tourists on a continuum of novelty-seeking and familiarity-seeking, with the drifter being located on the novelty-seeking end of the spectrum. This is similar to Stanley Plog's (1974) classification of *psychocentric* and *allocentric* tourists based on their personality and desire for novelty. He referred to psychocentric tourists as passive, risk averse and unadventurous. They do not exhibit high levels of curiosity, tend to return to familiar locations, prefer peaceful travel destinations and choose travel destinations that are perceived as safe. In contrast, he described allocentric tourists (which he further divided into explorers and drifters) as active and risk-taking tourists who travel for reasons of excitement and adventure. Not only are they comfortable meeting strangers, they actively seek unfamiliar situations. In this sense, Plog's distinction not only influences the traveler's destination choice but also has a strong influence on the traveler's mode of travel. Plog (2001) recently updated his model and re-labeled psychocentrics as *dependables* and allocentrics as *venturers*.

Likewise, the psychological concept of *optimal arousal* seeks to explain travel motivation. According to this theory, which was put forward by Wahlers & Etzel (1985), those travelers who are under-stimulated in their home environment seek travel experiences that are stimulating and novel, whereas those travelers who escape an overstimulated environment seek to obtain an optimal level of arousal by slowing down during their travels. Seeking to understand people's pre-travel daily life at home may yield valuable insights into travel motivation, travel behavior and style and life after one's return.

Kottler (1998) argued that for many, "intellectual curiosity" is a main motive for traveling. In other words, their main motivation springs from a strong intellectual desire to learn about many different aspects of the world. He argued that some people want to be stimulated by learning as much as possible about the world and get bored easily with their routine jobs at home. In a similar vein, Anderson (1970) termed this desire the "Ulysses factor", which expresses itself in an intense curiosity to explore new places and interact with different people. According to Anderson (1970), the independent traveler is not "looking for anything in particular and is not greatly concerned with what he discovers. It is in this sense that he is a true explorer" (p. 179, cf. Hyde & Lawson, 2003).

Some scholars have even suggested novelty-seeking is an innate quality in travelers (e.g. Cohen, 1979; Kottler, 1998; Lee & Crompton, 1992; Mayo & Jarvis, 1981), which is also reflected in popular travel writing. In the first paragraph of the book *Travels with Charlie*, Nobel-prize winner John Steinbeck (1962) described the desire for novel experience in this way:

> When I was very young and the urge to be someplace was on me, I was assured by mature people that maturity would cure this itch. When years described me as mature, the remedy prescribed was middle age. In middle age I

was assured that greater age would calm my fever and now that I am fifty-eight perhaps senility will do the job. Nothing has worked... In other words, I don't improve, in further words, once a bum always a bum. I fear the disease is incurable (p. 3).

In his mind, this "disease" or "incurable itch", as Steinbeck conceived of his desire to be someplace else, cannot be cured and does not disappear with maturity and greater age. Once infected with the "travel bug", one is trapped forever. This is echoed by Mayo & Jarvis (1981), who argued that some people may even be born with an innate desire to explore the world around them, and Lee & Crompton (1992), who maintain that some individuals have a genetic predisposition to novel experiences due to a certain level of arousal.

But why are some people on the lookout for new experiences while others are quite happy with how things are? While none of the above-mentioned researchers had any scientific proof for their assertion that novelty-seeking is a genetic trait, personality theory may provide an answer and is thus mentioned briefly here. The biological psychiatrist Robert Cloninger (1987, 1994) found that novelty-seeking behavior is related to specific neurotransmitter activity in the brain, which partially confirms the existence of an innate desire and genetic predisposition for novel experiences. In his psychobiological theory of personality, he identified novelty-seeking as one of four inherited temperament domains. Novelty seeking is characterized by the "tendency to engage in exploration of novel stimuli, [...] by impulsive decision making, intense responses to cues for potential rewards, and active avoidance of frustration. Individuals high in novelty seeking tend to be impulsive, exploratory, fickle, excitable, quick-tempered, and extravagant. Generally, they engage quickly in new activities, but are easily bored" (Cloninger, 1987, cf. Noggle, Rylander, Soltys, 2013, p. 354). Cloninger (1994) also found that high novelty-seeking personalities are also at risk of developing psychological personality disorders, such as addictive behaviors and attention deficits.

Links can be drawn between Cloninger's dimension of novelty-seeking personality and Hans Eysenck's (1967) differentiation between the two extremes of extraversion and introversion, which reflects individual differences in the cortical arousability of the brain. Eysenck argued that introverts are very sensitive to stimuli and as a result feel overstimulated and uncomfortable with high levels of stimulation, such as large crowds of people. In contrast, extroverts tend to prefer high levels of stimulations and are easily bored when under-stimulated. Instead, they are drawn to large groups of people, enjoy meeting other people, loud music, busy surroundings and novel situations.

As we have seen, there are many different perspectives on novelty-seeking as a key motivator for travel. While distinctions such as those between extroverts and introverts, allocentrics and psychocentrics and theories of optimal arousal may help explain why someone chooses to opt for a travel style that relishes a certain degree of uncertainty and risk, it is important to remember that many travelers fall somewhere between these extremes. Another point to remember is that personalities as well as personal ideas of what is novel can change over time and affect one's travel career over time. What is novel at first may soon become normal and therefore lose its attraction, - a point that will be more closely examined in the empirical part of this work.

4.1.3 Escapism

It is widely accepted that escape is one of the most important driving forces behind travel (e.g. Krippendorf, 1987; Mayo & Jarvis, 1981), and this is particularly true for long-term travelers. Molz (2012) even argued that the modern world requires an escape: "The modern individual can escape the stress and structure of modern work life, the conformity of consumer society, the constraints of moral norms and even the ordered hierarchies of social class identity" (p. 138). The reasons for escape identified in motivation literature are manifold: escape from mundane routine life at home, escape from an anomic society, escape from social constrictions and expectations, escape from one's personal or interpersonal life crises (Crompton, 1979; Dann, 1977; Krippendorf, 1987; Iso-Ahola, 1982; MacCannell, 1976; Turner & Ash, 1976). In order to foster a feeling of escape, Crompton (1979) argued that the travel destination must be physically and socially different from the home environment. This novel environment allows for a multitude of novel and unusual experiences, which is essential for self-discovery.

For many, the idea of being completely freed from the constraints and responsibilities of everyday life is the main impetus to escape. Crompton (1979), for example, argued that a "break from routine" (p. 414) provides the main impetus for many travelers, as people are increasingly dissatisfied with traditional concepts of life that revolve around work. Molz (2012) argued that "long-term independent travel, in particular, represents an escape from the overbearing monotony of a corporate career, epitomized by a 9-to-5 schedule worked in a non-descript office-cubicle" (p. 138). This was supported by Maoz (2007), who in her qualitative study on the motivations of young Israeli backpackers (aged 20-25) in India found that the majority of her subjects sought to escape the materialistic and stressed society, to "rest and do nothing" (p. 128), which is considered deviant in Israeli society.

4.1 Before travel: Motivational dimensions

Travel gave them the opportunity to break away from the rigidly structured routine of their home society.

In addition to escaping the monotony of daily life, escaping an anomic environment is still an important push factor three decades after Dann (1977) initially proposed it in the late 70s. Dann's anomic society bears resemblance to Gergen's (1991) state of multiphrenia, characterized by a fragmented and incoherent sense of self that is often overwhelmed by conflicting options, values, and motives and feelings of self-doubt, failure and permanent duty. Escaping an anomic society is also at the heart of MacCannell's (1976) proposition that traveler's alienated from Western society search for authenticity in other cultures with "purer, simpler life-styles" (p. 3) in order to find their place in the world. From this angle, this quest for authenticity is a reaction to fast-paced modern society. This was supported by Ateljevic and Doorne (2000a), who conducted focus groups with long-term travelers, and found that many travelers were increasingly dissatisfied with the global capitalist world, the Western way of life, the pressures of globalization and loss of control over their lives. Through long-term travel in more relaxed destinations, they hoped to find meaning in life by exploring other lifestyles.

Many young people in the life stage of emerging adulthood (Arnett, 2000b) see travel as a way to escape or postpone adult responsibilities. In some countries, such as the UK and Ireland, taking a "gap" year or more off after high school or study is quite common and socially accepted. Similarly, the "overseas experience" in Australia and New Zealand is commonly perceived as a rite of passage (O'Reilly, 2006), while many young Israelis take some time off to travel after their obligatory military service (Maoz, 2007; Noy, 2004). Similar to Cohen's (1973) drifter, who is on a "prolonged moratorium from adult middle-class responsibility" (p. 89), for many emerging adults, the long-term travel experience is comparable to Erikson's moratorium, which allows individuals to free themselves from socially constructed norms and expectations and enter a liminal space that provides opportunities for self-exploration (see section 4.1.4 for a discussion of the liminal space).

And finally, Iso-Ahola (1982) has argued that many people travel to escape from personal or interpersonal failures and problems. The motivation to travel may be induced by a disorienting dilemma, to use Mezirow's terminology, such as the death of a loved one, failed relationships or divorce, a career break or the loss of a job. Such trigger events can prompt the need or desire to make significant life changes and provide the energy to act. For some LITs in this study, the trigger events act as an energizing factor to disengage from unsustainable life circumstances in order to see things from a different perspective.

Such escape can provide a much-needed distance to reconsider one's life and choices. This is supported by Jeffrey Kottler (1998), who argued that many people are so threatened by change and find it so hard (e.g. changing one's lifestyle, working less), the only way out is to physically escape home in order to make radical changes in one's life. He quotes an example from his own therapeutic practice where alcohol abusers "escape" to in-patient alcohol withdrawal clinics or "health camps" lasting several weeks that separate people from their familiar environment in order to change something in their life. He argues that this separation from the familiar surroundings can help them reprogram their bad habits or lifestyle (at least for a certain period of time), and opens up new paths to a healthier life.

Although the escape motive is useful to understand the impetus for LITs to travel in this study, the forces of globalization and recent technological advances have blurred the lines between home and away, as separation from home is less strict than it used be when communication was difficult. When I set out on my first long-term travels in the mid-90s, staying in touch with friends and family at home was a tedious process that involved making expensive phone calls and mailing letters that would take weeks to arrive. Now, with e-mails, blogging, and internet phone calls, keeping in touch with home has become very easy. The increasing popularity of Facebook and Skype and the proliferation of internet cafes in what seem to be the most remote corners of the world now make it possible to chat in real time, share pictures and images with the rest of the world and stay up-to-date with what is going on at home and the rest of the world, thereby blurring the lines between home and away.

4.1.4 Freedom through liminality

The notion of escape within travel motivation studies has been paralleled by a discussion of seeking, as depicted in Iso-Ahola's (1982) escape-seeking framework. In her study on long-term budget travelers, Riley (1988) explained their motivations using "Paul Theroux's (1975) words, 'equal parts escape and pursuit' – that is, the result of both push and pull factors" (Riley 1988, p. 317), the latter including "an opportunity to experience real freedom" (p. 318). In this sense, travel offers not only an escape *from* something but also an escape *to* an environment of perceived freedom, choice and agency, a space that differs significantly from home and that allows freedom to explore and play out new versions of the self.

This is supported by Krippendorf (1987), who argued that travel provides the individual a sense of freedom which is not available in everyday life. Most travelers engage in long-term independent travel out of personal choice, and research has shown that perceived freedom features strongly in people's motivation to travel (Iso-Ahola, 1982; Kleiber, Walker, & Mannell, 2011). The notion of freedom, whether perceived or real, implies the ability to make decisions and to have options. This was shown by Naomi and Peter White (2004), who examined the motivations of mid-life and older long-term travelers and found that the sense of freedom inherent in long-term travel is not only a freedom from social constraints and pressures of everyday life but also "offers alternative ways of living, the chance to do things differently and most significantly to live spontaneously. Long-termers are not tied to one place; they are not bound by time. They can stay in one place for extended periods, or 'just up and move along'" (p. 212). The travel process itself is in some way characterized by a suspension of ordinary life in that the decision to stay in a place or move on is often based on opportunities that arise in the host environment (e.g. staying because someone offered a place to stay).

White & White (2004) found that long-term travel provides a transitional zone that acts as an "interval away from social pressures and new or different responsibilities or roles" (p. 201). They compared this transitional zone to "rites of passage" where individuals move from one life stage to another, as illustrated by Erikson's psychosocial moratorium. Arnold van Gennep (1960) was the first to conceive of travel as a rite of passage and proposed the three phases of preliminal, liminal and postliminal phases of the rite of passage. Victor Turner (e.g. 1969, 1973, 1974), who popularized the rite of passage model in the 1970s, re-labeled these stages of a rite of passage as *separation, margin* (or *limen*) and finally *reintegration* (or *re-aggregation*) that the individual passes through. The separation stage refers to the temporal and spatial movement in which one leaves the "normal" home environment and enters an unfamiliar one. The liminal stage is conceived of as a metaphorical threshold or transitory stage which separates the known from the unknown, in which one has to prove oneself in an unfamiliar environment and make decisions without the advice of parents, teachers, or any authoritative figure. This transitory state of liminality (Turner, 1974) is commonly viewed as a time frame free of obligations (Elsrud, 1998), a moratorial break and safe space away from the expectations and the scrutiny of modern Western societies. In the final stage of reintegration the individual returns home as a "new" person with a transformed identity.

White & White (2004) argued that the decision to travel for an extended period was usually precipitated by the end of a life stage. Many of the middle-age to older respondents were in between jobs or were burned out, experiencing empty nest syndrome or the death of a loved one, or were simply dissatisfied with the monotony of everyday life. Long-term travel was thus found to offer a form of escape and a way to regain personal control over one's life. This freedom includes indulging in activities that would be frowned upon at home, such as doing nothing, hanging around in cafes for days or weeks, writing journals or interacting with other travelers. In her study on Israeli backpackers in India, Maoz (2007) found that travel provided a "sense of total freedom and moratorium" and "escape from their former conformist behavior" (p. 130) bridging the gap between compulsory military service and adult life responsibilities.

The rite of passage model applied to travel is a useful heuristic device that can help understand the dynamics and function of traveling (Cohen, 2003). Historically, rites of passage, such as the Grand Tour or the 19th-century tramping culture, marked the transition from adolescence to adulthood. However, rites of passage often occur at critical junctures or periods of crisis at any point in life, and they are commonly triggered by a disorienting dilemma. Successful completion of the trip and resolution of difficult situations is viewed as an accomplishment and proves the individual's competence to manage her own affairs autonomously, which is also an important cornerstone of adulthood in Western society (Cohen, 2003).

Some researchers (e.g. Cohen, 2004; Noy & Cohen, 2005; Sørensen, 2003) have questioned the applicability of the rite of passage model and argued that the view of travel as a liminal and transitory experience that ends with the reintegration in one's home culture does not entirely hold true in the postmodern era. For one, the institutionalization of backpacking with the aforementioned enclaves that cater to the travelers' needs as well as the ease of staying in touch with home through modern communication technologies and extended social networks have made an escape from everyday life impossible and blurred the distinctions between home and away. Rather than viewing travel as a linear process between home and away with the suspension of everyday life at its core, they argue that it must be viewed as an extension of daily life, a "home plus experience" (Richards & Wilson, 2004c, p. 254). Similarly, despite the liberation from socio-cultural constraints imposed by their home societies that curtailed their freedom, the idea of complete freedom through travel is illusory as the travel environment is also defined by economic and socio-cultural constraints.

Furthermore, the discussion of long-term travel as a rite of passage with clearly marked boundaries between home and away has also been problematized by the fact that the re-integration stage does not apply to many travelers. This was shown by Scott Cohen's (2011) lifestyle travelers, for whom travel is no longer a liminal experience but has become a way of life, and Noy & Cohen (2005), who identified a growth of "serial" backpackers, who engage in repeated (long-term) travel and do not see it as a once in a lifetime experience. Further complicating this situation is the idea that the final "re-integration" stage of the rite of passage model assumes that the individual re-integrates seamlessly as a new and stable person (Turner, 1982). This is problematic, as many travelers may not want to return to their previously structured life at home and have retained some parts of the new cultures encountered, and therefore experience repatriation stress upon returning home (see section 4.3).

Despite these reservations of the applicability of the rite of passage model and the notion of travel as a liminal space, the perceived sense of freedom is crucial for the individual traveler and the meanings they attach to their experiences. Freedom in travel, whether perceived or real, may grant the feeling that they are free to pursue their desires, to take chances or risks, and transcend structural limitations. As Matthews (2016) pointed out "it is the freedom, licentiousness, creativity, indulgence and experimentation that liminality engenders and the intensified social bonds which may emerge from such experience, which leaves ritual participants changed, renewed or transformed" (p. 161). Thus, freedom through liminality is invariably conceived as a time and space away from the social structures at home, governed by different rules, values and behaviors that opens up opportunities to play out different versions of the self and may lead to possible transformations of self.

4.1.5 Self-development and personal growth

> Journeys lead us not only outwards in space, but inwards as well. Travel can be one of the most rewarding forms of introspection.
> Lawrence Durrell (1957, p. 15)

Another highly significant travel motive in the context of long-term travel is the notion of self-development and personal growth. Although the link between cross-cultural travel and the potential of personal growth is well established in academic literature, a "gaping hole" in empirical research has left this hypothesis unexplored (Hirschorn & Hefferon, 2013, p. 283). The assumption is that the anti-structural performance of traveling, characterized by freedom from "normal constraints on time and energy" (Stringer & McAvoy 1992, p. 17), offers manifold opportunities to experience the self in new environments and can thus provide increasing opportunities for self-development and transformation. These new environments or "spaces in-between" as Homi Bhaba (2001) calls them, provide the ideal playground for elaborating strategies of selfhood. This playground is the vantage point from which to examine our own personality and identity in action.

Empirical research attesting to the potential of personal growth and self-development resulting from extended cross-cultural encounters is derived largely from the fields of education, psychology, tourism and sociology. Backpacker research, in particular, has shown that the construction of a new sense of the self (Urry, 1990), even if temporary, is a central motivator for travel (Desforges, 1998, 2000; Cohen, 2004; Elsrud, 2001; Galani-Moutafi, 2000; White & White, 2004). As Maoz (2007) stated, "tourism provides the potential for a new form of identity, allowing individuals to define themselves according to their personal experiences of the world, rather than through paradigms offered by their society relating to their age, nationality, background, and gender" (p. 126). In other words, travel provides an arena for self-development and transformation by allowing individuals to experiment with new ways of being (Kottler, 1998), by creating conditions that are vastly different from those at home and by sampling different lifestyles. This may involve acting in the opposite way of how one would normally act, taking the hard route instead of the easy one, or going off the beaten track instead of following the safe and well-beaten tourist trail.

Turner (1982) called this freedom "experiential freedom", in which the individual is free to "play". The importance of play as a freely chosen experience in both children and adults was highlighted by Erikson (1963), who maintained that play is an important factor for ego-development and people can only "feel human" when they play (p. 214). Erikson (1963) equated play with leisure for the working adult and indicated that in play we let go of our pre-defined roles and scripts (p. 213). Likewise, Seligman & Csikszentmihalyi (2000), differentiated between pleasure and enjoyment, the latter of which plays a critical role in subjective well-being and personal growth:

> Pleasure is the good feeling that comes from satisfying homeostatic needs such as hunger, sex, and bodily comfort. Enjoyment, on the other hand, refers to the good feelings people experience when they break through the limits of homeostasis – when they do something that stretches them beyond what they were [...] Enjoyment, rather than pleasure, is what leads to personal growth and long term happiness (p. 12).

Csikszentmihalyi (1997) used the term *flow* to describe enjoyable experiences and differentiated them from states of boredom and anxiety. Csikszentmihalyi's flow experiences were an advancement of Abraham Maslow's (1971) *peak experiences,* which describe these rare moments of extreme happiness and excitement, in which the individual feels more integrated, whole, and feels meaningfulness in life, which may lead to self-actualization and growth. Both Csikszentmihalyi and Maslow found that people, regardless of their age, gender, culture, or social class, are capable of experiencing flow or peak moments. Not only are they capable of experiencing these peak moments, Csikszentmihalyi (1996) also found that the more peak experiences people had, the happier they were in life. Moreover, he did not attribute peak experiences to mere chance or luck, but rather contended that the happiest people worked hard to experience them and even devoted their lives to it:

> The feeling didn't come when they were relaxing, when they were taking drugs or alcohol, or when they were consuming the expensive privileges of wealth. Rather, it often involved painful, risky, difficult activities that stretched the person's capacity and involved an element of novelty and discovery (Csikszentmihalyi, 1996, p. 110).

Both Maslow and Csikszentmihalyi hold that peak and flow experiences are deeply rewarding and usually intrinsically motivated. The theme of intrinsic motivation is interesting in the context of travel because of its link to personal growth and transformation (Iso-Ahola, 1982). Intrinsically motivated activities are activities that are "undertaken purely for the interest inherent within them" (Hirschorn & Hefferon, 2013, p. 299), in contrast to extrinsically motivated ones, which are incentivized by external social pressure or rewards such as money. In their qualitative study on older career-break travelers taking time out for extended travel, Hirschorn & Hefferon (2013) confirmed that participants "reported heightened vitality and well-being by connecting to 'true self' and pursuing intrinsic will" (p. 299).

Hirschorn & Hefferon (2013) also found that the courage to pursue an intrinsic yearning to travel in the face of uncertainty played a vital role in experiencing personal growth and self-development. Finding the courage to change one's life circumstances and/or remove oneself from a difficult situation may be one of the hardest parts of the entire travel experience. Kottler (2014) argued that it is rarely one singular event that stimulates self-development and transformation, but rather a series of small events that may even feel unrelated, but eventually feed one another and push one in a certain direction. He explains:

> Change usually begins with someone feeling a level of desperation that leads him or her to take constructive risks and experiment with alternative ways of being that previously felt inaccessible. Motivation and drive are intensified by fear, and often we learn and grow as much from disappointments and failures as we ever do from successes and achievements. It is during conditions of vulnerability and feeling lost that our self-deceptions are confronted and new insights

generated. We try new things because we are now certain that what we've already been doing won't ever work (Kottler, 2014, p.9).

This courage to act upon significant trigger events and disorienting dilemmas (positive and negative), which are an inevitable impetus for long-term travel, takes us back to the vantage point of Jack Mezirow, who emphasized the importance of emancipatory learning for personal development and growth. Following Habermas (1971), Mezirow (1981) maintained that the desire to free oneself from (self-imposed) constraints and expectations is a fundamental human characteristic, and the ability to do so a sign of emancipatory learning. Mezirow (1981) defined emancipatory learning as "emancipation [...] from libidinal, institutional, or environmental forces which limit our options and rational control over our lives but have been taken for granted as beyond human control" (Mezirow, 1981, p. 5). However, in order for emancipatory learning to take place, one must not only be willing to free oneself from constraints but also have the capacity to do so, as emancipatory learning takes place through critically reflecting on one's assumptions. This implies that in order for travel to lead to transformation and personal growth, a person has to be willing and able to learn and reflect, which raises the question of whether travel can also be transformative even if people do not engage in critical reflection.

4.1.6 Summary

In summary, we can say that not all travelers are driven by the same needs and motives to travel, and many travelers seek to satisfy several needs at once. Thus, the self-development and personal growth motives most often work in tandem with other travel motives, such as escape, novelty and freedom-seeking. It has been argued that researching travel motivations is a difficult undertaking (Dann, 1981; Gee, Choy & Makens, 1984; Pearce, 2005), and tourist motivation theory development is rather limited and lacks widely accepted research methodology (Hsu & Songshan, 2008). This is largely attributed to the fact that much research on tourist motivation uses a positivistic and quantitative research paradigm, which relies on predetermined items that may not correspond to the actual motives of the respondents (Hsu & Songshan, 2008; Mannell & Iso-Ahola, 1987). Of course, this is problematic because the underlying motives for travel commonly reflect highly personal needs and are often covert (Gee, Choy & Makens, 1984). Dann (1981), for example, proposed four reasons, suggesting that people (1) may not wish to reflect on their travel motivations, (2) may be unable to reflect on their real motives, (3) they may not want to express them or (4) they may not be able to express them. While certainly not error-proof, a qualitative approach, as employed in the present study, may therefore be more useful to explore the underlying motivations for engaging in long-term independent travel. Also, it is important to consider that travel motivations may change over time along with socio-cultural changes (Hsu & Songshan, 2008) and changing life situations and situational triggers. Whether or not personal growth and transformation are the main motivations for travel or just a 'by-product', travel provides the ideal context for it.

4.2 During travel: Cross-cultural learning

> *What gives value to travel is fear. It is the fact that, at a certain moment, when we are so far from our own country ... we are seized by a vague fear, and the instinctive desire to go back to the protection of old habits. This is the most obvious benefit of travel. At that moment we are feverish but also porous, so that the slightest touch makes us quiver to the depths of our being. We come across a cascade of light, and there is eternity. This is why we should not say that we travel for pleasure. There is not pleasure in travelling, and I look upon it as an occasion for spiritual testing. [...] Travel, which is like a greater and graver science, brings us back to ourselves.*   Albert Camus, Notebooks, 1935-1942

In the passage above, Camus refers to fear that most individuals feel deep inside when venturing into unfamiliar territory and being confronted with the "other". This fear has the frightening potential to undermine our deeply held notions of ourselves and the world and to transform our worldviews, attitudes and behaviors. Camus tells us that by leaving behind the safe, predictable, and comfortable home world and confronting the "other", which is perceived as dangerous and unpredictable, we may well be able to rediscover the self and understand it more deeply and fully.

In order to examine potential transformations of self through traveling, we need to take a close look at the very nature of travel experiences and the meanings that are commonly attached to them. While the previous section looked at the main trigger factors associated with long-term travel, this section links the theoretical bases of identity formation and transformative learning with cross-cultural learning. In order to better understand the complexity of travel experiences, I focus on the nature of cross-cultural transitions with culture shock theory at its core and highlight the crucial element that links culture shock theory to the work of Erikson, Mezirow and others: the central importance of facing and overcoming a dilemma that challenges once core assumptions about oneself and one's place in the world.

4.2.1 Cross-cultural transitions

Mezirow (2000) postulates that being placed in dramatically different environments and cultures and being compelled to engage in critical reflection advances individuals to higher-level cognitive functioning and thus transforms them into more autonomous and mature thinkers (Merriam, 2004). This is because in our own culture, we are often unaware of deeply embedded patterns (Montuori, 2004, p. 244) and we take things just the way they are without giving them too much thought. However, so much of how we perceive ourselves, of who we think we are, is actually determined by our culture, and this becomes strikingly clear when encountering another culture with different values, attitudes and behaviors. Travelers are placed in cross-cultural situations which provoke them to challenge their assumptions of themselves and the world. When meaning perspectives collide with disorienting dilemmas (i.e. experiences that do not fit into existing meaning schemes), the meaning perspectives are questioned and need to be revised in order to accommodate the new experiences. The opportunity for transformation occurs when the meaning schemes are changed and a dilemma is negotiated.

In a cross-cultural context, culture shock is one possible disorienting dilemma that can disrupt an individual's view of reality. The study of cultural transitions, which has been permeated by the study of culture shock, tries to explain the processes at play when people are exposed to other cultures. This field of research started to flourish in the 1960s and 70s, and to date it has primarily focused on student sojourners, volunteers, religious missionaries and expatriates on foreign assignments, thereby largely ignoring the field of independent travelers.

Early culture shock research, as postulated by the North American anthropologist Kalvero Oberg (1960), defined culture shock as "the anxiety that results from losing all our familiar signs and symbol of social intercourse" (p.177) and viewed it as "an occupational disease of people who have been suddenly transplanted abroad" (p. 177). George Foster (1962) went even further and called it a form of mental illness of which the afflicted is usually unaware (p. 187). In an unfamiliar environment, much of one's existing knowledge becomes useless, and previously held opinions and interpretations of the world cannot be applied. Language, gestures, facial expressions, paralanguage, customs, values and behaviors are different, or their meanings have changed. Culture shock was thus commonly associated with negative psychological symptoms, such as fear, disorientation, confusion, helplessness, and a loss of frames of references or breakdown of familiar cues; in other words, it was seen as a medical condition that needed to be treated or cured.

4.2 During travel: Cross-cultural learning

Oberg based his culture shock theory on Lysgaard's (1955) study of human adjustment to foreign cultures, which resulted in the U-curve hypothesis of psychological adjustment. In his study on Norwegian Fulbright scholars in the United States, Lysgaard found that those sojourners who had stayed abroad for six to twelve months experienced the greatest adjustment difficulties compared to those who had been abroad for either less than six months or more than 18 months. In his U-curve hypothesis, which was based on time and level of adjustment, Oberg (1960) suggested a four-stage culture shock process that sojourners experience as they adapt to the foreign culture: (1) the *honeymoon phase,* where the sojourner feels excited to be in the new culture; (2) the *crisis* or culture shock phase, where the sojourner experiences feelings of frustration and anxiety in an attempt to adjust to the cultural stressors (e.g. language, culture, food, relationships) associated with an unfamiliar environment; (3) the *recovery phase,* where the sojourner addresses these stressors by employing several methods, such as learning the language and practicing new ways of thinking and acting in the new cultural environment; and finally (4) the *adjustment stage,* when the sojourner feels "at home" in the new culture and enjoys it.

Figure 1. U-Curve: Adjustment to a new culture over time (modified from Lysgaard, 1955)

Despite the continued popularity of the U-curve model, a number of scholars have pointed out weaknesses in the theory. For one, the majority of studies using the U-curve have yielded inconsistent results when applied in different contexts (Kim, 2012). For example, in a study on backpackers traveling in India and in Sri Lanka, Westerhausen (2002) found that the majority of backpackers had negative emotions at the beginning, rather than the feelings of euphoria proposed by the U-curve. A significant number of people decided to reduce the number of places visited or even returned home earlier than planned. Likewise, in their study of Japanese students in New Zealand, Ward et al. (2001) found no evidence of a euphoric honeymoon phase, but rather discovered that the levels of stress, anxiety and depression of were highest at the beginning of the study abroad experience.

In essence, even under similar circumstances, there are many factors involved in intercultural adaptation, including nationality, pre-travel expectations, previous intercultural experience, personality characteristics (e.g. patience, flexibility, empathy), psychological orientations (e.g. attitude, perception, motivation, uncertainty and anxiety), communication skills (e.g. language competence, listening skills, interpersonal relationship skills) and demographic characteristics (e.g. age, gender, socioeconomic background, marital status, etc.) (Kim, 2012). It is therefore problematic to depict the process of cultural adaptation as a linear, sequential process and generalize it across different groups of people crossing cultures.

In my view, one of the main shortcomings of culture shock theory is that it focuses on the negative initial shock experience at the expense of taking on a broader perspective wherein one could see intercultural experience as a catalyst for learning and personal growth. In this context, culture shock is not simply a pathological shock that must be avoided or treated (Hottola, 2004), but rather a valuable opportunity for learning.

One of the first scholars to re-conceptualize culture shock and emphasize the transformative and learning potential of cross-cultural experiences was Peter Adler (1975). In his view, culture shock should be viewed as a *transitional experience* that "begins with the encounter of another culture and evolves into the encounter with the self" (p. 18). He explained that a transitional experience such as traveling is inherently marked by difference and complexity. However, beyond possible negative feelings (e.g. helplessness, isolation), it can also lead to profound self-awareness, learning and personal growth. Having traveled extensively himself, he was one of the first to question the notion of culture shock as a form of anxiety, illness or even disease as it was traditionally perceived and instead consider it an opportunity for cultural learning and self-development.

Adler's (1975) transitional model starts with the initial contact with a second culture. This is followed by disintegration, which is characterized by confusion and disorientation. The next phase is the reintegration phase, which is marked by a strong rejection of the foreign culture and resorting to stereotyping and judgmental behaviors and attitudes. The individual then moves on to the autonomy stage, in which the individual has a heightened sensitivity towards the new culture, before finally reaching the independence stage, where the individual has learned to accept and even enjoy social, psychological and cultural differences. The individual can now exercise choice and responsibility and has learned to create meaning from experiences.

While the stages in Adler's human psychology approach to the transitional experience are similar to the instrumental approach of culture shock as pursued by Lysgaard (1955), Oberg (1960) and Gullahorn & Gullahorn (1963), the concepts differ in that no time sequence is attached to each stage. Rather than passing through a linear and sequential process, Adler (1975) contends that in his model of transitional experience an individual passes through a series of phases at different times. This is in line with other researchers (see for example Furnham & Bochner, 1986) who suggest that intercultural adaptation processes do not necessarily represent a linear U- curve, and that duration of the adaptation process varies greatly.

Adler (1987) envisioned the development of a *multicultural person*, who is characterized by a heightened sense of self and the ability to think and act in a culturally sensitive manner. A successful cross-cultural experience typically results "in the movement of personality and identity to new consciousness of values, attitudes, and understandings" (p. 15). Thus, Adler describes a movement from low cultural and self-awareness to high cultural and self-awareness. Since the encounter with another culture enables the individual to understand the roots of their own ethnocentrism and to gain a new perspective on the nature of culture (Adler, 1975, p. 22), it is essentially a journey into the self.

In accordance with Adler's humanistic view of transitional experience, several researchers have criticized the terminology of culture shock. For example, culture shock has been referred to as *culture learning* (Paige, 1993), and *cultural adjustment stress* (Anderson, 1994). Berry (2008) prefers to call it *acculturative stress* and point to the transformation an individual undergoes after having been exposed to different cultures for some time. These changes can affect a person's identity, attitudes and values and can be quite profound and life-changing. In a similar vein, Ward, Bochner & Furnham, (2001) simply refer to acculturation when describing the sojourner's experience abroad. They suggest that sojourners typically undergo both psychological adjustment and sociocultural adaptation during their experience abroad. Psychological adjustment involves emotional (affective) reactions, whereas sociocultural adaptation refers to learning the appropriate cultural skills (e.g. language, behaviors, social skills) in order to function well in the host culture (Ward et al., 2001, p. 42). Likewise, Hottola (2004) suggested reserving the term "culture shock" for situations of genuine shock and proposed the more general term *culture confu-*

sion for less shocking experiences. He contends that culture confusion "focuses both on the problematic part of the adaptation process and on the frequently simultaneous presence of enjoyment, success and learning" (p. 453) and maintains that people experience culture confusion throughout the travel process, from the beginning, during travel and even when they return home.

Similarly, in cases where the contrast between the home and host culture is significant, as often true when individuals travel to less developed regions of the world, Hottola (2004) proposes the term *life shock* instead of culture shock. Travelers may experience this kind of shock when confronted with "less desirable facts of human life, from which people in Western society often are shielded by social security and state institutions" (p. 454). Encountering poverty, disability and death for the first time can be a truly disturbing emotional shock, but Hottola (2004) reminds us that this is an elitist concept this is only relevant to the well-to-do citizens of the world who can afford to travel to less developed parts of the world.

In her discussion on self-identity and cross-cultural adaptation, Jannet Bennett (1977) suggests expanding culture shock by viewing it as *transition shock*. People experience transition shock, for example, when they lose a partner through death or divorce, change their lifestyle, lose a familiar frame of reference in an intercultural encounter, or experience a change in values due to rapid social innovation (p. 45). She contends that "during any transition experience, the quandary is frequently: 'Who am I?' There is a loss of continuity in one's purpose and direction" (p. 48). She maintains that those with a firm sense of identity are most likely to successfully master intercultural experiences. Bennett's more general concept of transition shock is essentially a re-statement of Mezirow's disorienting dilemma, which has the potential to trigger a transformed worldview or perspective in any significant transition phase, regardless of whether or not a different culture is involved.

Although the conceptualizations of culture shock vary widely, one can identify some points of consensus. First, researchers agree that culture shock is generally not triggered by a single event, but rather by the accumulation of a series of smaller events (Ward et al., 2001) in which pre-existing meaning structures cannot be applied to interpret new experiences. In addition, researchers have shown that the demands of adapting to a new culture exist on a variety of levels, including the emotional, cognitive, social and physiological levels, and each traveler will experience a different mix of these pressures, depending on factors such as the traveler's background, personality type, and life situation, as well as the specific characteristics of the host culture(s) (Chapdelaine & Alexitch, 2004,

p. 168). In this context, it is important to mention that the "host cultures" include not only the cultures of the various locations a traveler may visit, but also the traveler culture, which is itself a complex construct with values and rules that vary widely, as seen in the aforementioned discussion of the traveler/tourist dichotomy.

4.2.2 Learning through experiences and challenges

The notion that travel offers many opportunities for learning through negotiating challenging situations is reflected in the etymology of the words "experience" and "travel". The word "experience" derives from the PIE root (Proto Indo-European language) *per (the asterisk marks reconstructed PIE words), which has been construed as "to attempt", "to risk", "to test" - all words that are cognates for the English word peril, which connotes risk and danger. *Per appears in the Latin words for "experience" experior and experimentum which is conceived as passing through an ordeal, a test, suffering or undergoing a series of events that have an effect on the person living through it. In this sense, *per is also linked to liminality and the passing of a threshold (Leed, 1991; Turner, 1974).

This notion of experience as an ordeal or suffering also describes one of the first and most general conceptualizations of the effects of travel on the traveler and this understanding is reflected in the original English word for travel, travail. Here, the conceptualization of travel as a transformation that strips, wastes and reduces the traveler, while testing the heroism of the traveler is implicit. The German word for experience Erfahrung is derived from the Old High German irfaran which means "to travel", "to traverse", or "to wander". (Leed 1991, pp.5-6) The deeply ingrained presumption that travel is an experience that puts the traveler's character to a test while at the same time refining it, is exemplified by the German adjective bewandert, which means "proficient", "knowledgeable", or "clever", but originally - in 15th century texts – merely meant "well traveled".(Leed 1991, p.6).

Learning from experience is also at the heart of transformative learning: "It is experience, particularly prior experience (that happened in one's past), that is the primary medium of transformation, and it is the revision of the meaning of experience that is the essence of learning" (Taylor & Cranton, 2013, p. 35). In particular, experiences that are unexpected, surprising, unfamiliar and even disorienting often induce dissonance, and travel experiences can be all of these.

Experiential learning, is "education that occurs as a direct participation in the events of life" (Houle 1980, p.221). This type of learning does not take place in a formal educational institution, but is rather achieved by the individuals reflecting on concrete lived experiences and attaching meaning to them. Learning from travel is therefore a reflective and interpretive exercise, whereby individual must examine their own experiences with new social systems, new cultures, and new meanings in an effort to assign significance and meaning to these experiences and integrate them into new or existing meaning schemes.

Turner (1986) contended that travel gives rise to "unique structures of experience (p. 41). The diverse and multi-faceted nature of travel experience contrasts strongly with travelers' "normal" realms of experience and are therefore at the heart of learning and transformation. Travel involves transcending the boundaries of that which is existentially familiar while seeking the sublime, authentic "Other" (Noy, 2004, p. 92). Novel and challenging experiences that test one's boundaries are commonly viewed as critical for an evolving self (Csikszenthmihaly, 1993). "The fatigues of travel, the sufferings of the journey, remain a cause and a measure of the extent to which a traveler is marked and tested by experience, becoming *bewandert* – 'skilled' and 'wise'" (Leed 2001, p. 7, highlight in original).

Leed (2001) argues that it is exactly this hardship and suffering that distinguishes the tourist from the genuine traveler, who does not merely travel for pleasure, but rather seeks a personal test. Westerhausen (2002) agrees and points to the growth potential of long-term independent travel:

> In contrast to mass tourism's offer of a temporary escape from the pressures of an ordered existence, long-term travel instead provides a whole way of life whose demands on body and mind tend to be far more challenging to the individual. As a tourism experience, it offers the opportunity for semi-autonomy, personal growth, continuous learning, adventure and self-testing at an affordable price. (pp. ix–x)

Independent travel is rarely predictable, and the constant need to adapt to an ever-changing environment entails many potential challenges, including enduring physical hardship, arduous journeys, dealing with perceived or real dangers, coping with unexpected problems (e.g. getting stranded by a train strike or missing a bus connection), getting lost, finding no accommodation, adjusting to a different lifestyle, learning to communicate with people from different cultures, or encountering angry locals or aggressive hagglers.

Experiences and perceptions of risk and hardship are also highly subjective and personal. In the late nineties, Pine and Gilmore (1998, 2011), who heralded the era of the experience economy as a successor of the agrarian and industrial economy, held that "experiences are inherently personal, existing only in the mind of an individual who has been engaged on an emotional, physical, intellectual, or even spiritual level" (p.99). They contend that when discussing engaging experiences, it is important to consider many dimensions, including the multisensory nature of experiences, their duration and intensity, simplicity or complexity, their level of personal meaningfulness, and the ways in which experiences are shared with others (if at all). They go on to explain that experiences are always co-created, as they happen within the individual person and in reaction to what is presented outside that person (Pine & Gilmore, 2011 p. xx). Moreover, experiences are constantly being (re)interpreted and (re)constructed (Schwandt, 2000; Urry, 1990, 2002). From this we can conclude that no two people have the same experience because prior life experiences, cultural, national and local aspects all impact how these experiences are perceived (Pine & Gilmore, 2011 p. xxi).

4.3 After travel: Reentry

The whole object of travel is not to set foot on foreign land; it is at last to set foot on one's own country as a foreign land.
    G. K. Chesterton, (1901-1903, p. 89)

Returning to one's home country after having been gone for an extended period can be a difficult and challenging experience. It has been well established that most people expect challenges and maybe even a certain amount of shock when crossing cultures, but few people expect the same to happen when they return to their home cultures (Mitchell, 2006). In fact, returnees may expect the exact opposite experience; namely, that coming home will be exciting (Storti, 2003). However, returning to one's home culture has often been found to be even more challenging than adjusting to a new culture and has been associated with emotional upheaval and periods of distress (e.g. Martin, 1993; Sussman, 1986; Szkudlarek, 2010; Ward et al., 2001). This phenomenon has been termed "reverse culture shock" (Gaw, 2000; Mitchell, 2006; Samovar et al., 1998) or "repatriation distress" (Sussman, 2001). Some researchers have taken a more neutral stance and referred to the concept of readjusting to one's home culture after an extended period abroad as "cross-cultural readjustment" (Adler, 1981; Rogers & Ward, 1993; Ward & Kennedy, 2001), "reacculturation" (Martin, 1984), and "reentry" (Brabant, et al., 1990; Callahan, 2010; Mitchell, 2006; Rohrlich and Martin, 1991; Smith, 2002). Many researchers have posited that the unexpectedness of reentry shock is its distinguishing feature (e.g. Martin, 1993; Smith, 1998; Storti, 2003; Sussman; 2001).

As early as 1963, Gullahorn & Gullahorn (1963) expanded the Oberg's U-curve into a W-curve that included the phase of returning to one's native culture. According to the W-curve hypothesis, the reentry process is similar to the culture shock process. The returnee initially feels euphoric about being home, but soon becomes frustrated and anxious when realizing that home is not as expected. This leads to reentry shock, which is followed by a gradual readjustment to the home environment and eventually feeling satisfied and content (Gullahorn & Gullahorn, 1963). The W-curve model continues to receive strong support among scholars and practitioners, despite limited empirical evidence of its validity (Martin & Harrell, 2004; Szkudlarek, 2010). In addition, none of these theories were developed or have been tested with long-term independent travelers in mind, and their validity can therefore only be speculative.

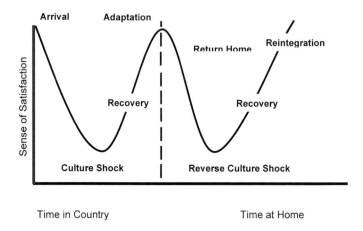

Figure 2. W-Cure: Stages of transition shock (modified from Gullahorn & Gullahorn, 1963)

It is important to point out that in this thesis, reentry does not necessarily represent an endpoint in a linear process of leaving home, traveling abroad, and returning. Many travelers leave and return to their cultural contexts multiple times (Martin & Harrell, 2004), and for many travelers the re-acculturation to their home culture can become a life-long process. In this thesis, the terms reacculturation, readjustment and reentry are used interchangeably, as they are within the wider reentry literature.

4.3 After travel: Reentry

Compared to other phases of travel, there is a dearth of academic literature on the "return" phase. Although the growing number of people returning to their home countries following an extended period abroad has prompted a growing body of literature on the reentry experience, the vast majority of reentry literature has centered primarily on student sojourners, migrants, missionaries and expatriates and their re-adaptation to the home culture. Repatriation of long-term travelers remains relatively unexamined within academic scholarship, and several researchers have called for the need to study traveler's return to their home societies (Pearce, 2006; Richards & Wilson, 2004c). Indeed, it seems that this is a major shortcoming, as the post-travel phase is one of the most critical phases. Just as traveling to a completely different culture functions as the "disorienting dilemma" that can precipitate a perspective transformation, returning home frequently presents another disorienting dilemma, and it is often not until one returns home that changes in identity become apparent and the true perspective change takes place (Smith, 2002). Moreover, I argue that returning to one's home country must be viewed as a longer transitional experience rather than a singular event. Although the return has immediate effects on the traveler, it can also produce lasting changes that have significant influence on important decisions throughout a person's post-travel existence.

4.3.1 Reentry challenges

Reverse culture shock has been described as "the psychological, physical, and emotional symptoms of feeling like a foreigner in their own country" (Hurn, 1999, p. 227). Nancy Adler (1981), who was one of the pioneers in reentry research, studied the reentry process of 200 employees returning to Canada after working overseas for an average of two years and found that the readjustment to their home culture was perceived to be more difficult than the transition to the foreign culture (p. 341). This distress results from the realization that home did not stand still while one was gone. When leaving home, sojourners often take with them a static mental and emotional snapshot of home, and they are unprepared for the changes that occurred while they were gone (Mitchell, 2006, p. 5). Even more importantly, in the context of the present study, not only do returnees realize that home has changed, they often become aware of how much they have changed when they return home. This lack of understanding of one's identity change can lead to re-acculturation problems or reentry shock. A review of the reentry literature confirms that many sojourners experience transitional distress or even periods of depression or trauma that can be broadly linked to the two dimensions of psychological (emotional) and sociocultural (behavioral) re-acculturation challenges.

Psychological reacculturation challenges identified in the literature include frustration, anger, hostility, lethargy, helplessness, boredom, restlessness, loneliness, anxiety and depression (Allison, Davis-Berman & Berman, 2011; Foust, Fieg, Koester, Sarbaugh, & Wendinger, 1981; Gaw, 2000; Rogers & Ward, 1993; Walling et al., 2006). Foust, et al. (1981) found that the transient travel lifestyle abroad is commonly viewed in a more favorable light than the sedentary home environment, which leaves travelers feeling bored and restless. This was confirmed by Riley (1988), who noted that "the experience of extreme freedom can make the regimentation of daily home life difficult because of the dramatic contrast" (p. 325). Allison et al. (2011) and Gaw (2000) observed that student sojourners felt isolation and loneliness after the return home. Kartoshkina (2015) explored the reentry experience of US college students who studied abroad for up to one year and described the reentry experience of the participants as bitter-sweet, with participants reporting a wide range of reentry experiences, from feeling lost, frustrated, annoyed, confused, alienated and depressed to more positive ones, including feelings of excitement, happiness, relief and comfort.

Sociocultural reacculturation challenges revolve around changed relationships with family and friends, as well as alienation from their home society. Returnees may soon find out that they cannot just pick up where they left off (Freedman, 1986), which can lead to frustration or disappointment. Interpersonal tensions may arise mainly due to unrealistic expectations of both the returnee and family and friends at home. Returnees often do not expect friends and family to have moved on or changed while they were gone (Gaw, 2000). Moreover, many returnees experience communication difficulties with friends and family and feel that those who stayed at home are either not interested in hearing about their experiences abroad or are unable to relate to them. What is more, many returnees feel their sojourn abroad was so unique that they cannot explain it to others in a meaningful way (Allison et al. 2011; Gaw, 2000).

Another social reacculturation challenge involves returnee's alienation from their home culture. Intercultural experiences often give travelers a different vantage point "from which it becomes possible to see the inadequacies of [one's] own society more sharply (Turner & Ash, 1976, p. 49). This can be disorienting for some travelers, especially as the spiritually rewarding experiences of travel may render life at home unattractive. Pritchard (2011) studied the reentry of Taiwanese and Sri Lankan graduates after completing their studies

4.3 After travel: Reentry

in the West and found that the majority of the people in the sample did not experience any reentry trauma or emotional distress, but rather experienced conflicting values between traditionalism and modernist or collectivism and individualism (p. 108). One of the main reasons for this dissonance was that returnees no longer conformed to the typical stereotypes of their home cultures. Similarly, Sussman (2001) investigated experiences of corporate returnees and found that the less one identified with their home country, the more severe the return distress. She confirmed these results a year later in a study of American teachers returning from an overseas assignment in Japan (Sussman, 2002).

This highlights the change in an individual's cultural identity upon returning to one's home culture. Sussman (2002) defines cultural identity as "the degree to which an individual identifies with the home country and the host country" (p. 392) and adds that cultural identity is a key variable in successful cultural adjustment. Naturally, we are all a product of the particular circumstances of our lives, as well as the social and cultural conditioning we experienced growing up.

This "cultural self" is our frame of reference, which serves as a basis for our values, attitudes and behaviors. At home, this frame of reference is often beyond our awareness because we are rarely stimulated to reflect on our cultural selves. When encountering a different culture and actively engaging with different norms, values and behaviors, we automatically notice that which is different and compare it to our own frame of reference. We notice different habits, behaviors and value systems, and we see our own cultural selves in action. Inevitably, we may adopt some new values, attitudes and behaviors and shed some old ones. Shelly Smith (1998), for example, noted that some returnees need to relearn certain norms and social skills that they had forgotten while away (e.g. shaking hands or kissing when greeting someone). Naturally, these conscious or subconscious changes may contribute to reentry shock, which may be stronger, the greater the difference between the old and new values, behaviors and attitudes are. Reentry can therefore never be seen as complete assimilation, which involves giving up the new cultural self, but rather must be viewed as a complex process in which home and host cultural elements are integrated (Berry, 1980, 2008; Kim, 2001; Martin & Harrell, 2004; Ward, et al., 2001).

When returning home, Craig Storti (2003) argues, we are "something of a cultural hybrid, viewing and responding to the world around you from the perspective of two different realities, partaking of each but not fully belonging to either" (p. 54). Storti (2003) goes on to explain that the returnee has become what is called a "marginal person, functioning more

– and better – at the edges of your society rather than at the center, more likely to be an observer of, rather than a participant in, the scene around you" (p. 54). Storti compared the situation of a returnee to that of a minority, in that the majority of people may see things differently from the returnee, react or feel differently to certain things or may fail to see certain things altogether. This is in line with Adler (1975, 1987) and later J. Bennett (1993), whose cognitive development model of the "multicultural person" lends insight into the cultural identity development. They contend that the ideal model of a multicultural person often lives on the margins of a culture, maintains several frames of references (i.e. values or belief systems), and is capable of successfully mediating between cultures. However, the adoption of a new cultural identity abroad commonly results in cognitive dissonance and viewing the home culture through a new lens, which can be challenging and disorienting for many returnees. Zaharna (1989), even argued that, given the emotionally unsettling and uncertain experience of the return, the returnees experience a kind of "self-shock" that forces them to "renegotiate viable identities" in their old or new homes (p. 501).

Despite the oft-mentioned reentry challenges fraught with negative emotions, it is important to not lose sight of the tremendous transformative potential of cross-cultural transitions. As with other adult life transitions, cross-cultural transitions are associated with loss and change for the individual and are therefore very often a precursor to personal growth and self-development (Kim, 2001; Martin & Harrell, 2004). To date, only a small number of studies have pointed to the positive aspects of reentry. Walling et al. (2006) indicated that some of the returned students experienced a new-found appreciation for their home country. In his study of 40 backpackers who had traveled for a minimum of three months, Noy (2004) found that all of the backpackers reported positive personal changes as a result of this trip. These changes included increased self-confidence, self-knowledge and knowledge of other cultures, and a more positive outlook on life in general.

4.3.2 Factors affecting readjustment

Of course, when considering the reentry experience of returnees, it is important to keep in mind the various factors that influence the reentry experience and the coping mechanisms applied. Reentry experiences may be influenced by general factors, such as age, gender, ethnicity, and socio-economic background, or the length of stay abroad, as well as cultural factors, including previous intercultural experience and the cultural distance between the host and home cultures (Christofi & Thompson, 2007; Gaw, 2000; Martin & Harrell, 2004; Uehara, 1986).

Another important factor identified in repatriation literature is an individual's personality, which includes aspects such as level of extroversion, openness to novel experiences and adventure, risk-adversity, perseverance, emotional stability, and social skills. Emotional stability, for example, refers to an individual's ability to cope with the daily stresses of navigating through a new cultural environment and, in turn, the ability to re-adapt to one's home culture. Openness has been found to be important when relating to and seeking to interact with people who are different than oneself, whereas extraversion influences a sojourner's desire to seek adventure and excitement abroad (Arthur & Bennett, 1997). Some researchers have proposed that some people have a "mobile personality" in that they seek change in their lives when dissatisfied with the current situation, while others are resistant to such change, regardless of how dire the situation becomes (Boneva & Frieze, 2001; Frieze & Yu Li, 2010; Tartakovsky & Schwartz, 2001). Furthermore, it has been argued that those people who find it hard to cope with change, difference and uncertainty are also more likely to struggle with reacculturation to their home societies (Foust et al., 1981). Sussman (1986) suggested that reentry becomes easier and less stressful the more often it is experienced because the individual has already learned and can now refine adaptation skills and strategies (p. 242). However, more empirical research needs to be carried out in order to verify these claims on the link between personality and ease of (re)adaptation.

One of the major factors influencing the reentry experience is the social support the returnee receives when returning home, as well as the degree to which the traveler stayed connected with family and friends while away (Mitchell, 2006; Ward, et al., 2001). The ubiquitous access to information technologies and social networks enables travelers to never completely disconnect from their home cultures, and it has been suggested that this may ameliorate the reentry shock in terms of expectations. By remaining in contact and engaging with the lives of those who stayed at home, the returnee knows what to expect, rather than being left with a feeling of being "out of sight, out of mind". Similarly, the ability to use modern communication technologies to maintain contact with likeminded people encountered during travel often provides an outlet to share travel experience and gives travelers the feeling of being "on the same page" with people who have had similar experiences.

One useful conceptualizing of reentry is Martin & Harrell's (2004) *Systems Theory of Intercultural Reentry* (see table 2), which is based on Kim's (2001) integrative theory of communication and cross-cultural adaptation. Their theory integrates the affective, behavioral and cognitive aspects of reentry and identifies factors that influence the readjustment outcome. Martin and Harrell (2004) identified five dimensions of the reentry experience. These are (1) sojourner characteristics (demographic and personality attributes and level of preparedness), (2) host environment characteristics (host society receptiveness, cultural difference, and amount of contact with home), (3) home (reentry) environment characteristics (support during and after reentry), (4) communication during reentry, and (5) re-adaptation outcomes.

The outcomes are the most important component of the theory and comprise four re-adaptation outcomes. The first one, "psychological health", which is the affective component, is important for both sojourners abroad and returnees. For example, in a study of American foreign exchange students returning home, Gaw (2000) found that many felt lonely, depressed, alienated and confused. The second outcome, "Functional fitness", incorporates the behavioral aspect and refers to the ability to carry out every day social and professional activities. The third outcome is the cognitive development of "realistic expectations" when readapting to the home environment. There is broad agreement in the reentry literature on the importance of expectations in reentry. It has been argued that the larger the gap between sojourner's expectations and reality at home, the more distressful the reentry experience (e.g. Martin, 1993; Smith, 1998; Storti, 2003; Sussman; 2001). Expectations that are met or even exceeded lead to psychological well-being (Rogers & Ward, 1993), whereas unfulfilled expectations result in poorer adjustment (Martin & Harrell, 2004). And finally, "intercultural identity" is a cognitive outcome that refers to the identity transformation that may take place as a result of the intercultural experience and re-adaptation. As Kim (2001) explains,

> Unlike the original cultural identity that had been largely preprogrammed into the stranger through childhood socialization experiences, the emerging identity is one that develops out of the many challenging, and often painful experiences of self-re-organization under the demands of a new milieu. Through prolonged experiences of trial and error, the stranger begins to 'earn' a new, expanded identity that is more than either the original cultural identity or the identity of the host culture. (p. 65)

Drawing on Adler's (1982) multicultural identity, this emergent intercultural identity is what Kim (2001) calls *interculturalness*, which is not to be understood as a fixed psychological state, but rather a developmental process whereby identities become increasingly flexible. Through prolonged intercultural exposure, an individual's identity may undergo two interrelated transformative processes, namely *individuation* and *universalization*. Kim (2009) describes these processes as follows:

> *Individuation* involves a clear self-definition and definition of the other as a singular individual rather than a member of a conventional social category. With this capacity, one is better able to transcend conventional in-group and out-group categories and to see oneself and others on the basis of unique individual qualities. Accompanying individuation is universalization, a parallel development of a synergistic cognition born out of an awareness of the relative nature of values and the universal aspect of human nature (p. 56).

According to Kim (2009), individuals who have undergone these transformational processes and developed an intercultural identity may have also become interculturally competent in terms of having the ability to make "deliberate choices of constructive actions rather than simply being dictated by the prevailing norms of a particular culture." They feel secure in their identity and without surrendering their own cultural integrity they are able to transcend traditional group boundaries and can better cultivate meaningful relationships with people who are different (p. 62).

Table 2. Systems Theory of Intercultural Reentry (Source: Martin & Harrell, 2004, p. 315.)

Sojourner Characteristics	Host Environment Characteristics	Home (Reentry) Environment Characteristics	Communication during Reentry	Re-adaptation Outcomes
Sojourner background Nationality Age Gender Religion Ethnicity Socioeconomic status Personality attributes Openness Personality strength Positivity Preparedness for change Training Prior experience Voluntariness of transition	Receptiveness of society Host-home culture difference Amount of contact with home	Amount of relational support	Communication with family, friends, and coworkers	Psychological health Functional fitness Realistic expectations Intercultural identity

It is important to point out that none of the theories mentioned in this section were developed with long-term travelers in mind, but rather focused on the reentry of student and corporate sojourners. This is probably because travel is commonly associated with notions of pleasure, free-time, recreation and play, but rarely associated with more negative concepts of homelessness, uncertainty, identity crises and reentry distress. Although the latter may apply in a limited way to short-term travelers, these concepts may be particularly relevant for long-term travelers, who sometimes give up everything prior to departure and return to a world of uncertainty. The level of uncertainty may be even larger than that of students or professionals, who are likely to be returning to their university or their old job. Hence, these models serve as a useful theoretical framework that may help understand the empirical findings discussed in this thesis.

4.4 Summary

This chapter showed that the transformative processes involved in contemporary long-term independent travel are complex and go beyond the physical travel experience. Disorienting dilemmas, or trigger events, arise before, during and after travel and offer opportunities for learning and identity transformation. Although these phases cannot be clearly separated, they serve as a useful guideline to structure this research.

For the pre-travel phase, this chapter drew upon the relevant literature in tourism studies to describe the wide variety of motivations that drive travelers out onto the road. In the context of transformative learning theory, these motivations often involve disorienting dilemmas that trigger the learning process.

The chapter then looked at the travel experience itself, and offered some insight into cross-cultural learning theories and the work on culture shock and cross-cultural transition. The need to adapt to different cultures (including the traveler culture itself) can itself serve as a disorienting dilemma. Experiencing different ways of being and overcoming this challenge can involve perspective change an identity transformation.

Finally, the discussion of the post-travel phase examined literature on the reentry process and the factors that affect readjustment to one's home culture or to post-travel life in a new culture. For many people, the return home serves as a secondary, or perhaps even the primary disorienting dilemma of the entire long-term travel cycle. In fact, the readjustment involved in this phase may be the time where the real transformation occurs, as the fundamental perspective shift that may have first transpired during the travel experience is brought into harmony with the traveler's "home" existence by adapting values, attitudes, behaviors and even life goals.

With the theoretical framework now in place, the following chapter moves into the empirical part of the present study and describes the methodology deployed in the present research.

5 Methodology

This chapter discusses and justifies the methodological framework within which the empirical part of this study was conducted and highlights some of the issues that affected both the type and amount of data collected during field work. In order to make sense of the extremely rich research setting and to capture the complexity of the topic, I sought a research method that could explore long-term travelers' understanding of their lived experiences and the stories they tell by stimulating their reflection on this sense-making process. To this end, a multi-faceted, qualitative interpretive research approach (Sarantakos, 1998) was deemed appropriate.

The following sections describe the individual steps involved in the empirical research strategy, from the initial approach to the topic to the task of making sense of the complexity of the meanings people give to the world (Holliday, 2002, p.137). First, section 5.1. delineates the research design and highlights some of the most pertinent theoretical perspectives surrounding this study. Section 5.2 then describes the data collection process and explains in detail the qualitative methods adopted for data collection. Section 5.3 then outlines the demographics of the participants, and the remaining sections describe the techniques used to analyze and validate the data.

5.1 The research paradigm: An interpretive approach

The methodological framework for the present thesis evolved gradually in the course of experiencing first-hand the individual stages of long-term traveling, as well as interviewing and spending time with long-term travelers. The period of information gathering consisted of several years of actively experiencing and observing the research setting. This enabled me to survey the scope of the topic and then identify key areas of inquiry. Moreover, this first-hand experience helped me to understand the connections between the different stages and processes of the travel experience, which in turn contributed to the formation of effective research questions and strategies for following up on these connections and emerging themes (Holliday, 2002, p. 75).

Before deciding on the appropriate data collection method, it is important for researchers to consider their personal understanding of what constitutes knowledge because the paradigmatic debate surrounding the two extremes of interpretive and positivist research philosophies is ultimately rooted in the researcher's own philosophical assumptions. In this context, I agree with Guba & Lincoln (1994), who argue that "questions of method are secondary to questions of paradigm, which we define as the basic belief system or worldview that guides the investigator, not only in choices of method, but in ontologically and epistemologically fundamental ways" (p. 105). Thus, identifying the researcher's perspective on what we can know about the world (ontology) and how we can know it (epistemology) is critical, as it provides the guiding principle to justify the adoption of a specific research paradigm.

As this research seeks to explore the transformative potential of long-term independent travel, I adopted an emic (insider) approach that privileges the participants' voices over the researcher's perspective and allows for inquiry into the meanings the travelers attach to their experiences. This approach is premised on the assumption that objective research on human behavior and their social world is impossible (Willis 2007 p. 110), as there are not only multiple realities (ontology) but also multiple possible explanations of a phenomenon (epistemology). This view stands in contrast to the positivist paradigm, which holds that there is an objective truth that is generalizable. The interpretivist research paradigm, with some of its philosophical foundations in Immanuel Kant's *Critique of Pure Reason* (1781), holds that humans interpret what they feel rather than directly experiencing the world as it is (Willis, 2007). This view is echoed by Willis (2007), who asserts that human behavior is strongly influenced by the subjective perception of the world. Thus, an individual's perception of the world and what the world means to that person is vitally important for effective research in the social sciences.

Imagine the following situation: Five travelers are on their way to visit the Mayan temple site of Tikal, located in the jungle in the Guatemalan Biosphere Reserve. When they get off the bus, they pay the entrance fee and set off to explore the vast temple premises. It may be logical to think that everyone involved would have the same experience. Perhaps someone videotaped the event and thereby produced a permanent record of this "reality". A positivist would attempt to look at the situation objectively, for example by examining the visual documentation or the transcript of the spoken words. An interpretivist, however, would take the opposite approach of inquiry and consider that, even though all individuals were exposed to the same situation, they may still walk away with very subjective and different experiences and therefore very different knowledge about the event. Perhaps the first traveler has never traveled before and thus experiences the excitement and novelty of the place, whereas the second traveler is immediately reminded of her visit to the Great Pyramids in Egypt years ago and may then feel nostalgia for times past. The third traveler, although fascinated by the sheer size of the place, is tremendously saddened by the

5.1 The research paradigm: An interpretive approach

environmental and cultural damage done by the thousands of tourists visiting each year, while the fourth traveler revels in the mystical and spiritual power of seeing the pyramids. For this fourth traveler, experiencing the serenity of this sacred site with her own senses might constitute a true journey inward and may even become a life-changing event in the long run. Finally, a hypothetical fifth traveler may be well seasoned and have just completed extensive and tiresome travels through the Yucatan peninsula in Mexico, visiting every Mayan temple on her bucket list. Therefore, she may simply feel "templed out" or incapable of enjoying the experience. Thus, as a result of past experiences and knowledge, worldviews, psychological and physiological states, each individual person experiences the Tikal temple site differently. These different interpretations can be considered meaning systems (Mezirow 1991a), the organizing structure with which meaning and significance are constructed. From an interpretive point of view, the experience can be examined from each individual's perspective, rather than seeing the visit as one unifying event that can be documented and codified.

Since the interpretive paradigm embraces methodologies that are well-suited to understanding the lived experiences of those being researched (Lincoln & Guba, 2013, p. 88), it was deemed the most appropriate for the present study. However, favoring an interpretive research philosophy does not vilify or defame positivist research approaches. Quite the contrary: interpretive researchers argue that the research question should drive the choice of method (Yanow & Schwarz-Shea, 2011). The highly subjective nature of the research question "*How does long-term independent travel transform the values and identities of travelers?*" makes it impossible to seek one universal truth, but rather *requires* a research approach that is shaped and co-created by both the researcher and those being researched (Denzin & Lincoln, 2005). Interpretive inquiry allows the researcher to look deeply into the behavior of people and discover unforeseen events, and to "explore, catch glimpses, illuminate and then try to interpret bits of reality" (Holliday, 2002, p. 5).

Proponents of the quantitative-positivist research vein might argue that there are few differences between interpretive research and fiction writing (Denzin & Lincoln, 2008). However, Yanow & Schwarz-Shea (2011) argue that "interpretive researchers, unlike novelists, undertake an explicit and conscious effort to produce an understanding that is a faithful rendering of lived experience. Interpreting words or acts or objects in a scientific fashion may be an act of creating meaning, but it is not an act of imagination *ex nihilo*. In this sense, interpretive work is as methodical as any other", (highlight in original, p. 385) and provides a greater understanding of how experience is created and meaning assigned to them.

Qualitative researchers deploy a wide variety of interconnected interpretive practices in an attempt to examine the world through the experiences and perceptions of the participants, as well as via their own backgrounds and experiences (Creswell 2003, Yanow & Schwarz-Shea, 2011). It is commonly agreed that while all of the approaches provide insights and knowledge, each one uncovers the world in a different way. For this reason, qualitative research is "inherently multimethod" and facilitates creativity, innovation and reflexivity (Denzin & Lincoln, 2011), depending on the specific research questions and the relevant context.

In fact, many social scientists now favor a pluralistic approach, arguing that it is important to "employ many perspectives, hear many voices, before we can achieve a deep understanding of social phenomena and before we can assert that a narrative is complete" (Lincoln & Denzin 2000, p. 1055). This approach involves the synthesis of diverse information sources and the use of a variety of data gathering techniques. The goal is to produce a "thick description" (Geertz, 1973), which captures the deeper cultural meaning of an experience by explaining its context, rather than simply reporting facts, irrespective of intentions or circumstances: "A thick description... gives the context of an experience, states the intentions and meanings that organized the experience, and reveals the experience as a process" (Denzin, 1994, p. 505).

Norm Denzin and Yvonne Lincoln (1994, 2005, 2008, 2011), central figures in the field of qualitative research in the social sciences, have suggested that the multiple-method approach of qualitative research may be regarded as bricolage and the contemporary qualitative researcher as a *bricoleur* (1994, p. 3). Drawing on the anthropologist Claude Levi-Strauss (1966), who defined the bricoleur as a "Jack of all trades, a kind of professional do-it-yourself person" (p.17), they redefined bricolage as "the combination of multiple methods, empirical materials, perspectives and observers in a single study" which adds "rigor, breadth complexity, richness and depth to any inquiry" (Denzin & Lincoln 2005, p. 5). The bricoleur approach thus involves borrowing from a variety of different disciplines and utilizing a variety of research tools, methods and perspectives, which opens up alternate paths to new forms of knowledge and acknowledges the complexities of the research process. By adopting this approach, the researcher rejects externally imposed research methods that try to justify reductionist universal knowledge and instead seeks to penetrate more deeply into the complexities of lived existence (Denzin & Lincoln 2011). The research activity becomes "a pieced-together, close-knit set of practices that provide solutions to a problem in a concrete situation" (Denzin & Lincoln, 1994, p.2). This offers the flexibility necessary for dealing with the complexities of postmodern society by working "with elements of randomness, spontaneity, self-organization, far-from-equilibrium conditions, feedback looping and bifurcations, all features of the world of chaos and complexity" (Berry, 2006, p. 89). In the end, the research should yield "a complex, dense, reflexive collage-like creation that represents the researcher's images, understandings and interpretations of the world or phenomenon under analysis" (Denzin & Lincoln, 2005, p. 6). While the artistic freedom inherent in qualitative research facilitates creativity, innovation and reflexivity (Denzin & Lincoln, 2011), it is all the more important for the researcher to provide an adequate description of the methods used and the theoretical paradigms underpinning the research design.

5.2 Data collection methods

In addition to taking the epistemological and ontological considerations into account, the research design of this study is based on the assumption that a triangulation of theories and data will provide the best understanding of the topic and strengthen the quality and reliability of the research findings. The concept of triangulation refers to the combination of several methods or theories in order to compensate for weaknesses or blind spots of each individual method and to examine an issue from various vantage points (Flick, 2009). The richness, depth (Denzin & Lincoln, 2008) and exploratory power of qualitative approaches also make it possible to adopt a flexible research design, which was necessary in this case due to the limited knowledge about LITs.

For the current study, I drew on concepts from various fields. Thus, narrative identity comes from psychology, transformative learning from the field of adult learning and lifelong learning, and many of the concepts presented in the main section (e.g. culture shock, reverse culture shock, self-development) have their origin in cultural or inter-cultural studies. By blending these together, I have attempted to present a multi-faceted picture of the travel process and its effect on individual identities that captures some of the complexities of the subject. In addition to drawing on a variety of theoretical concepts, I also deemed it necessary to diversify my sources of information and data gathering techniques, which are outlined in greater detail further below.

The diversification of techniques is in accordance with the concept of triangulation across data, methods and theories, by which different theories and sources of data are compared and contrasted to extract common themes and to ensure the integrity of the conclusions drawn. The following sections take a closer look at the various data collection methods and discuss the rationale behind the selection of these methods and the means by which they were carried out.

5.2.1 Field observation and autoethnography

The exploratory interpretive research paradigm involves getting out in the field and talking to real people. Researchers cannot hide behind surveys, numbers and abstractions, all of which offer the (dis)advantage of antiseptic distance (Yanow & Schwarz-Shea, 2011). The key assumption of field observation is that by actively participating in the lives of the research subjects, the researcher can reach a better understanding of their motives, beliefs, value systems, behavior etc. (Creswell, 2003; Cohen, 2000). The goal is to produce a contextualized and integrated synthesis of theory and experience (Denzin & Lincoln, 1994). The researcher takes part in the participant's everyday life and in this way explores the patterns of interaction and value systems as part of the investigative process (Lamnek, 2005, p. 549). Hammersley and Atkinson (1983) assert that, in a sense, all social research is a form of field observation because we cannot study the world without being a part of it.

Here again, it is important to be clear about the research paradigm that I employed. In contrast to positivist research, which seeks to remove the researcher from the research setting and acts as though the researcher were not there, the qualitative interpretive research paradigm that I employed in this study recognizes the researcher's presence and acknowledges its effects on the research. As mentioned earlier, I have taken this a step further by adopting the autoethnographic perspective, which views the researcher as "a *resource*, which must be capitalized upon" (Holliday, 2002, p. 145, original emphasis). In this sense, I am in agreement with many postmodern humanistic researchers, who believe that there is no such thing as value-free research and that the researcher always impacts the research process.

In this context, it is important to explain my own experience with the research setting. As mentioned at the outset of this study, the initial impetus to conduct this study came from my early childhood and short-term (i.e. 2-3 months) travel experiences to countries like Venezuela, Indonesia, Malaysia, Vietnam, Cambodia, and Laos. Furthermore, while the majority of my field observation was conducted in the course of my 4 years of travel through Latin America and a three-month trip to India several years later, it is important to realize that these were not exclusively "research trips" per se. Although I observed and

5.2 Data collection methods

interviewed others throughout these trips, in Latin America I was also experiencing my own first long-term (i.e. more than six months) independent travel experience. This means that I was traveling with a backpack on a very limited budget, and I often had to stop in my travels to work and make money.

In addition, I was not only interested in learning about traveler culture, but rather I also wanted to learn about the host cultures of the countries that I visited. To this end, I took part in the "typical" activities by which long-term travelers interact with host cultures (e.g. excursions, attending cultural events, home-stays), often going out of my way to avoid other travelers. Such avoidance of fellow travelers is actually a common practice for long-term travelers, and this representative example highlights the crucial point: namely, that I experienced first-hand most of the challenges and processes described in chapter 4 (e.g. culture shock, adaptation stress, reverse culture shock).

A further example may clarify the point. When I returned to my native culture after over four years of travel and experienced first-hand the difficulties of the transition to my home country, this significantly altered my perspective on the research and forced me to re-evaluate some of the information and re-formulate some of my research questions. In short, I realized that many of the identity changes experienced on the road do not completely "take effect" until one returns "home" and tries to integrate the "new self" with the "old self," which lingers in both one's own mind and the cultural surroundings themselves (e.g. the expectations of others and the cultural environment).[1] In fact, in this context, one can see even the terminology of methodology begin to breakdown. The word "field" in the term "field observation" in traditional ethnography would normally be defined in terms of a physical location (e.g. some setting that is different from the researcher's "native" setting). In the present case, however, the research setting actually consists of the psychological state of the research subjects, which does not end when the trip ends. That is to say that the observations I made in my own life upon returning to my native culture (e.g. talking to friends and family, re-integrating into society), as well as the discussions and interactions with other "returnees", also make up part of what would be considered the "field observations" for this study. In other words, in order to get a full understanding of the identity changes precipitated by long-term travel, I found it necessary to expand the field of study into the post-travel experiences of the research subject (including myself, in this case).

---

[1] Note: the liberal use of quotation marks in this sentence is intended to emphasize the relative, flexible nature of all of these concepts, particularly for people undergoing reverse culture shock.

Although I believe that my personal experiences have contributed greatly to my understanding of the topic and the subsequent depth of the conclusions drawn herein, it is still incumbent upon me to address the relations between myself and those whom I was observing in the field, as this is an essential aspect of the research (Holliday, 2002, p. 145). In general, upon first contact with other travelers, my practice was to behave like any other traveler, since this was essentially the life that I was living at the time. Therefore, I was simply observing my fellow travelers in their native habitat, so to speak. However, I also did not go out of my way to conceal my research interest. Thus, in answering the typical traveler questions ("Where are you from?" "Where have you been?" "Where are you going?" "Why are you here?"), I would often mention my project and the basic premise of my research (i.e. "I am studying the effects of long-term travel on individual identity constructs."). Most often, this proved to be helpful, as travelers were usually eager to contribute to my research. In these cases, I believe my status as a fellow traveler helped me connect to the subjects and encouraged open, honest communication. In fact, countless conversations ensued at the spur of the moment, many times in places where I did not have access to my recording equipment (e.g. during hikes, on bus rides, at the beach, in bars), and these conversations often provided important new insights or suggested new avenues of inquiry.

In some cases, this led to more intense social interactions between myself and other travelers based on shared travel experiences. Although such situations introduce the risk of allowing one's personal emotions to influence interpretations of events, it is my belief that this is a risk worth taking. In fact, I would agree with Jeffrey Cohen (2000), who suggested that efforts to preserve neutrality and distance in research may even complicate the researcher's life and may be interpreted as a lack of involvement or trust. As trust developed between myself and some other travelers, they often began to open up more and offer some deeper insights than those that first surfaced upon the initial, sometimes largely superficial encounter. For this reason, I believe that such personal connections can add to our "understanding of the ethnographic moment and need not 'contaminate' or lessen the scientific value of our work" (Cohen, 2000, p. 327, original emphasis). What was important in these cases was to keep this within the perspective provided by the broader field of research. If new ideas were suggested in this context, it was important to pursue them further in contacts with other subjects or to follow up in a more structured manner. For this reason, particularly thought-provoking interactions with other travelers often provided the impetus for arranging interviews.

5.2.2 Life-world interviews

Since field observation does not constitute an adequate method in itself (Cohen, 2000) to examine the research questions guiding this study, semi-structured, "life-world interviews" (Kvale & Brinkmann, 2009) were the second method used to expand the toolkit of primary data collection. This method is appropriate for gathering detailed views and perspectives from participants and "seeks to obtain descriptions of the life-world of the interviewee with respect to interpreting the meaning of the described phenomena" (Kvale & Brinkmann, 2009, p. 124). Life-world interviews depict an interpersonal situation that comes close to an everyday conversation between two partners about a topic of mutual interest. Although the semi-structured life-world interview has a sequence of themes to be covered and some suggested questions, the interviewer determines the interview process by asking probing questions and maintains flexibility in terms of the sequence and forms of questions. This allows the interviewer to follow up on the specific answers given and the stories told by the respondents (Kvale & Brinkmann, 2009, p. 125). The interviewee is viewed as an expert on the topic and is given the opportunity to provide as much information as possible. The following passage captures the mindset behind the open phenomenological approach of the life-world interview:

> I want to understand the world from your point of view. I want to know what you know in the way you know it. I want to understand the meaning of your experience, to walk in your shoes, to feel things as you feel them, to explain things as you explain them. Will you become my teacher and help me understand? (Spradley, 1979, 34, cited in Kvale & Brinkmann, 2009)

The life-world interview operates under the assumption that the most influential meaning for the individual is that which he or she *perceives* to be reality (Kvale & Brinkmann, 2009, p. 26). Thus, the life-world interview is not concerned with judging the efficacy or "truth" of these perceptions against any pre-determined ethical or scientific standard, but rather seeks to understand reality as perceived by the subject.

Kvale & Brinkmann (2009) mention twelve aspects that constitute the main points of qualitative research interviews, which I adopted for this study. These points can be summarized as follows:

- The interview topic relates to important themes in the *life-world* of the interviewee and his or her relation to it.

- The goal of the interview is to understand the *meaning* of these themes from the interviewee's life-world. Aside from looking at factual information, the interviewee also interprets what was said and how it was said.

- The interview aims to gather *qualitative* knowledge in everyday language, without aiming for quantification.
- The interview is *descriptive* in nature, since it seeks open descriptions of important themes in the interviewee's life-world.
- The interview develops *specificity* about certain themes and situations that occurred in the interviewee's life-world, and not general opinions about events.
- The interviewer exhibits a certain *deliberate naiveté* in order to remain open to unexpected phenomena and to encourage the interviewee to disclose more of his/her life-world.
- The interview must be *focused* on the particular themes of study, which means it is neither rigidly structured with ready-made questions nor completely open or without directive.
- Statements by the interviewees can sometimes reflect *ambiguity*. It is the interviewer's responsibility to determine whether contradictory statements are genuine inconsistencies in the life-world of the interviewee or whether they are due to faulty communication in the interview.
- Interviewees may re-evaluate and *change* their attitudes toward and descriptions of certain themes discussed in the interview. This is indicative of new insights and awareness gained in the course of the interview. The interview can thus be a learning process for both the interviewee and the interviewer.
- The interview can differ depending on the level of *sensitivity* of the interviewer and his or her knowledge of the topic. Hence, it is important for the interviewer to be sensitive to the comments made by the interviewees.
- The qualitative interview constitutes an interpersonal situation, where knowledge is produced via the social interaction between two individuals. In addition to producing knowledge, this interview type may provoke anxieties and defense mechanisms in both the interviewer and interviewee.
- A well-conducted life-world interview may be a positive experience for the interviewee, who may gain new insights into his or her life-world through the interview. (Kvale & Brinkmann, 2009, pp. 28-32)

The interview format in my study is consistent with Kvale & Brinkmann's (2009) qualitative interview. In accordance with these principles, it would appear at first glance that the interview occurs as a conversation between two equal partners. However, it is important to recognize that the life-world is not a "completely open and free dialogue between egalitarian partners" (Kvale & Brinkmann, 2009, p. 33). All scientific interviews bestow certain levels of power upon the two participants. For example, the roles of the interviewer and interviewee are clearly defined. The interviewer is granted the power to determine the topic, probe further into certain issues, and terminate discussion on other issues that are seemingly of less interest. In the life-world interview, the researcher must wield this power carefully. For my part, I was generally inclined to err on the side of leniency, allowing tangential discussions to proceed in the event that they might yield some useful insights (a fact which is reflected in the length of the interviews, which sometimes stretched to 3 hours).

On the other hand, the interviewee has the power to withhold information or to refuse to address certain topics. I experienced this on rare occasions, when the interviewee was either unwilling to open up about a certain topic or genuinely believed that he or she had nothing meaningful to say about a certain topic. More problematic are the cases of exaggeration or falsification. Stories may be anchored in reality but rarely reflect travel experiences as fixed certainties. Thus we can never be sure of their accuracy and sincerity. They may be distorted, exaggerated or simplified, personal setbacks may be played down, and risks may be blown out of proportion.

Here, it is important to distinguish between two forms of "misinformation" – unintentional and intentional. In the case of unintentional misinformation (i.e. the respondent's memory of an event does not correspond exactly to the actual facts), it is important to remember that what "actually happened" is not the point here. What is important is the meaning the speaker has assigned to the event. Ellis & Bochner (2000) address this question of what they call "narrative truth" and point out that "one narrative interpretation of events can be judged against another, but there is no standard by which to measure any narrative against the meaning of events themselves, because the meaning of prenarrative experience is constituted in its narrative expression" (p. 745). Thus, by narrating their experiences, the speakers are assigning them meanings which serve to support their own identity constructs.

In the case of deliberate falsification (e.g. the common tendency either to exaggerate or downplay certain events), the first task of the interviewer is to establish an atmosphere in which respondents feel that they can express any idea without the risk of being judged or criticized. Nevertheless, it must be conceded that there is an inherent risk in any social research. There is always the possibility that people will lie on questionnaires or in interviews. In the case of interviews, the researcher can at least probe deeper into apparently false statements. Often, this can provide valuable data, since the image that a subject attempts to convey to those around him or her (including an interviewer) can often reveal important things about the subject's desires or the values of the subject's or the interviewer's culture.

5.2.2.1 First interview

The sample for the present study comprises 41 long-term independent travelers from economically developed countries, the majority of whom I met traveling in Central and South America between 2003 and 2007. As shown in Table 5, I conducted 30 interviews in Central and South America, while some interviews took place in Austria (n=8), Easter Island (n=2), and India (n=1). The interviews, which I conducted in Austria and India, occurred after my own return from traveling between 2008 and 2010, and they were shorter, more focused and aimed at covering the categories that had emerged from the first round in greater depth. In addition, I also interviewed 2 LITs who had returned from their extended journeys between 15 and 25 years ago. However, these two LITs were not contacted again to participate in the follow-up interview.

The interviews emphasized three central themes: (1) motivation for engaging in long-term independent travel (2) experiences on the road and (3) returning home (or settling down elsewhere). I asked the respondents to discuss these research topics and offer their personal views and opinions regarding the research questions. As most respondents spoke English quite fluently, most interviews were conducted in English, and some in German.

The interview guide was divided into four distinct sections (see appendix 12.1):

- PART ONE: *Biographical information* about the participants, including their age, country of origin, where they grew up, educational background (highest degree), and travel background (e.g. number and length of long-term trips)

- PART TWO: *Motivation* for going on a long-term trip, including information about the living conditions at the time of departure (e.g. employment status), motivations, trigger events, etc.

- PART THREE: *Experiences on the road,* including topics such as dangerous situations, taking risks, feeling out of place, loneliness, interacting with other travelers, highlights, poverty, lessons learned, etc.

5.2 Data collection methods

- PART FOUR: *Returning home*, or settling down somewhere else, including topics such as expectations before returning, relationships with friends/family, perceptions of one's home country, support networks, etc. Part four also includes general questions on perceived learning through travel.

Part four (i.e. returning home) was particularly relevant for those LITs who had traveled before and could therefore share stories about previous reentry experiences. For those LITS who were on their first trip, only the questions about learning outcomes were relevant in part four.

It is important to mention that the interview guide evolved over time. During the interviews, new aspects or ideas often emerged. In this case, I would amend the interview guide to allow for the collection of relevant information on new or refined questions. When no new information was forthcoming and I felt that a saturation level of information was reached, I concluded the interview part of the study.

The face-to-face, open-ended, interviews lasted between one and three hours, depending on the information offered by the respondents. After providing some background information on the research, I promised to preserve their anonymity by allocating pseudonyms instead of their full names and by not disclosing information that may identify them in this research. The interviews were recorded with different audio recording devices. The first interviews in 2003 and 2004 were taped using a mini-disc player. This was somewhat cumbersome, but it was the best available option at the time. Subsequent interviews were recorded using an mp3 player/recorder and eventually a smart phone. The latter two options had the significant advantage of obtaining an mp3 file immediately after recording, rather than an actual mini-disc that could hold a maximum of 120 minutes per disc and needed to be sent home, relying on the various postal services of the countries I was traveling in at the time.

Stories are often the lifeblood of travelers, whether still on the road or upon return. If we conceive of identity as the story that we tell ourselves and others about who we are and what we are, then this narrative is often unconsciously affected by forces that are beyond our awareness and control (Jenkins, 2013). In this context, the researcher plays a critical role. It was therefore my role to help shape the subjects' narratives by framing their stories, prodding them for more details, eliciting emotions and strong reactions and producing thick descriptions and compelling narratives of personal travel experiences and perceived transformations.

The levels of detail offered depended on the interviewees' assumptions on how well I understood their experiences, as well as their own self-reflective skills. Moreover, as explained in section 1.4, my own personal history, worldview and experiences as a LIT without doubt influenced my relationship with the interviewees and reaction to their stories. In most cases, it was easy to build a rapport with the interviewees, which was maybe due to an unspoken mutual understanding of the topic under discussion. This connection may have had a positive effect on how openly the subjects shared their stories with me, and this allowed me to gather rich and at times deeply personal data. I tried to listen actively and attentively and remain open to perspectives that differed from my own, which also contributed to creating rapport and trust.

The majority of the phase-one interviews took place on the road, usually in guesthouses, restaurants, beaches, mountains, or by campfires. The relaxed atmosphere allowed for emotional safety, enabled the participants to speak freely and openly, and the interview thus took the form of a casual conversation rather than a pre-defined question and answer format. Moreover, this interview format allowed the incorporation of new questions based on input from both the researcher and the interviewee. This means that, in order to gain additional information from the interviewee or to clarify ambiguous or incomplete answers, I asked specific questions and probed them for more details. In some cases, I had traveled with the participants for several days or even weeks and gotten to know them quite well before sitting down for the actual interview. The vast majority of the participants showed a genuine interest in the research project, and some specifically stated that the interview had a cathartic effect and that they found it a valuable reflection exercise. Some also asked me for preliminary findings.

5.2.2.2 Second Interview

One of the main problems of longitudinal research is the fact that not all initial interview partners are available for a follow-up interview many years later. This is also the case in the current study, which is why the number of respondents whom I interviewed a second time is smaller. Although I stayed in contact with some of the respondents from the initial interview over the years, others were gone from the radar, possibly because they had changed their email addresses, changed their names through marriage or were unavailable due to other factors unknown to me. Nonetheless, I managed to contact some of them through public profiles available on social networking sites, such as Facebook, LinkedIn or Xing.

5.2 Data collection methods

In total, I obtained follow-up information from 23 LITs, 13 interviews and 10 questionnaires (see section 5.2.3). The interviews took place in early 2017 and apart from one face-to face interview, the other 12 interviews were conducted via skype or in the case of one – via Facebook video chat - as personal interviews were not a viable option due to geographical distance between us.

The second interview (see appendix 11.2 for the interview guide) focused on the LITs post-travel life, their reentry experiences in their home societies, their relationships with friends and family, coping strategies and professional life. In particular, during the second interview, participants were asked to elaborate on the perceived changes that had happened in their lives since the first interview, and on whether they had experienced any further transformations, either through travel or other life events. This was critical in determining whether the experiences on the road had a lasting effect on the lifestyle, attitude, behaviors and values of the participants.

Before the interview took place, I re-read the interview transcripts from the first interview in order to ask specific follow-up questions. For example, one LIT mentioned in the first interview that she wanted to pursue a Master's Degree after traveling, and in the second interview I referred to this intention in order to find out whether her plans were put into practice. What is more, during the second round, I also fed back some interview segments from the first interview to the participants, asking them to comment on the passages. I applied the same procedure for the written questionnaire and compiled individual questionnaires for each individual traveler.

5.2.3 Questionnaires

Several participants ($n = 10$) preferred to do the second round of interviews in writing, indicating they would have more time to think about the questions, or in the case of one, simply because they were not familiar with the synchronous phone technology. In that case, I prepared an individualized questionnaire with a number of questions, which they returned as a Word or PDF document attached to an email or Facebook message. As mentioned above, in addition to the standard questions (see appendix 11.3 for sample questionnaire), the questionnaire also comprised segments from the first interview, and I asked the respondents to comment on them.

Both questionnaires and interviews have their benefits and drawbacks. Email interviews allow the interviewees more time to reflect and engage more in depth with the interview questions, whereas participants in "face-to-face" interviews often formulated their ideas as they were speaking. The main advantage of face-to face interviews is that I could clarify particular issues right away or prod subjects to elaborate on a specific topic. Overall, the interview transcripts from the second round of interviews were much longer than the returned questionnaires, with the longest interview running 4.5 hours (until 2 in the morning in my case, considering the 9 hour time difference). There were several instances with the written interviews where certain elements were unclear, and I had to ask the subjects in follow-up emails to clarify or elaborate on particular issues.

It can be argued that the time lapse between the first and the second interview may affect the comparability of the data. However, the mobility of many participants in this study does not follow a simple home-away-home framework, and the vast differences among the participants in terms of previous travel experiences, trip lengths, exposure to other cultures, educational and socio-cultural backgrounds and post-travel life events actually provides a richness and depth to the overall perspective offered here. In fact, some of the respondents I interviewed never even returned home, but were still traveling or settled down elsewhere. Perhaps most importantly, the point of this research is not to aggregate information by comparing traveler accounts to derive some sort of "objective" truth about travelers in general, but rather to present a rich tapestry of the different ways in which travel can affect different people in the short and long term.

5.2.4 Blogs, email and social media

It is worth mentioning that this research would not have been possible to this extent without the help of new media, such as blogs, email and social media. Although travel blogs were still in their infancy at the time when the majority of interviews were conducted, several LITs were among the early adopters and gave me an insight into their blogs (private and public) which they maintained during and in some cases until briefly after their travel. That being said, I refrained from using verbatim quotes from their public blogs in order to protect their anonymity.

Other LITs sent mass emails to friends and family and included me on their list or would stay in touch via private emails during their travels and afterwards. Three LITs, for example, who unfortunately did not respond to my request for a second interview in 2017, shared their personal reentry experiences with me in several emails up until three years after their return, thereby giving me a valuable insight into their early post-travel life and re-adaptation process. However, they are not part of the 23 LITs of the second round, since they were unavailable for a second interview in 2017 and therefore did not provide me with a long-term perspective on the impact their travels had on their lives.

And finally, social networking sites such as Facebook, LinkedIn, Xing, and private websites proved helpful to track down many of the LITs that volunteered to participate in the second round, and their public profiles gave me a glimpse into their lives since the first interview. Of the 41 LITs who participated in the first interview, I managed to obtain information primarily revolving around their professional careers and private lives of 38 LITs.

Table 3. Interviews and questionnaires

Type	No.
Interviews 1st round	41
Interviews 2nd round	13
Questionnaires 2nd round	10

5.3 Participant demographics

The participants are pivotal to the success of this study, as they constitute the main source of data. They are the people who "define, explain, interpret and construct reality, and as such they are as important as, if not more important than, the researcher" (Sarantakos, 1998, p. 51).

As shown in Figure 5, 41 LITs participated in the first round of the study. In terms of demographics, 25 were male, 16 were female. Their ages ranged from 23 to 51 with an average age of 34. Furthermore, all LITs come from Western countries, and their nationalities include English ($n=8$), Austria ($n=7$), Germany, ($n=7$), Canada ($n=4$), USA ($n=4$), Australia ($n=2$), Denmark ($n=2$), Switzerland ($n=2$), Belgium ($n=1$), Czech Republic ($n=1$), Ireland ($n=1$), New Zealand ($n=1$), Sweden ($n=1$).

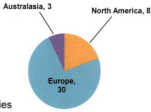

Figure 3: 1st round LITs' nationalities

Of the 23 LITs who participated in the second round, 13 are male and 10 are female. Their ages during the second round ranged from 36 to 59, with an average age of 47 years. The majority are from European countries (Germany (*n=6*), England, (*n=4*), Austria (*n=4*), Ireland (*n=1*), Denmark (*n=1*)), six are from North America (Canada (*n=3*), USA (*n=3*)) and one from New Zealand.

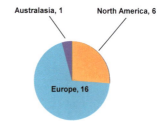

Figure 4: 2nd round LITs' nationalities

Participants were chosen through non-random methods based on their travel experience and willingness to share their perspectives. Although one of the requirements to participate in this research was to have a minimum of 6 months of long-term independent travel experience, the majority of participants had extensive long-term independent travel experience and the length of travel time was one of the greatest variables among the participants. One LIT was interviewed two months prior to his departure to an open-ended journey and had no previous travel experience. While some of the LITs interviewed were still on their first long-term journey (*n= 31*), others had accumulated previous travel experience and could talk both about their experiences on the road as well as the reentry experiences. Their long-term independent travel experience at the time of the interview ranged from 6 months to 7.5 years, with an average time spent on the road of 33 months, i.e. 2 years and 9 months.

In terms of their educational background, the majority of the respondents had a university degree (*n =29*). One LIT had a doctorate, 12 a Master's degree, and 16 a Bachelor' de-

5.3 Participant demographics

gree (see table 4). Three LITs studied for a few years but did not complete their degrees, 7 have an apprenticeship and 2 LITs have completed high school. The rather high overall educational background of the LITs came as a surprise and it was not until I analyzed the data and put the demographic information in an excel sheet, that I became aware of it. I believe I was surprised because when traveling, most LITs do not define themselves by typical status factors deemed important in mainstream Western society as LITs have their own status factors by which they define themselves. This will be more closely examined in section 7.4.3 of this thesis.

Table 4. LIT's educational background

Educational background	LITs (41 total)
Doctorate	1
Master's Degree	12
Bachelor's Degree	16
Some university	3
Apprenticeship	7
High school	2

The following table gives a brief overview of the demographic information of the interview participants:

Table 5. LIT's key characteristics

Pseudonym	Follow-up*	Gender	Age 1st round	Age 2nd round	Nationality	Education	LIT experience**	Interview when	Interview where
Nadine	Q	F	23	36	Canada	Bachelors	8m	2004	Costa Rica
Chelsea	I	F	25	37	England	Bachelors	1y 3m	2005	Brazil
Glen	Q	M	26	38	England	Bachelors	2y	2005	Bolivia
Emma	Q	F	41	53	England	Apprenticeship	1y 7m	2005	Bolivia
Jake	Q	M	45	57	England	Apprenticeship	4y 3m	2005	Bolivia
Nick	Q	M	34	47	Ireland	Masters	10m	2004	Argentina
Eric	Q	M	48	59	Canada	Masters	2y 10m	2006	Brazil
Dana	I	F	39	51	Denmark	Bachelors	1y 9m	2005	Bolivian
Sarah	Q	F	37	45	Austrian	Masters	3y 6m	2009	Austria
Lukas	I	M	27	39	German	Masters	1y 1m	2005	Argentina
Matt	I	M	28	39	USA	Bachelors	2y 6m	2005	Bolivia
Julia	I	F	37	50	Germany	Bachelors	6 y	2004	Honduras
Tom	Q	M	46	59	Germany	Bachelors	1y 6m	2004	Panama
Brian	I	M	43	55	USA	Bachelors	3y	2004	Panama
Nora	I	F	49	57	Germany	Masters	6y 5m	2009	India
Max	I	M	30	36	Austria	Masters	0	2011	Austria
Ryan	Q	M	26	40	Canada	some university	1y 9m	2003	Honduras
Lena	I	F	26	41	Germany	Masters	1 y	2003	Honduras
Oliver	I	M	51	59	Austria	Apprenticeship	4y 6m	2009	Austria
Veronica	I	F	35	43	Austria	Bachelors	4y 6m	2009	Austria
Emilia	I	F	36	49	Germany	Apprenticeship	4y 9m	2004	Uruguay
Alan	Q	M	42	56	New Zealand	Bachelors	1y 4m	2003	Nicaragua

5.3 Participant demographics

Pseudonym	Follow-up*	Gender	Age 1st round	Age 2nd round	Nationality	Education	LIT experience**	Interview when	Interview where
Andy	I	M	30	42	USA	Bachelors	3y	2005	Bolivia
Jakob	NO	M	34		Austria	Bachelors	3y 7m	2009	Austria
Dan	NO	M	34		England	Masters	1 y	2008	Austria
Aimee	NO	F	26		England	Bachelors	2y	2005	Bolivia
Heather	NO	F	36		Australia	Bachelors	7y 6m	2004	Bolivia
Ally	NO	F	33		Switzerland	Apprenticeship	2y 7m	2005	Easter Island
Syd	NO	M	32		Switzerland	Masters	2y	2005	Easter Island
Lilly	NO	F	31		England	Masters	1y	2005	Bolivian
Andy	NO	M	30		USA	Bachelors	2y	2005	Bolivia
Aaron	NO	M	35		USA	Bachelors	9m	2005	Peru
Ben	NO	M	31		England	Doctorate	3y	2004	Panama
Eva	NO	F	26		Germany	Apprenticeship	2y 6m	2005	Chile
Keith	NO	M	23		Australia	Bachelors	1y	2004	Honduras
Philipp	NO	M	46		Austrian	Masters	2y	2010	Austria
Chris	NO	M	36		Czech Republic	Apprenticeship	3y	2003	Honduras
Theo	NO	M	33		Canada	some university	2y 4m	2003	Honduras
Magnus	NO	M	25		Denmark	High school	5y	2004	Honduras
Lars	NO	M	28		Belgium	some university	3y 8m	2005	Chile
Patrick	NO	M	37		Austria	Masters	3y	2010	Austria
Alice	NO	F	29		Sweden	High school	6y	2003	Honduras

* **Follow-up** refers to the type of follow up information received: Q = questionnaire, I= interview

** **LIT experience** refers to the number of months (m) or years (y) traveled at the time of the interview.

5.4 Interpreting the empirical data

One of the main goals of qualitative data analysis is to capture the complexity and richness of lived experience. This does not seek objectivity, but instead it assumes subjectivity and positionality (Riessman, 2002, p. 696), where the perspectives of both the participant and the researcher can come into the foreground. However, one of the main challenges of data analysis is to make the familiar strange. Wittgenstein (1968) suggests that "the aspects of things that are most important for us are hidden because of their simplicity and familiarity (para. 129). Similarly, Gubrium and Holstein (2000) assert that the researcher "must temporarily set aside belief in its reality" (p. 498). In other words, it is important not to be blinded by one's own assumptions and to look for small and seemingly unimportant details that would otherwise be overlooked.

The primary goal of data analysis is to "make sense out of information gathered through the previous stages of the research and to identify the meaning the data contain" (Sarantakos, 1998, p. 313). This represents a formidable task for the qualitative researcher and is a time-consuming and at times ambiguous but also fascinating process. The ongoing process of data analysis involves studying data and identifying trends and patterns and relationships pertinent to the research topic. It entails condensing data and discarding unnecessary information and requires continual reflection about the data and posing analytical questions (Creswell, 2003). Data must be interpreted in such a manner that it enables the researcher to move deeper and deeper into understanding and interpreting the larger meaning of it.

Due to the fluid and emergent nature of qualitative analysis and the bricolage approach to research, the first steps of data analysis are already made during the process of data collection. New insights and ideas about how to make sense of data emerge, and patterns take shape while still in the field. Hence, the early stages of field work tend to be emergent, while later stages of data collection deepen insights and move towards confirming or disconfirming patterns (Patton, 2005, p. 436). While data analysis begins early on in research, it is important not to rush to any premature conclusions in the early stages of research. Instead of trying to confirm preliminary findings and hypotheses, "the inquiry should become particularly sensitive to looking for alternative explanations and patterns that would invalidate initial insights" (Patton, 2005, p. 437).

In accordance with Sarantakos (1998, p. 315), I employed the following three broad steps in analyzing data in this paper, which describe the processes of induction (field material), deduction (conceptual framework) and verification in a cyclical manner:

5.4 Interpreting the empirical data

1. *Data reduction:* This involves carefully reading the recorded information (i.e. field notes, interview transcripts and online narratives), summarizing, identifying recurring and important themes and categorizing the material for analysis. This first step also helped to decide what further material to collect and how and whom to interview next.

2. *Data organization:* This entails finding similarities, arranging information according to relevant themes and sub-themes, and clustering together information more specifically. It also involves presenting the results in text.

3. *Interpretation:* The final step involves identifying patterns, trends and explanations, which lead to making decisions and reaching conclusions related to the research questions. These conclusions can be tested again through more data collection, reduction, organization and interpretation. This process continues until a point of saturation is reached and no new information is forthcoming.

I chose this cyclical process of data analysis primarily for its simplicity and conciseness. Thematic analysis as a way to organize the data seemed appropriate for the purpose of this study. This entailed identifying and organizing distinctive sets of thematic meaning units before, during and after the data collection process. The themes gradually emerged in the research process and were influenced by my own experience and field observations, as well as the interviews and literature reviews. While my field notes and travel diaries proved invaluable material for the research design, the rich data gathered through interviews provided even deeper insights into the window of human experience. For example, an answer from one interview often created a new idea, which led to a new question to probe further in the next interview. Furthermore, information from subsequent interviews caused me to go back and re-read older interview transcripts, and this led to a re-evaluation of the original conclusions based on the new information or context gained from the newer interview. Also, with repeated reading and scrutinizing of the transcriptions, particular topics and broader themes became apparent and were further developed as the research proceeded. Due to the large amount of data, this study would not have been possible without the assistance of data analysis software. To this end, I opted for the *f4 analyse* software, which enables the structured creation of color-codes, writings of summaries and memos as well as export of quotations. The *f4 analyse* memo function, which enables one to record ideas as they emerge while reading the transcripts, proved to be particularly helpful in developing codes and identifying patterns, similarities and dissimilarities.

After multiple readings of the data, I assigned a code to these topics and then grouped them together (using the F4 software program). In the early stage of data analysis, I fed back some data to the participants for comment and to ensure validity. The main goal was to make sure that my interpretation of an idea corresponds with the respondent's interpretation. Aside from adding to the validity of the data, actively involving participants in the co-construction of meaning is appropriate, since it also represents a necessary dialogue between the participants and the researcher and helps provide a structure for writing (Holliday, 2002, p. 104). I subsequently examined the data in order to identify how these common themes are linked together. Finally, I interpreted the data, identified patterns, commonalities as well as differences, and drew conclusions, which are presented in the following chapters of this thesis.

Overall, the entire research process spanned more than a decade. The time commitment resulted largely from the extended time spent in the field, writing field notes and hundreds of pages of interview transcriptions, as well as communication with participants and travel to and from interview sites. The second interview required me to re-read the first interview transcript and create targeted, individualized questions based on the first interview in order to follow up on it. For example, if an interviewee indicated an interest in pursuing a different career after travel in the first interview, I addressed this aspect in the follow-up interview years later. Thus, it was necessary to modify the broad interview questions for each individual follow-up interview. While this study contributes to the scant existing literature on the long-term transformative power of travel, the time aspect makes it hard to replicate the present research.

5.5 Validating the accuracy of findings

The fundamentally interpretive nature of qualitative research necessitates employing verification strategies to ensure the validity of findings. In this thesis, I employed a number of verification strategies in accordance with Creswell (2003, pp. 196-197):

- *Spending prolonged time in the field* to provide an in-depth understanding of the phenomenon: Field observation was an essential part of this research, as it helped to formulate and refine the research questions and also yielded the conceptual framework upon which the study was then built (see section 3.3.1)
- *Participant-checking* by feeding specific descriptions or themes back to the participants and determining whether these participants feel that they are accurate: This

was done in two ways, primarily during the interview process. First, if answers were ambiguous, I probed further to try to clarify the idea. However, in some cases, these misunderstandings did not arise until the second or third time I reviewed the transcript. In this case, I employed the second method – I contacted the respondent and read back the relevant section of the transcript and followed up to see if I had interpreted their words correctly.

- Using *peer debriefing* to enhance the accuracy of the account: In order to make sure that the account resonates with people other than the researcher, I regularly attended university-run PhD seminars within the interdisciplinary PhD program "Lifelong learning" of the University Klagenfurt, where I received useful feedback from both my peers and my supervisors about my study.

- *Using an external auditor* to review the entire project: Since my topic cannot be ascribed to a single field and falls into interdisciplinary studies, both supervisors, who have a well-established interdisciplinary track record, also functioned as auditors who assessed the project through an "outside lens."

- *Triangulating* different sources of information (field observations at different times and in different locations, life-world interviews and employment of different theoretical perspectives) by examining evidence from the sources and using it to build a coherent justification for themes (see section 5.3)

- *Clarifying the bias* the researcher brings to the study in order to create an open and honest narrative: Section 1.4. clarifies my role in the research project, in particular as it relates to the concept of autoethnography.

- *Presenting negative and discrepant information* that runs counter to the themes: Different perspectives do not always coalesce, and discussing contrary information adds to the credibility of an account. As mentioned in section 5.3, I tried to interview many different types of travelers with different viewpoints and opinions in order to promote intersubjectivity and to obtain a well-rounded picture of long-term travelers.

- *Using rich, thick description* to convey these findings: Such descriptions may transport readers to the setting and give the discussion an element of shared experiences. I hope that this study produces thick description by giving the context of an experience and capturing its cultural meaning.

5.6 Summary

To summarize, I chose a qualitative, interpretive and (auto)ethnographic research design because it affords the opportunity to focus on understanding how long-term travelers create meaning and make sense of their own realities. The study began with long-term field observation, in which I was immersed in the traveler culture I was studying. This was in line with the recommendation of Denzin & Lincoln (2008), advocates of postmodern approaches to ethnography, who suggest immersing oneself in the research setting and the lives of the research participants in order to gain a deep understanding of them. This immersion also gave rise to some personal experiences which are integrated in the sections below and represent an autoethnographic element that serves to enrich the text and broaden the perspective offered.

However, the central focus of the research is on the semi-structured life-world interviews conducted with a wide variety of LITs. Kvale & Brinkmann's (2009) semi-structured "life-world interview" aims to obtain an understanding of the respondent's complex social world. They allow the researcher to acquire detailed information about the interviewee's personal beliefs and perceptions of a particular topic by providing access to various narratives in which people describe their lived experiences and how these experiences contribute to meaning making. The interviews are particularly revealing in that they contain emotive and personal elements and can therefore function as triggers for self-discovery by both the researcher and the participants.

With regard to data analysis, multiple theories and methods were triangulated to enhance the validity of the interpretation. In addition, I followed Sarantakos' (1998) cyclical approach, which deploys a process of data reduction, organization and interpretation to separate relevant information from irrelevant information and identify common themes for subsequent interpretation. The following chapter will discuss the results of this analysis using the tripartite structure established in chapter 4 (pre-travel, on the road, and post-travel) to show how the challenges experienced in these different phases help to shape and transform the identities of LITs.

6 Findings

In the following four chapters, I will look at the results from my interviews with LITs and use their responses (as well as some autobiographical elements) to demonstrate how the transformative learning process plays out in the course of long-term independent travel. Drawing on the structure established in chapter 4, this chapter is also first divided into three main sections corresponding to the three phases of long-term travel. Thus, the chapter begins with an examination of the reasons why LITs decide to engage in this specific type of travel in the first place and which specific experiences "get them out the door". The second section then discusses LITs' experiences on the road and the challenges faced there, while the third section focuses on the post-travel phase, during which LITs must figure out how their new values or meaning schemes can be integrated with their native culture.

For each of these phases, I will look at the disorienting experiences, the LITs' efforts to resolve these dilemmas, and the learning outcomes in terms of altered values or identity constructs. It is important to emphasize here that there is no fixed chronological correspondence between these basic phases of (transformative) learning and the phases of travel. Rather, disorienting experiences can (and usually do) occur in any phase, and most LITs actually experience multiple disorienting dilemmas over the course of the long-term travel experience. Similarly, there are no simple "before and after" identities. In most cases, the transformation process is, in fact, far more complex and can involve multiple phases of relative levels of identity synthesis and confusion (Erikson, 1968) along the way. Indeed, this will ultimately emerge as the key message of this chapter: the complete long-term independent travel experience, as conceived here with its three phases, presents a multitude of challenges, each of which represents an opportunity for learning, and all of which can interact in complex ways.

Finally, in the final results chapter, I will outline the final outcomes of the overall long-term independent travel experience, with a particular focus on the meanings, identities and competences developed by travelers through the transformative learning process.

Throughout this chapter, I will also highlight the narrative identity construction process in action. This process can be seen in the answers given and the stories told throughout an interview. As we will see, this sheds light on the role of critical reflection on the learning process. In some cases, one can "see" a LIT essentially "re-telling" a story that they constructed before the interview, indicating that the LIT has already at least partially processed the experience and established the related meaning. In other cases, one can "see" the participant struggling to construct both story and meaning while answering the question, or perhaps allowing the meaning to unfold over the course of the interview as the trust and comfort level increases. Finally, and perhaps most interestingly, thanks to the longitudinal nature of this study, in many cases we can trace the evolution of values and identities by comparing two interviews with the same subject conducted at different phases of the (transformative) learning process.

Before proceeding, there are a few small points to clear up about the interview quotes contained in the sections below. First, each quote is labeled with the speaker's name, nationality and age at the time of the interview in which the quote occurred. If the quote came from the second interview with a subject, this is indicated with a "2nd" after the age. In addition, any quotes that came from questionnaires, blogs, or emails are also indicated in the citation after the age. Second, I would remind the reader that the subjects were speaking freely during the interviews, and many of them are not native English speakers. For this reason, there are, of course, occasional grammar and syntax mistakes. As I think it is important to let the speakers voices come through here, I have not corrected these errors. In addition, to keep the quotes cleaner, I have also chosen not to use the condescending academic [sic] to indicate every error. Finally, for those interviews conducted in German, I have translated the responses into English.

Figure 5: The transformative learning process in long-term independent travel

7 Reaching the Tipping Point

This chapter seeks to answer the research question "What are the critical motivating factors for extended travel?" Thus, the focus here is on disorienting dilemmas, while the outcome for this chapter is simply the decision to embark upon the journey. For the purpose of the discussion below, I will be substituting the term "disorienting experience" for Mezirow's more conceptually loaded term "disorienting dilemma", or to go back a bit further, Erikson's concept of a "life crisis". Since these terms imply a serious problem that urgently demands a rapid decision or solution, from a narrative standpoint they are quite attractive for both individuals thinking about their own life stories and researchers who are trying to explain those life stories. A traumatic experience that launches the protagonist onto a journey of self-discovery is a very comfortable and easily comprehensible narrative device that we have "seen" in countless narratives (books, films, oral stories, etc.). However, my research among LITs suggests that this kind of shocking experience is more the exception than the norm. Rather than one single catastrophic problem that triggers the decision to travel, the far more common pattern I found was a gradual accumulation of disturbances that lead to some level of cognitive dissonance and eventually to the decision to begin traveling.

For this reason, I prefer to think of the decision to embark on long-term travel as a kind of tipping point. The term "tipping point" was coined by the sociologist Morton Grodzins in the 1950s and popularized by Malcolm Gladwell in the early 2000s. While both employed the concept to describe social change, here I use the term to emphasize the necessary accumulation of disorienting experiences that must occur before the trigger event can release the energy needed to motivate an individual to embark on a long-term independent journey. In essence, almost all LITs had some feeling of dissonance with their cultural environment, a sense that their roles in society were somehow not in accord with their personal values and desires. While such feelings are nearly universal, they have to reach a certain level before one considers a radical decision such as leaving society for an extended period of time, and this level is essentially the tipping point. Of course, as we will see below, this level varies widely from one individual to the next, due to a wide range of factors, including personality, background, predispositions, and intellectual curiosity.

Thus, in order to provide a more complete picture of travel motivations, this chapter will start with what I call "seed experiences." These are disorienting experiences that occur well before the decision to travel is made, but that plant the seed of the idea to look beyond one's cultural setting – a kind of curiosity or even longing to know what is beyond the borders of one's world. I then move on to the more general category of "lifestyle dissonance". This section discusses the creeping feeling of dissatisfaction that emerges over time if one's identity gradually comes out of alignment with the values and norms of the cultural environment. For those who had previous seed experiences, this lifestyle dissonance is a kind of fertilizer that nurtures the feeling of discontent. Next, I will cover some of the more common trigger events. These are the experiences that researchers tend to focus on. As the "straw that broke the camel's back" (or the "last drop that made the cup overflow", to use the expression from German, French, Italian, Spanish, etc.), these are experiences that LITs tend to remember, and they are the ones that often emerge first in an interview.

Two final sub-sections round out this section on travel motivations. First, I will discuss the process of overcoming the final obstacles to departure that often arise either internally (i.e. from their own fears) or externally (i.e. from important figures in their lives) even after LITs have made the conscious decision to go traveling. And second, I will discuss the rewards that LITs expect to gain by traveling.

Before proceeding, it is important to emphasize here that I am not suggesting that the sections outlined above represent a universal "pre-travel" process through which all LITs pass. On the contrary, no two experiences are alike, and this section is simply intended to highlight some of the main feelings and mechanisms that lead people to decide on a non-traditional form of further development such as long-term independent travel.

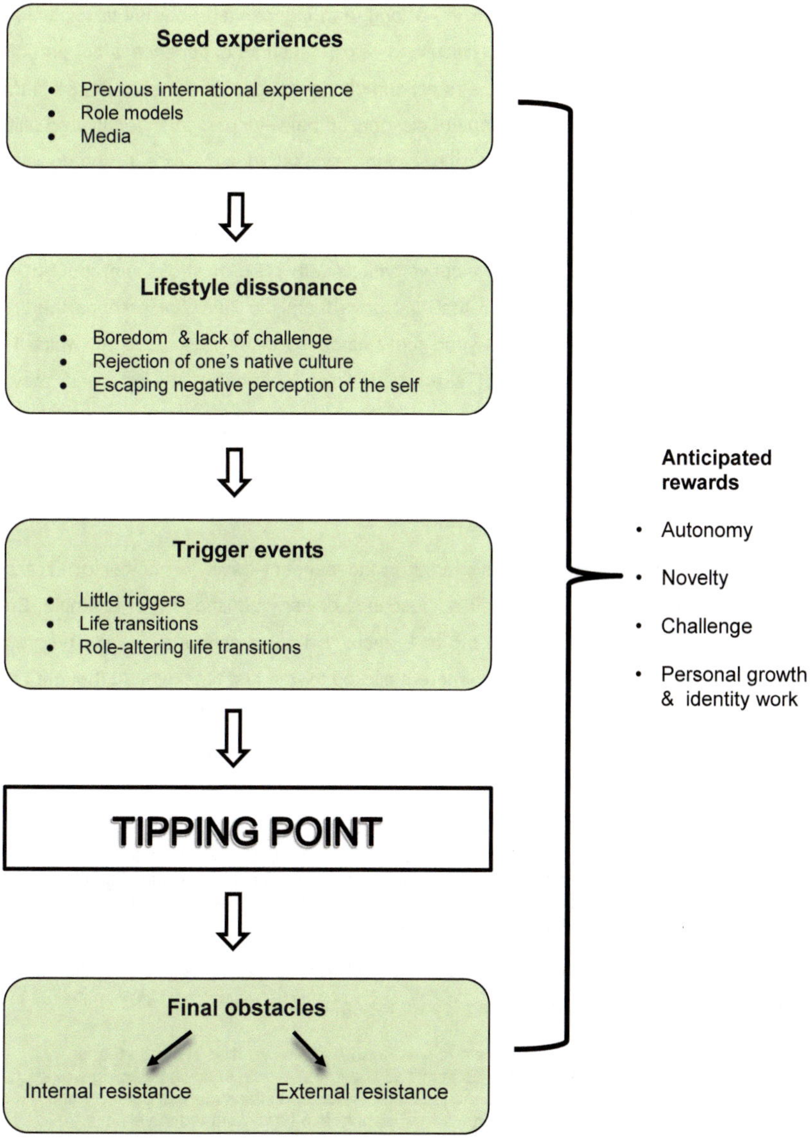

7 Reaching the Tipping Point

```
┌─────────────────────────────────────┐
│         Seed experiences            │
│  • Previous international experience│
│  • Role models                      │
│  • Media                            │
└─────────────────────────────────────┘
              ⇩
┌─────────────────────────────────────┐
│        Lifestyle dissonance         │
│  • Boredom & lack of challenge      │
│  • Rejection of one's native culture│
│  • Escaping negative perception of  │
│    the self                         │
└─────────────────────────────────────┘
              ⇩
┌─────────────────────────────────────┐
│           Trigger events            │
│  • Little triggers                  │
│  • Life transitions                 │
│  • Role-altering life transitions   │
└─────────────────────────────────────┘
              ⇩
┌─────────────────────────────────────┐
│          TIPPING POINT              │
└─────────────────────────────────────┘
              ⇩
┌─────────────────────────────────────┐
│          Final obstacles            │
│   Internal resistance   External    │
│                         resistance  │
└─────────────────────────────────────┘
```

Anticipated rewards

- Autonomy
- Novelty
- Challenge
- Personal growth & identity work

Figure 6: Reaching the tipping point

7.1 Seed experiences

Obviously, the decision to embark on a long-term independent journey is relatively uncommon. With some exceptions (discussed below), such an experience is not part of the socially accepted life plan, and it is rarely something that people are encouraged to do by their communities. So while feelings of dissonance between personal identity and cultural surroundings are common (and perhaps even universal, to some extent), the decision to deal with those feelings by leaving one's cultural setting for an extended period of time is rare. This raises the question of why certain individuals hit upon this particular strategy for addressing their discontent. In my conversations with LITs, most of them could point to some experience or experiences that first gave them the idea that perhaps there was something useful to be found beyond the boundaries of their own culture, which I call "seed experiences". Within the LITs' answers, three main categories emerged: previous international experience, media (e.g. books, films), and encounters with role models.

7.1.1 Previous international experience

When asked what sparked their interest in independent travel, a number or LITs cited international experience from their adolescence or early adulthood. For example, Emilia (36, Germany) recalled her first trip to France: "I did this school exchange program in France when I was 14, and that's where it clicked for the first time, when I thought I have to get out; there's other things aside from home". Andy (30, USA), who had only traveled domestically within the United States as a child, vividly remembers his first short backpacking trip abroad:

> I think I got the travel bug, the idea to go traveling, back when I went to France when I was 17, when I went to southern France and I stayed in hostels, saw the beautiful beaches, and talked to interesting people, and it really just kind of grabbed my attention. The adventure, the unknown, trying different foods, different music, different cultures just grabbed my attention.

Similarly, although Matt (28, USA) did not start traveling until his mid-twenties, a trip to Costa Rica at the age of 17 was an "eye-opening" experience:

> I didn't really realize what the world was like. I had always lived in the States, grew up in Texas and then I ended up in this village in the middle of nowhere being woken up by monkeys. And after that, I just sort of started to think more about the world and my place in it. And it took me a few years before I really started traveling.

When I interviewed Matt a second time twelve years after the first interview, he still thought of this event as the *"defining moment"* and turning point that made him see be yond his cultural boundaries and provided a main impetus to leave his country many years later.

In Aaron's (35, USA) case, he had never really been interested in traveling or working abroad and was focused on getting his career on track, when his company suddenly compelled him to work abroad in London and Tokyo for 9 months. He reported that this international experience fueled his wanderlust, and it is also what keeps him traveling, as the memory provides a constant reminder that "there's bigger and better things out there aside from the office". He explained this process as follows:

> It's through this living abroad that I definitely started to get my taste for my wanderlust for truly traveling... [....] and between London and Tokyo, that's when I acquired not only my enjoyment of not only living abroad, being comfortable being out of the US, integrating with people of completely different cultures, and I think it started from there, that's when the passion existed.

Finally, Chelsea (25, England) discovered her love of independent travel when she went abroad for the first time in her life at the age of 17 to visit a friend in Greece and then backpacked around on her own: "It was the first time I felt 'wow I can actually do whatever I want to here'. It was such a wonderful experience for me [...] It felt like a playground. My playground had enlarged." The independent part of her trip (i.e. after having said goodbye to her friend) was what struck her as an exceptional experience that sparked her desire for more—a desire which she would ultimately fulfill in subsequent, extended independent travel experiences.

In all of these cases, the disorienting experience (i.e. previous international experience) occurred long before the actual decision to travel long-term, but the LITs nonetheless considered them a crucial aspect in their decision to travel.

7.1.2 Media

Although an under-researched topic in the field of tourist motivation, the inspirational and motivational power of media has recently been pointed out by several researchers. For example, with reference to travel writing, Müller (2006) argued that such works are the *sine qua non* for arousing interest in travel destinations and attaching meaning to them, and Laing & Frost (2012) asserted that the immersive nature of travel writing promotes ideas of yearning, exploration, escape and personal transformation. On a more general level, Rossiter (2002) views authentic stories as an instrument of transformation: "Because stories lead from the familiar to the unfamiliar, they provide an entryway into personal growth and change". She further argues that by confronting people with new knowledge, expanded possibilities and broader perspectives, they can act as a motivator and source of encouragement.

In my research, a number of LITs mentioned drawing inspiration from media, including books, films (both fictional and documentary), travel blogs or other websites, which portrayed qualities they wished to cultivate within themselves or aspects of life that they wanted to experience. "Books and documentaries make me dreaming, but I want to see for myself" (Ally, 33, Switzerland). Experiencing stories of foreign cultures can be disorienting because they highlight experiences or aspects of life that might be different or even lacking from the audience's own lives. Although the mediated nature of the experience may mute the feeling of disorientation, these seemingly insignificant experiences can provide an inspiration or plant a seed that can grow over time into dreams of travel and eventually into transformative experiences. For example, Ryan (26, Canada) cited a well-known magazine as one of his primary early motivators:

> I've always wanted to [travel]. I just remember looking at *National Geographic* when I was a kid...and...looking at the pictures and stuff and thinking, "That's beautiful, but I bet it looks a lot better in person". And I'm sure you know that pictures can't do any justification for anything you see in person.

Similarly, Oliver (51, Austria) mentioned the profound effect of books on his imagination, saying, "Books were definitely the decisive motive and inspiration", and Julia (37, Germany) reported, "I had a beautiful book about adventures at home – and I think this is what inspired me to travel – where two people were on the road by bike, and it sounded great".

This last example from Julia mentions a particularly powerful kind of literature – the travel narrative. When reading travel narratives, readers can live vicariously through the author and imagine themselves in the same position, thereby forming a kind of quasi-memory. Like real memories, these can remain dormant for an extended period of time before some trigger event causes them to re-surface. In other cases, the feelings associated with reading such narratives remain in the subconscious, but still exert influence, which is evident in the following interview quote from Nick (34, Ireland):

> My entire bookshelf at home is travel writing. I didn't even notice it until about two years ago, when somebody pointed out that every book on my shelf was – apart from the odd standards of literature, or whatever – was travel writing.

This quote also highlights the fact that not all people independently engage in the kind of critical self-reflection that would make them analyze their early motivations and incorporate them into their own identity narratives.

However, in other cases, LITs were very conscious of the influence of their own "media experiences", as evidenced by the fact that such experiences often have a direct effect on

7.1 Seed experiences

the eventual choice of a destination. Thus, Alice (29, Sweden) mentioned this effect when describing her feelings upon returning from a six-month work stint in Canada: "I never even thought about going to Scotland, and it was after coming home from Canada, and I didn't know what to do, and I was reading a book at the time that was about Scotland". Reading the book about Scotland was a decisive factor that contributed significantly to the decision-making process. In a similar vein, Syd (32, Switzerland), whom I interviewed on Easter Island about two years into his three year journey around the world, associated the books he had read in his childhood with the destinations that he was drawn to: "Isla de Pasqua [*Easter Island*] is a dream from my childhood. I had read *Great Mysteries of Humanity*, and I had that in mind. I used to read Jack London as a child, and I wanted to see the Yukon." Likewise, Jake (45, England) linked his ambition to climb a 5,800-meter peak in Ecuador to the books he had read about climbing Mount Everest.

Finally, it is important to point out that a disorienting media experience does not always come from a media text directly pertaining to travel. Max (30, Austria), for example, talked about a documentary he had watched at the age of 12, from which he learned that the average person in the world grows up, works and dies within a 40-km radius.

> When I saw that, it was so unbelievable to me and I thought, "How can this be, that out there is the entire world, there is so much to see and discover, and we spend our entire lives in 40 km radii?" And somehow that stuck with me. I am mentioning this now because I think there were probably 100 individual events that accumulated to this specific point, which I will tell you later about, and then broke open.

Max's final words in the quote above provide a good end point for this sub-section, as he emphasizes that these media experiences can contribute to the accumulation of motivational influences that eventually lead to the tipping point.

7.1.3 Role models

In addition to books and other media, some LITs mentioned specific role models who provided an essential motivation to leave. Role models are an important factor in stirring interest and providing encouragement, as they provide a concrete example to follow or, in some cases, to avoid following. By means of social comparison (i.e. comparing oneself to others), role models play a crucial role in the socialization process and often positively influence the mindset of LITs. For example, Aimee (26, England) mentioned, "I'd heard of people, like family friends, who'd done it, and I was like, oh that sounds wicked".

The example of Heather (36, Australia) sheds light on the motivational force of positive role models. Heather was very happy with her teaching job at a local school in Australia.

She thought of herself as an ambitious and career-oriented person and had never considered traveling any longer than the usual two-week holidays, until she encountered her colleague who had just returned from a two and a half year trip around the world:

> She said "Oh my God, you gotta do it. You gotta get out and experience the world." She is another teacher and teaches drama, completely opposite fields, and I just admired her so much that I was inspired to go and do it, if this [traveling] could create a person that's so marvelous.

Heather, who was 29 at the time she encountered this role model, was enthralled by her colleague's stories, personality and encouragement, and she realized there were so many things she had not done or seen. This encounter would prove definitive in her eventual decision to leave Australia.

On the other hand, some LITs referred to what I would call negative role models. These are individuals who affect one's mindset by revealing a possible life outcome that one wishes to *avoid*. The following three accounts testify to the motivational influence of such negative role models:

> This [desire to travel] probably comes from my father's frustrations about all the things he would have done in his life if he etc. etc. I just told myself when I was a kid that I would never have the same life, and that I would open my eyes and open my mind. (Syd, 32, Switzerland)

> My dad didn't get out of our northern industrial working class town early enough, and it's affected him now, basically. And it's affected his marriage later on. [For him], nothing was ever good enough, the grass is always greener on the other side of the fence. And I didn't wanna have that in my life. (Glen, 26, England)

> I saw a friend of mine, who [...] I was in the Masters programs with and also worked where I worked. And she got promoted, and it just sucks you in, and I could see that happening to her, and I could see her starting to get really, you know, sleepless nights about really banal, stupid things at work and I was like, "I don't want this to happen to me, I'm not that bothered", and I actually had to keep on asking myself, "what did you start out thinking you wanted to do?" (Chelsea, 25, England)

These LITs were inspired by people who exemplified a "feared, to-be-avoided-self, pointing to possible future disasters, and highlighting mistakes that must be avoided so as to prevent them" (Lockwood, 2000, cf. Lockwood, Jordan & Kunda, 2002).

These final examples lead us to the next section, which discusses the more general feeling of lifestyle dissonance. In the examples above, the future LITs were essentially witnessing this lifestyle dissonance in other important figures in their lives. But for many, this feeling creeps into their own lives, as discussed below.

7.2 Lifestyle dissonance

In many cases, the LITs I interviewed were unable to pinpoint specific events that gave rise to their desire to travel, but rather referred to a general sense of dissonance that seemed to grow over time. That is, over time they began to feel that their personal desires and values were no longer aligned with those of their cultural environment. In the interviews, I was able to detect three important trends within this general category of lifestyle dissonance: boredom or lack of challenge, an active rejection of one's native culture, and frustrations targeted towards one's own identity.

7.2.1 Boredom or lack of challenge

Crompton (1979) has asserted that too much routine and repetitive action can result in a state of socio-psychological disequilibrium, which acts as a main factor that encourages individuals to leave behind their schedule-driven lives. My interviews showed that long-term travel is definitely one of the ways people choose to escape the routine of their daily lives. As "serial" LIT Brian (43, USA) summarized:

> There's a huge thing where I get really, ... I am very, very susceptible to monotony. It makes me crazy so quickly. So, the escape from that is really kind of what helps fuel that as well. Like, when you go through a month of like everything is the same it makes me nuts.

Similarly, Jake (45, England) stated that he had "had enough of work and the daily grind", and Lars (28, Belgium) cited boredom with routine as his prime travel motivation: "I don't like routine. And that's what all my life was like. It was just routine. So I just said, 'I wanna get out of here.'"

The case of Nadine (23, Canada) provides an even more dramatic example of someone who was not only bored with the routine of her job, but also tired of the entire culture and the homogeneity of the people in her native setting.

> I was really not feeling well...and everything was just boring. Everything was just ordinary and normal, and I needed a change, something new, and people that are talking about something else... because, you know, people are like you. They're living the same thing...They live in the same city, the same country and are doing the same thing and liking the same thing. So I really needed people that are completely different.

In some cases, this boredom is accompanied by not only a longing for variety, but also a more conscious awareness of the lack of meaningful life challenges. Such individuals are consciously frustrated with their lack of opportunities for personal growth. For example, in describing his early work career, Nick (34, Ireland) stated:

> At the beginning of my work life I never really had any jobs that I cared about at all. I was doing these marketing jobs and there was nothing to challenge me either. And people would be like 'Wow, you have a real gift for this marketing thing'. And to me, you know, you've gotta be a fucking idiot not to do marketing. You know, you just need a tiny bit of creativity and a little bit of brains, and that's it.

While above, Chelsea saw the dreaded future of corporate monotony in her co-worker, Nick experienced it in his own life. This was a common theme in the interview. Thus, Jake (45, England) mentioned a fear of getting "stuck" in the "rat race", while Lily (31, England) stated:

> I got a bit stuck…well, I chose one path which was a career path and was doing quite well and so…. I sort of went that way but always needling in the back of my mind was "you really should just strap a rucksack to your back and just go", and that did scare me definitely a little bit as well.

7.2.2 Rejecting one's native culture

While the LITs discussed above experienced feelings of general dissatisfaction with their lives, for other LITs this feeling leads to a more conscious rejection of one's native culture and its associated values. For example, Chelsea (25, England) described how her budding career was actually trapping her in a value system that was far removed from her longing to become a filmmaker. She mentioned that her "priorities were totally skewed", a situation which she partly attributed to the materialism and class consciousness of her native culture. Thus, she mentioned that in England, "status is a big thing", but she wanted "to get away from sort of modern trappings a little bit" and "get back to thinking, actually, what is really important". She went on to explain her feelings of dissatisfaction:

> It ended with me thinking that if I stayed for another year or two, I would get promoted again. And I would have more money, and it would be more difficult to back out. […] I knew that didn't want to work in advertising, I knew I didn't want to be media strategist. But I was so fuck close to becoming one, that I thought if I gave it one or two more years, it would be more difficult to go back to the original point of me making films.

In a more specific and explicit case of value dissonance between individual and native culture, Jakob (34, Austria) referred to the disgust he felt towards the Austrian political system when a right-wing party joined the conservative-led government in 2000: "I wanted to see what it's like to live somewhere else, and as far away as possible, so that I can see the differences". Similarly, Max (30, Austria) referenced the concept of a social contract, i.e. the idea that individuals consent to collectively enforced social arrangements (D'Agostino, 2017). I interviewed Max 2 months before his initial departure, and he was already quite clear about his motivation to travel: "I don't want to squeeze myself into a system. I don't want anyone to dictate what my day and life rhythm should be like". The

7.2 Lifestyle dissonance

central figure who embodied the values that Max sought to escape was his mother, and it was clear that he had given a good deal of thought to the origin of the values she represented:

> For her as a child from the post-war generation it's all about an academic education, a job for life with a good salary and a fat belly because it's always full. But for me, I need fulfillment, satisfaction. There has to be a purpose. I completely reject the post-war concept of life, which only looks at the material side of things. So you suck it up for 35 years, and then you can do whatever you want when you retire. I utterly detest this concept. I understand it from a historic point of view, how it came about and why they are all about security. I am completely aware of this. But I am a child of the 80s, and not the 40s or 50s. I understand my parent generation but I strongly reject their way of thinking.

Indeed, Max falls in the age demographic of the so-called generation Y, also referred to as the Millennials, Echo Boomers, Nexters, Generation Next, or the Digital Generation (Beckendorff, Moscardo, Pendergast, 2010, p. x). Generation theorists, such as Wang & Dennett (2014), have argued that in contrast to the baby boomers, who sought achievement at work, members of Generation Y consider a healthy work-life balance and personal time important. They grew up observing their parents' strong work ethic, which limited their personal free time, and then often saw their parents "downsized" later. Thus, it is not surprising that Max felt that changing roles within the system (e.g. by switching jobs) would not be enough. What he needed was a "radical break": "So I sat down and pictured my life as a white sheet of paper, blank, without guidelines, start from scratch as the saying goes". What emerged was a vague plan, which at the time of our first interview, was to "head north".

From the standpoint of narrative identity, what is fascinating about Max is that he was already engaged in the process of integrating his travel experiences, and the values he believed they represented, into his life story before he even went traveling. In particular, he mentioned his efforts to persuade his worried and disappointed mother of the value of the trip on which he was about to embark:

> I offer her so many positive ways of looking at it by saying "Be happy that you raised someone who dares to leave everything behind to travel", because I think if I come back, I will manage again, and this requires a good portion of chutzpah, but she refuses to see all these things.

Considering the generation gap between Max and his mother, which Max himself pointed out, Max's failure to convince his mother is not surprising, but it is nevertheless a prime example of an individual trying to re-shape his identity via negotiation with a representative of his native cultural value system, accomplished by telling stories of himself as the brave rebel which had not even transpired at that point.

In the cases discussed above, it is clear that the LITs were dissatisfied with their cultural environment, and these LITs clearly identified escape as a main push factor, rather than destination-specific motives that pulled them towards a specific destination. This finding provides support for Crompton (1979), who pointed out that destination is often secondary and often serves "as a medium through which these motives could be satisfied" (Crompton, 1979, p. 415). As Max stated in the second interview, which took place six years after the first one: "There was definitely a running-away aspect at the beginning. There was no place where I said I wanted to go to; it was just that I wanted to leave. That's how it all started." Thus, the need to satisfy certain psychological needs was stronger than the pull factor of a certain destination.

In telling their stories, some LITs embrace this concept of "escape" as a motivation because they were comfortable in their belief that the surroundings from which they were escaping were truly lacking or even detrimental to their well-being. Thus, they could embrace the concept of escape as defined, for example, by the Cambridge Dictionary (2017): "the act of successfully getting out of a place or a dangerous or bad situation". That is, from the perspective of the prisoners, escape is a noble accomplishment. Thus, people like Max could take pride in their ability to free themselves from the bondage of an unjust (or at least unfulfilling) reality.

On the other hand, it is important to mention here that many LITs were not so willing to accept the "escape" motivation, but were rather haunted by the more negatively charged term "escapism". The Merriam-Webster Dictionary (2017) defines escapism as "an activity or form of entertainment that allows people to forget about the real problems of life". Where "escape" evokes the value system of the prisoner, "escapism" evokes the value system of the prison and the society it represents. The term has the same connotation as the more common phrasal verb "to run away", which the Cambridge Dictionary (2017) defines as "to avoid dealing with a problem or difficult situation", which constructs a role of a person who is unable or unwilling to handle the problem. In telling their life stories, and thereby constructing their own identities, it was clear that many LITs had been unable to shake society's implied judgment. Thus, Nick mentioned that he was seen as a gifted marketer, and Lilly was careful to point out that her career was going "quite well." Similarly, Heather (36, Australia) emphasized her successful career, and even mentioned that she enjoyed it, before describing her decision to leave:

> I was happy at my job, it was a great job. It was real cushy and completely secure. I could have stayed there for the rest of my life. [...] A lot of people say it's a matter of running away [...] And for me it wasn't like that at all. It was more like, "Oh my god, this is something I have to do before I'm too old."

7.2 Lifestyle dissonance

Here, Heather uses the term "cushy", which the Oxford Dictionary (2017) defines as "undemanding, easy, or secure". As the word evokes weakness or visions of a pampered person with little tolerance for risk and no sense of adventure, it subtly supports her rejection of the accusation that she was running away from something. Similar to Max, she moves the discussion back towards "escape" and away from "escapism". Or perhaps more precisely, she rejects escape entirely and positions her motivation as a pull factor: it was the thirst for something new, exciting or challenging that drew her towards her travel experience. Naturally, escape from boredom/dissatisfaction and pursuit of excitement/adventure are two sides of the same coin. However, rather than focusing on the classification of push vs pull, the point here is to look at the way in which the travelers' narratives construct these meanings to support their desired identity constructs.

In this context, perhaps the most interesting case is that of Oliver (51, Austria), who left Austria at the age of 45 to sail around the world with his wife and son for almost five years. With no prompting on my part, Oliver forcefully rejected society's implied accusation of "escapism", pointing out that "What is of particular importance is that we never escaped from anything. We loved our life in Austria before we left". This forceful statement caught me by surprise, but as we spoke further, it emerged that his self-proclaimed "love" for his pre-travel life was perhaps not as pure as he liked to believe. As a successful self-employed technician with his own business, Oliver stated, "I worked 50, 60 hours [a week], and there is no way to get out of this system. You can't just say, 'No, I'd just like to work 30 hours'. It doesn't work." Thus, it seems there was, in fact, at least one aspect of Oliver's life from which he definitely wanted to escape. However, his strong rejection of the term "escape" shows a lingering discomfort with the common perception that long-term travelers are just running away from a reality that they are either too weak or too lazy to handle. In this case, without attacking the fundamental values of his native culture, Oliver uses his narrative to push back against this assumption by constructing an image of himself as a person who made rational decisions based on a desire for expanded experience. Below, I will discuss further how Oliver's post-travel lifestyle likely affected the development of this attitude, but for the moment, we can just point out that Oliver's narrative negotiates a middle ground that preserves his own sense of identity by criticizing a specific value of his native culture, without condemning that culture wholesale, as other LITs frequently do.

7.2.3 Escaping negative perceptions of the self

In the examples above, we first saw LITs who were stricken by a nebulous sense of disharmony with their cultural environment, and then heard from a group of LITs who had more consciously identified the source of their uneasiness (i.e. the value or aspect of society with which they were not in agreement). In contrast, the final group of LITs discussed here showed a different tendency, whereby the negative energy generated from the sense of disharmony with the cultural environment tended to be directed inward back on the individuals themselves. Although they often recognized a social root to their problems, they tended to lay the blame at their own feet and expressed frustration or disappointment with themselves. Several participants described personal problems as the disorienting experience they wanted to get away from, which included depression, substance abuse, low self-esteem, being bullied, and a general sense of meaningless of life. For example, Chelsea (25, England), who above expressed her frustrations with the materialism and class consciousness of her native culture, also pointed out a fundamental dissatisfaction with her own identity within that setting: "I wasn't happy with who I was in London". And Max (30, Austria), whose struggles with his mother's value system were described above, pointed to his problems with "low self-esteem":

> I had the feeling that everyone is better than me. I was always in competition with everyone, and I couldn't find people fascinating for what they did, but I immediately thought, either I'm gonna lambast them, I'll bash them, because it's not that great anyway what they're doing, or I'll try to be better than them. And this almost turned into a mania. And when something becomes manic, it's very difficult to say, "now I've achieved something."

This was echoed by Theo (33, Canada), who grew up under rather poor conditions with his parents and three siblings. He feels that he's always been very different from everyone he's ever known and has a rather low self-image:

> Oh my God! You have never met anybody that fucks up everything. I cannot do anything. I am just so absent-minded and so ditzy and lazy, like I can't fit into a normal kind of... I can't do 9 to 5. I lose every drive I get. [laughs] I can't hold a job, and I tried. I got tired and frustrated and upset about it. [...] I kept trying to do something that I can't do. And that just wears you out after a while.

Similarly, Julia (37, Germany) stated that she "always had this complex that she's not good at anything", while Matt, (28, USA), despite his comfortable middle-class upbringing, described himself as a "suicidal kid" who "didn't have any friends in high school". As he stated, "I was always really a confused boy. I never did fit in high school. I never fit in any school at any time."

7.2 Lifestyle dissonance

Nadine (23, Canada) represents a variation on this theme of dissatisfaction with one's own sense of identity and one's roles in society. She was yearning for a change in her everyday existence because of the effect her life was having on her:

> I really, really needed a change in my life because I was too much partying [...]. I didn't have the motivation to stop and get serious with my life. So I was just working and spending my money and partying...and always drinking and doing drugs, and I was also really depressed because I guess I knew it wasn't doing me any good... and I really needed a change in my life.

The unsustainable life circumstances and unhealthy patterns described in the examples created a state of disequilibrium that needed to be balanced. Hence, these examples provide support for Mannell & Iso-Ahola's (1987) assertion that some individuals are motivated to travel because they seek to escape personal or interpersonal problems in their everyday lives.

It is interesting to note that these negative self-perceptions tended to emerge later in the interview, when a certain level of trust and comfort had been established. Since the questions of motivation came up relatively early in the interview, when such a comfort level may not have been established, I realized the importance of broaching the topic again later in the interview. Thus, at a later stage in the interview, I would return to the questions about motivation and associated contextual factors. It was then, after having shared numerous personal travel stories with me, that many LITs were willing to open up more and share these highly personal perceptions of themselves and how these perceptions affected their initial decision to engage in long-term independent travel. This pattern of delayed response was also illuminating in that it showed that the personal stories people tell to express their values and construct their own identities vary greatly depending on the audience for the stories and the relationship between narrator and audience.

Finally, it is also worth highlighting that, as with the cases in the previous two sections, the participants did not suggest that their self-image problems were the primary factor that drove them out on the road, so to speak. Rather, it was clear that, as with the previous cases of people who felt a general dissatisfaction with their cultural surroundings, the negative self-image was lingering in the background, and was something that they had unwillingly learned to live with. In a sense, in terms of the narratives the participants were constructing, all of the factors described in this section were the background. They were setting the scene for the main action of the story, which usually involved some kind of key event that they could point to that finally tipped them over the edge and into a life of travel. These events are the subject of the following section.

7.3 Trigger experiences

This section examines the trigger events that provided the final impetus for the decision to leave. In contrast to the seed experiences mentioned above, which may linger in the subconscious for an extended period of time, trigger events spur conscious reflection and provide the final energy to act. As we will see, these trigger events can also range from seemingly minor occurrences to major events. Here again, it is important to mention the concept of the tipping point and perhaps use the metaphor of the overflowing glass to illustrate the concept. In some cases, the lifestyle dissonance mentioned above has already reached a high level—i.e. the glass is already quite full—and a minor occurrence, a metaphorical drop of water, is enough to make the glass overflow and get people out the door. On the other hand, in cases where a less acute sense of dissatisfaction or disharmony is present—i.e. the glass is only two thirds or three quarters full—a more significant event, a metaphorical shot-glass of disturbance may be necessary to push the individual to leave. In short, the relationship between existing circumstances and the nature of the tipping point can vary greatly, but the important thing to recognize is that the narratives of almost all LITs contain some event that they can identify that finally convinced them to travel.

7.3.1 Little triggers

The header of this section (borrowed from an Elvis Costello song) is simply meant to show that, if the level of underlying dissonance is great enough, certain trigger events may indeed be relatively minor experiences. The aforementioned case of Max (30, Austria), who ultimately rejected the values of his native culture as espoused by his mother, is a good example of a relatively minor trigger event. Max had a high-powered job, was advancing swiftly on the career ladder, and had sought some sense of fulfilment by spending his money on the latest technological gadgets and other material items. Subconsciously, an elusive feeling of dissatisfaction was brewing inside of him, but a very minor occurrence was what ultimately caused this feeling to bubble up into his conscious mind. When leaving his apartment, he did something he had never done before—he double-locked the apartment door:

> Then I thought, "OK, something is different now, something just happened in my life". And I realized that all these things that I had been buying to have fun and to distract myself started to occupy me, even control me. For example, I always carried my new iPad with me in my backpack, and I constantly kept an eye on it, no matter where I was. And I wasn't consciously thinking of it, but it permanently stressed me out on a subconscious level. I feared that somebody might break into

7.3 Trigger experiences

the apartment and steal my TV. I had all these material possessions and realized that I have anxieties about losing them. And this was the point when I realized I had to change something.

In fact, Max talked at great length about this seemingly minor incident, which he called a "turning point" that forced him to critically reflect on his life and realize that his approach to life was gradually making him "a slave to the system". He was overcome with a sense of urgency to quit his job, sell everything he owned, pack up and leave in order to explore the world. This sudden insight even led him to imagine and embrace his own death while traveling: "Before I sit here and waste away in safety and security, I'd rather die in danger. At least then I know why. And life is too precious". The courage to act upon an intrinsic yearning for change recalls Habermas (1971) and Mezirow (1991a), who maintained that the willingness and ability to liberate oneself from (self-imposed) constraints is a sign of emancipatory learning and leads to personal growth and transformation. Thus, the present case is a good example of taking the first steps in transformative learning, as it led to a reevaluation of previously held values and worldviews and the adoption of a new meaning perspective, which would then be put to the test during Max's travels.

In addition to exemplifying transformative learning, the aforementioned example also highlights the importance of key events/experiences in narrative identity construction. Although the underlying factors (i.e. dissatisfaction with his life, discomfort with the "postwar" values of his culture) came up as the interview proceeded, the key story was the first thing that Max mentioned, and a theme to which he returned again and again during the interview. In fact, in our second interview, which took place seven years later, Max again brought up this key incident when the topic of motivations came up in our interview. It was clear to me that this event had become part of the standard narrative that he used to explain himself and his travels to the repeated inquiries about his life decisions that he faced before, during and after his travels. In a Hollywood movie, this kind of epiphany moment might be attacked by film critics, who would likely argue that it is a rather artificial or contrived plot element. However, the audience itself, which is far less focused on critically deconstructing the film, would likely nod its head and accept it without too much thought. For the fact is that such tidy events make for easily comprehensible narratives. For Max, it is clearly much easier to explain his motivations and express his values via this quick trigger event rather than elaborating on the details of his relationship with his mother and his culture. By constructing and refining this key-turning story over multiple repetitions, Max shows the ability to make connections between the self and the events in one's environment, which is important for establishing autobiographical coherence (Habermas & Bluck, 2000). Establishing autobiographical coherence by generating thematic similarities and causal relationships and integrating them within a larger narrative is important, as it provides meaning and purpose to an individual's life (Habermas & Bluck, 2000, McAdams, 2011).

To take another example of a relatively minor event, Jake's (45, England) trigger event was a short trip through Greece and Turkey. He explained it as follows:

> I'd worked from the age of 16 until I was 23, bought my first house, struggled with the bills and mortgage as everybody does in England and then just thought there must be a little bit more to life than this. So, I went on a small trip, starting in Greece, traveling up through Greece, Turkey, which was nice and simple. And then I say, bitten by the bug, I always wanted to go to India, somewhere completely different. And that was it. Once I realized that, I went home and then to India.

For others, this trip might have served as a seed experience, but for Jake the time was right, as his feeling of lifestyle dissonance had already reached a relatively significant level by the time he took his short European trip. As he explained later:

> I'd been working for a long time, and ah, managed to buy a first house, and worked very hard to put the money down to buy it and decided enough is enough and there's more to life than just working and owning a house. And that's why I wanted to escape.

Jake's quote illustrates another point that was significant for several of the participants: financial security. Jake mentioned that owning his house also contributed to his decision to leave, as it gave him the feeling of security that he would have something to return to when the trip ended. A similar dynamic was at play with Oliver's (59, Austria, 2nd) decision to take his family on a sailing trip around the world. In reviewing his initial interview, I noticed that he had not mentioned a specific trigger event, focusing instead, as mentioned above, on how he was NOT running away from anything. In our follow-up interview, I therefore asked if he could put a finger on a specific event that finally pushed him over the edge. After a moment's pause, he replied that it was the moment when he inherited a decent sum of money that finally convinced him to leave:

> If I had been alone, I would not have needed the money. [...] But because of [my family], this simply gave me a feeling of security so I could say, "If something goes wrong, and we have to break off the trip, we can come back and we will have enough money to survive for a year."

Although this was not the kind of life-altering, multi-million-Euro lottery prize that completely changes people's lives, it was enough to give Oliver the courage to take the risk of making some changes to his relatively comfortable and financially successful life. It is perhaps illuminating that he did not mention this in our initial interview. Here again, we see narrative construction via careful selection of key events. As we will see below, part of the ethos of most travelers is the importance of having the courage to take risks and challenge established value systems. However, being handed a large sum of money rather diminishes one's right to claim this courage, evoking instead images of "cushy" travel by spoiled rich people. Thus, it is not surprising that Oliver, either consciously or subconsciously, omitted this plot detail in his original account of his initial travel decision.

For my own part, I can relate to this tension between security and risk. When I left for my big Central/South America trip, I had worked hard to earn around 6,000 Euros, which was earmarked for my trip. When people would ask about my travels (before, during and after my trip), this is the number I would mention. However, the fact was that through many years of hard waitressing work and careful budgeting, I had managed to accumulate over 10,000 Euros, which I held in another account and, in my mind, reserved as a cushion for my return to "society." Even though I had worked hard for that money, I still omitted that from my discussion with other travelers, so as not to appear a "wealthy" traveler. In my case, although this financial cushion was not the trigger that set me off on my travels, it definitely played a role in my decision. Having that financial cushion helped reinforce my decision to embark on my planned journey when the trigger event happened, which was my graduation from university. However, this trigger event leads us into the next section.

7.3.2 Life transitions

In this section, we move into more significant events in life that can trigger transformative learning experiences. Here, we look at "standard" life transitions – moments when one moves from one phase of life to another. As discussed above, the transformative potential of these moments is evident in Erikson's initial focus on adolescence, which marks the transition from childhood to adulthood, as well as Gail Sheehy's expansion of this concept into other stages of life via her concept of "passages." A common theme that runs through many LITs' narratives is the disorienting experience of finishing one's education and moving into the working world. Completing school/university can be highly disorienting, as individuals must transition from the relatively structured academic world with its fixed values and externally imposed rules and expectations, to the professional world, which is far less clearly defined and places new demands on people. For example, Chelsea (25, England), who was a good student and enjoyed her university life, was thrown off balance after graduating because "At uni it's different, you know, you always got structure, and you're always being told how good you are, and stuff. So you're always happy." Similarly, Glen and Aimee (26, England) saw travel as a good way to postpone adult responsibilities, although they knew that they eventually wanted to settle down somewhere in England: "We didn't want to start work straight away, although we knew work was approaching".

In fact, taking a moratorial break in between life phases is a well-established practice in many Anglophone countries. Before setting out on her first long-term independent trip in her mid-twenties, Chelsea (25, England) went to India with one of the many companies offering organized gap-year packages for privileged emerging adults. She referred to herself as a "gap kid": "You know, it's one of these things for a lot of the middle-class kids going on to university. So a lot of the friends I made at university were gap kids." Alan (New Zealand, 42) mentioned that this practice is similarly well-established in his home country:

> It's one of those things for a lot of New Zealanders to do what they call "OE", which is Overseas Experience. So it's very much in the New Zealand psyche to finish something big and then go traveling. And I guess a lot of it rubs off with whether you individually want to travel yourself or not. And there is a certain element of almost like social expectation to do it. It's a common thing to do, so you'll do it.

Alan theorizes that the OE has become a common practice "amongst educated people, generally people who had gone to University" because "New Zealand is so isolated from the rest of the world". This echoes the views of previous researchers who have conceptualized backpacking as a rite of passage (e.g. O'Reilly, 2006; Maoz, 2007; Noy, 2004).

In other countries, though, the idea of heading off to travel for a year or more is not so well received. The tension a traveler faces in such a country is evident in the following quote from Lukas (27), who left Germany to postpone his entry into the daily grind:

> The point was right after university you have to think about whether you want to start applying for jobs and work from Monday to Friday or you just set out and explore the world first. And of course then you think about whether you could build a life somewhere else. And then I just thought it's easier and more beautiful anywhere else in the world outside of Germany.

Lukas's decision to travel to South America was made rather spontaneously and with the clear goal in mind of having an adventure and finding out about himself. However, people in Germany viewed his decision as an attempt to escape from "reality". This attitude can be even more pronounced when people decide to travel even after they have started a career. For example, Syd (32, Switzerland), who quit his corporate job to travel around the world for two years with his girlfriend, reported, "I know that most people at home think that you're incapable of being in society, and that's why you have to go to travel and so on. It's not something viewed as positive, normally. At least in formal traditional type of jobs."

The same can be said for my own home country (Austria), where long-term travel is commonly viewed as a "cop-out". Although I started my travels with three friends from university, none of them was ready to forgo potential career opportunities awaiting them at home. The same can be said for my larger circle of friends. While I received a great deal of admiration and sometimes envy, none of my friends were ready or willing to take the leap into uncertainty for a certain period. Of course, while I was gone I received periodic emails from my mother reminding me about the years and earnings missed for my "retirement account". For me, however, taking a moratorial break was an important stepping stone in the maturation process. Thanks to my earlier, shorter travel experiences (lasting up to 3 months), by the time I graduated from university, there was no question that I would go traveling. I was simply not ready for a structured life with all the responsibilities it entails and felt there were many years left to work, whereas the time to travel was that moment. Like Erikson, I was already convinced that the moratorial break between life phases would offer valuable opportunities to engage in self-exploration to find out more about my purpose and place in this world.

7.3.3 Role-altering life transitions

Similar to the transition from student life to working life, there are other events that can radically alter the role or roles one is playing or expecting to play in life and thereby provide a stimulus to embark on an extended journey. In fact, While & White (2004) argued that the decision to travel for an extended period is often precipitated by the end of a life stage (e.g. between jobs, burnout, empty nest syndrome, death of a loved one). Unlike the little triggers described above, these events tend to be more significant. In cases where the individual feels only a mild sense of lifestyle dissonance, a more significant trigger event is often required to get them out the door. One obvious example of such a disorienting trigger event is losing one's job. For most people, their occupations contribute greatly to their sense of identity, not to mention that they take up a significant amount of their time and mental energy. When this factor is suddenly removed, this opens up mental space, and it is likely that largely repressed feelings of general dissatisfaction may surface and trigger critical reflection on one's life and place in society. Aaron (35, USA) described this process when he spoke about losing his job in his mid-thirties. He started to reflect on the story of his life to that point, and these reflections gave rise to an increased sense of urgency to travel:

> It was starting to build up that I needed to do this because you never know when you're gonna have the chance in your life to do it. And there are an endless number

of stories of people that I know who died young, and you spend too much time planning life and not enough time…you know planning for yourself.

This sense of awareness about one's own mortality, the feeling that life is passing you by, often accompanies role-altering life experiences and is a theme that will re-surface in the examples below.

Of course, beyond one's job, personal relationships with the key individuals in one's life play a crucial role in defining and maintaining one's sense of identity within society. Thus, changes in these relationships also serve as role-altering life experiences that may contribute to the desire to travel. For example, Andy (30, USA) mentioned, "I was in a relationship for a while and that had ended, and I had closure, which was nice. So that wasn't holding me back anymore." In a more potent example, Dana (39, Denmark) remarked that after her marriage ended in divorce, she wanted to "get away, as far away from Denmark as possible". She had to move out of the house they owned together, and since they both worked together as well, she was also facing pressure to find a new job so she would not have to interact with her ex-husband on a daily basis. Not only had she lost major life roles as a wife and homeowner, but the part of her identity that was defined by her job had also been cast into uncertainty. Thus, she decided it was a good time to get away and spend some time re-evaluating her past and future life.

The loss of a friend or loved one can have a similar effect of profoundly altering one's roles in life and thereby calling one's life path into question. For example, Jake (45, England) described the loss of an important friend to cancer, which forced him to contemplate his own mortality and ask some difficult questions about how he had spent his life to that point: "[The death of my friend] was a big thing for me, and that really sold it that I must get out of England and do a bit more traveling."

This effect is perhaps even stronger when a family member dies. Alan (42) had been working overseas for several years, but returned to New Zealand after learning that his mother had been diagnosed with cancer:

> Unfortunately, she died within a month of my return. It was shocking for me to see how fast it all went down. She was diagnosed with cancer and was dead 4 months later. That was a bit of a wake-up call, and it really made me think about my own life. I mean, I was earning tons of money, I own a house in London, and never really had to think about money. But then one night I also remembered why I went overseas in the first place, to travel. Which I never really did. I mean yes, I went on short trips, but never really more than three or four weeks. And that's when I decided that I didn't want to wait any longer."

Even though Alan had a successful career and seemingly a successful life, he still felt that something was missing, and the death of his mother brought this feeling to the surface. It

7.3 Trigger experiences

reignited his long-standing desire to explore the world via extended travel – a dream which had receded into his subconscious as soon as he had found his first job overseas.

Similarly, Dana (39) cared for her dying grandmother in her adolescence, and several years later moved in with her mother, who was dying of cancer. The emotional strain of these times in her life was evident in her interview responses:

> And I did everything for her. I fed her; I put diapers on her [...], she pissed in bed and all of that. When she finally died, I went down. I went seriously down. And I tried everything to get back up, like real shrinks, and I went to all kinds of spiritual women. And then I left.

Dana initially sought help from psychologists and spiritual healers, but eventually decided she needed to completely liberate herself from her ordinary surroundings and take a substantial break from everything. She had always harbored the dream of long-term travel but thought of it as a rather selfish endeavor. The death of her mother eliminated what had been a primary role in her life (i.e. as a caregiver for her grandmother and then her mother), and the release from this obligation gave her the "permission" she needed to travel: "Because [*the death of my mother*] is what may have set me free to be not selfish, or to not view my travels as selfish".

While the death of a parent is almost always a disturbing emotional experience, the death of a child is an even more powerful experience. Although we never stop being sons and daughters, assuming our parents live until our own adulthoods, by the time they die, the role of son or daughter has normally been overshadowed by other roles in our lives (e.g. employee, spouse, parent). However, losing a child, and particularly a young child, removes a primary role from one's immediate life (i.e. parent), a role which was still expected to have a significant influence on one's present and future life for many years to come. Such an experience almost forces one to re-evaluate one's life course, and such was the case with Sarah (37, Austria), whose infant daughter died when Sarah herself was just in her low thirties. Sara and her husband had always dreamed about traveling, but decided to postpone these plans to a later point in life. When their infant daughter died, their lives were turned upside down, and they were forced to reconsider their life choices:

> That was, then we said, there's nothing worse that can happen to us anymore. We couldn't lose more than we had just lost. And that was the point when we said there's no point of return, let's go for it. I'm not sure if we would have made that step. Our plans were to have two kids and then, when we were 50 or 55, to move to another country. But then when she died, there was nothing holding us back anymore to leave at the very moment.

The narratives above illustrate how a significant life event can profoundly alter the roles one plays in life, and thereby force one to evaluate those roles and how they match with one's personal identity concept. Such events can provide an important impetus to travel, but even when individuals make the conscious decision to travel, they often face unexpected resistance, which is discussed in the following section.

7.4 Final obstacles – Preparing for the unexpected

The preceding sections highlighted the various factors that prompted the LITs in this study to change their life circumstances and engage in long-term independent travel. These factors are important, as they reveal the complex forces underpinning the decision to leave. However, most pre-travel narratives do not end with the decision to leave, but rather continue with expressions of a wide range of emotions, ranging from "fear", "anxiety" and "apprehension" to "excitement", "anticipation" and "euphoria".

Even after making the conscious decision to travel, the plan must still be put into motion. For Ryan (26, Canada), this meant paying off his bills and university debt, which took him a year and a half. He was one of the few LITs who described his pre-travel emotions in a positive way: "I couldn't wait to get out of the country. Yeah. I've been looking forward to this for so long. I was bouncing off the walls for a month before I left". For Alan (43, New Zealand), taking to the road meant opening a new chapter in his life: "It's almost like starting a new life, a new chapter of your life. Everything's ahead of you, and that's sort of like a euphoric feeling." In a similar vein, Keith (23, Australia), was excited to start his adventure, although he was sad to leave his girlfriend behind, who was supposed to join him four months later:

> I had a lot of money in the bank account, and I was just like, "fuck it, I got the cash and the plane tickets, so I'm gonna be ok. At least for, you know, this amount of time." So I was just happy and excited to get out of Sydney. At the same time, I was leaving my girlfriend and other commitments or semi-commitments back home. So that was sad, but it was mostly excitement.

Accounts like these three are rare in the present data. In fact, only four LITs indicated that the overriding emotion was excitement and joyful anticipation of their extended travels. This may be due to their relatively young age. At the time of leaving, all four were in their early twenties, which may indicate a relation between pre-travel anxieties and age.

In contrast, the overwhelming majority of LITs expressed mixed emotions ranging from moderate to severe anxieties about the uncertainty that lay ahead of them. This is hardly surprising, as extended travel is always a leap into the unknown; it separates one from

7.4 Final obstacles – Preparing for the unexpected

the care of loved ones and from the safety of home—which is often seen as a place of continuity, comfort, control, refuge and belonging. In contrast, the LITs in this study sought experiences that lie beyond the parameters of life at home, in places where everything is different, including the language, food, culture, customs, climate, etc. Many LITs expressed unspecific fears about leaving. Aaron (35, USA), for example, despite having traveled extensively on business, had never engaged in independent travel and was "nervously excited" about it. For him, it "just felt like this humongous thing that was sort of exciting but also challenging and a bit scary". Not only was he wondering about "how it actually gets done", but also whether he was going to enjoy it:

> I was worried am I gonna burn out? How do you really, in these Asian countries, get around, like when you're in the middle of nowhere? What do you do when you're in India and the train doesn't work? You know, how do you get around the crowds? How do you get around the city busses? Am I gonna like that? Am I gonna like – cause one of my goals was to see how people really live – and am I gonna be able to do that? Do I like that because of all this business travel, where I stayed in nice hotels and I traveled by planes? Can I sit on a shitty bus for seven hours? I am spoiled, so can I do these things? How do you do this without getting tired? Am I gonna need to be concerned about my safety?

While Aaron was worried about getting tired of traveling, Dana (39, Denmark), felt "damn tired" before she even left. After her divorce, it took a long time to make up her mind about travel and to let go of her old life: "It was a process for me to give everything up and let everything go, like my house, my job. It was a certain process, but when I figured out I wanted to do that, I also knew I wanted to travel". This feeling was shared by Lilly (31, England), who also struggled with the decision to travel and leave behind the creature comforts of her life:

> And then I realized I was quite attached to my house, and it was another excuse, to be honest, you know...another excuse, not to go traveling. You know: 'I can't leave my house. I can't possibly have anyone else live in my house.' I mean I've got as many books as this [points to a large bookshelf in the room]). I can't possibly pack all those books and put them in the lot, you know.

Although Lilly felt relieved once the decision was made, she was still haunted by pre-travel anxieties:

> I was shitting myself to be honest. Yeah, in my last month, I remember very vividly, [...] it was nuts... I think I enjoyed it because everyone was so lovely to me. Everyone at work knew I was going. I had a lovely Christmas and New Year with my family. Stupid, busy, packing up the house, painting the house, trying to organize everything, sell my car...that was .... I sold my car 20 min. before I left for the airport. That's how much I was cutting it dry [laughs]. I was just getting all the paperwork ready to give to my friends saying 'I'm really sorry you have to sell my car.' And then a couple of young kids rang, and I sold the car.

Like many other LITs in this study, Lilly had to break down the tents at home, which can be a challenging task, especially when one embarks on an open-ended journey. When asked about the specifics of her anxieties, she said, "I don't know what I was scared of. Well, maybe if I think about it, that I wouldn't enjoy it or that I'd hate it or that I'd get murdered, or I mean, stupid stuff, you know... or that I wouldn't enjoy being on my own." Later in the interview, Lilly pointed out that it required an enormous amount of commitment to put her plan into action: "It's more in your head. It's not the organization. It's not all the decisions of where to go and all that. It's just in your head. You gotta commit to it." She points out that destination choice was secondary to making up her mind about leaving in the first place, which is supported by several other LITs, who indicated that the hardest part of the entire travel process is leaving:

> The hardest part is when you're sitting in the office going "I hate my job. I really wish I was, you know, in Ushuaia for example." And the hard part is actually that moment when you are struggling to make up your mind. (Nick, 34, Ireland)

> The first big challenge is not just to think about it and say 'I'll drop out' or 'I'll take a big trip', or 'I'll go away for several months', but to actually summon the courage to really book the flight. (Lukas, 27, Germany)

Many LITs were caught up in feelings of self-doubt, questioning their decision to make such a radical change in their lives. This self-doubt is exemplified by Chelsea (25, England), who remembered the struggle of self-doubt about the decision to leave:

> I felt like there was more at risk and there was more to lose. And this trip has been the biggest because there are so many uncertainties hanging over this particular one. But to leave at this time in my life's stage, at the beginning of the potential career that I don't really want but that is very lucrative. And do I really want it or not? Not really, but actually, it would be a very easy path to take. And the one I'm taking is very uncertain because who knows what's gonna happen when I return, you know, who knows?

Clearly, Chelsea was experiencing an identity crisis, in that her previous identity was no longer suitable, but a "new" identity had not yet been established, as discussed in section 2.1. By taking a "psychosocial moratorium" (Erikson, 1980) through extended travel, Chelsea was hoping to explore her identity and find answers to fundamental questions about her place in this world. She also fits well into Arnett's (2000b, 2004) profile of "emerging adulthood", which is a period "when people explore various possibilities in love and work as they move toward making enduring choices" (p. 12). Throughout the interview, Chelsea highlighted the importance of succeeding professionally, and that she was hoping that this trip would bring more clarity in her life about her future professional life. Interestingly, when referring to the decision to travel, which meant taking the "uncertain path", she was not too concerned about the uncertainty she might encounter while traveling, but rather the uncertainty she would encounter upon returning home. This contrasts with many LITs who did not express any concerns about the "post-travel" life, but ex-

7.4 Final obstacles – Preparing for the unexpected

pressed more fears about what they might encounter due to having chosen a travel style that values a certain degree of uncertainty and risk.

Long-term independent travel also means fending for oneself, usually with limited money and resources, while being exposed to potentially harmful situations and personal dangers. Like Cohen's (1972) drifters, the LITs in this study all traveled to distant destinations, which are often underdeveloped and which allowed them to venture off the beaten tourist path. Such less-developed destinations are commonly associated with higher levels of risk (Elsrud, 2001) and perceived as perilous. In Plog's (2001) terms, LITs are "venturers", who actively seek adventure and embrace risk. While travel types have been studied widely, the topic of pre-travel anxiety and risk perception has received little attention from researchers. Despite an overwhelmingly positive determination to travel, which often involves overcoming significant hurdles to put this plan into action, the majority of LITs expressed anxiety regarding destination-specific fears and travel-related anxieties. This anxiety revolves around fears of physical danger, (injuries, accidents, violence, contracting diseases) and financial risks (losing or running out of money), as well as sociocultural factors (cultural misunderstandings, differences in non-verbal communication), language barriers (failure to communicate with locals) and situational risks (destination-specific laws and regulations, road safety, domestic conflicts). The following narratives illustrate these fears:

> I didn't know what to expect. I was kind of scared, for money for example. I didn't know if I would have enough money, I didn't even know what to carry. And after two weeks there, I sent most of my stuff back home and bought other stuff there, cause what I had was just wrong. (Lars, 28, Belgium)

> I will be scared, I will freeze to death, I will starve, I will fear for my life. [...] It can end well, or not well at all. Yes, these are things that I worry about at the moment. What if I bite the dust? [...] With a simple appendicitis it makes a difference if you are in Kazakhstan 1500 km from the nearest village shaman, or here in [*home town*] 5 minutes by ambulance to the hospital. (Max, 30, Austria)

As Brian (43, USA) summed it up: "The mystery and the lack of knowledge about something can...You can build a fear, and the fear is so strong that it paralyzes you. And that happens to me on trips. I leave very scared. I don't know what's gonna happen."

Pre-travel anxiety and self-doubt were often reinforced by friends and family. When Chris (36, Czech Republic) decided to take to the road, he was criticized by his friends: "When I sold everything, dissolved the entire household and just gave everything away to friends, sold my motorbike, all the tools from the garage... They all said 'Are you crazy, you give up everything?'" In addition, family, and in particular parents, often have difficulty in coming to terms with their son's or daughter's decision to travel long-term: "Then I had many discussions and I had to justify myself a lot why I wanted to do this. My dad said it was the biggest nonsense that I have ever come up with" (Lukas, 27, Germany). This need to justify one's choice was expressed by several other LITs, as exemplified in the following narratives:

> I was scared because a lot of people were telling me "you're crazy, you're going alone, and you're a girl, and you're going for six months, it's a long time and you're gonna miss people... What are you gonna do all this time? And maybe you're not gonna have enough money or maybe you get robbed or raped." And people were always saying things like that to you, but you have to stick to it and just say "No, I wanna go, I wanna go, I wanna go." (Nadine, 23, Canada)

> Everyone is going "Oh fuck, it's really dangerous and why do you want to go to Brazil? Rio? Have you heard what's going on in Rio?" Yeah, you're not so immortal as you get older. You're immortal when you're younger, and you think you are. And the stupid things I did in my early... you know when I was younger, traveling, and you look back again, fuck that, what was I thinking? Now I wouldn't do this. It feels like now I have more fear. But that's just what all adults have I think when you get into adulthood. (Chelsea, 25, England)

This raises the question of whether pre-travel anxiety changes with accumulated travel experience. One might hypothesize that after several months or even years on the road, one is familiar with the ins and outs of independent travel, and embarking on a new adventure may cause less pre-travel anxiety. Surprisingly, the stories of the majority of LITs in this study do not support this assertion. Tom, (46, Germany), who periodically takes one-year sabbaticals to travel and therefore has extensive travel experience, explains: "I am always nervous; I'm always a bit scared. Once I'm at the airport or on my way to the airport, then it's all good, and then I look forward to it. But when I'm still at home, packing my backpack, then I'm always a bit scared." Another viewpoint was given by "serial LIT" Brian (43, USA), who has been on several extended travels.

> I get into this worry thing before I leave. What if this happens? What if I lose my money? What if I get sick? Where am I gonna be for Christmas? And it all works out. It's just something I do. Is she gonna be fun to travel with? I think also,...there was a certain amount of excitement. But the excitement for me happens more in the planning process, like when I plan the trip, then I buy the ticket and that's the height of it, when the ticket's bought...that weekend, I remember that's such a great feeling...and that'll last for a week. And then the month before, it's like complete denial....and then the week before I don't want to go. I go into this thing of "oh my god, all this stuff is going on, and I don't want to leave this."

Brian's narrative describes the rollercoaster ride of emotions that he experiences in the period leading up to departure, including emotions of anxiety, excitement, denial, not wanting to leave and feeling overwhelmed. His pre-travel anxiety is only eased when embarking on smaller trips of about 5 weeks or fewer. This indicates that there may be a correlation between the length of the trip and pre-travel anxiety.

Previous research on travel anxiety and travel intentions has argued that the need for security, safety and stress-free travel is a core factor in determining destination choice or future travel intentions. In other words, when travelers' anxiety is high and the host environment is perceived as less safe, travelers will withdraw from it, and travel intentions decrease (Gudykunst & Hammer, 1988; Reisinger & Mavondo, 2005). This does not seem to hold true for the LITs in this study. While the majority of LITs indicated moderate to severe pre-travel anxiety, it did not deter them from choosing this particular travel style or a particular destination, nor did it inhibit intentions of engaging in future long-term independent travel.

What seems paramount is the LITs' strong determination to engage in long-term independent travel. Despite their different demographic profiles, motivational patterns, disorienting experiences, trigger events and obstacles they had to overcome, the willingness to change is what all LITs in this study have in common. According to self-determination theory (Ryan & Deci, 2000), individuals who are proactive and willing to determine their own destiny are intrinsically motivated. The LITs in this study are intrinsically motivated individuals who engage in long-term travel for its own sake because it is perceived as interesting and enjoyable and may potentially lead to personal growth and transformation. Of course, not all travelers will be transformed in the same places or on the same journeys, but transformation always depends on an individual's mindset and willingness to let go, to embrace risk and ambiguity, and to broaden one's worldview (Poutiatine, 2008). Thus, the notable sense of strong determination to engage in long-term independent travel evident in the LITs stories may pave the way for authentic experiences that allow them to re-invent themselves and experience personal growth and transformation. The next section will look at how such experiences play out on the road, but first it is important to mention the rewards which LITs consciously expected to derive from their travels.

7.5 Anticipated rewards

The participants mentioned a wide variety of anticipated rewards, many of which correlated directly with the disorienting experiences and lifestyle dissonance mentioned above. That is to say, in some cases they phrased the reward as a release from a disturbing state at home, while in other cases they phrased it as a longing for a specifically different (or even opposite) condition that they believed they would encounter during their travels. For example, a consistent theme throughout the interviews was a longing for autonomy, which some phrased as a "pull factor" (e.g. a longing for the freedom of independent travel) and others phrased as a "push factor" (e.g. a longing to escape from the restrictions of their regular lives). Beyond this near universal factor of autonomy, the other anticipated rewards can be roughly divided into two categories. On the one hand, many participants were focused on the novel experiences they expected to have. They were, in a sense, more externally focused on "broadening their horizons" and learning about different cultures and different modes of existence. On the other hand, some participants were focused more on the anticipated outcomes of these experiences. In other words, they expressed a conscious desire to use their travel experiences to effect a change in their values and identities. The following sections explore these themes in greater detail.

7.5.1 Autonomy

The desire for a certain degree of autonomy and independence was mentioned frequently, often in association with the desire to escape from a way of life that was perceived as monotonous, stressful or meaningless. For example, Jake (45, England) clearly identified escape as his main motivation to leave and did not have many expectations other than "freedom, no stress, no worries about paying bills, just to meet some interesting people", while Lilly (31, England) had been looking forward to breaking free from the routines and confines of work, and having the freedom to do what she wanted to do:

> I wanted to have no constraints of work. I wanted to be free. I mean, basically, I worked my ass off for eight years to save lots of money so I could go be free for a couple of years, and ..... I did work hard and I did save sufficient funds, just so I could... I mean every night it's Saturday night when you're traveling. You can drink beer every night. There's no reason not to. And that sort of thing. [...] You know, I wanted to live, organize that for myself.

Similarly, Chris (36, Czech Republic) just wanted to "drop out" in order to "be independent, think independently" and make his own decisions. Traveling to Asia for a couple of months every year from his mid-twenties onwards had given him a taste for life outside his familiar context, and he had increasingly contemplated the idea of leaving everything behind.

In Max's (30, Austria) case, he described his relationship with his parents as "something like Moscow against Washington", and how he "fought to be viewed as independent and autonomous, and my parents never wanted to give me that". He explains further:

> My mother just can't let go. She simply can't do it, and this is the recurring theme of my life. She always wants to be in control, wants to have her say, and talks herself into believing that I can't survive without her. Well, that sucks for her; I'll just take off and travel around the entire planet without her.

7.5 Anticipated rewards

It is interesting to note that Max felt strongly that he could only achieve this independence by leaving his native culture for a minimum of one year because "when you say you drop out for a whole year, and this was important for me, I can tick it off in my head, and I don't have to think about anything. I don't have to attend any birthdays, no annual festivities, nothing".

In discussions about independence, one consistent theme that emerged was the contrast between independent travel and more organized forms of travel. This topic is covered in much greater detail below, but for now it is enough to simply mention that the participants had strong feelings of antipathy towards package tourism or all-inclusive holidays, and one of the main reasons was the lack of autonomy. For example, Alan (42, New Zealand) stated, "I don't like the idea of being stuck with people who might have different interests than me." Brian (43, USA) expressed this sentiment a bit more colorfully:

> I hate these organized tours, here's where you're gonna eat, here's where you're gonna shop for jewelry. I hate that. [...] A lot of it has to do with the fact that you're too lazy or too stupid to do it yourself. And I have no fear about anything like that.

As we saw above, escape from people telling you what to do and when or how to do it is a main motivator for LITs, so it is not surprising that their anticipated reward is a release from these forms of control.

7.5.2 Novelty

To one degree or another, all LITs were motivated to travel by a desire to see new places and have novel experiences, which supports Richards & Wilson's (2004b) claim that independent travelers are particularly "experience hungry" tourists. In some cases, this novelty-seeking was focused on the natural environment. For example, Dana (39, Denmark) expressed her hope to find something that she felt lacked in her home environment: "[*In Denmark*] there is no nature and no wildlife. I hoped that I would find a place in South America where I could work for a long time with wildlife or animal protection and learn a lot about it." In a similar vein, Eric (48, Canada) "was just curious, interested in nature, mountains and things like this", and Andy (30, USA) stated, "I wanted to see the jungle, the rainforest, I wanted to see the Amazon, I wanted to see a volcano. I'm a child at heart [*laughs*]."

While nature was a factor for some LITs, the majority were focused more on the different cultures and people whom they expected to meet. In this way, they fit the profile of Cohen's (1972) drifters and explorers, as well as Plog's (1974, 2001) allocentric travelers or venturers, who have an intrinsic "intellectual curiosity" (Kottler, 1998) to explore new cultures and actively seek out novel experiences. For example, Alice (29, Sweden) stated:

> I like to meet new people and see new places and learn about...I think, basically I think I want to know things and to broaden my horizons, and by talking to people who got a completely different background and culture, and have been brought up in a completely different part of the world, I think that gives you ... talking to people just give you new ideas about everything, about how to live life and about what's important (Alice, 29, Sweden)

Similarly, Lena (26, Germany) expressed a desire to see more of the world:

> The world is so damn huge, but I've only seen such a tiny, tiny, tiny fraction, and there's soooo much that I still want to see. It's just so diverse. There are so many corners I'd like to go to, where life is just completely different than what I know. Gain new experiences, broaden your horizons (Lena, 26, Germany).

It is important to mention here that the LITs were specifically interested in experiencing cultures that were fundamentally different to their own. Since all of them were from more developed countries, this usually meant traveling to less developed countries, a pattern that supports Plog's (2001) assertion that venturers tend to be attracted to underdeveloped destinations. For example, Lilly (31, England) reported:

> England is western world. Everything is shiny and tarmacked, and you know, that sort of thing. And I've never seen a third world country or things that are very different to the UK and Europe. And I wanted to see, physically see other people getting on with their lives in different ways. That was one of the things. I wanted to meet loads of cool people.

In a related vein, Aaron (35, USA) stated:

> The main goal of this trip was certainly to see interesting places, but... primarily to see how people live, you know, in a completely different environment than what I'd seen previously. And as I said earlier, most of the trips I'd taken were mostly business trips, and, you know, you stay in luxury hotels in cities, and you're doing business, or it's been to go diving or doing sightseeing or something like that. Certainly in the third world countries or countries that are distinctly different than us and so I wanna see things from a different perspective.

Be it unfamiliar cultures or unfamiliar natural settings, we could say that these expected rewards were more externally focused. These LITs expected to have novel and exciting experiences from which they could learn something new.

7.5.3 Challenge

Whereas the LITs in the previous section focused on the perceived novelty of the expected experiences they would have, others phrased their anticipated rewards more in terms of the challenges they expected to face and their desire to test their limits or abilities. Even unprompted, several participants expressed an explicit desire to go beyond their comfort zones. For the more nature-oriented participants, this often took the form of

7.5 Anticipated rewards

physically challenging tasks which they set for themselves, which including climbing high mountains, kayaking dangerous rivers, or going on extended hikes in remote national parks far from civilization. Lukas (27, Germany) is a good example. As an avid mountain climber, he wanted to attempt a first ascent of a mountain in Pakistan. The desire for physical challenge is evident in the following excerpt: "It was very important to do this [*first ascent*] on our own power, on our own, which means without porters and guides and all those things, but truly independently."

While many LITs reported engaging in certain "nature-related" physically challenging activities, for the majority the focus was more on taking on the challenge of surviving in a new culture and learning how to adapt to the ways of long-term independent travel. Here again, some LITs phrased this anticipated reward as an escape from what they perceived as the excessively cushy existence they were leading at home. For example, in England, Lilly (31) owned a house, had a stable career and had relative financial security. In discussing her decision to travel on a low-budget, she stated:

> So one of the things I wanted to do is try and live on a smaller budget, coming away. You know, I can't buy loads of clothes cause I have to carry them. And I am just gonna take busses and try that, so.... It was something I thought I wanted to reinforce when abroad. I definitely had those thoughts in England because my life in England was getting a bit too comfortable. And I wanted to reinforce that you can live without television, you can bike to places or take a horse [*laughs*], rather than having to have your own car and your own transport.

Similarly, Aaron (35, USA) had done a good deal of travel, but always in the form of comfortable business travel or short holidays. In the interview, he expressed a longing to challenge himself to take on a more challenging form of travel: "So, the main purpose of this trip, in a lot of ways, was to take myself out of the comfort zone. You know, I tend to kind of challenge myself, and I wanted to travel in a way that I am not used to traveling". While this form of travel is clearly a novel experience for Aaron, the difference between the people in this section and those in the previous section is that here the focus is more on anticipating how they are going to manage, as opposed to what they are going to see. Thus, the anticipated reward of this group of people is more consciously articulated as an opportunity to place oneself in disorienting or challenging situations, which is of course typically the first step in transformative learning.

7.5.4 Personal growth and identity work

The distinguishing factor of this final type of anticipated reward is that the participants express a conscious expectation that their travels will change them in some meaningful and desirable way. That is to say, whereas the participants above were focused on the experiences they hoped to have, some participants sights were more firmly set on the learning and growth outcomes of these experiences. In some cases, this was expressed as a general expectation that travel will make one "grow as a person" (Magnus, 25, Denmark). In other cases, travelers mentioned what they perceived as specific personality flaws that they hoped they would be able to change through travel. For example, Chelsea (25, England) mentioned that, despite her budding successful career, her self-confidence had decreases since leaving university: "So, I'm trying to find and getting my confidence back by traveling". She also wanted to learn how to slow down and adopt a more relaxed approach toward life: "But I'm so fucking impatient. And this is another thing that I want this journey to teach me. It's just Shanti, shanti, slow down". Finally, Chelsea discussed her anticipated reward in terms of dealing with a crisis about her own personal and cultural values. Raised a devout Christian, she had an experience that led her to renounce Christianity, which left her in a state of profound disorientation:

> It literally crushed down right around me, and I was left thinking, I don't know what I believe in then. [...] People build different structures around their lives to feel that they have meaning.... and when that structure is gone—and that was my religion—then you don't feel like you have meaning, and it's still taking some time to find that meaning again. So, it's totally crap though, cause it's like yeah... I'm traveling to find myself, to find where I fit in.

In line with Chelsea's comment about "fitting in", the following quote from Max (36, Austria, 2nd) also highlights the crucial social aspect of identity work and travel.

> Basically, I also left for highly egotistical reasons. An important fuel, especially in the first months, was that I wanted to show them that I was able to break out of the centrifugal force of the familiar, it was the "I'll show you", this petulant, stubborn "I can do this. Kiss my ass."

Here, Max is focused on the importance of proving to "them" that he has the courage to take a risk by leaving his comfortable life and heading out into the relative unknown. Thus, this statement highlights the importance of social context for the individual's identity concept, a common theme in the interview responses.

This is also interesting because it shows that some LITs were already looking forward to the effect travel would have on their lives after the travel experience (i.e. when they return to their home culture) and how it might help them fit into their home cultures in a more meaningful, satisfying way. For example, Theo (33, Canada) described the frustration of not fitting in with his environment: "I've always been so different anyways". He had studied art at university, but dropped out shortly before graduating, which left him with a rather poor self-image. He was hoping travel would help him find a purpose in life and perhaps the courage to pursue his artistic aspirations: "I'm trying to find inspiration to paint my paintings. And I'm so .... I don't know. I'm trying to find something that I can do." In cases such as these, the LITs essentially view their travels as a psychosocial moratorium (Erikson, 1980) and a period of "experiential freedom" (Turner, 1982) which they hope will allow them to experience themselves in new environments, experiment with new ways of being and encounter opportunities for elaborating strategies of selfhood, which they hope will ultimately help them fit in better when they are back in their home cultures.

On the other hand, rather than learning to fit in, some LITs expressed an expectation that their travel experiences would help them stand out when they returned to their home cultures. This fits in with the essential concept of uniqueness theory (Snyder & Fromkin, 1980), which suggests that some people seek to establish and maintain a sense of interpersonal difference or uniqueness which contributes to their self-identity, self-esteem, social status and attracts attention (Lynn & Snyder, 2002, p. 395). In fact, it has been argued that people with a high need for uniqueness are more likely to act in ways that run counter to social expectations and yield less to majority influence than those who do not have this need (Imhoff & Erb, 2009; Lynn & Snyder, 2002). Indeed, for those bored or dissatisfied with their lives or their social standing in their home cultures, long-term independent travel offers them a way to stake a claim to their own exceptionalism. For Max (30, Austria), even before leaving he had already begun to enjoy the changed social status that came from "publicly" (i.e. among his family and friends) announcing his intention to travel:

> The thought occurred to me that I might want to attain a distinguishing attribute through [*travel*], just to be awesome. Just the fact that I am being interviewed, I mean... if I didn't go away now, you wouldn't interview me now [*laughs*]. I mean, in terms of that, I feel desired now, and that alone confirms it.

Similarly, in discussing her expected rewards, Julia (37, Germany) stated, "I think the real trigger was that I just wanted to do something special, you know, where you stand out in your town." As a committed traveler myself, this is a motive that I can relate to. As described earlier, in my case I discovered this feeling at a very young age when my father took the family on trips to other countries, and it definitely altered our status in our hometown. From the perspective of the villagers, it did not necessarily "improve" that status, as most people just thought we were crazy and eccentric; but from the perspective of a young girl who wanted to feel different and special, this small-town disapproval was something I took pride in.

7.6 Summary

This section examined the pre-travel experiences that ultimately motivate certain individuals to embark on long-term, independent travel. We have seen that these experiences are highly diverse and that, in most cases, for each individual there is an accumulation of major and minor experiences and feelings that contribute to the ultimate decision to head out on the road. In order to make some sense out of this complex body of motivations, I proposed dividing them into: seed experiences, which are usually relatively minor experiences that plant the idea of travel in the individual's head and then may lay dormant for long periods of time; lifestyle dissonance, which is the gradually growing feeling of disharmony with one's cultural surroundings; and trigger experiences, which are more specific events that somehow release the energy accumulated through the other two categories and provide the final impetus to take a break from one's regular life and go traveling. We then looked at the significant effort required in some cases to overcome final obstacles that arise even after the decision to travel has been made, and finished up with some of the important rewards that travelers expect to gain from their travel experiences. All of these factors can play a role in the initial travel decision. It is now time to move on to the experiences long-term independent travelers have on the road.

8 Experiences on the Road

As we saw in the previous section, people set out to travel with different motivations, prior disorienting experiences, and varying degrees of previous intercultural experience, as well as different goals and expectations – all of which strongly influence the learning process. This wide range of backgrounds, as well as the different destinations and travel styles chosen, result in an immense variety of learning and growth experiences that occur during travel. This section attempts to bring some order into this great variety by identifying some common themes in terms of both the mechanisms and the outcomes of learning.

As this study draws on narrative modes of thought (Bruner, 1986, 2002) and stories of lived experiences, I focus on peak experiences, which are sometimes referred to as "defining moments" in everyday conversation. As we will see below, these peak experiences provide the key events in people's identity narratives. In almost any narrative, be it a book, film, or play, the classic dramatic structure consists of a problem, a struggle with the problem and the subsequent resolution of the problem. Similarly, LITs' stories are full of peak experiences that trigger learning and have a lasting effect. This is because such experiences occur in the interstices between the "old" and the "new" culture and create an intense internal disequilibrium "in which our mental and behavioral habits are brought into awareness and called into question (Kim, 2008, p. 363).

It is important to emphasize that these events can be either positive or negative, and thus should perhaps be called "peak or valley experiences". In "regular life" (i.e. non-travel-specific settings), these include positive experiences, such as a first kiss, the first day on the job, the wedding day, or the birth of a child, and negative experiences, such as the death of a loved one, a serious illness, or an embarrassing moment. Similarly, in "traveler life", these experiences can range from the intense joy of reaching a mountain summit to the overwhelming confusion and frustration that can arise when one finds oneself in a culture where everything is foreign. These are the moments that linger in the memory, and by synthesizing and integrating stories of these events into their personal narratives, LITs seek to provide meaning and coherence to their identities (McAdams, 2011).

As with the previous chapter, and in keeping with the model of transformative learning that informs this work, I have chosen to structure this section roughly around the types of disorienting experiences that open up learning opportunities. The first type of disorienting experience arises from encounters with the natural environment, and this section therefore describes LITs' experiences with nature. The second sub-section, *Encounters with*

© Springer Fachmedien Wiesbaden GmbH, part of Springer Nature 2019
B. Phillips, *Learning by Going: Transformative Learning through Long-term Independent Travel*, https://doi.org/10.1007/978-3-658-25773-6_8

the self, focuses on experiencing loneliness, dealing with the accompanying emotions, and learning to appreciate solitude. The third sub-section then examines interactions with a foreign culture and the negotiation of inter-cultural difference, while the fourth subsection examines the tension between the individual and the traveler community, as well as the adoption of a (temporary) traveler identity and that identity's evolution over the course of one's travels. A final section offers a summary of the many learning outcomes derived from these many forms of experience

8.1 Encounters with nature

Central to the concept of learning through long-term independent travel is the notion that experience lies at the core of transformation and personal growth. Although many LITs embark on their journey with the primary goal of learning about other cultures, a certain subset of LITs are inspired primarily by the desire to experience something novel in the natural environment. Furthermore, even among those whose primary focus is on intercultural experience, the majority still end up participating in some activity that causes them to have a meaningful interaction with the natural environment, such as scuba diving, mountain climbing, trekking, jungle tours or boat journeys. The following subsections describe the key themes that emerged in LITs' stories of their experiences in nature and the learning and personal growth that these experiences often trigger.

8.1.1 Appreciating the beauty of nature

The first theme to emerge was simply an expanded awareness of the beauty of the landscape and a new appreciation for the aesthetic beauty of nature. In some cases, this could even occur from scenery glimpsed from the window of a moving train or bus:

> I was on a bus in Ecuador, can't remember where I was going. I was looking out the window, listening to music, and the landscape was just so ravishingly beautiful, such a breathtaking landscape, it was unbelievable. And I was just sitting there and watching the landscape for hours. And then, I don't know if you know this feeling when you just start crying because everything is so beautiful, and you can hardly believe that you are there now, doing all these things, ... these are the highlights of traveling. (Lena, 26, Germany)

Such rushes of emotion triggered by the natural beauty of the surroundings were a common theme throughout the interviews. Thus, Julia (37, Germany) got "goosebumps" when witnessing the towering Angel Falls in Venezuela, while Lilly (31, England) was almost crying when she saw her first cloud forest on a lone trek in northern Peru because "it was

8.1 Encounters with nature

soooo beautiful". Similarly, Magnus (25, Denmark) was so impressed by the beauty of the lagoons and mountains of northern Peru that he "could have died up there", and Glen (26, England) described getting "natural highs" when immersed in beautiful natural environments. Finally, Brian (43, USA), had his breath taken away in places like Torres del Paine national park in Chile and felt incredibly grateful for being able to see it, while Lukas (27, German) was overwhelmed with joy and gratitude when watching the sun set behind the impressive Fitz Roy in Patagonia.

Through all these experiences, many travelers developed a new appreciation for natural beauty that they had never particularly noticed before. Matt (28, USA) reported that he had spent the majority of his life "inside with [his] Nintendo", but traveling changed that, as he explained: "I've become much more nature-oriented since I started traveling. I've never been more interested in [nature] than on this trip". Independent travel forced him out of his Nintendo bubble, stimulated his senses and fostered an appreciation for the natural environment. Many other LITs described how travel had heightened their awareness and appreciation for nature:

> I went to the Grand Canyon. It was amazing. You know there's no way you can ever express that in however many movies or TV programs you watch or anything like photographs. You have to feel it and see it for yourself. And that's something that I'll never forget. It's awesome. (Alan, 42, New Zealand)

> In Switzerland, I went biking and was not aware of the natural environment I was in. That's changed now completely. When I go back, I will do both, and if I go on a hike, I will see birds or other animals, plants, flowers and trees as part of the experience, whereas before it was all about sport. (Syd, 32, Switzerland)

Both Alan and Syd come from countries that are internationally renowned for their natural landscapes, yet they had to leave their home countries to finally open their eyes to the beauty of the natural world. It seems there are two factors that account for this: first, travel affords people the time to slow down their lives and notice the things around them; and second, travel works against the tendency for the "natural" surroundings in one's native environment to take on the other meaning of the word natural: i.e. normal or expected (Cambridge Dictionary, 2017). This calls to mind the common saying (usually attributed to Aesop's fable of the Fox and the Lion) "Familiarity breeds contempt", although perhaps Huxley's more neutral rendition is more appropriate in this context:

> Familiarity breeds indifference. We have seen too much pure, bright color at Woolworth's to find it intrinsically transporting. And here we may note that, by its amazing capacity to give us too much of the best things, modern technology has tended to devaluate the traditional vision-inducing materials. (Huxley, 1956, p. 33).

While Huxley's essay criticized the deadening of the human sense of wonder caused by overexposure to artificial beauty, the same process can occur with natural beauty or with anything to which we are continuously exposed, particularly if we grow up in certain surroundings.

For myself, the stories of Syd and Alan ring true, as I had a similar experience. Austria, my native land, is full of stunning and picturesque mountain villages, hiking trails and outdoors activities, yet I had to travel to South America to discover the joy of experiencing the beauty of nature. I had never had any interest in hiking in Austria, but in Argentina my travel companion (and now husband) Mike convinced me to go on a five-day hike in southern Argentina's Parque Nacional los Glaciares. The beauty of the landscape on this hike, which included gorgeous glaciers, stunning mountaintops, lakes, and an abundance of flora and fauna, made a lasting impression on me and led to an interest in further hikes later in our travels—an interest that carried over to my post-travel life back in Austria.

8.1.2 Connecting with nature

Beyond the appreciation for the beauty of nature, the emotions released by these experiences also testify to another process at work: a feeling of connection with nature. Dana (39, Denmark) described this feeling in trying to express the meaning of nature for her personally:

> This is what I love about traveling. The happiest moments that I have enjoyed in my life have been on this trip in nature. Because sometimes, many times, I think this world is way too cruel and way to evil, and I fucking hated it, and I yelled at God or whatever it is. But then going outside in nature here, it's just so big and so beautiful and so magical, it's so incredible. And yes. I can't describe it. It's just complete happiness.

In her travels, Dana had witnessed great poverty, as well as the cruel treatment of animals by people who were supposed to be helping them, all of which had left her feeling disillusioned about the world. The "God" she yells at is human society and the evils it perpetuates, which come to feel like the "natural" order of the world when one spends too much time among them. Getting away from this environment can remind us that there is something bigger and purer than human society and its problems.

Dana showed a closer awareness of this effect in a later story involving an adventure in nature. During a solo hike in northern Argentina, she found herself unable to cross a river that had been swollen by heavy rains. What was meant to be a 4-day hike turned into 11 days stuck alone in the snowy wilderness. Fortunately, she discovered a small refuge where people had left some food she could eat. Oblivious to the fact that there was a search and rescue team of firefighters and policemen searching for her, she found the

8.1 Encounters with nature

situation "extreme" because she was alone, it was freezing and she was cold. However, the story was full of positive details:

> Taking a bath, because there was no shower or nothing, but taking a shower, butt naked with a mountain in your face, condors flying over you, and just dipping down, and the pain of the cold water was so intense, but the whole experience was just so extremely, extremely, extremely, I can't tell you, beautiful. And coming up, and you are warm, and you can run around again without clothes on cause your whole body and blood is just hammering. No it's fantastic.

Rather than remembering the situation as an experience of despair or hardship, Dana describes the restorative power of nature. By leaving behind the disturbing environment of the social circumstances in which she had found herself, she was able to connect with something bigger than humanity, an experience which helps her to feel alive and renew her faith in existence. In essence, her experience in nature helps put the problems of life in society in a new perspective. Of course, her words "I can't tell you" are revealing. Her struggles to find words to express her ideas show that she experiences this perspective shift on an emotional level rather than an intellectual level. That is to say, she would most likely need more contemplation to grasp this idea intellectually, and in some ways the interview itself was helping her move towards this greater understanding—which is a testament to the power of narration, or the struggle to articulate one's experiences in narrative form, to push an individual to greater understanding and coherence. Nevertheless, whether or not she grasps this intellectually, the fact that this peak experience remains in her memory as a building block for constructing meaning shows the transformative potential in such traveler activities.

In other instances, the LITs showed a conscious awareness of the power of connecting with nature and the positive effect it has on their lives and spoke of this connection as a stated goal or benefit of their travels. Thus, Aimee (26, England) stated, "Lots of our highlights of our travels have been kind of spiritual... kind of on a mindset level, being one with the environment." Similarly, Chelsea (25, England) spoke at great length about the effect of the natural environment on her life perspective and even her sense of identity. I met Chelsea in northern Brazil, where we traveled together up the Amazon River from the estuary mouth all the way to Manaus. We slept in hammocks on a clunky old passenger boat traveling upstream, took refreshing baths in the Amazon, watched indescribably beautiful sunsets and sunrises, and even got stuck for a couple days in a remote Amazon river community when the boat broke down and we had to wait to be towed to a larger community further upstream. In our interviews during this time, Chelsea related how she had grown up in the English countryside but moved to London in her late adolescent years. In discussing the role of nature in her travel experience, she had the following to say:

> It's about this feeling of just being really close to nature, and really close to actually the hum of what makes us all tick and being close to really what it's all about [...] One of the reasons why I wanted to come to the Amazon was because I wanted to reconnect with the environment, because I've lost all, I've been divorced from it. That's what happens when you live in cities. When I lived in [hometown] you know what the tide's doing, and in London you've got no fucking clue. [...] You can't see the stars or anything, and I just wanted to reconnect with the earth because I think,...I am changing my ideas, my ideologies, my faith and everything is changing and I thought this would be a better place for that to happen.

Chelsea refers to her crisis of faith mentioned above and the identity crisis it caused, commenting, "And that's what I was really looking forward to, to actually just getting to a stage where I felt comfortable again with who I was." For Chelsea, it was not enough to get into a different cultural environment. Rather, she wanted a true escape from all cultural environments to give her some space to reconsider her life.

8.1.3 Nature as a source of personal challenge

While the stories in the previous section showed LITs positioning nature as a nurturing force or a source of energy or peace, in many traveler stories the natural environment takes on a different role—a difficult or even dangerous space rife with challenges that one must overcome. In the context of the near-universal agreement among LITs regarding the importance of leaving one's personal comfort zone to foster significant learning experiences, nature becomes a perfect foil for stories in which the travelers take on these personal challenges and test their abilities and limits. And indeed, it has been argued that pushing one's boundaries is crucial for an evolving self (e.g. Csikszentmihalyi, 1993), and experiences in nature that involve testing one's physical or emotional limits have the capacity to reveal previously hidden aspects of the self and can take on deep meaning by providing a sense of mastery (Bosangit, Hibbert, McCabe, 2015). Furthermore, due to the intense emotions usually involved in testing one's limits, these events tend to make a lasting impression on the travelers themselves. Finally, from a narrative identity perspective, events in which an individual overcomes adversity to achieve something important obviously fit perfectly into the most common of all narrative templates and are very attractive additions to the repertoire of personal anecdotes that LITs use to construct and reinforce their identities for others and for themselves. The following examples will shed some light on the types of nature-oriented traveler experience that LITs most frequently cite.

8.1 Encounters with nature

In some cases, such experiences may involve a deliberate effort to overcome a known weakness by pushing not one's physical boundaries, but rather one's psychological anxieties and engaging in novel experiences (Hopkins & Putnam, 2012). For example, Philipp (46, Austria), who had been scared of the dark all his life, decided to confront this fear by going into the rainforest at night:

> In Indonesia I was invited to dinner in the middle of a rainforest. When I wanted to leave, they almost didn't let me go. The family said it was too dangerous to roam through the woods at night. At night, I slept near the path in my sleeping bag behind a bush. Then, I realized that in this rainforest, I had even lost my fear [of the dark] that had been with me since my childhood.

Here, the local host family who warns him against his plan adds a nice narrative touch that deepens the sense of danger and thereby enhances the drama and the resulting sense of accomplishment.

In a similar vein, when I worked for a time as a divemaster in Honduras, I heard many stories (and witnessed many experiences first-hand) of people testing their limits by learning scuba diving. Experienced divers will be aware that most recreational diving is hardly physically challenging. In fact, due to the combination of deep breathing, weightlessness, and (often) beautiful underwater scenery, recreational diving usually has more in common with peaceful meditation than strenuous mountain climbing. However, many (if not most) people have some level of innate fear of drowning, and overcoming the feelings of anxiety and even panic that some people experience when first attempting to breathe through a regulator underwater can be extremely challenging. Thus, Brian (43, USA) struggled mightily when he first tried scuba diving, but he persisted because he wanted to prove to himself he could do it. When he was finally certified, he was very pleased, noting, "I didn't know I had that in myself". Similarly, like myself, Ryan (26, Canada) took advantage of the flexibility afforded by his long-term trip and decided spontaneously to learn how to dive. Although it was not easy, he stuck with it and eventually received his divemaster certification. As he recounted this experience, one could see his surprise and satisfaction about this achievement: "I didn't even dive before I got here, and now I'm a divemaster".

While the LITs in the stories above set out into nature to conquer a fear, sometimes nature comes to the travelers and inflicts them with a different kind of fear: fear of sickness or even death. This is perhaps one of the favorite "genres" of traveler stories, and I have been around many campfires or (unfortunately) dinner tables where travelers will get into their dueling sickness stories, each one trying to outdo the other with the worst tale of suffering. Although frequently disturbing (and often highly unappetizing), these stories obviously make perfect identity narratives because they cast the traveler as the hero overcoming intense physical hardship. The stories I heard included various insect and spider bites, skin infections or mysterious rashes, dehydration, heat exhaustion, altitude sickness, various intestinal disorders, and even some serious diseases, such as typhoid fever, dengue fever and malaria. These stories, often accompanied by plenty of gory details, evoke the confusion and fear travelers experience when they contract these illnesses, as well as the steps they had to take to overcome them and, in many cases, the way their perspectives or behaviors changed during or after the sickness. For example, Max (30, Austria) described a "funny story" (his actual words) in which he got "mega severe antibiotic-resistant salmonella poisoning":

> It tore me apart for a whole month, and I lost 10 kg in one week alone, that was the worst week. They tried to get me back on my feet with infusions, but nothing worked. I didn't eat or drink anything for an entire month. I was just on an IV drip. I went down, and at the end, I only had 66kg. The doctors said they couldn't get any nourishment to stay inside me because it just came right out the other end. I knew that I was reaching my limits, and I knew that it was gonna be fucking close. But I knew, I really never found it threatening for a second because when you die, there's nothing better than biting the dust in India, with all this Hindu, ascension, and what not. I think I was on a spiritual trip back then, and I was also just ready to accept things the way they were.

This well-crafted story, which Max had clearly told a time or two before the interview, features plenty of detail to build suspense and then a surprise ending. Obviously, the listener (me, in this case) knows that Max is going to survive, but one is not expecting to hear that he had overcome his fear of death by traveling to India and engaging with the Hindu religion. Although it may seem a bit unlikely, it certainly seemed that Max believed it, which would make this a prime example of a perspective change brought on by an intense disorienting situation.

In fact, research has shown that experiencing a traumatic life event, such as a serious illness or disease, is often followed by periods of intense reflection, spiritual searching and efforts to make sense of the trauma, all of which can lead to posttraumatic growth (Tedeschi & Calhoun, 1998), as the individual finds a way to incorporate the newly created meaning into his or her sense of self. A story from Julia (37, Germany) displays this process even more clearly. During a three-day boat trip from Sumatra to Singapore, Julia came down with malaria. She soon fell into a coma and was hospitalized immediately upon arrival in Singapore. Although she eventually woke up, it soon became clear that her condition was life-threatening: "It went on for ten days, although doctors had told me that normally people die after seven days." Recounting this story years later, Julia described not only the intense fear, but also her clear recollection of her release from the hospital once she had recovered, including how intensely she perceived smells and sounds: "When you experience and survive a near-death experience, you get a sort of life adrena-

8.1 Encounters with nature

line. It's almost like a drug. The perception changes." However, beyond that burst of adrenaline, it was also clear that Julia had told this story often, and that perhaps in telling it, she had drawn a clear lesson from this experience which she had incorporated into her value system and which had a lasting effect on how she responds to life's challenges. She reported that after such an experience, "You don't get worked up about things so easily. Many problems concern you marginally because you know there are bigger things out there."

Of course, viruses are just one of the natural hazards travelers face. In the next story, Philipp (46, Austria) tells of his experience swimming in New Zealand. In this case, Philipp did not particularly go looking for adventure or challenge, but it found him nonetheless:

> I'm sitting here because of sheer luck. In New Zealand close to Christchurch on the southern island I went swimming with a bunch of others. We all swam out together, and on the way back, a large wave came and I panicked. Somebody from that group saved me and pulled me out of that wave. It turned out that in my panic I was breathing completely the wrong way. Later I found out that the bay is very dangerous. Not panicking and being consciously aware at all times of what's going on is your only chance of getting out of a hairy situation like that.

This traumatic experience taught Philipp an important lesson about being cautious and staying calm in frightening situations (as I used to teach new scuba divers: "stop, breathe, think, act"). In a coda to the story, he even drew a related lesson that many people in modern society would do well to heed:

> That's why I think that cell phones are so dangerous, because they distract you. When you are consciously aware of everything around you, you have more possibilities of getting out of a hairy situation alive.

Perhaps it is worth mentioning the unstated lesson of this episode—choose your travel/swimming companions wisely because they might have to save your life at some point. However, from the perspective of narrative identity building, it is not surprising that Philipp glosses over this detail, since that rather shifts the focus of the story to a new protagonist—the swimmer who saved him.

Of course, challenging encounters with nature are rarely life-threatening. However, although the suffering involved is normally far less traumatic, any event in which an individual must overcome hardship holds the potential for learning and identity development. For those who have little experience with outdoors activities, simply taking on a longer hike, with the unfamiliar experience of walking all day and sleeping in a tent, can prove very rewarding. Thus, Lilly (31, England) described her ten-day, high-altitude trek in Peru: "I've never walked or camped for that long in my life, and it was a big challenge for me to do that. And it doesn't sound that exciting or anything, but it was amazing, and I loved it. That made me feel proud". Emma (41, England) described a similar long-distance trek, including some dramatic details to emphasize the challenge: "Sometimes in the middle I'm just thinking, 'What the hell am I doing? This is like really hard work.' And I'm getting blisters, and my feet are killing me. But then, once I've done it, I'm really sort of ...yeah, I'm so glad I've done it."

Aimee (26, England) adds some nice details about the dangers she faced and the fears she had to overcome:

> It was really, really remote, [...] and like the most spectacular scenery we saw in New Zealand. But there were things like we had to cross a river that was like 30 meters wide and up to there on me [points to her chest]. It was a really strong river, and it was scaring me, and we crossed it with our big backpacks. [...] in a couple of points that path had just totally diminished, and then every step that you took you were like sliding down and there was a three hundred meter drop and it was really muddy, and me being scared of heights, it was crazy.

For Nadine (23, Canada), it was an experience hiking in Peru's Colca Canyon:

> That was so hard... really, really hard. We had to get down in this canyon, it's really deep, it's one of the deepest canyons in the world. It's really something [...] And first we had to go 4 hours down and walk all day in the sun, and after going back up for three hours and with the altitude it was really difficult. But you know, you just finish it, and you are so satisfied about yourself, and it's such a good sensation, and so you just wanna do it again and again and again, even if it's difficult. And the more you're doing it, the more it's easy.

Here, Nadine shows how the feeling of self-satisfaction leads to a desire to repeat the experience, as well as her recognition of the gradual improvement that comes from taking on repeated challenges.

While Nadine went down, Tom (46, Germany) described challenging himself to go higher and higher into the mountains. When asked if he remembered doing anything that had made him feel proud, he immediately answered with great enthusiasm:

> Yes! Climbing on a high mountain and standing on the summit, thinking "Wow, you just climbed up here! Incredible!" And that also just got more, the mountains [...] in [hometown] there are no mountains, other than coal mountains, and when I got up there for the first time,... First, they were small, but then the got bigger and bigger, and I thought "Wow!" That is, I mean I think that is just the best feeling to know that you did that, to have accomplished that. And that's a real achievement.

Along with the obvious emotion linked to the memory, Tom's story emphasizes that this was not an opportunity that was available to him at home, as well as the extended effort it required for him to build up to bigger and bigger mountains.

Andy (30, USA) heightens the drama even more:

> Climbing the volcano in Chile. But not because of the physical ... it was a tough climb to get up, but because of the reward at the end. I was staring down at a vol-

cano that was erupting. Like people burned their clothes up there. That was just mind-boggling. That was adventurous and rewarding.

For Ben (31, England), the mountain may not have been on fire, but he made sure to do a little "name dropping" and back it up with some altitude statistics, just in case I was not familiar with the peak:

> Mountains thrill me, and one of the things that really excited me was climbing Aconcagua. It's the highest mountain outside of the Himalayas, and I just did it with a friend, no guide, no nothing. That was a huge sense of achievement.

Beyond the height of the mountain, Ben's story also includes a key detail worth pointing out—they did it without a guide. In the sections below, we will see the crucial importance of autonomy and self-reliance, which are values that lie at the core of many travelers' value systems and self-identity concepts.

However, before moving on, there is one last way that nature can offer a challenge—namely, by providing LITs with a setting that is devoid of human contact and may therefore be conducive to personal reflection. Patrick (37, Austria) emphasized this concept when he spoke of the months he spent alone in the Andes: "The spiritual component was a huge change on this trip. [...] Being alone high up in the Andes for many months helped create this spiritual foundation, on which I can always build now". Of course, isolating themselves in a natural environment is just one way that travelers can create space for self-contemplation and reflection. Since this is an important element of the learning process, the following section will cover this issue from a wider perspective of examining how individuals come into contact with themselves and the effects such experiences can have.

8.2 Encounters with the self

For most LITs, travel is primarily a social experience. This is evident from their stories, which normally feature a diverse supporting cast of memorable locals and fellow travelers. However, almost every travel experience also features at least some periods of time where the traveler is not interacting with other people. Such time isolated from the direct influence of other people offers space for LITs to engage in the type of reflection that Mezirow and others have posited is often a key component of transformative learning. In the context of long-term travel, this can be particularly useful for processing the experiences travelers have on the road—that is, making meaning out of these experiences and then figuring out how those meanings fit into the big picture of the traveler's identity and concept of how she fits into the world. As Richards and Wilson (2004b) have suggested, periods of "passive activity" (e.g. long bus/boat/train journeys, waiting times, hiking, or simply relaxing at a beach or in a café) are an important part of the travel experience and offer time to reflect on the travel experiences and on life in general (p. 27).

In some cases, LITs actively seek out alone time due to a recognition, either conscious or subconscious, of the potential value of such periods, while in others cases people find themselves unwillingly forced into isolation by circumstances beyond their control. However, regardless of how the isolation may come about, these experiences seem to leave a deep impression on the LITs as memories of either peak or valley experiences, and the related stories in the interviews often mention the effect these moments alone had on their meaning schemes and perspectives.

8.2.1 Loneliness

While many travelers actively seek out moments of solitude, even the most introverted or independent LITs reported struggles with feelings of loneliness. Even though most of them were at least partially motivated by a desire to escape from the restrictions or, in some cases, the boredom or excessive comfort of their home environment, the complete removal of this social support system proves challenging at some point for most of them, particularly when they have nobody else to replace this support or distract them from its absence, so to speak. Of course, it is important to point out that loneliness does not necessarily involve the absence of fellow human beings. On the contrary, one of the lessons of intercultural travel for many travelers is seeing how the presence of a multitude of people with whom one cannot communicate, either due to a language barrier (in the case of locals) or shyness and insecurity (in the case of other travelers), can intensify feelings of loneliness. Thus, Ben (31, England) described his experience traveling through northern Brazil, where he met no travelers and could not speak Portuguese: "So I was quite...yeah, what am I doing? I've got so many good friends and family at home, and now I'm here and I can't even say anything to anyone. So that was tough."

Similarly, although overall Ryan (26, Canada) speaks of his extended solo cycling trip through Central America as a positive and even transformative experience, he still had some powerful stories of loneliness to relate, such as the following event, which transpired after 8 days of cycling alone across "the most atrocious roads ever":

> I had no one I could talk to, no one I could express to. No one I had anything in common with. And I hadn't felt that lonely in a long time. And then on day 9, I biked into this small community, ...beach town in El Salvador [...] and this guy comes up on a dirt bike, and he got off and he was very visibly, I mean he was a white person obviously, so I ran after him and chased him down and I went up to him and I said right into his face "Please God tell me you speak English" [laughs]. And he looked

8.2 Encounters with the self

at me and he said "Yeah", and then I spent an hour just...just...nonstop talking to this guy.

Interestingly, Chelsea (25, England) described a similar feeling of intense need for companionship, but it was not to help her get through a difficult period, but rather to help her appreciate a peak experience:

> That one time I felt bitterly lonely when I'd had the most extraordinary day, beautiful day, and at the end of the day there was no one I could tell. I ended up going to a café, the restaurant I always went to, and telling the chef all about it. And I ended up crying, and he gave me a hug, and he cooked me a nice meal. And you know, he was the only person I vaguely knew, cause I'd been to [the restaurant] a couple of times, and he'd always been friendly. So I ended up telling him about my day. But that day I felt very lonely. It was in Mozambique....the most beautiful day.

These stories demonstrate clearly the powerful inherent need many people have to share their experiences, both positive and negative, with other people. In the context of narrative identity, it is worth noting that beyond human connection, both Chelsea and Ryan essentially needed an audience for their stories, so that they could use the act of storytelling to process these experiences and create meaning out of them.

8.2.2 Reflective writing

When deprived of an audience for their stories, or a person with whom they could share and process experiences, many LITs mentioned turning to reflective writing, which has been called "one of the most widely-used and effective forms of reflection that exists" (Wright & Bolton, 2012, p. xi). For example, widely traveled LIT Brian (43, USA), who described his drawer full of travel journals at home, stated that he sees his journal as a kind of surrogate travel companion: "It's kinda like bringing along another person". In fact, about two thirds of the LITs indicated that they keep a private travel journal, and almost all LITs engage in some sort of travel writing, either through a blog or emails. While some people tend to focus on the memory value of such writing (i.e. creating a permanent record of one's experiences and feelings), most LITs were keenly aware of the meaning-making function of such writing as well. Reflective writing can take the form of a private journal (written, electronic, or even audio recordings) or may even have an audience, such as emails to friends or relatives or online blogs for "public consumption." In fact, one of the themes that emerged from the interviews was that some LITs practice multiple forms of reflective writing, and they were quite articulate about the differences between them. Whereas one form involves a more conscious construction of a public persona via mass email or a blog, keeping a journal serves more as a meta-cognitive support strategy to cope with disorienting experiences, be they positive or negative. Eric (48, Canada), who practices both forms of writing, summed up the difference nicely:

> I write two kinds of journals. I write my journal of traveling, you know experiences and everything. But this I write on the internet, and I send it to people in my country. But in my paper journal, it's more how I feel and the reflections. Sometimes I see something and, it's like a mirror for me, and I talk about myself. So I think about it, and I write about it, sometimes to unblock something, to uncover something inside. Writing it, it often comes and just comes out. Sometimes you know, and sometimes you don't know why. But this journal is more personal.

Heather (36, Australia), who at the time of our interview had been faithfully maintaining a travel blog for seven and a half years of travel, described how her blog could embrace both styles and functions. Depending on her inner feelings her writing is sometimes "very thoughtful, sometimes it's lots of pictures, sometimes it's just a description of what I did in a given day or week, so quite boring." Lena (26, Germany) also described how her journal mixes mundane details of daily life and deeper reflections on experiences and meanings:

> I write about myself, about my own feelings, when I feel real shitty sometimes, or when I feel extremely well, or things like that. I can write three pages about... I don't know, fish that I saw while diving, how great they are, and I'm like a child then. It depends, sometimes I write half a page. Sometimes I write ten pages.

While Lena, like Brian with his drawer of journals, was a conscientious journal writer who embraced this mix of styles and function, Heather (36, Australia) described how her journal-writing practices had evolved over seven and a half years of travel:

> I don't feel overwhelmed by the information coming in. I do ... the first year I had a journal and I faithfully wrote in it, like I had to have an entry every day. But then it was just too hard. It's like, oh my god I have to go back and fill in the last seven days. I don't feel like that now. I actually have a journal online where I put photos and where there are private entries and public entries and other people can read it and comment. And I'm pretty good at keeping up with it. And I just write down, sometimes just how you're feeling in a city or a town or a place and what I did ... just notes.

While the true reflexive meaning-making function of writing faded for Heather, most LITs who have not traveled quite as long as Heather expressed a continuing deep appreciation for the therapeutic value of reflective writing, which allows writers to stand back and examine their lives from a wider angle. Writing encourages travelers to listen to their innermost feelings and often forces them to re-evaluate meaning structures or mental habits. Nadine (23, Canada) expressed this concept in her interview:

> When you're feeling alone, or when you're feeling really mixed up in your head, or you don't know where to go, or you have problems with people, or you're feeling really alone or sad, I think the best way is to write it to be clear in your head. [...] I really like to write, and it's really a way for me, when I'm really mixed up in my head, and all these emotions and confusion...just writing, and just putting it on paper. And after that it's like, it's on paper now, and it becomes clear, and you can

8.2 Encounters with the self

> read it later and take some lesson of it. You learn from that too, cause you're always growing and you're always changing.

Nadine mentions another benefit of journal writing, which is that travelers can go back and re-read what they have written, which can lead to new ideas and realizations. As Wright & Bolton (2012) have argued, reflective writing externalizes thoughts, ideas, phrases, images, and feelings and opens them to scrutiny, which can disturb habitual ways of thinking, a necessary first step towards change and evolution. This assertion was supported by Dana (39, Denmark):

> It's healthy re-thinking [your travel experiences]. And that's why the journal might be healthy too. Cause you might not think about how you have changed and how your outlook has changed in your everyday travels. Sometimes it takes a conversation with someone or writing your diary to bring you back to that and to realize that you do think different today.

In the long run, this has the potential to alter meaning schemes significantly and bring about a new or renewed sense of autobiographical coherence. Nadine (23, Canada) pointed to just such a significant change, when her journal writing during a period of extended travel actually helped her resolve a conflict from her "pre-travel" life. Nadine described her "really bad" relationship with her sister, with whom she had been competing since her childhood. She states that for the first few months of her travels, she refused to communicate with her sister due to long-standing negative emotions associated with her. However, she reported that the time for solitary contemplation that she gained via her travels, along with the ongoing reflective journal writing that accompanied it, set in motion a transformative process that ultimately led to a perspective change about her sister: "I just realized that she is such a good person, and that I really don't have any time to lose hating her or not having such a good relation with her. So that changed my mind. And I just grew up like that." Travel writing helped Nadine engage in the most profound form of reflection – premise reflection – whereby she sought to understand why she perceived, acted, thought or felt the way she did (Mezirow, 1991), which led to a resolution to make a new start with her sister and to start respecting and loving her. This experience supports the findings of Pennebaker & Chung, (2007), who have suggested that, in addition to enhancing both physiological wellbeing (e.g. sleep and immune function, reduced alcohol consumption) and psychological wellbeing, reflective writing can improve communication and social relationships with others.

8.2.3 Discovering the value of solitude

In the context of narrative identity, Beach (2010) has argued that "We are all preoccupied with the flow of our own and others' experience, which we think about in the form of stories. We tell stories to one another when we're together, and we tell stories to ourselves when we're alone" (p. 20). Ultimately, private travel journals (and to some extent even public blogs) are a form of communication with the self. While some travelers forego writing, they are nevertheless engaged in a continuous internal narrative construction, with the ultimate goal of constructing an identity that provides a sense of purpose in life. As Brinthaupt and Lipka (1992) explain: "On some level we are the stories we tell about ourselves. This is so whether the tales are accurate or inaccurate" (p. 25). Solitary moments and experiences provide the best forum for such self-storytelling, which can be extremely satisfying and productive.

Of course, personality and attitude towards alone time affect this process. For example, Andy (30, USA) initially described his coping strategies for dealing with loneliness during his three-year motorcycle journey across Latin America: "I read, I move. You're constantly packing your bags, and even though I have very little stuff, it's 45 minutes getting the bike ready. Get out my music, go to a bar one night, there's always somebody to talk to." Andy's description of his coping strategy reveals that introspection is perhaps not his preferred pastime. However, he nevertheless went on to acknowledge the benefits of solitude:

> So I'm pretty outgoing. Being alone is good, though, because you think, and being depressed is good because you think more about life, and you see things sometimes more realistically than they are. Sometimes depression sucks, but when you're happy, it's even better, and you have more insights. You learn a lot more about yourself.

Although Andy's extroverted value system causes him to equate solitude with depression in some way, even so he is able to recognize the value of this form of "depression", and later in the quote, he tacitly acknowledges the possibility that one might even be happy when one is alone—not the kind of realization that comes easily to many extroverts.

In a classic example of "passive activity", Eva (26, Germany) described how she could experience solitude on a crowded bus and the benefit she derived from this experience:

> I was homesick, but I incredibly enjoyed this time when I traveled alone, in the sense that you don't talk, you have personal privacy when you sit alone on a bus. Sometimes I walked through the countryside for four weeks all alone, and your experiences are significantly richer than when you travel with someone. You experience yourself in a much more emotional, much more intensive way, the way you react to the environment.

8.2 Encounters with the self

Eric (48, Canada), who was definitely more introverted by temperament, described how he had to overcome an initial tendency to drown his loneliness in drinking and learn to appreciate his alone time:

> All the time I am alone I want to look inside and see what's happening. Why am I feeling this way? I want to learn about it. Sometimes, you know, I can drink for three nights because I don't want to think about it. But traveling, I discovered the beauty of solitude. The good side of solitude. And now I can appreciate it more than earlier. And now I need it, and it is good for me. I was alone many times before, but I didn't appreciate it. But now, yes, and I need it.

In fact, Eric specifically credited travel with teaching him to treasure his time alone and use it productively, including by integrating reflective writing into his routine:

> You have a lot of time, and because I am traveling alone, I can be three weeks without speaking with any travelers, and I like that, and I need that. And during that time I can think more, I can write more, and I can read some books that give me an idea of how to work on myself more. And I can practice these things and be more introspective.

While Eric learned to treasure his alone time, for some travelers it was more a matter of making a kind of uneasy peace with loneliness. The internal struggle is evident in the following revealing story from Lilly (31, England):

> But I'm aware of being on my own a lot. But I think, "When you're two people, three people, then you're not aware of individual people around". So I always think, "Well, I might be sitting there, looking like Billy No-mates, but those people haven't even noticed I'm here anyway," and that sort of thing. So, but you do worry about what other people think about you a little bit. But you like try and rationalize it that when you're in a group, you're so busy talking to each other you don't notice the people around you. So I just pretend I was anonymous. I do, yeah, Huaraz… I can still picture myself being on my own, and I don't know. You're still…you just structure your day around where will I have lunch, and then where will I have dinner? [laughs] Where will I have food? And I need to write my diary, and that will take time. And I console myself in that you wanted to travel on your own for a bit. And you wanted to see what it's like. This is what it's like. So feel it, enjoy it while you're there.

Here, Heather tries to laugh at her own insecurities, and describes the process by which she rationalizes being by herself in a crowded room by convincing herself that nobody notices her anyway, and then dealing with her feelings of isolation by introducing some comforting structure or routine into her daily life. From the perspective of narrative identity, this story is a perfect illustration of internal narrative meaning making in action, as Heather describes her internal struggle to come to terms with her uncomfortable feelings of loneliness. This example also illustrates the premise of narrative learning, which is that "the nature of experience is always prelinguistic; it is 'languaged' after the fact, and the process of narrating it is how learners give meaning to experience" (Clark & Rossiter, 2008, p. 64). Clark and Rossiter go on to explain the process further:

The process of constructing the narrative, the story, is how we can see our understanding of something come together and make sense. It's a complex process in which we identify and struggle with the pieces we cannot make fit together (that is, what we do not understand yet), and we see the gaps (what we still do not know).

Of particular note is that this story of internal value negotiation features to two different "characters" who personify different sides of her personality; one is nervous and insecure, while the other "consoles" her by suggesting a different way to interpret her feelings (i.e. embrace this experience that you said you wanted). In fact, these types of internal conversations are common, whereby the individual can create characters to represent "sides" of their own personalities or the "voices" of other external influences, such as society, parents, friends, religions. This is essentially a form of conflict resolution (one thinks of the common cartoon trope in which the little devil and the little angel pop up on opposite shoulders of the character to debate the next course of action). In principle, the ideal outcome with this kind of internal conversation is that eventually, after similar experiences trigger similar internal conversations, the comforting voice will gradually win out, and Heather will learn to truly appreciate or at least more comfortably accept the experience of being alone in a social setting. However, on a different level, we can see Heather using this story about internal storytelling to express to me, the interviewer, very honestly how she still struggles with the insecurity and loneliness in social situations, inviting me to share a sympathetic laugh both with her and at her (which I did).

8.2.4 Outcomes

Before proceeding to the next sections, which explore what travelers learn by interacting with others during their travels, it is perhaps useful to mention some of the key learning outcomes that LITs mention when describing their experiences with loneliness and solitude.

One interesting outcome mentioned by Lukas (27, Germany) was that his experience solo trekking had heightened his awareness of the effect of his environment on his emotions:

> When you're alone, in the 'pampa', the feelings depend on the weather or the situation. When the sun is shining, and you see an endless grass steppe, then I feel great and free. I can run in any direction. The sun is everywhere. It's great, and you think "wow, I can do whatever I want". But once I sat in the rain, surrounded by this grass steppe, and you just see the horizon. It's totally flat. Everything is grey in grey, it's raining, and you sit in your tent for six hours. The mood is gloomy, not really depressive but pretty low, and your only sunshine is the granola bar that you allow yourself once a day. And when you run around there, then you just feel bleak and lost. And it's the same landscape, but just because the sun isn't shining, it's much more extreme.

8.2 Encounters with the self

While the idea that bad weather affects one's mood is hardly shocking, as Lukas continued his story, a more interesting observation emerged:

> Then I wrote in my journal, feeling depressed. But when the sun comes out the next day, and you put your sleeping bag out to dry and you get warm and realize, hey, this is beautiful, that's great. And afterwards this was a real great experience that I wouldn't want to miss. And that's something you just can't do in Europe, because when you're feeling down then you always have some people around you or else you get a stupid video or something, you can always distract yourself. But real self-reflection, that just happens when you are somewhere in the pampa, in a tent, and there's nothing else to do.

Here, Lukas describes how he learned to appreciate the value of his alone time as a time for self-reflection. In fact, it is interesting to note that the German phrase that I have here rendered as "self-reflection" ("mit dir auseinandersetzen") is based on a German word that essentially has connotations of grappling with, dealing with, or even arguing about an issue with a person (in this case himself). Thus, it again calls to mind the internal dialogic process discussed above. However, perhaps more valuable as a perspective change is the recognition of the valuable role the valley moments play in enhancing one's enjoyment of the peak experiences to come later. Finally, his quote even highlights a valuable lesson about learning to beware of the meaningless distractions that surround him back in his native culture.

In the case of Tom (46, Germany), the outcome for him was simply learning how to enjoy being by himself: "Sometimes I thought, 'There must be something wrong with me.' Because I can do this so well. That is, that I am good at being alone. I can really enjoy being by myself. But that just came with traveling." Tom's quote shows the specter of his previous cultural value system hovering over his consciousness, which had likely been telling him his whole life that being an introvert who enjoys alone time is something anti-social about which he should feel guilty. Thus, traveling freed him from the dominant extrovert mentality of his native culture.

Dana (39, Denmark) describes a similar outcome:

> I am like down in a whole other, more peaceful state, energy field. I don't feel any stress and I haven't for a long time. I never thought this is possible. Which also means that I, yes that I haven't been really like, people would still be able to piss me off, and I can see again, and that's why I might be avoiding relationships. I do not wanna re-do what I did before. Which was hysterical. But I am more calm now....being with myself for so long has really helped me to chill me out, to bring me down a bit. So....so, I have changed now, if I have changed for good, I couldn't promise you that. I wish I could, but I guess I'll find out once I stop traveling and live a different life again.

In addition to her slight struggles with English, Dana's slightly chaotic account reveals how emotionally charged this issue is for her. Nevertheless, she believes that the alone time afforded by her travels has fundamentally altered her mindset and her ability to deal with problematic situations in her life, although her final sentence shows that she appreciates the challenge that lies ahead when she returns to Denmark.

Moving one step beyond being at peace with themselves, some travelers even reported an increase in their confidence and self-efficacy (i.e. their belief in their ability to handle situations in life). Thus, Alan (42, New Zealand) stated, "You gotta get used to being by yourself [...], which means becoming more self-reliant, believing you can achieve something, you can do what you need to do. You can go where you need to go." And Lukas (27, Germany) describes how the freedom of travel has taught him to increase his focus and accept responsibility for his own choices and actions: "You have absolute freedom, freedom of choice, you can do whatever you want to, maybe you have to be....you are a bit more attentive and behave responsibly, because if something happens, then you're on your own."

Eric (48, Canada) described how a negative travel experience ultimately boosted his self-confidence and self-efficacy. For his first significant trip to a less-developed country, he went to Nepal to visit a friend who was living there. However, his friend turned out to be "totally egotistical" and of "no help", leaving Eric to fend for himself in this truly foreign environment:

> So the first day I was really shocked. But at the end of the day, I decided that I could manage by myself. So after that, I decided to do things by myself. And it was no problem after that. I discovered that..., that I was able to adapt myself to any kind of situation. That was the first time I discovered that. It was a real big moment.

In the long run, Eric turned a highly disorienting and disturbing experience when he was left to his own devices ("I was crying [...] I was shocked, totally shocked. When I arrived in Kathmandu, totally shocked.") into a narrative of personal achievement and growth, which he was proud to share with me in his interview.

Of course, although this section has highlighted some important strides made by travelers in terms of understanding themselves better and being better able to handle or even appreciate solitude, it is important to emphasize that this is not a universal outcome. Long-term travel does not turn every LIT into a solitary wanderer who pauses only for moments of peaceful meditation and reflection. In fact, some travelers only learn to endure the interludes of solitude, remaining firmly committed to their outgoing natures and focus on meeting people throughout their travels. For example, Lilly (31, England) expressed a very limited desire for solitude: "I am not here to be on my own. I like my own time, but it only has to be a few hours a day on my own, or in the evening or a night on my own. Or whatever."

8.2 Encounters with the self

And even most of those who grow to appreciate their moments of solitude also develop a healthy appreciation for the importance of companionship or even a new understanding that ultimately completely solo travel (more on the meaning of that term in the next section) is not for them. For example, Lars (28, Belgium), who had been traveling for two years at the time of the interview, said "I'm sick of being alone. I won't go alone anymore. I just need somebody else. I'm done traveling by myself." Ally (33, Switzerland), who had also traveled alone for an extended period of time on her first trip, was traveling with a long-term boyfriend she had met on the road when I interviewed her 2 years into her latest trip. When asked if she wanted to travel alone again, she explained what her early trip had taught her: "I need people, I need to share, I don't care if it's with a girlfriend, or with my boyfriend. (…) I'm boring with myself. [laughs] I need to share, to say 'look, that's nice!'" Julia (37, Germany), an even more experienced traveler, described this evolution in attitude towards solo travel even more clearly:

> I have to say that over the years, I do not like to travel alone so much anymore. Earlier, I didn't mind so much. Sometimes I really enjoyed these moments of solitude. But it's just really nice when you can really laugh with someone. I think this is what I miss the most. It's not even the talking, but more the poking fun at something, cracking up, or contemplating something, being embarrassed about something, raving about something, that's what I like.

For both Ally and Julia, it is clear that over time the internal storytelling had grown tiresome or in some way unfulfilling and they now wanted a real conversation partner to share their experiences with. It is interesting that Julia even uses the German word for "contemplate". This shows that, for her, this reflective thinking process, which above was described as a task for solitary times, is now an activity that she prefers to do in tandem, as she and her travel companion can and build meaning from their shared experiences and grow together.

8.2.5 A note on "solo travel" and "traveling alone"

The evolution of travel habits alluded to in the previous sub-section is described in greater detail in the following sections. However, before proceeding, there is one final topic related to encounters with the self that is important to mention here. Travelers often use phrases such as "solo travel" or "traveling alone", which for many people evoke images of some kind of lonely warrior traveling from place to place making little effort to interact with other human beings or form any meaningful relationships. Although there are the rare individuals who fit this model, a closer look reveals that travelers do not use these terms to connote completely solitary travel, but rather to limit the set of "allowable" companions to people met on the road, which usually means shorter-term, more casual friendships. In fact, some travelers even get more specific when defining which people must be excluded for the travel to count as "solo" or "alone." For some, this is defined as a travel experience that plays out with no companions from one's life *before* that particular travel experience. This definition still embraces relationships made on the road with fellow travelers, which are implicitly sanctioned as having some meaning and value. Chelsea (25, England) demonstrates the use of this meaning in the following quote, whereby she uses the phrase "on my own":

> The richer experiences have been on my own, cause you have to interact with people you don't know, you have to trust people and you end up taking more risks by traveling on your own. But it pays off because you end up having more extraordinary experiences.

On the other hand, the more restrictive use of the concept of "solo travel" is demonstrated in the following quote from Emilia (36, Germany) about her travels in El Salvador, where very few foreigners travel:

> It was great because the people there are not used to tourism, and that means I had such great contact with all kinds of people, drank coffee somewhere, people sitting down, lots of questions, but super friendly people. And I get so much more out of this, even if it means that I have to sit in my room alone in the evening. But during the day, I had so many impressions and I get more out of that than being glued to some European tourist.

Here, Emilia implicitly rejects relationships formed with other travelers while privileging travel experiences that involve only people from the local culture(s).

The important thing to recognize about both of these usages of the terms "solo travel" or "traveling alone" is that both of them advocate limiting one's travel companions in one way or another to compel oneself to focus one's attention outwards towards other people. In other words, by prohibiting a comfortable protective social circle or even individual travel companion, travelers are challenged to exercise their powers of socialization to meet and interact with new people. Thus, unlike the discussion above, which focused on the ways in which long-term independent travel can direct a traveler's intention inwards and foster introspection and reflection, the sections below focus on the specific *external* sources of disorientation or stimulation that trigger the learning and development processes. However, since most travelers distinguish between experiences with locals and experiences with other travelers, as shown above, I have separated the types of experience into two sections: encounters with local cultures and encounters with the traveler culture itself.

8.3 Encounters with local cultures

Clearly, experiencing other cultures is one of the primary motivations for engaging in independent travel. Because intercultural interactions occur in unfamiliar places, they require LITs to behave in ways that are different to those considered normal or acceptable in their home cultures, which can be a daunting task. When exposed to a novel environment, people enter a heightened state of attunement and automatically become much more conscious of stimuli, such as smells, tastes, sights, behaviors and feelings; they become aware of things they would essentially ignore at home (Kottler, 2014). It is this heightened state of awareness and enhanced cognitive function that facilitates potentially transformative experiences (Mezirow, 2000; Merriam, 2004). Thus, the greater the difference between home and host country (e.g. in terms of climate, natural environment, ease of travel, sociocultural values and behaviors), the greater the likelihood of experiences conducive to transformation.

The LITs in this study are all from developed countries and, as discussed above, were driven to travel to cultures that are markedly different from their own. The novelty factor associated with cultural difference, and in particular underdeveloped destinations, acted as a pull factor for alienated individuals searching for authentic native cultures which are "thought to remain incarcerated into the space of primitiveness and timelessness" (Vrasti, 2009). As one LIT put it: "Although it's always a bigger shock and more difficult when traveling to a completely different world, I think the experiences you have and the journey itself are just much better the further away you are" (Lukas, 27, Germany).

Despite the strong passion for experiencing unfamiliar environments, all LITs told stories of dissonance and incongruence that resulted in different kinds of learning, not least because of the emotional nature of such experiences. Such dissonance between host culture and home culture can elicit a variety of feelings, ranging from humor, elation, and joy, to discomfort, guilt, embarrassment, anxiety, frustration and even shock. In addition, journeys were mostly unplanned, chaotic and often dangerous, and in their quest for "authentic" experiences, many LITs actively tried to "live like locals" by taking the cheapest bus available, eating at local food stalls, sleeping in cheap accommodations and so forth. Many deliberately subjected themselves to situations they would otherwise avoid at home, thereby paving the way for both heartening and disturbing experiences.

The following sections describe some of the experiences LITs described and effects these experiences had on them. Although there is some overlap, I have attempted to group these responses into common themes that recurred frequently in our conversations.

8.3.1 Realizing the limits of one's knowledge

Several LITs discussed disturbing moments that made them realize either how little they knew or how what they had learned back home did not match what they learned on their travels. For example, Matt, (28, USA), a high school history teacher before taking to the road, had been studying wars his entire life, but was nonetheless shocked when he saw the effects of war *in situ:*

> Mostar in Bosnia opened up my eyes to what war looked like. I never knew what war looked like before. [...] And it opened my eyes more than any other place that I'd been to, just to see, you could see it. Not only in all the buildings, the houses, the barbed wire, the shrapnel, the way the war had been horrid, and torn this place apart. But you could also see it in people's eyes, too. Just the way the war had torn the people's souls apart. And it really opened my eyes to what happened in 1991, 1992 in ex-Yugoslavia.

Matt was so emotionally affected by visiting war sites that his views on war have changed from an interest in the practical and tactical side of wars to the social aspect: "That's how travel's changed my view on history. I'm interested in how people felt." He noticed that his experiences of seeing war sites such as Auschwitz and Mostar had made him realize how little he knew of wars, despite having been fascinated by them and having studied them for a large part of his life. He also noticed how the experience of physically seeing evidence of the wars made him more critical of what is written in history books: "It's just totally different in history books. And history books are always written by the victors, by the people who won."

A similar example was described by Aaron (35, USA), who had a strong interest in history, as well as Hinduism and Buddhism, and had taken college courses on eastern religions. When he visited Angkor Wat, he was surprised at how little he knew about Cambodia, despite having learned about it at university.

> The big shock for me was, you know, Cambodia is a Buddhist country, so I thought I was going to see a bunch of Buddhist artifacts and things like that, but it actually turns out that most of the temples in Angkor were built by the Hindus. [...] You really see at Angkor the connection between Hinduism and Buddhism, because so many of the myths have migrated from Hinduism to Buddhism. So that's an example of the history sinking in. Having no concept of the history, or actually having the wrong notion of it. Because it is the national symbol of a Buddhist country but most of it is actually Hindu innovation.

Aaron explained that one of the pull factors for choosing Cambodia was to "recover" some of what he had learned at university, "because what you actually retain of what you have learned is minimal, because it has no practical use in your life, and I think you tend to retain things more when you experience them." Aaron's narrative is an example of cultural learning through the transformation of a meaning scheme in that the new experience can-

8.3 Encounters with local cultures

not be interpreted by applying previous knowledge about Cambodia, and the old meaning scheme is therefore transformed. The difference between meaning schemes and meaning perspectives lies in the broader manifestation of beliefs, values and attitudes (Mezirow, 1991a) characteristic of the latter, as shown in the next example.

Andy (30, USA) is interested in the recent history of a country, which he would find out about by reading books while traveling as well as going to museums. When traveling in El Salvador, he was truly disturbed about how little he knew about America's involvement in civil wars in Latin America:

> I was quite surprised to learn about the US involvement in all the civil wars in Central and South America. That's something we didn't learn in school. Pretty shocking. Shocking that I had so little knowledge regarding a subject that were historical events that the US were so involved in. US involvement is pretty shady in all of Central and South America, and it's probably not one of our shining moments in history. So it's like the skeleton in the closet, something they don't wanna teach their kids.

This example illustrates how a premise reflection led to a transformation of his perspective on his home country. First, his experiences in El Salvador resulted in a reexamination of his presuppositions about America's standing in the world. Andy was shocked about how little he knew about the USA's involvement in several civil wars throughout Latin America. Second, he came to understand that the USA is not very proud of this part of its history, which is why it is not taught in school. Overall, the premise reflection "leads to a more fully developed meaning perspective, that is, meaning perspectives that are more inclusive, discriminating, permeable (open), and integrative of experience" (Mezirow, 1991a, p. 111). This experience led Andy to alter his perception of his own country and also to begin thinking more critically about what he had been taught back home, which he had previously trusted and accepted relatively blindly. Since "American" is part of Andy's identity construct, we can also see this identity being destabilized as he seeks to distance himself from the negative aspects of that culture of which he has now learned. This is even evident in the quote above when one looks closely at the pronouns he uses. Although he partially accepts responsibility for past transgressions by labeling them "*our* history", he signals his rejection of the subsequent whitewashing of these events that occurs daily in American schools when he mentions that "*they* don't wanna teach it to *their* kids." Here we see an active transformation, as Andy alters his meaning scheme for his home culture.

8.3.2 Language barriers

Traveling independently to a country with a different language clearly poses certain problems, considering one has to find accommodation, shop for food and use transportation to get around. Although LITs, who fall in Plog's (2001) category of venturers (i.e. novelty seekers), differ from dependables (i.e. familiarity seekers) in terms of the importance they attach to language difference when choosing a travel destination, language barriers nonetheless were identified as a source of some degree of frustration across all parties.

While language barriers most often occur between speakers of different languages, they may also cause confusion between speakers of "the same" language. When Dan (34, England) arrived in the United States at the beginning of his extended journey at the age of 18, he experienced a true culture shock, not least because of the language difference, which he did not expect:

> I distinctly remember in the first few days in America, walking into a fast food place, and they didn't understand me. It's a totally different language. [...] I remember with the trains, saying things like 'I'd like a return ticket' and they just stared at me, and they would just look at me like 'There and back again?', and then finally realizing it's a round-trip. I struggled with that in America at first.

Dan was taken by surprise when, for the first time in his life, he realized the differences in English. He also became aware of his "thick southern accent" for the first time, and made a strong effort to shed this accent as a result of his travel experience. This is an example of learning through transforming meaning schemes that results in changed behavior, where Dan reflects on his assumptions and finds out that his "specific points of view or beliefs have become dysfunctional" and he experiences an increasing sense of inadequacy of his old views of understanding meaning (Mezirow, 1991a, p. 94). Since the new experiences cannot be interpreted using his existing meaning schemes, the individual is compelled to transform the meaning scheme to incorporate new knowledge gained by his travel experience. As evidenced by Dan's case, such transformations are often accompanied by discomfort and confusion.

Similarly, Alice (29, Sweden), who had a good command of English before she left for Canada, was frustrated when she realized her language ability was not as good as she thought and even questioned her decision to travel to Canada: "It was the first time I was away on my own, and I didn't understand everything people were saying to me. And for the first week I was really thinking that I made a mistake, but then it went away." In the case of Dan and Alice, the unexpected language barrier contributed to their transition shock at the beginning of their travels, but subsided within the first week or two of being in

8.3 Encounters with local cultures

the new country, when they had become more familiar with themselves and their new role as travelers.

The majority of LITs, however, described their frustrations with language barriers in countries where a completely different language is spoken. For Nora (49, Germany), the inability to make herself understood is "the worst" part of traveling. This is corroborated by Emilia (36, Germany), who feels that having "no exchange with locals is really heavy and is a real challenge", and Brian (43, USA), who found traveling in Russia and China hard because of his inability to connect with locals:

> It's a drag, cause it holds you back. And you can't really speak to locals when you don't speak the language, which usually means the locals you meet are in some sort of job involved with tourism. Or they went to school and are young. Sometimes it can be a real drag, the language thing, cause you really want to connect more and you can't.

The language barrier and associated inability to interact with locals were seen as a major deterrent to having meaningful encounters with the local population, as the following three LITs explained:

> When you speak the language, it is much easier to get in contact with locals, get to know their way of life. If, for example, you travel in Central America and you speak no Spanish, or very little Spanish, you have very limited contact with locals, and that's a whole different level of travel. (Lena, 26, Germany)

> Without speaking the language of the country, I think it's pretty difficult to get down to the grassroots of it. You can get around and stay in the backpacker hostels and stuff, meet other travelers, which is a very valid interaction with traveling, but being able to speak the language gives you so much more option about where you go, what you do, what's happening in the place when talking to locals is a huge benefit. (Alan, 42, New Zealand)

> For me personally, the language barrier is one of the biggest obstacles because you can be as interested as possible in people, and try to get in touch with them, but if you don't speak a word in their language, and depend on sign language, a pen and a piece of paper, then it's tough. (Lukas, 27, Germany)

Although interacting with locals was not the primary stated goal of all LITs in this study, failure to communicate with locals was seen as a main source of frustration for many. Lukas (27, Germany) also pointed out that when traveling alone "you definitely rely on communicating with people, and if they don't speak any English, then you have to get by with your 5 words in Spanish". Despite calling it "one of the biggest obstacles" earlier, he goes on to explain that for him, the language barrier creates an interesting challenge because it forces you outside of your comfort zone:

> And you learn much more and have many more experiences. When I was sitting at a bus stop and talked to this woman for half an hour, who just wanted to know where I came from and why I was sitting here all by myself waiting for a bus, I was as proud as never before on this trip that all of a sudden I could speak Spanish,

> and I think we could understand each other, even if she didn't speak any English and my Spanish is below poor. But you just get instant gratification.

Such learning outside of one's comfort zone was described by several other LITs, whose perceived inability to communicate forced them to push their boundaries and overcome some of their long-held inhibitions. Eric's (48, Canada) learning curve may help illustrate the point. On his first travels to Nepal, Eric "didn't want to know nothing about the people", because:

> At that time, I didn't know how to talk with people. I was a bit afraid of local people. I couldn't go near them. I was just looking at them but from afar, far away from them. I was observing them. I'm like this. I observe a lot. And I didn't want to talk to them because I was afraid, not of them, but the difficulty to communicate and not to be understood and not to understand them, and I was really nervous about that.

Over time and through cumulative travel experience, Eric learned to overcome his shyness and the personal distance he had maintained between himself and the local population:

> Now, the more traveling I do, the more I joke with people, just by gesturing, using body language and so on. So now, the more I'm traveling, the more I try to do that, and I like to laugh with people, and talk with people. But slowly, slowly this happened.

Traveling showed Eric a new side of himself that he did not know existed: "I discovered all the resources I had inside, and I've just become much more resourceful overall."

8.3.3 Dealing with different cultural values and practices

While Oberg's (1960) model of culture shock starts with a positive "honeymoon phase", many LITs who travel to cultures that are radically different to their own essentially skip this phase and proceed straight into the "crisis" phase. For example, Dana (39, Denmark) described her inability to even process the environment she was experiencing because it was so extremely different:

> At the beginning it was so unreal that I couldn't even take it as a culture shock. At the beginning I was just standing and laughing because the things were just so extreme. It was just so…like the lady, you know, just picking up the sari and pissing on the street. And the cows coming into where I was sitting and eating. And everything was just soooo extreme that it was hard for me to picture that I wasn't in a movie. It seemed like I was in a movie. It was just so incredibly far out.

Where Dana felt mild bemusement, Lukas (27, Germany) felt a more conscious feeling of disturbance during his first days in Pakistan:

> At the beginning in Pakistan, when we arrived and everything just crashes in on you, I just felt out of place. And of course you are a stranger, you look totally different than everyone else, you have no clue, and are completely overwhelmed with

8.3 Encounters with local cultures

everything that's going on. So in that moment, I was thinking "Hey, what am I doing here?"

Lukas even considered aborting his trip and returning to Germany after a week in Pakistan due to the intense feeling of disorientation he felt in this completely foreign environment. Crossing into a new culture severely disrupts one's sense of belonging, as one comes face to face with completely "abnormal" (from the traveler perspective) values and practices that make it very clear that one does not fit in. Here we will look at some of the most commonly mentioned aspects of host cultures that caused LITs inner turmoil and forced them to confront values they had perhaps taken for granted.

Perhaps a good place to begin is with an area that many LITs mentioned: environmental awareness. Most LITs come from cultures with active movements seeking to sensitize people to humanity's effects on the environment (e.g. through education programs that in many cases begin in elementary school or even kindergarten) and minimize this impact (e.g. through environmental regulations). With this background, it is quite disturbing when they are confronted with the local population's seemingly careless attitude towards the natural environment. As an example, Andy (30, USA) described his experience on a long-distance bus through the Paraguayan Chaco (a pristine desert environment largely devoid of human inhabitants). As part of the bus ride, they were served food:

> So the stewardess comes to collect all the Styrofoam trays to collect them in a huge plastic bag, and then she walks up to the front of the bus, opens the door and throws the whole bag out. And I was just like OH MY GOD. It was so depressing. You're driving through this crazy wilderness, and every once in a while there's this huge pile of Styrofoam trays and trash. That was a culture shock. Definitely. (Andy, 30, USA)

Nadine (23, Canada) described a similar experience in which she was in the jungle and the local inhabitants were throwing all kinds of garbage on the ground. As she spoke of this incident, she became very emotional, and it was evident that she was still struggling to work out how this experience fit into her ideas about her own culture and the host culture:

> They're just throwing everything on the [...] ground... that's just... but they don't have the education...nobody telling them that that's bad. Or they all wash themselves with soap in the river, and that's really bad, but they don't know. They don't care. No, not because they don't care, just because they don't know about it. And they don't know that you have to be careful. And they don't have all these laws that protect the environment. So I think it's really bad, really bad. And now in countries that are really poor, it's very important to make money than to protect the environment.

In this quote, one can see Nadine struggling to overcome her initial inclination to apply her own cultural perspective and condemn this behavior as a sign that the people have no respect for their environment. However, using her empathy, she can see the scene from their perspective and realize that it is a lack of education and guidance from the social (i.e. political) system. In the final sentence, she even goes a step further by recognizing that, to some extent, environmental protection may be a luxury that people who are struggling to have a decent existence cannot afford – an unpleasant but possibly true idea. Heather (36, Australia) echoed this sentiment when she described her frustration when she learned that the government of the African country where she was traveling was refusing food from aid organizations because it was from genetically modified grain: "So they've got a reason which may be a valid reason, but when you're starving, you want anything. And it really, it did strike me that so many people were starving and dying, and you could see the people were about to die."

On the topic of eating and food, this was also clearly an area that proved to be quite challenging for many LITs. For example, on his first night in a small village in Argentina, Matt (28, USA) had a culinary surprise: "We had sheep's head. A little tiny bit of meat. You could see right through the eye sockets. There were teeth on it still. The most disgusting thing I've ever had put in front of me. I looked at it, and tried a bit. It was disgusting". Hearing this story reminded me right away of the time in Indonesia when I found out after a meal that I had eaten dog. Naturally, I was disturbed when I found this out, but it also forced me to think about why I was disturbed. Ultimately, the food had tasted good, and meat is meat; there is no difference between killing a cow to eat or killing a dog, except that my culture defines dogs as pets which are not to be eaten. However, I cannot say that I became a regular consumer of dog dishes, as I found that particular cultural programming was too difficult to overcome. So instead, I learned the local word for dog to make sure I would not mistakenly order it again. Nevertheless, it did force me to examine my own cultural biases and made me more aware of the socially constructed nature of what I considered "normal."

For Dana (39, Denmark), her eye-opening experience did not deal with eating animals, but rather with taking care of them. As a true animal lover, Dana volunteered to work in an animal shelter in Northern Argentina, thinking she could do something good for animals and learn a bit about the culture's attitude towards animals. The reality turned out to be a bit different:

> So even the animal protection people, even the people here that are supposed to work with and for animals, the way they treat animals is just not only below what I can accept, it is cruel. It is brutal, from my little Danish view. And that was a shock to me that the ones that I was supposed to work with, to help and better this place for the animals, the way they look upon animals. […] I am just too fucking naïve.

8.3 Encounters with local cultures

Dana explained that the people at the shelter were only in it for the money and would pocket the money they received from various organizations. When asked whether she thought this lack of animal welfare was particularly prevalent in Latin America, she put it in perspective by referring to European countries such as France, where they use brutal methods for catching sharks. In fact, although the treatment of the animals disturbed her, as the conversation proceeded it became clear that what really bothered her was the effect this experience had on her own beliefs about humanity and her self-image, from her comment about her "little Danish view" to her concluding expression of anger: "I'm just so fucking naive". Here, Dana was forced to give up a cherished belief about the inherent goodness and trustworthiness of humanity, and especially alleged animal lovers, and to realize that she needed to stop being so trusting herself if she was to survive in this new culture.

This final realization is one that almost all new LITs experience at one point. At some point, almost all travelers learn that they have to be careful about whom they trust. In short, almost every traveler I talked with had an experience about being deceived by people from the host culture. For example, speaking of her travels in Africa, Sarah (37, Austria) reported that one of the biggest lessons she learned was "that you cannot trust anybody. That was actually a big shock to us. You cannot trust anybody's word." She went on to describe her frustration with receiving bad directions from locals about how to get to places. Although they originally thought people were doing this intentionally to be mean, she went on to describe how she eventually learned to shift her perspective and understand the likely reason for the bad directions:

> They don't know how long something is. Like they would tell you the next village is 1 hour away but then it's 5, because they have no watch or no concept of how long something takes. So that was a big problem in the beginning. Once we found out that you cannot ask an African for time or distance, you could ask how many mango trees are there from one village to another.

While this is a relatively benign example of deception, most travelers have more significant examples of being lied to or taken advantage of. This is a source of frustration for many LITs that causes resentment, but some of them learn to accept it over time, usually by learning to engage their empathy. For example, after describing an experience in which he heard that some less-experienced fellow travelers had been grossly overcharged for a wilderness trip by a dodgy guide, Glen (26, England), a somewhat more seasoned traveler at the time of the interview, paused and then stated:

> But you gotta put yourself in their perspective as well...because in a foreign country they see you as just a walking dollar. [...] Yeah, you just gotta be more skeptical, which is a shame cause you just don't trust people. But if you do, then you get ripped off and then you hate them even more, you know [laughs].

In this quote, we see Glen trying to find the balance between his desire to trust and enjoy the local people, while still preserving his self-image as someone who is not so naïve that he can be taken advantage of. In another example, Sarah (37, Austria) described how she took this a step further by changing her behavior to survive in the different culture.

> We had to get used to lying a lot [...] People lied to us all the time, and we had to lie as well. It depended on the situation. Like when a policeman stopped us on the road, you know, just because we were white, we had to lie. About how much money we carried, what's in the back of our car, like a computer, and I wasn't able to say a computer because they would have taken it away. At the beginning, we didn't know that and always told them the truth, and we always got in trouble. But once we started lying ...and the funny thing about the lying was, the more we lied and the more utopian the answer was, the more they believed it. Like when we told them little lies, they'd be like, "no, you're lying", but when we told them big lies, like once we said we're from Russia, we're teachers, or I'm a politician and I'm fighting against corruption, that's what they believed. So the huge, the big lies they all believed. And you had to come up with those.

Here we see a classic example of a LIT learning to adapt both her underlying value structures (i.e. concept of truth) and the related behaviors (i.e. lying) to survive in a foreign culture.

A final aspect commonly mentioned in the LITs' narratives was the significant difference between the gender role definitions of their home cultures and those of the host cultures where they traveled. Although female travelers bore the brunt of repressive concepts of female gender roles, male travelers were also disturbed by this inequality. For example, Syd (32, Switzerland), who traveled throughout Latin America with his girlfriend, described how the local men would often talk only to him and refuse to incorporate his girlfriend in the conversation:

> All over Latin America, mostly in countries like El Salvador, a bit in Brazil, a bit in Peru, the patriarchal model is so present that it disturbs me [...] You see that in the main attitude. They don't care that Ally [his girlfriend] is here. I try to be diplomatic and to put her in the conversation all the time. But you feel that.

Nadine (23, Canada) experienced this first-hand when she interrupted her travels to start a relationship with an Ecuadorian man. Needless to say, this triggered a different level of inter-cultural experience that forced her to "work on herself" and learn how to negotiate difference. She described how she had learned to accept things about him that she "could have never, never accepted in a boy in Canada." Nadine's boyfriend sometimes displayed what she labeled "a real macho thing", and to be clear, this was not something she just accepted. Rather, she learned how to understand it and how to deal with the conflicts that arose. She described the process of managing difficult incidents vividly in her interview:

> But here, [takes a deep breath] relax, just think about it. Maybe it's not so bad. Maybe he's right about this. Maybe I'm right about that, but we have to compromise. I learned a lot about that, about myself. And that's why I'm saying that I can

8.3 Encounters with local cultures

> adapt to a lot of situations. Because I'm always thinking that I don't have the ultimate, like the better way of living, of doing things. You always have to learn about other people, even if sometimes it's real difficult.

This new style of conflict management, including the deep breaths which she acted out several times during the interview when talking about conflicts, was something she was quite proud to have mastered. Of course, a crucial part of that was learning to understand her boyfriend's perspective, which she described as follows:

> The guys there they are so used to women who just don't say anything [...] Like his sister. She was like a slave. And I was like, "No, I'm not a slave. [...] I'm really pleased to do things for you because I love you, but you have to ask me in the right way. And I'm accepting of a lot of things about your culture, but I have a different culture, too. You have to accept it."

Fortunately for Nadine, it seemed that her boyfriend was also able to understand this, and thus they could help alter each other's perspectives and find a way that worked for both of them:

> But always, when we had a hard time like that, after that it was so nice because we just talked about it, and you know, we just grew, and that was really difficult at the beginning, but after that it was better because we understand more each other.

Perhaps the most important change in Nadine's identity was gaining confidence in her ability to "adapt to a lot of situations", as she mentioned in the quote above.

While the issue of restricted female gender roles was a consistent theme for people who traveled in Latin America, the problem was far more severe for many who had traveled in majority-Muslim cultures. Here again, even male travelers found this inequality disturbing. For example, Lukas (27, Germany), who traveled to Pakistan with a male and a female friend, noticed the gender power imbalance in the way the Pakistani women were treated. For a traveler, the Pakistani women basically did not exist, as they were forbidden even the most cursory contact with male travelers:

> Women had to leave [the room], and it was like that at home with the peasant population where that was very strict; they leave when you eat. You eat with the man, you eat with his sons, maybe with the mayor, but the women stayed outside most of the time, unless they get to know you much better, and you've lived in their village for maybe 2, 3 months. Otherwise you never get to see them, other than as a waitress. But even then they cover up. They'll sit around in the house without the veil, but even after a week, when I walked by, they'd still put it on. So it was practically impossible to get in touch with them. Also, they had gone to school for a maximum of 4 years, and didn't speak any English and all that. So there's just no contact.

Despite his best intentions, as a man Lukas was forced to conform to the local norms pertaining to gender roles. Thus, he was compelled into the role of what for him, due to his own personal values, felt like that of an oppressor. Needless to say, although this experience was discomfiting for Lukas, his female traveling companion suffered even more. It is one thing to be compelled to play a dominant role that one is uncomfortable with, but quite a different thing to be forced into a submissive role that robs you of your autonomy and even your identity completely. Such was the plight of Lukas's female travel companion:

> All business, handing over money when buying stuff and so on, that all takes place between men, and the women may at the most stand next to the man. Even though her Urdu was better than ours, when we bought bread, they only negotiated with us, and that escalated a few times when she wanted to hand over the money, but they refused to take it from her.

Essentially, her efforts to "blend in", including learning the local language, basically earned her the right to be treated the same as the local women, which was difficult for her to swallow.

One might expect experiences such as this to have the effect of reinforcing negative stereotypes of Islam that are prevalent in many "western" countries. However, it is important to emphasize that, at least among my participants, this was not generally the case. When I asked Lukas why he thought the Pakistani women accepted this situation, he replied:

> I don't know, I don't want to make any kind of universal statement about whether or not [the Pakistani women] accept it, but I think they don't really have the awareness, because they don't know, for example, how things are in Europe, and therefore they don't really feel the need to break free, because they just don't really know. For them it is mainly something unknown that maybe frightens them a bit, or maybe they haven't even thought about the fact that they are basically enslaved, to speak frankly.

This quote displays a kind of cautious empathy. That is to say, Lukas is attempting to think beyond his own perspective and imagine the perspective of a completely different group of people, but he is also cognizant of the limitations of his ability to understand what these women might be thinking.

Of course, the strong word "enslaved" shows that he still holds strongly to his own values about gender equality, but this does not mean he has learned nothing from his travel experience. On the contrary, Lukas has had a chance to practice the key emotional/intellectual skill of empathy, and his response shows that this exercise has already helped him focus on the *causes* of the problem of gender inequality, which can contribute to the search for solutions (e.g. promoting education of girls and women in such countries). Furthermore, the more diverse experience he gained through his travels gave him a more nuanced understanding of the complex question of women's rights in Muslim cultures. He was quick to point out what else he had learned about the culture:

> For example, that there are 15% Taliban in Pakistan, and that there are many different religious groups, and that "Muslim" is not a homogenous term. And that the

8.3 Encounters with local cultures

Taliban aren't that liked in Pakistan, but that they just occupied the country. These are the things that you learn. (Lukas, 27, Germany)

The ability to see beyond one's own cultural stereotypes was even more evident in the story of Eva (26, Germany), who spent some time in the United Arab Emirates. Since her story is quite revealing, it is worth quoting here at some length:

> A big surprise happened in the United Arab Emirates. That was our first contact with Islam, with Muslims, and that Islam itself is not an absolutely discriminating and misogynistic, and not a militant religion, which is what we learn in the West from media, newspapers and TV. We lived with an imam for a week, and we got to know Islam as an absolutely peaceful, democratic and respectful religion. And that was a big surprise for me. I did not expect that. Islam has a very deep faith in God, but also in reason. If God is the truth, if God is unique, it is a very deep, deep love for truth, which I found in Islam, and which I love.
>
> A simple thing, for example, which fascinated me was that there are Muslims who don't see the fact that women have to cover up as misogynistic. A woman who knows that she is beautiful doesn't constantly have to show it. For example, in the Emirates, not a single man shook my hand. For me this was totally strange. I felt despised. But in the end, Abdullah explained that it was a sign of respect for a woman, that a woman is respected as an autonomous person and has her place, in which men with all their militancy don't enter. Instead, the woman simply has her place, and one does not touch a woman. No one violates her private sphere. And sometimes in the two weeks in the Emirates, I felt more respected as a woman than in the West. And that was a surprising experience, extremely surprising. (Eva, 26, Germany)

This quote shows a radical perspective transformation. Not only does Eva come to understand her host's view of a woman's role, but she even seems to embrace it, going so far as to express a preference for the way she was treated in this different culture. Of course, as a woman, it is a bit difficult to let this perspective pass without comment. I would have to at least point out that putting women on a pedestal as objects of "respectful" worship is an age-old patriarchal tactic for limiting their freedom. Or one might point out that the specious paternalistic argument about not needing to display one's beauty cleverly smuggles in the assumption that covered faces are somehow the natural state of affairs, thereby placing an obligation on women to provide some compelling justification for uncovering their faces. On the other hand, in the context of the present study, this story is perhaps a testament to the transformative potential of the travel experience, as it seems likely that the imam's arguments would be far less convincing delivered in the context of an "Islamic studies" classroom at some "Western" university.

8.3.4 Out of place – From discomfort to danger

While the women in the stories above faced gender-based discrimination, many travelers also reported experiencing discrimination based on their status as outsiders. On the "lower" end of the danger scale, we have the simple experience of feeling out of place. Thus, many LITs told stories of how their physical differences from the local people triggered curiosity that led to unwanted attention. Alice (29, Sweden), for example, found it difficult to travel in the less touristy parts of Asia and Latin America because her blond hair and blue eyes made her stick out "like a sore thumb" amongst the local population and resulted in her being frequently stared at, which made her quite uncomfortable.

In some cases, this curiosity about foreigners can take on the form of more overt racism and discrimination. For example, Emilia (36, Germany), who is one of the most widely traveled LITs in this study and had a strong interest in engaging with locals, found that this was impossible in China. Although she had faced some negative racial sentiments before, she reported that "It's never been as cold as in China. I would say they are quite racist towards white people [...], and that was quite hard."

In a similar vein, Chris (36, Czech Republic) discovered the dark side of travel first hand. In a bar in Thailand, a drunk Thai man suddenly started shouting about his hatred for "farang" (i.e. foreigners) and saying that he wanted to kill them all. Fortunately, he did not make good on his threats. Despite his fears, the next day Chris sought the man out to ask about his hatred of foreigners because he wanted to understand what could cause such rage: "We talked the entire afternoon, and he told me about his village and that he had lost his house and everything, and his job too, because a tourist hotel was built there. And that really opened my eyes." Here we see the learning potential behind even these negative experiences, as Chris's efforts to engage with the other culture and seek an explanation helped him to understand a different perspective, which ultimately gave him a new awareness of the power mechanisms at play in a touristic environment.

In Bogota, Colombia, Max (30, Austria) experienced a similar form of racism, but targeted directly at him. Although he had traveled around the world for nearly three years, he talked about Bogota as the one place where he felt acutely out of place:

> Because I am a white person, a 'gringo face'. Apparently they have a massive problem with that. I don't find that good at all, but it was important. I thought, OK, that's what it's like. When you're being screamed at on the street because of the color of your skin, even though you're not doing anything and your intentions are good. [...] People stopped on the street and called me "son of bitch".

In this case, the learning-effect went beyond the immediate setting. Max felt the experience was "important" because it helped him understand the experience and feelings of people of color (e.g. foreigners, migrants, refugees) in his own country. Thus, for both Max and Emilia, being on the receiving end of racism was ultimately a valuable experience because, as Max put it, "I realized what it feels like when you are discriminated against as a foreigner".

In Max's case, he felt genuinely threatened by the local people, and he was far from the only traveler to have this experience. Indeed, the overwhelming majority of LITs told stories about situations involving personal danger, which ranged from comparatively minor incidents of witnessing crime and petty theft, to more disturbing incidents of being drugged and robbed in a public space, physical attacks, muggings at knifepoint or at gunpoint. Before looking at some of these experiences and what LITs learned from them, it is important to mention that some travelers even seek out danger as part of their efforts to push boundaries and experiment with their own limits. For example, Magnus (25, Denmark) told this story about an experience in Morocco:

> Got robbed in Tangier the first night there. And these two guys came up and rammed us and took all of our stuff. So we had to sleep out in the streets of Tangier the first night. They took all our money. We still had the visa card, but we wanted to be adventurous as well, and so we slept in the cemetery and woke up at 5 o'clock in the morning to the Muslim prayers.

After a disturbing experience, rather than using the credit card to bail them out of danger, they chose to up the adventure and danger even further by sleeping in a cemetery. In the way Magnus recounted the story, including mentioning the credit card and the nice dramatic detail of waking up to the Muslim prayers, it was evident that this was not the first time he had told this story. Here, we see a traveler using a story from a key experience to construct a valued part of his identity—namely that he was not in the least daunted by the robbery. Indeed, many travelers use stories about dangerous situations to display their courage and adventurousness, two traits which can increase one's status in traveler culture.

However, despite the subtle pride sometimes expressed through tales of danger, most travelers described real shock, surprise and fear about such experiences, as a few select examples will make clear. Within two weeks of travel, Andy, (30, USA) witnessed three different violent crimes in two different countries: "Leaving El Salvador, the day before, I saw a dead guy on the street in a pool of blood with a pistol like two feet from his hand, and they had the guy just laying out on the sidewalk, police walking around. That was shocking." Despite this deeply disturbing experience, he boarded the bus to Guatemala City, where he had the following experience just one day later:

> I was grabbing my lunch at the terminal and I heard in the street 'bang, bang, and I thought there were fireworks. And then the music stopped. And everybody's looking around. And a couple of drunk Guatemalans invited me to their table. It was the World Cup at the time, and I think Mexico had just played the States, and so they were like, 'come have a beer, have a beer'. So I said, "Ok". And they said, "Sit.

> Don't go anywhere. There's a drive-by shooting outside." And they were carrying the third guy to the ambulance. The guy was dead. And it turns out it was a gang shooting but they missed their target and they shot some poor guy who was selling shoes. And I was pretty shook up about that and realized this place wasn't for me.

Nevertheless, Andy remained in Guatemala City, and few days later witnessed yet another drive-by shooting outside a shopping mall: "There was a guy shot dead in a drive-by, the body laying out and they were doing forensics on the sidewalk. And that in ten days, compressed, that blew my mind. It was complete culture shock".

Ryan (26, Canada) had a similar experience in Honduras, where he witnessed a fatal shooting outside of his guesthouse in Honduras, which shook his confidence, despite already having a significant amount of travel experience at the time: "It's so easy to forget where you are in Central America. Cause you feel so safe. [...] I cycled 4000 km through 5 countries or 6 countries, and if anybody was vulnerable at any point on this trip it was me". Honduras was also the scene of one of the most shocking stories I heard in my interviews. Heather (36, Australia) was on a daytime bus from Copan to San Pedro Sula, when the following events transpired:

> Three guys standing on the side of the bus waved down the bus and got on. Two guys got on and just shot the first guy in the first seat and killed him, without saying a word. And then, I was sitting in the third row, so one guy died immediately, straight away. He was shot in the head. So there was no question of survival. He was dead. At first I was in disbelief. I couldn't believe that that actually happened, until you know, 10 seconds later when they shot the next guy. And then I realized, no this really is happening. So they shot the guy that was sitting in the seat in front of me. They shot him in the stomach. He fell on the floor. I was the only foreigner on the bus. Third row, first guy's dead, the second guy was shot in the stomach and falls on the floor in the isle. Then they shot the guy across the aisle from him in the stomach as well, you know, stomach region. It was all very, very quick, bang, bang.... bang. And then, I was in the third seat and they grabbed my bag. They saw that I had a bag, and they just grabbed it. My little daypack. The guy was shaking the gun in my face and ahm, was yelling, and I didn't understand a word, not a word. One guy didn't actually get on the bus. He stood at the door. They were all armed. The second guy got on the bus but stayed in the front. And the third guy came down the aisle, and he was the one shooting. So he's shaking this gun in my face, and I was scared to death at this point. I'm thinking, "this is my last moment on Earth". And two seats behind me, a man who was traveling with his son got a gun out of his bag, which again, is quite normal cause everyone has weapons, and shot the guy standing next to me in the shoulder area. And with that, they still had hold of my bag with his other arm, and they all got off the bus, and then there was more gunfire from the bus to the bandits and the bandits back to the bus. So then, people just grabbed their cell phones and decided to call the police, hospitals. They tried to pick up the dead man who had fallen onto the stairway, trying to pick up the guy who had been shot in the stomach. This was about an hour from San Pedro Sula, where we then drove. I was in shock, just complete shock. I was just like, I can't stay here. I was in disbelief [...] I had lost all my valuables, camera, passport and everything. The other people in front of me were robbed, they took money, but they didn't take their bags. The only bag they took was mine. And I probably, as a tourist, I stand out, I mean, I do stand out.

8.3 Encounters with local cultures

Heather's story, which she told me in Bolivia approximately two years after it occurred, struck me personally because I had taken the exact same bus several times and had traveled extensively in Honduras in the 18 months I spent in Central America. Although I never experienced crime of that severity, the potential danger of traveling in countries with exceptionally high crime rates was always with me, a feeling shared by many of the LITs I interviewed.

Although truly terrifying, Heather's story also serves as an important example of the willpower and resilience LITs sometimes develop when faced with such dangerous experiences. Rather than going to the Honduran police and finding a way out of the country as soon as possible, she immediately went to the next airport and, using her spare credit card, booked a ticket to a small island in Honduras, where she spent a whole month scuba diving. As she described it, this month helped her process the experience: "I just went diving. My whole brain was just like,...just dive, just enjoy diving, I was so happy to just be alive, thinking you can't do anything, you can't leave the country, you can't actually do anything else except exist here until things get sorted out." Although she was traumatized by the deadly shooting on the bus, and having to endure a six month ordeal involving embassies in three different countries and traveling between them with various preliminary passports issued by countries of the Commonwealth (at the time there were only two Australian embassies in all of Latin America), she rationalized the experience as bad luck and taking the wrong bus and continued her travels for another two years in Latin America.

Scuba diving is perhaps one of the more creative coping styles devised by travelers, but time after time LITs told me stories of how they devised strategies to persevere after experiencing danger or violence. The need to safeguard one's few precious possessions (and particularly travel documents) brought out the creativity in many travelers, such as Keith (23, Australia), who had secret pockets sewn into various areas of his clothes and gear that contained small amounts of money and copies of important documents. This was a strategy I deployed myself as well, with a 100 dollar bill and copies of my passport in a plastic bag sewn into the pants I always wore on longer travel days. In terms of personal safety, at the most basic level, LITs told how they learned to identify dangerous situations (e.g. night buses on certain routes, bad parts of town) by talking to locals and fellow travelers, and to develop a greater awareness of their own surroundings. Thus, Emilia (36, Germany) reported:

> And here in Zimbabwe, Botswana, there were many situations, there were many black marketeers, dealers, where I said, "I don't feel right here." It was just a feeling, something's not right here, I think I better turn around. And this happens a lot when traveling, that I say, I gotta get out, I don't feel good here.

Others took more proactive measures to protect themselves. Ryan, the avid cyclist mentioned above, mounted a machete on his mountain bike because "it's great for opening coconuts and as a visual warning". This was also something I could relate to, as I carried a pepper spray with me on my travels in Central and South America, which I would have in my hand in my pocket with the my finger on the button in situations I felt were dangerous.

Of course, not surprisingly, women seemed to suffer disproportionately from this kind of violence and intimidation, particularly in the Middle East or Latin America. As discussed above, as areas that tend to be male-dominated cultures, the gender role definitions in these countries provide sanction for aggressive behavior by men against women. One coping strategy adopted by many women is to travel with one or more male companions, but even this does not help in some cases. Speaking of her travels in Cairo, Alice (29, Sweden) reported:

> I didn't like Cairo much, mainly because I couldn't walk down the streets without men grabbing me and touching me and it was really annoying. If we – me and my boyfriend - stood beside each other, looking at something, people would come up behind me and grab my ass and stroke my back and just touch me in a sexual way, and I felt very uncomfortable.

Alice found that the Egyptians were not deterred by her boyfriend, as he, too, was a foreigner and therefore not deemed worthy of respect. The Global Gender Report, published annually by the World Economic Forum, ranks Egypt 132 out of 144 in the gender gap, whereas Sweden has occupied the fourth position for almost a decade (2016). Thus, this values clash is not surprising, and in Alice's case, it resulted in a professed dislike for the country and no desire to ever return there again.

Other stories related to me in the interviews were even more disturbing. On a night bus ride in India, Julia (37, Germany) woke up and saw the man sitting next to her masturbating while staring at her. She instinctively smacked him in the face, which almost resulted in her getting kicked out by the bus driver: "The bus driver yelled at me in English, 'How dare you. You're just a woman,' and stuff like that." The story had a positive twist when the female bus passengers took her side and started to defend her and eventually prevented the bus driver from kicking her out of the bus in the middle of the night. She was struck by the intense female solidarity that she encountered several times during her travels: "That's one thing I learned from traveling. If you make it clear to the local women that your intentions are sound, and I was always dressed decently, always long T-shirts and a bra and all that, then they were always on my side."

8.3 Encounters with local cultures

This final point shows an important lesson that many travelers learned, which goes beyond specific gender concerns and will serve as a closing thought for this subsection: While many LITs developed a healthy fear of the local culture, in many cases they also discovered that the local community was sometimes the best source of guidance and protection, if one learned to interact with them effectively. Thus, Brian (43, USA) mentioned the importance of learning "from the locals, about where to go, how to act and all that," and later went on to emphasize the importance of "trusting the locals, because you know, they're the ones that know what's going on, they're the ones that can drop you in a bad neighborhood." As we will see below, most travelers also had wonderful experiences as well, which is one of the things that keeps them traveling. But before moving on to these positive experiences, it is necessary to cover one final shocking aspect of travel which was perhaps the most commonly mentioned factor of all—poverty.

8.3.5 Poverty

As mentioned above, most LITs end up traveling in countries where the standards of living are significantly lower than those of their home cultures due to their desire to experience cultural difference and, to some extent, simple budget constraints. Many of them come into the experience with no idea what to expect, but in most cases they arrive with romanticized images of exotic cultures. Even in times of mass media and constant exposure to images from around the world, when one might expect a higher degree of awareness about the real living conditions of people around the world, these romanticized fantasies persist. Researchers have pointed out the existence of such orientalist tropes and fantasies about the primitive "Other". O'Reilly (2006), for example, described these romantic, orientalist views of "the simple, 'happy' native who gets by with very little and appears not to mind living in poverty – a corollary being that their culture or religious beliefs somehow inure them to suffering" (p. 1003), emphasizing that these images are particularly popular among travelers in India and, to some extent, in Africa. These fantasies emerged in the interviews. For example, Eva (26, Germany) admitted that she had an illusory image of exotic and adventurous places prior to her arrival. Although she had seen plenty of images of India before she traveled there, her main impression was that "these pictures are always so colorful". With these expectations, she confessed that she was quite surprised by the "real" India.

Indeed, many LITs, having either no idea what to expect or only a romanticized image, experience a "life shock" (Hottola, 2004) when actually encountering the high levels of poverty, disability, diseases and even death in the countries to which they travel. This shock is often accompanied by strong emotional reactions, including confusion, depression, disillusionment, and mental or sensory overload, as evidenced by the following narratives:

> I was crying. I discovered that the world was so different for me. For me, I was in a place 500 years ago. So for me, I was shocked, totally shocked. [...] For one day, I was like this, it's incredible...I called my sister and I was crying. It's incredible that people can live like this. (Eric, 48, Canada)

> It's really tough. What depressed me the most were those millions of street kids in Nairobi. That was real heavy. [...] There were these two boys, maybe nine or ten years old, and they were sniffing on a bottle and were living on a garbage dump, and that was just crazy extreme. And I bought them food sometimes. I just couldn't walk past them. And then they had this sparkle in their eyes, just because someone was talking to them and giving them something, that they are still a part of this world, and this sparkle...you never forget that. But when you see how many there are, then your money's not enough. That was real tough. (Lena, 26, Germany)

It was evident from the stories I heard that these encounters with poverty affected the LITs strongly and in most cases triggered the beginning of a profound change of perspective. In essence, experiencing the living conditions in the less developed world gave them a new appreciation for their own cultures. For example, Theo (33), who grew up in what he described as "very poor circumstances" in his Canadian hometown, realized on his travels through Mexico that the poverty he saw in Mexico is quite different from the poverty in his home country: "The children really suffer the most, for sure, cause don't forget, kids here don't have a childhood. [...] And I mean, I grew up very poor but I could go to school, and I never starved." Theo experienced a shift in his meaning scheme that defines his concept of "poverty" when he saw that being poor in a developed country with a functional social safety net is quite different than bring poor in an underdeveloped country that lacks the resources or social structures to alleviate the suffering of its least fortunate people.

Lilly (31, England) also described the shock of recognizing the vast difference between living standards in her native England and Bolivia:

> Poverty is incredible here [...] We have so much gluttony in England. People like me, there are poor people in England, but I always have enough food on my place. I always have my own space, my own bed, my own roof, you know. I have things, objects. And I'm not even materialistic, I don't even have that many things. But I still have stuff. And I have liberty, which these people don't have. (Lilly, 31, England)

Similarly, Ben (31, England) described the feelings of gratitude he felt for being born in England after doing a tour in which he went down into the mines in Potosi, Bolivia and witnessed the terrible conditions under which the miners labored:

> You can't ever describe it to people at home what it's like unless you see it with your own eyes. But I'm glad I did see it with my own eyes. I'm glad I'm not in their

8.3 Encounters with local cultures 211

> unfortunate position to be doing what they're doing. It makes you look at your own life, and realize how fortunate you are to be born in a country like England, when you see people in a situation like they are

Ben's story evokes a controversial topic: poverty tourism. In short, the very existence of an organized tour for foreign tourists that takes them into the workplace of suffering Bolivian miners to witness their appalling work conditions cannot help but raise some ethical questions. Indeed, with the rise of organized tours of this nature, including well-known examples in infamous slums such as Rio de Janeiro's Rocinha favela or Mumbai's Dharavi slum, the issue of "poverty tourism" has gained increased attention and condemnation from various parties, who argue that "it might seem the pinnacle of cynicism when slums become tourist attractions" (Frenzel, 2016, p. 3). Although LITs rarely participate in the kinds of organized slum tours that have drawn the most stringent protests, it cannot be denied that, in the vast majority of cases, even professed low-budget travelers such as those studied here are in a position of far greater relative wealth and mobility than most people in the cultures to which they travel. Regarding their impact on the host cultures, there is no clear black and white answer, as there are both pros and cons to this type of travel, both culturally and economically. Perhaps not surprisingly, my personal inclination is that the benefits outweigh the drawbacks. However, a full discussion of this important issue is beyond the scope of this thesis, and for now I must keep the focus on how this issue affects the perceptions and identity developments of the LITs in this study.

In that context, as mentioned above, the overwhelming prevalence of this issue in my interviews shows that experiencing poverty had a dramatic effect on the LITs in this study. This illustrates the importance of emotions in learning, which has been pointed out by several researchers (Dirkx, 2001, 2008; Jarvis, 2006, Merriam, et al., 2007). And as we see in Ben's quote above about "seeing it with your own eyes", it is clear that this in-person experience far exceeds anything they may have learned via their traditional educations in their home cultures. Eric (48, Canada) described the difference between formal learning or even learning via media accounts and travel (i.e. informal) learning: "It's not the same, it's really not the same to see it for yourself. And to be there and to feel it, and to smell it...it's totally different, really different" (Eric, 48, Canada). If a movie or news report or classroom lesson causes a feeling of dissonance, we can switch off the TV or walk out of the classroom and go right back to our "normal" surroundings, where plenty of tailor-made distractions are waiting to ease us back into a pleasant state of psychological comfort. In contrast, travelers are immersed in the culture, and the psychological dissonance that comes from witnessing poverty, suffering and living conditions that are shocking when contrasted with the comfortable standards of home cannot be easily diffused by comforting surroundings replete with reassuring reinforcement of their "normal" accepted values.

And indeed, the interviews featured many instances of travelers describing the confusion and even guilt they felt when holding these two vastly different images—living standards at home and in the foreign culture—in their heads. For example, after elaborating on the poverty he experienced in Islamabad, Lukas (27, Germany) reflected on his role as a traveler and the dissonance it created within him.

> You get there as a tourist or as a long-term traveler or whatever you are, you paid a ton of money for the flight and you carry with you many valuables, even if it's just your backpack, but compared with what they have in Pakistan, well, I could probably buy three little huts just for the price of my flight ticket. And the people there are totally poor, they fight for survival, they are starving, and you get there and travel through their country [...] Especially when I drove out of the city, through Islamabad, and you drive through a slum for half an hour and you see all the misery and the poverty. And then of course, all the kids and all the people they come on the road and want to beg for a few cents. And every time you go shopping, you're happy, thinking "Wow, that was so cheap". And for you, everything's cheap, but for them it's a chunk of money, and to see this relation, and the poverty and the problems that result from it. I don't know, it's just shocking to see this difference. And these are unpleasant things, and I don't think anyone likes that.

The appreciation for one's home culture that arises from this experience with poverty is certainly a positive development. Countless philosophers and religions have stressed the benefits of cultivating a sense of gratitude, both for the individual and the community at large. However, in the moment, this gratitude cannot relieve the cognitive dissonance felt so strongly by travelers in these situations. Due to their long-term travel plans, dreams and goals, simply turning around and returning to their comfortable native culture is not an option. Thus, they must come up with some other coping strategies if they wish to continue traveling. These coping strategies take many forms, the most common of which I will mention here.

First, to overcome the initial shock, many travelers feel a strong need to discuss their feelings with some supportive contact from their pre-travel value system. Thus, Eric (48, Canada) called one of his siblings to describe his experiences and receive some form of comfort or understanding, while Both Aaron (35, USA) and Ben (31, England) described how they processed their feelings and emotions by writing in their travel journals. Others retreat to the more comfortable setting of traveler enclaves, where they can discuss their feelings with other travelers, many of whom are likely experiencing or have already experienced the feelings they are struggling with. All of these coping strategies show the role of narrative in processing experiences and adapting meaning structures, as they each involve telling stories to an audience (i.e. people from home, fellow travelers, or oneself in

8.3 Encounters with local cultures

the case of journals). As Clark & Rossiter (2008) have pointed out, through such storytelling we "craft our sense of self, our identity" (p. 62).

These strategies can help dampen the initial shock, but in order to continue traveling, travelers have to find a way to manage the cognitive dissonance created by the vast disparity in material circumstances on a day-to-day basis during their travels. Several LITs described how they attempted to repress the disturbing emotions by training themselves to block out the upsetting scenes they confronted each day. For example, Aaron (35, USA) said that he could not allow himself "to be emotionally impacted by it" if he wanted to keep traveling: "It's the only way I could deal with it. Cause if you sort of let it sink into your system, you can't enjoy India worth a second". Similarly, Eva (26, Germany), who experienced a real culture shock upon her arrival in India, described how she learned to live with the harsh conditions she witnessed by shifting her focus to more pleasant things: "I got used to [the discomfort of seeing poverty] after some time. You notice other beautiful things. You try to distract yourself from this poverty, from this misery." Perhaps the ultimate form of this coping strategy is to minimize contact with the host culture by retreating completely into comfortable spaces occupied by fellow travelers (i.e. traveler enclaves).

Other travelers did not want to hide from the cognitive dissonance, but rather sought active strategies to alleviate their discomfort by changing the way they interact with the host culture. On the most self-oriented level, many learned to hide their material circumstances or at least minimize their displays of material wealth. This partially accounts for the decision of some travelers to avoid ostentatious clothing and equipment, but perhaps more important is learning how to downplay one's material circumstances in conversations with local people. Most travelers soon learn that people in the local culture have very little concept of the massive extent of the wealth disparity between cultures. Thus, Lilly (31, England) described a conversation with a Bolivian who asked her how much she earned back home: "When I told him that I'd probably earned 4,000 dollars a month, in England, he nearly fell over. And I felt, I instantly felt stupid for having said it, you know. To someone who earns a couple hundred bolivianos [around 30 dollars] a week." Like many travelers, Lilly soon learned to avoid the topic or just plain lie about it to avoid uncomfortable situations. Here again, we see the importance of narrative. Travelers learn to "adjust their narratives" (a nice euphemism for deception, in this case) such that they can construct an identity that they can show to local people that will not offend them or make them feel uncomfortable, and thereby make the travelers feel uncomfortable as well. This shows that "narratives are always tentative and evolving, which is appropriate because learning has not endpoint" (Clark & Rossiter, 2008, p. 66).

Other travelers find ways to reduce their discomfort by finding rationalizations that they essentially work out in conversations with themselves. In the interviews, I specifically asked about this issue, and the responses revealed the thought processes the LITs had undergone to help them assuage their guilt about the issue of poverty. One popular rationalization is to come to the decision that the scope of the poverty problem is simply too massive. Thus, on the topic of giving money to travelers, Chelsea (25, England) reported:

> The guilt factor has passed. I don't feel the guilt anymore, and in Africa I had it a great deal. But when we went in Philippines, and here [in South America] again. I don't feel that guilt anymore, I just think this is how it is. I can be you know.... You give money to people when they ask for it sometimes, but on the whole, and I think eventually I want to do something that's a bit more meaningful, worthwhile that will do good to greater good but on the whole I don't feel guilty anymore. Part of that to me is a fatigue, and part of that is just thinking there's nothing I can do. There are thousands and millions of people. And we're just a tiny percentage who have this amount of money, and we are very lucky.

The argument here is that if a problem is too large, one is relieved of the obligation to even attempt to solve it. Others take this argument even farther by arguing not just that giving money to poor people is futile, but that it can actually aggravate the problem. When asked if he gives money to beggars, Ryan (23, Canada) explained this rationale as follows:

> That's always a very... that's a tricky question...ahm... There have been a few people that I've given money to, but as a general rule, no, because my thinking, and whether right or wrong, I mean you might have different opinions on this, everyone does. My thinking is that by giving someone money when they beg, you teach them to beg more. You teach them that white people have money. Yeah, especially with children, and it, yeah, exactly. You're teaching them not to work and to put their hand out and ask for money from us. And it's a torturous thing for me because I have the money to give to them and it doesn't amount to very much, but I'm teaching them all the wrong lessons, and I wish it wasn't like that, but I think me giving them money doesn't solve anything. I think it makes things worse. There have been a few people in particular that have pulled on my heart strings a little bit too much, and I had to give them money, but as a general rule, I don't give money to anybody.

It was evident in the hesitation and hedging language Ryan used when answering this question that this was a sensitive topic, which he had spent a good deal of time contemplating. It also shows that Ryan himself is not completely convinced about the arguments he presents. When asked a similar question, Alan (42, New Zealand) showed a similar hesitancy, but he also put a different twist on his rationalization about not giving money to people:

> There's physically nothing really you can do about it. If you were to give people money just for whatever reason... you don't have dependence on tourists so an attitude towards tourists so they are just a money machine... That's not helping them

8.3 Encounters with local cultures 215

> either... So there is that guilt factor I guess. But once again, it depends on what you do with it. Just... visiting the country and distributing some money through travel, you know, is a bonus, as a bonus....as long as you don't give it to.... take advantage of the situation then ...that's all good. Tourist dollars are obviously very welcome in any country.

The argument about tourist dollars is a familiar one for anyone who has looked into the question of responsible tourism. Of course, the idea that simply spending money in another country has an inherently positive effect on the economy and the people is far too simplistic, as it fails to account for the many negative externalities associated with many forms of tourism. However, the point here is not to judge the merits of the various narratives which LITs construct. Indeed, their words and manner of speaking make it clear that the LITs themselves are not 100% convinced by their own arguments. Rather, the point here is to highlight the way in which these narratives are composed with a goal of making themselves feel better about their relationships with the host cultures and more comfortable with their identities as long-term independent travelers.

Some backpackers, recognizing the ethical complexities at the heart of intercultural travel, made a conscious effort to travel in the most responsible way possible. For some, this meant refraining from the cutthroat negotiation styles often associated with first-world travelers or even willingly paying above fair price just to contribute to the local economy. In discussing this habit, Lukas (27, Germany) stated, "I think any reasonable person would say, I'd rather pay twice as much for an onion, or I pay as much as I pay at home, I would do that at home anyway, but then at least the people there have a better life." Many struggled with this practice, as it brought two fundamental aspects of their desired self-identity into conflict. On the one hand, they have the desire to see themselves as generous people, while on the other hand, they also want to see themselves as savvy independent travelers who cannot be easily deceived or taken advantage of. Many who were unable to overcome that particular dissonance found other ways to contribute more responsibly to the local economy, such as purchasing goods from local artisans, tipping local service providers more generously than they normally would, or simply making every effort to patronize locally owned and operated businesses, including restaurants, accommodations, tourism services, and local food markets.

Still other LITs found non-monetary ways to give back to the local community. For example, Lena (26, Germany) often bought food for the local people, and particularly the children in need, a common practice among LITs. Others found more creative ways to meet a local need, as was the case with Keith (21, Australia), who recounted the following story:

> I prefer to do more action-oriented stuff; I don't like to give out money so much. My brother and his fiancé, who are now living in Cambodia, she works for an aid organization...but they needed tampons in Cambodia. So we bought a bunch in Hong Kong, and I was traveling though Vietnam, Southeast Asia with about 30 packets of tampons in my backpack. So stuff like that...that's how I... and to my mind... I mean, you can't help everyone, and I could help a little bit or everyone, but I'd rather just put all my efforts into one thing, and that's how I'd justify it to myself.

Here again, the use of the phrase "justify it to myself" alludes to Keith's internal dialog, as he uses key events and stories from his life to construct a coherent narrative that supports a self-image of himself as a good person and a responsible traveler.

As a final form of giving back to the local country, some travelers decided to give their time and effort by volunteering with local organizations. Thus, Aaron (35, USA), whom I cited above talking about how he had to harden himself to the sight of poverty if he wanted to enjoy India, later in his trip volunteered with an organization that helped poor children in Paraguay, an experience which he "loved". And Dana (39, Denmark) described her experiences volunteering with a British doctor in Calcutta who treated the local people free of charge at his clinic. In a similar vein, although many of the travelers did not make the time to volunteer during their travels, many of them expressed their intentions to volunteer or donate money to good causes when they returned home or perhaps on future trips.

The stories above show LITs deploying various coping strategies to manage the guilt and general cognitive dissonance they feel when encountering poverty. Each of these techniques helps the LIT construct a meaning scheme that defines their chosen role of long-term independent traveler as something of social and personal value, or at least something that they can live with. As a final note on poverty, we can look at how dealing with this disturbing topic comes to alter people's perceptions of the host culture. In some cases, LITs showed the temptation of subscribing to the romanticized view of poverty mentioned at the beginning of this section. Thus, in speaking of Indian people, Eva (26, Germany) stated:

> For them it's not just about material things. It doesn't matter at all how you look, which clothes you have, and you start talking about other things. Sometimes you start talking about other topics, the weather, philosophical things, God and the world [...] how the cow's doing.

Similarly, Brian (43, USA) described a night out with a friend in India in a way that clearly seeks to minimize or perhaps trivialize the difference in wealth standards between America and USA:

> I went to his house one day and just hung out, and his house was the size of my bathroom at home. You know...you could lay down in it and that was it. And we

went to an Indian movie one night, and I met all his friends and we got drunk. And they have lives just like us, just with less money. And they have much more acceptance of poverty than we do, cause it's part of their culture and part of their religion.

While these responses contain a disturbing element of cultural condescension and self-justification, others come away with a respect for the local people that is not tainted with rationalizations for their poverty. Thus, Aaron (35, USA) stated:

I've learned and I've seen, you know, tremendous, you know strength and perseverance of people, I've seen you know the utmost of despair and poverty, and those are the things that I've learned. I mean those are the things that I take with me, is how people really do live.

This final observation from Aaron serves as an appropriate bridge into the next two sections, where we will look at some of the positive experiences LITs had with their host culture.

8.3.6 The nature of positive intercultural experience

Although, as mentioned above, experiencing inferior material living conditions in less developed countries tended to foster an appreciation for some of the material comforts of home, this should not be interpreted as a simple confirmation of the "superiority" of the LITs' home cultures. On the contrary, the interviews were replete with stories of highly positive, or peak experiences, and it is important to recognize that these positive experiences can be just as disorienting as the negative experiences described in the previous sections. It was evident in the interviews that these positive experiences, which range from brief experiences with individual locals whom the LITs barely knew to deep connections made with entire local communities, were firmly lodged in the LITs' memories and, as with the traumatic or disturbing experiences mentioned above, had had a profound effect on their worldviews and even identity constructs. Listening to these stories, it was clear that these were usually constructed narratives that had most likely been refined via repeated re-telling, and in most cases, little or no prompting was required to uncover the lessons learned via these experiences.

Before proceeding to the specific values and experiences encountered by the LITs, it is also necessary to mention two key factors that the participants consistently cited as essential for promoting these deeper learning experiences. The first is that they found it crucial to maintain an attitude of openness and flexibility, so that they could recognize and seize any opportunities that might arise. Indeed, the most meaningful experiences usually took the participants by surprise. Here, both the duration and relatively unplanned nature of long-term independent travel are particular advantages. While it is certainly possible to have experiences of this nature on shorter, more structured travels, the flexibility that long-term travel provides makes it much more likely that one has such encounters.

From my own travels, I could cite several examples, but perhaps the greatest occurred in Paraguay. After a 35-hour bus ride through the Chaco, we stumbled into a small restaurant in Asuncion for dinner, where we struck up a conversation with the two brothers who ran the restaurant. A day later, we returned for another salad (which is hard to come by in Paraguay, due to the carnivorous tendencies of the Paraguayan people) and mentioned a music festival/barbecue festival/rodeo we had heard of in some remote part of Paraguay. It turned out the festival was in the brothers' rural hometown. One thing led to another, and after a bus ride and some hitchhiking we soon found ourselves honored guests in their parents' house during the time of the festival and for some time after that. Furthermore, one year later, we traveled three days from Peru back to Paraguay to attend their youngest sister's *fiesta de quinceañera* (a 15th birthday party which is a momentous event for Paraguayan girls), a true peak experience for me as well. And none of this would have happened if we had not been completely improvising our Paraguay visit (note: most South America travelers skip Paraguay entirely, a grave error), and if we had not had the schedule flexibility to spontaneously decide to spend a few weeks in a small village in the middle of nowhere.

This final phrase leads to the next key factor which is common in many of these peak experiences with the local culture: the need to get off the beaten path. Independent travelers are a rarity in Paraguay, and there is very little in the way of "traveler infrastructure". This forces travelers to engage more deeply with the local culture just to survive and take care of the basic travel needs. In addition, it has an effect on the local people, who are less jaded about independent travelers. Ryan (23, Canada), who biked through Central America, described the reception he often got in small towns in the remote parts of the countries through which he traveled, where the local people

> ... would respect me for some reason that I was riding through the countries and they were more interested in where I come from and why I was doing it than actually going after my money. Whereas, if you're on a chicken bus, no one cares because you're doing the same thing everyone else is, so they don't mind robbing you. Cause I know a lot of people that got robbed on chicken busses...,but...I'd bike through these small towns and literally people would scream and yell and clap and cheer and run to the side of the highway and I felt like a rock star [laughs]. I honestly felt like a rock star, through all these towns, I would spend my days riding with one hand on my handlebar and the other hand waving and yelling at people all the time [...] I ended up in the small towns in the middle of nowhere. I met the most interesting people who've never seen travelers before. And they just wanna tell you so much...they wanna talk to you, they want you to stay at their house, they wanna cook for you, they want you....it's just incredible.

8.3 Encounters with local cultures

Indeed, although this is not a universal rule, and some travelers certainly reported less-than-positive experiences in remote areas, in general, if travelers are still a rarity in a particular area, the locals tend to be more open and curious about foreigners, which often makes them more willing to engage with the travelers in a more meaningful way.

However, it is also important to note that far-flung rural areas are not the only place where tourists generally do not go. Chelsea (25, England) told of accepting an invitation to visit a family in one of Rio de Janeiro's infamous favelas (i.e. slums):

> And you realize, well, Ok, it might be dodgy to go with this person to his house in the favela, but actually, you end up having an amazing time and meeting the neighbors and getting a real insight into these people's lives. But it probably isn't the best decision to make. But then you go with them, and you have a lovely evening, and you see all their photographs. You get a real idea of what their lives are like, and they're friendly, and you see them again.

As Chelsea described her experience, it brought back memories of my own nearly identical experience in the same city. I can still remember the genuine fear I felt, even in broad daylight, as we passed through the gate to enter the favela squinting at a scrap of paper where our recently made "friend" had scribbled down a rough map (there is not much in the way of street addresses in the favela), and then what turned out to be a lovely afternoon spent with the entire family learning about their culture and everything from their favorite samba school and football team (of roughly equal importance in Rio) to their feelings about political corruption. Far from the favela tours mentioned earlier, this was an interaction that was completely devoid of economic motive. And we found, as many of my participants also reported, that the profit motive was not only absent, but rather replaced by the opposite: an overpowering giving motive, which brings us to our next topic.

8.3.7 Generosity/Hospitality

Almost every traveler I talked to had a story to tell about the amazing generosity they encountered on the road. For example, despite having his share of troubling encounters on the road, Nick (34, Ireland) was left with an overall positive view of the people he met: "People are amazingly kind and generous, and you've heard it a million times, but until you see it for yourself." Experiencing this generosity, particularly from people who were often far poorer than the travelers themselves, was a moving experience for many travelers, which forced them to ask some tough questions about their own cultural and personal values. As Brian (43, USA) said, "I've had people do things for me that were so nice, and they don't even know me. And that makes me stop and think 'would I do that for a complete stranger?'" And Lena (26, Germany), reflecting on her conversations with an Ecuadorian woman she met who owned and basically lived in a comedor (a small, very basic street food stall), mentioned something similar:

> And this is what fascinates me most, and especially with the poorest people that I've met. They were the nicest people that I've met, the most open-minded and most content, open-hearted. Oh it was incredible. And they welcomed me with open arms, even though they had to feed another mouth. The Europeans can really learn a thing or two.

In this context, perhaps one of the more surprising stories I heard involved travel to the USA, as one does not typically associate the USA with poverty conditions. Magnus (25) came from an upper-middle-class Danish family and grew up in very comfortable circumstances. In his 20s, he decided they were too comfortable, and he resolved to engage in long-term independent travel that would require him to get by on a small budget and live in a way that was utterly foreign to him. Upon arriving in New York City, he found that his Brooklyn accommodations for the first night had fallen through, and he decided to sleep in the streets of Brooklyn. After a sleepless night on a bench and a long and tiresome walk all the way to Central Park at dawn, he had the following experience:

> I arrived in Central Park and I was devastated, exhausted, cause I was also wearing my backpack and all my stuff. And this guy comes along and he says "Do you want a sandwich?" and first I say, oh no… but then he gives it to me, and I eat it, and then I get filled with all this energy, and then the sun comes out, and I'm like, I fucking feel this energy, getting stronger. So I sit there and go to a public toilet. And I see the guy there who gave me the sandwich, and the guy was a homeless guy. He was standing there, and I go over and we talked for like an hour. And it turned out he'd been homeless for like 40 years. And you know, I had money, I could've bought a sandwich. But I was battling myself, I was testing myself in this way. I go on these power trips to test myself. I felt so guilty. And for him to give that sandwich to me, that was like, he was like an angel, and that just stuck with me.

This experience caused Magnus to question his own values and motives for the trip, as well as his personal feelings about money and generosity. Similarly, Chelsea (25 England), whose favela experience was described above, arrived at a similar conclusion when reflecting on her experience, not about herself, but rather about her entire culture:

> You're invited into people's houses you've never even met, you know, and they just invite you for dinner, and suddenly you're having dinner with somebody you've just met, and it just doesn't happen at home. We don't have the same kind of hospitality.

Finally, the experience of Aimee and Glenn (26, England) shows the deep impact such hospitality experiences can have on travelers. They met a farmer in Patagonia, hundreds of kilometers from the nearest town, and ended up staying with his family for two weeks, where they helped slaughter sheep and milk cows and had experiences that they had never had before. Aimee called it the most "humbling" experience when she talked about how the family took them in:

8.3 Encounters with local cultures

> We were really, really part of their family, and I mean... it was only 14 days, but it was 14 days of, I'm having the best time of my life and these people want me there, and they've invited me, and you know...each day was like "Ok, we'll do this...we'll do that, and we'll show you this, we'll show you that", and it was just amazing.

To emphasize the importance of this experience for the two of them, Aimee told a story about saying goodbye to the family when they had to leave: "When we left them, we were both in tears. Like, we weren't even in tears when we left our family [in England], and we knew we weren't gonna see them for two years. It was such an amazing experience." Both Aimee and Glen, who had been on the road for over 18 months at the time I interviewed them, mentioned these two weeks with a Patagonian family as a true peak experience they would remember forever.

To reinforce a point made above, Glen also emphasized that this was a "two-way thing", meaning that he believed the Patagonian family enjoyed and benefited from the experience as well. He believed that was at least partially due to the remoteness of the area. As he put it, "We're getting to see a part of Argentina that you know for a fact no other gringos go to." For this reason, he felt that the family had a genuine interest in their lives as well: "The whole family were interested in what goes on in Europe, what goes on in England, how fast we live. It's a two-way cultural inter-exchange, definitely".

8.3.8 Community and family

Beyond the generous hospitality from which the LITs themselves so richly benefited, travel into other cultures, and particularly off-the-beaten-path destinations, provided them a valuable insight into the lives of the local people. The consistent theme from these experiences, which emerged again and again in my interviews, was the strong sense of community that characterized many of the towns and villages where LITs found themselves. Ryan (26, Canada) described the following scene from a small Central American village where he stopped at the end of a long day of cycling:

> This town was like the most incredible place because everybody in that town was friends. It was almost like a big, big family. Nobody was excluded. There were probably a couple of hundred kids. I would guess 400 people in this town maybe [...] And all the older people were sitting around in chairs and stuff, watching the sun go down and just relaxing, cause they looked like they had earned it. And every kid in town was playing soccer or basketball. There were three soccer pitches and two basketball courts, and everybody was playing at the same time. And it was just....Everyone from 5 to 25 to 30, everyone who wanted to play, played. And I just remember the laughter coming from everywhere, cause everyone laughed, and the sun was setting behind the mountains, and all lit up behind them, and it was just like...it was perfect. It was absolutely perfect. I absolutely loved it.

Cynics will point out that it is unlikely that every person in the town was friends, and no doubt the town had some interpersonal conflicts. However, the words Ryan uses and the details he remembered so clearly leave little doubt about the strong impression the experience made on him, and the scene of unstructured community play was clearly something that he had not witnessed back home in Canada. Dana (39, Denmark) directly pointed out the difference between communities in Paraguay and her own native culture, and then recounted an even more profound example of community spirit that affected her deeply:

> We don't know our neighbors in Copenhagen. We don't know our neighbors, we are inside a lot. And it's definitely a different life. With different values that comes with that [...] I don't agree with the value systems in Denmark. I don't agree with...so what I do like better here is the way that they upgrade their families. Family is very important to them. And they don't have a social system to catch them. So the things I've seen in Paraguay, small villages, there was this one lady and she was very sick. She's been in bed for seven months and how like the neighbors took turns in taking care of her. And by trying to save this little bit of money that they possibly could so that she could get treatment in the hospital, otherwise she would die. But the whole community came together for this one woman. To give her the treatment, and it was just this natural thing, like, now it was your turn to cook for her this night or whatever. So the whole family system, the extended family system in small communities, I think we could learn a lot from.

Dana's story makes it clear that her experiences on the road have altered her own values and created an awareness of an element of community that is lacking in her native culture. Jake (45, England) had the same clear impression of the difference between the communities he encountered in both Asia and South America and his own community back home:

> The whole community rallies together, the families rally together. Things that we have now lost, I would say, in Europe, sort of team spirit effort. This is something that I miss at home, but I didn't really think about that until seeing it here and realizing how much that means to me as well. The community coming together to help out.

Jake alludes to another aspect closely related to community that made a deep and lasting impression on many LITs—family structures. For example, Aimee (26, England), in elaborating on the strong emotions they felt upon saying goodbye to their Patagonian host family, stated:

> [South Americans] just seem to have such strong family units [...] But if you think of the typical Western family now, anyway, whether you are traveling or not, you've either got parents that are divorced or if they are still together they've got one daughter who's not here, or... you know...we just maybe get together for Christmas, but the kind of intensity of South Americans that we've kind of encountered ... they have such strong, strong family units, and I really admire that, and I realized that this is what I want for myself in my future

8.3 Encounters with local cultures

Here we see a traveler making a conscious link between her experiences on the road and her own intended life path for the future—a clear indication of a shift in her perspective on the importance of family.

Lena (26, Germany) also described the different family values she experienced there:

> And one day the mother said to me, and I'll never forget that, "As long as my kids are healthy, and I manage to get enough food on the table to feed them, I am the happiest woman in this world." And that really made me think, this totally different perspective that they have. I mean, when you look at the country we grew up in, where it's all about material things and money, and about who has more and so on...and there, people are happy when they have food to eat. They have completely different problems.

Here, Lena makes the link between reduced living circumstances and the strength of family bonds, which opens up a whole host of other questions related to materialism, suffering, inter-personal bonds, the nature of happiness and several other related issues. There are no simple answers to these questions, which philosophers, scholars and researchers have grappled with for ages, and Lena does not offer any, but her story shows that her experience has raised her awareness and compelled her to begin applying her analytical, reflective capacity to generate some solutions or ideas that she can accept. On this level, Andy (30, USA) demonstrated a similar level of awareness about these problematic issues and showed that he had examined the difference between American and Ecuadorian cultures on a different level:

> The lifestyle at least in Virginia is very accelerated, and people here in Latin America just value the family a lot more. But I think that also it depends on the economics as well, because when you get into the elite of a country, it's very similar to back in the States... identical, if not worse... more materialistic, more cut-throat, and more greedy. More than in the States. But then what I realized... people that have nothing, but they have their family, poverty isn't that bad. Life goes on, and life is simpler, and they live maybe in a small house, but they still have food, but they spend time with their kids. They spend time with their family. Food's cheap. There's always food. As opposed to life in the States, where people have money, but their 16-year-olds are rebellious, but their parents work. The kids never spend time with their family. They are resentful. It shows that either extreme is bad, I think. (Andy, 30, USA)

Here, Andy acknowledges some important ideas. First, he rejects the idea of a monolithic "Ecuadorian" culture by mentioning that the values and lifestyles of poor Ecuadorians are very different to those of the wealthier part of society. Second, we can see him struggling with this tendency to romanticize a "simpler" life. He has deduced that the family bonds he witnessed in South America, upon which he clearly places a significant value, are somehow related to the people's limited living circumstances, but the implied conclusion that poverty leads to happiness is so foreign to his cultural programming that he can't fully accept it. When he mentions two "extremes" at the end, he seems to be saying that people should be neither too rich nor too poor, but we can see Andy struggling with an inherent dilemma. There are plenty of people in America who are not super rich (by American standards) but neither are they extremely poor (i.e. facing starvation). Andy himself was clearly part of that group, and yet neither he, nor most of the people he knew from that segment of society, seemed particularly satisfied with their lives. By Ecuadorian standards, they were unimaginably wealthy, but they were still dissatisfied. Why is that? Is it a fault of the individual (i.e. Andy himself), the society (i.e. America), or some combination thereof? Like Lena, Andy's meaning schemes were still in conflict, and he had yet to reach a satisfying resolution to this value problem, but it was clear that he had begun to contemplate this issue. Learning had already taken place, and the next step would be to transform his meaning perspective itself and find a way to incorporate his new knowledge into a self-identity concept and lifestyle that he can feel comfortable with. Andy's story provides an appropriate bridge into the next section, which examines the fundamental value questions and even transformations that arose due to travelers' experience of other cultures.

8.3.9 Materialism, values and lifestyle

As one would expect from the previous sections, the most fundamental social value that was called into question during LITs' travels was the materialism of their own societies, which was forced into their conscious awareness by experiencing the immense difference between their own cultures and those they encountered on the road. Glen and Aimee (26, England) talked about the value disruption they felt when seeing the standards and lifestyles in South America:

> Whereas if you come to these countries, that kind of thing [materialism] just pales into insignificance because they're so poor and they don't really care about having a TV with Dolby surround sound or … it's not much of an issue. What the issue is, …cause they've all got six or seven kids, you know, they gotta feed them first. The perspective is totally put on its head.

Glen came back to this troubling idea later in the interview, expressing his frustration with "the thought process of wanting, it's the wanting process, the greed". He had clearly spent time contemplating the meaning of the difference in living standards and mentalities that he had seen and come to a conclusion that was highly critical of his own culture. Chris (36, Czech Republic) came to a similar conclusion about materialism and happiness:

> Where life is much simpler than Western life, you see people are much happier with their life that they have, and without all the shit that we have at home. They are just happier and get along much better because there is no envy. 'You have that and I have that'.

8.3 Encounters with local cultures

Of course, this raises the question of whether or not these LITs will actually put these ideas into practice when they return to their home societies. In fact, even before returning home several LITs expressed a firm intention to apply the lessons they have learned traveling when making future life decisions. For example, Glen (26, England) pointed out how travel had changed his and Aimee's life aspirations:

> That's probably the biggest value system change we've had because I know if we hadn't gone traveling, [buying a nice car] would be something we would have aspired to. But because we've seen what we've seen, since we've been traveling, it becomes less and less important. But it also becomes more and more clear and concise to see it for what it is. You can see that that car is worth that much, and yeah you've worked damn hard to get it, and yeah that's fine because you've wanted to get it. But at the end of the day you really have to ask yourself, "Do I really need it?" A 1982 Ford Sierra in England still gets you to the same place that you get in that car.

At the time of the interview, Glen and Aimee were still at an early stage of life, before they had taken such steps as buying a home or starting a family, and their careers were still in their infancy, so these lessons went on to play an important role in their later lives (more on that below). However, in the spirit of lifelong learning, the next example shows that travel can lead to this kind of perspective change later in life as well. Dana (Denmark) was 39 at the time of our interview and had already experienced great career success and the wealth that sometimes comes with it. She described how travel helped put that whole lifestyle into a new perspective:

> I did get the house I wanted, a beautiful wooden house. I got the beautiful wooden house right next to the ocean. At least my nature value was still there. I did get my beautiful house, and my big fat-ass four-wheel-drive, the one that I always wanted, the biggest four-wheel-drive that you could ever buy, that has lots of room for my dogs. It was a practical thing, too. So all of these things I did get, and I was not happy. I really wasn't happy. I always dreamed about something else and wanted different things. And I'm not saying I wanted more, because I actually didn't. And I did my ways, my job, always my job has been around people with a whole lot more money than I had. So I've always been with super rich people. And it's a very, very, very superficial world.

In a later story, Dana described a discussion in which a Paraguayan directly challenged her cultural assumptions by pointing out the advantages of the simple life in Paraguay:

> And [the Paraguayan guy] said, "You know, the people who live here, you might call them lazy, but they don't want much. You can go around and see. Now we do have electricity. Most of the houses don't have it, because they don't want it. Why would they want electricity? You know. They want an easy life. They want to take it easy. They want to sit on the chair all day long and talk. [...] You may think it's extremely poor, but it's not. They have their houses, they have their chickens, they have their one pig or whatever, and they don't want any more." The guy told me that the average they have is at least eight kids per family, and that this is part of the whole deal. And again, none of them starve. All of them have a roof over their head. And they have nothing, and they don't want more. He even told me that they don't want electricity, they don't want TV and radio and things like that.

> So when I'm looking for a piece of land or something like that, I do want some water, but I would like to do without electricity for a year or two. Because it keeps you… YES, I love being there with my candles, and they cook like in Paraguay. I learned how to cook Paraguayan. It takes forever. It takes 3 fucking hours to cook 3 tortillas. And first you make the fire outside, there is no fire inside. There is no electricity in these small villages. And how you know their whole thing, the whole talk is around you stand with the fire and you wait until the oil boils, but you stand there. Yes, she was cooking that night, we were cooking that night for four people, and I bet we stood there for 3 hours. It was only tortillas. It was dough in oil. It took that long to cook. But yeah. [laughs]

Here we can see Dana taking the next step to reject not just the materialist values of her home country, but also the lifestyle to which the thirst for material goods condemns many people. As Dana put it, "My life in Copenhagen was so stressful. It was about work all the time […] So it is about working and making money and buying my values." Nadine (23, Canada) expressed a similar appreciation for the approach to life in Latin America: "Here people can pass the day just sitting by the window or sitting outside, and that's ok, and it's not a bad thing. They don't have this stress that we have, this anxiety of always, always having to do something." This same contrast between the pace of life at home and in South America struck Lilly (31, England) when she was in rural Bolivia:

> When I imagine England in my head now, it's so full […] We haven't got a lot of land. We've got 17 million people. Everyone's got a car or two. And I think of Bolivia, and then having lots of space, and I walk a lot faster than anybody in this village. Like, I can walk here….and I notice all the Bolivian's thinking "slow down". And people have said that to me. I do walk a lot faster, and I still do. And I need to slow down. And it might happen while I'm here. I'm making an effort.

This final example is a good place to end, as it shows a LIT who not only learns an important lesson from experiencing a different culture, but already processes what it means for her personally and commits herself to making a change while she is still on the road.

8.4 Encounters with the traveler culture

While learning about and adapting to the values and conditions of the local cultures is a key aspect of long-term independent travel, there is another culture that also plays an important role—traveler culture. In fact, as far as the travel experience itself is concerned, traveler culture can be more important than the local culture for many LITs. For the great majority of LITs, long-term independent travel, even if it is performed as "solo travel", is inherently a social activity. That is to say, as much as they may set out to escape from the rules and values of a particular culture, it is difficult to completely turn off the basic human desire for contact with other people and some sense of belonging to a bigger community. And while some seek full immersion in the local cultures or travel to places where there is truly no traveler community or infrastructure, the great majority of LITs end up finding some sense of belonging within the traveler community itself.

In fact, although the degree to which LITs engage with the traveler community tends to vary as their level of travel experience grows, all of the 41 LITs in this study had encounters with the traveler culture and found their own place within it. This is important in terms of identity negotiation because adopting a lifestyle of perpetual motion means liberating oneself from social roles, pressures and established home identities in order to create a new sense of self and find a niche within the traveler community – a very diverse culture. In fact, when LITs first start out traveling, a significant part of their learning curve involves adapting to the traveler culture, the traveler lifestyle and the traveler value system. For this reason, this section looks at the rich tapestry of learning opportunities associated with encounters with the traveler culture.

8.4.1 Learning about other travelers' cultures

As with the previous section about encounters with local cultures, this section begins with some simple, yet important, fact-based learning. In this case, we focus not on the traveler culture itself, but on the native cultures of the individual travelers. One obvious defining characteristic of traveler culture is that it is inherently multi-cultural, as it consists of people from a wide range of different countries and cultures. Thus, in the course of their travels, many LITs find themselves in multi-cultural groups full of people from countries about which they know relatively little. Even travelers who came from multi-cultural communities noted a difference in the travel community, as noted by Nadine (23, Canada):

> Sure, in Montreal there's a lot of people from everywhere, but you never really mix because they are all in communities and they are all separate. So here, everybody is together, everybody is talking and that is really nice. And you're meeting... you're always making friends in other countries... so if I'm going to France, now I have a friend from there.

Despite the diversity of traveler culture, they all tend to share a similar socio-economic background (i.e. being from relatively wealthy, developed countries) and are united by at least their common role as travelers. As such, this makes traveler enclaves a potential comfort zone, which can be particularly attractive for people just starting out on their travels. The following story from Alan (42, New Zealand) is representative of many LITs who told similar stories of engaging with other travelers to get their feet wet in travel culture:

> At the very beginning of my trip, when I went to Brazil, I was definitely in that party mode. I sat and smoked weed for two weeks in Salvador. But I would say, I mean, there is something, there was for me at that time to be learned from this, just to be

> like it's ok, I don't have to run around. [...] And for me, those two or three weeks were a big learning experience, because yeah, I sat and got high with people from Italy and France, and I met these people from cultures that I had no concept of. So it wasn't that I was, you know, I wasn't learning about Brazilian culture, to be honest, but I was learning about all this other stuff. And now that I got that out of my system, I am much more relaxed and have started to enjoy the little things more.

For Alan, spending time with others was a way to ease into the traveler lifestyle, but also a way to learn about their cultures as well. The value of learning about cultures other than the ones to which one actually travels was a theme the recurred often in my interviews. Here is a small sampling of those stories:

> The guy in Machu Picchu told us a bit about Korea, and you just get a taste for the country from what they tell you. And you are intrigued. 80% of the people in Korea live in Seoul, and they've like never been out of Seoul, so it was like really huge for him to go traveling. (Aimee, 26, England)

> I've never been to Europe, and I never met a lot of people from Europe. And on this trip I met a lot of people from England, from France and from Germany, and we're always talking about the way we're living in our country, and it's always interesting. There's always a new thing that I didn't know "ah, I didn't know it was like that, I never learned about that." (Nadine, 23, Canada)

> I think that's the big thing...when traveling, not only do you meet locals, but the foreigners too, you start to learn so much more about other countries. You sort of get your little opinion of people when you meet them. And I think that's sort of what I learned. (Matt, 28, USA)

The final quote from Matt highlights another important aspect of this type of intercultural interaction among travelers. In addition to encountering people from cultures about which they knew almost nothing, many LITs met people from countries about which they had strong pre-conceived ideas. Such interactions often proved even more revealing for the LITs. For example, Glen (26, England) described meeting a traveler from Hungary:

> I [had] never met anyone from Hungary [...] so I asked a lot of questions about Hungary. [...] It's like watching a documentary, but better, cause the person's right in your face. [...] I remember I was surprised at how modern the infrastructure was in Hungary. I thought, "This is an Eastern Bloc country that's just become westernized." And this girl worked for like a media empire, whose biggest client was this guy who owns a magazine in London, and she was doing loads of interesting stuff. And I thought, "Shit, you actually have jobs like that in Hungary?" And it was a bit snobbish of me to think that, like, you know, I am English, and you are Eastern European.

Not only did Glen learn something new about Hungary, but he was also forced to confront the ignorance of his own preconceived ideas about Eastern Europe and acknowledge the condescending nature of those ideas. Lily (31, England) had a similar experience regarding her views of Americans. As I learned from years of traveling with an American, the USA is perhaps the one country about which everyone in the world has an opinion, and

8.4 Encounters with the traveler culture

Lily was no different. She spoke passionately about how much she hated Americans before her travels:

> I hated America, and I hated everything about it, and I hated every person in it. I just thought, ignorant, look at their terrible president and the terrible things he does. Americans are ignorant. They don't have very good education, none of them travel, I hate their accent, hate the dollar.

She then went on to describe how meeting Americans on the road had changed her perception of the country:

> I've met so many really nice couples or individual Americans [...] It's a different breed, and that's what I needed to see. I mean there are so many [Americans] who disagree with what's going on [in America], and it was important for me to see that. Cause you never hear or read about that. It's always just about "Americans as a whole". And I had to eat my words. I learned a lot, cause you know, the travelers they are intelligent people. They have a view on society.

Not only did she change her view of Americans, but we can also see from her phrase "you never hear or read about that" that she had also begun to question the sources of information she had back home that had contributed to the formation of her American stereotype in the first place. Of course, she would perhaps be pleased to hear that the stereotypes run both ways across the Atlantic. Andy (30, USA) described how his experiences traveling with English people had completely shattered his stereotype about the country:

> I always thought the English were kind of uptight and stuck-up people who have no sense of humor. And traveling, the English have been some of the greatest people I've met traveling. Phenomenal, hysterical. I mean some of the funniest people I've met, and I always thought they were dry, stuck-up, no sense of humor, uptight and condescending, and they are the complete opposite. They take the piss out of themselves.

The one group that does not fare so well in terms of stereotypes with fellow travelers is the Israelis. It would be disingenuous to pretend that I had not heard plenty of stories about problems with Israeli tourists, who have a reputation for being overly hard negotiators and inconsiderate about the needs of others, both fellow travelers and locals alike. Of course, the harshest criticisms I heard about Israelis tended to come from other Israelis with whom I traveled, a pattern which also applies in academia, as one can see from the many critical papers about Israeli travelers written by Israelis (e.g. Cohen, 2004; Maoz, 2005, 2007; Noy & Cohen, 2005; Uriely & Belhassen, 2005). For the purpose of the present discussion, it is important to make an important distinction that shows the learning process of travelers. Follow-up questions about Israeli travelers almost inevitably get to the root of the problem—namely, the well-documented tendency of Israelis to travel in larger groups (Cohen, 2004; Maoz, 2005, 2007; Noy & Cohen, 2005). Thus, I heard plenty of positive stories about traveling with Israelis. For example, Eva (26, Germany) reported,

"I met this Israeli and tramped with him for a while. That was really interesting, because I learned about Israel. I imagined there were about 60, 70 million Israelis, but the country is really small." And Lilly (31, England) specifically mentioned the group travel dynamic: "I like Israelis in ones and twos. I met some very nice ones. But you get three or more….it's the worst night's sleep I've had."

In essence, traveling in homogenous groups violates fundamental values of the LIT community, including the embrace of multi-culturalism and a professed interest in getting away from one's own culture to explore other cultures, as opposed to taking a little slice of your own culture with you on the road. Indeed, this was the exact criticism I heard from most of the Israelis I met and traveled with, who made a conscious effort to avoid groups of their countrymen because they wanted to meet people from other cultures.

8.4.2 Learning the ropes

While travelers obviously bring their individual cultural backgrounds with them when they travel, being part of the traveler culture itself, as mentioned above, involves putting aside that home cultural value system and embracing a new one. Here, it is important to point out that, although this culture, like any other, is highly diverse, it still exerts the same pressure to conform that all cultures exert. As mentioned above, in the long run many if not most travelers seek integration in the traveler community more than in the local community. Try as they may, it is more or less impossible for travelers to be accepted as a "Thai" or "Bolivian" person within the relatively short duration of their trips. As many expatriates will attest, years or even half a lifetime spent in another culture is sometimes still not enough to feel fully assimilated. However, as traveler culture is more open and flexible, it is reasonable to expect that individuals can find acceptance in the traveler community within the span of an extended trip.

Nevertheless, the initial exposure to the traveler community and lifestyle can be disorienting for many LITs. No matter how positive they may be or how eager to confront new challenges and unfamiliar environments, almost all of them experience some form of confusion at the onset. At the most basic level, this springs from a lack of understanding about of how to even accomplish the basic tasks involved with the traveler life. As Aaron (35, USA) put it: "It was this vague blob of what it is and how you do it" (Aaron, 35, USA). If one thinks in terms of Maslow's (1954, 1970) well-known pyramid of needs, the first two levels address the most basic human needs—physiological needs and safety. In inde-

8.4 Encounters with the traveler culture

pendent, unplanned travel, even these aspects are challenging at the beginning, as Eva (26, Germany) remembered vividly:

> The shock was the first moment when I got off the airplane, and shit, what am I going to do now? I have to sleep somewhere. I can't sleep under the bridge like all these people. I can't huddle together with the others on the street. I am not used to that. [...] There are no markets, well, there are markets, but no supermarkets. Everything kind of lies around on the street. First you think that you have to get your food from the dirt on the street. (Eva, 26, Germany)

Similarly, Dan (34, England), who traveled to the USA, a relatively "comfortable" country, described the difficulty of performing a very basic task:

> So I got off the plane and couldn't for the life of me work out how to dial an American phone, cause you got all the different codes. So I just, you know, all the people who wait with signs for youth hostels, so I just grabbed one of them and went to a different hostel [...] I understood that things were different, but I didn't understand what it was like to actually sort of, you know, shop for food in a different country, something simple like that.

For the first time in his life, Dan was forced manage his affairs autonomously. The situation was profoundly destabilizing for him, and he was "terrified" for the first few days and felt like he was "in prison in this youth hostel in Venice Beach". He describes his feelings as follows:

> I don't know if it was culture shock, it was just total shock. I didn't know anything about my situation. I didn't even have a guidebook. I was just there, and it took me, it literally took me a couple of days to actually pick myself up, work out... I mean, I knew that I had 9 or ten months ahead of me, which at the beginning of the trip seemed like they were never gonna end, and there was no one in this hostel either. I didn't know what to expect. I didn't even realize that the other people were not Americans, to be quite honest. And it took me a couple of days to really work out what was going on.

Indeed, there is significant amount of instrumental learning (Habermas, 1971, Mezirow, 1991, 2000) at play in the early stages, as travelers must learn how to find accommodation and food, and the learning curve is often steep. In most cases, there is a certain amount of trial and error, as Eva (26, Germany) pointed out: "You get an insight. You've tried the first things and know what tastes good and what doesn't. You haven't had diarrhea yet, and learn what you can eat. You also find out that these things they have are totally tasty." However, this trial-and-error transition phase can be strenuous, as is evident in the following story recounted by Lars (28, Belgium) about his first month traveling in Indonesia:

> I was not eating enough, really just going too fast. I know I was on a paddle boat and I even passed out. And then after the whole trip with my sister, maybe after a month, I remember I went to sleep in the evening and I woke up not the next day but the day after in the morning, which I'd never done in my life. I was just completely exhausted, the culture shock and everything together.

Still feeling the pressure of his value system from home, which emphasizes the need to keep busy and be "productive", Lars threw himself into too many activities and ended up on the verge of a physical breakdown.

To cope with the adjustment period, one common strategy mentioned by almost all of the LITs in this study was to seek guidance from more experienced travelers. In rare cases, the LITs had the opportunity to seek this kind of consultation even before embarking on their trips, as was the case with Aaron (35, USA), who before the trip met with a friend who had traveled for almost two years to pick his brain about "the day in and day out" of traveling. However, most LITs end up turning to a more experienced fellow traveler met on the road to learn the ropes of long-term independent travel. Dan (34, England) remembers the first few weeks of his year-long journey, when he teamed up with another traveler he met in a hostel:

> I was probably just like a puppy dog for a couple of weeks and literally just following him for a couple of weeks for everything that he did. I certainly, I do remember, I didn't have any opinions myself. I was fairly in awe of him, just because he knew what he was doing, and I didn't. I was fairly confused at one point about what was I going to do with myself.

Similarly, despite his aforementioned pre-travel "briefing" about traveler life, Aaron (35, USA) ultimately needed an "on-site" assist from a fellow traveler he met on the road to "figure out travel". He related how he had "teamed up with a German guy who had also been to Nepal" on his first day in India, which turned out to be packed with powerful, disorienting sights and experiences:

> We saw everything... naked people pissing everywhere, people...little kids picking up like cow shit and turning it into cow paddies for making chapattis, which is what I found out later that it's actually used to cook you know... you turn that into fuel, ah... you know half naked people, people drinking the water in the Ganges which would kill us, ah, you know...people burning, you know cremated bodies, people lying to you [...] I mean, it was everything. It was good, bad and ugly. It was a huge shock, but it was a great training ground, cause like I said, once I've done something, you know my nervousness is only not knowing what it is....you know, I am a very detailed-oriented person. So once I've done something, I can explain to people how it's done, and I can repeat it, I can enhance it, and I can improve it. But until somebody explains to me the details, it's this vague and nebulous thing, and I don't understand it. And so once I'd seen everything in full force in Varanasi, everything else was sort of repeatable, and I could sort of wipe away the things that I didn't want to repeat or have done, and repeat the circumstances or the mannerisms or the mechanisms whereby which I was traveling.

This story has all the hallmarks of a carefully constructed identity narrative. Aaron describes in vivid detail how his fundamental self-identity concept (i.e. "a detail-oriented person" who can "explain", "enhance" and "improve" things) was challenged by the completely alien environment, but a little guidance from an experienced mentor helped him see how he could apply his skills to master challenges he had never even imagined. Although

8.4 Encounters with the traveler culture

his fundamental identity concept of being a detail-oriented problem solver remained intact, the experience clearly gave him a deeper understanding of that side of his personality and the potential applications of this skill, all of which contributed to an increase in confidence and pride in this fundamental competence. However, it is also important to point out that he demonstrates the self-awareness of his own limitations (i.e. his nervousness about new things and the need for some guidance at the onset), which his experience with his German travel companion helped him understand. Nevertheless, nine months after this experience, Aaron was happy to report that "[independent travel] is second nature to me now."

Finally, while some people find an individual mentor, many learn quickly to lean on the traveler community as a whole to get them through their initial initiation into the independent traveler lifestyle. Nora (49, Germany) described her initiation as follows:

> In India I really learned how to travel. Yes, OK, you know where you arrive, you drift a bit, and you meet people. And I didn't know where I would be the following week. And then I met people, and they gave me tips, or said, 'just come with us'. And I did that. They were other travelers.

And Alan (42, New Zealand) described how fellow travelers help each figure out where to sleep, where to eat, what to see, and how to travel:

> Other travelers will help other travelers out; they will offer information freely; they will quite happily tell you where's the best place to go; they'll offer you information even if you don't ask for it. So I think there is a bit of a culture in there.

Indeed, long-term independent travelers do form their own culture. However, learning the practical skills and approaches needed to survive in this culture is only the first step in becoming part of this culture. This essentially takes care of the bottom two levels of Maslow's pyramid of needs, but to move to the next level of "Love/Belonging" needs, one has to learn the deeper values that determine acceptance into the community, which are discussed in the following section.

8.4.3 The traveler value system

By engaging in long-term independent travel in another culture, travelers remove themselves from their own cultural contexts, thereby leaving behind the values and behavioral norms that strongly influence their day-to-day lives. Although escaping from these constraints is a stated goal of most travelers, it nevertheless leaves a void behind that can cause disorientation—what Aaron described above as a "vague blob", or the uncertainty about what being a "traveler" even means. While learning the basics of survival (as described in the previous section) is helpful, to truly orient themselves in the traveler culture, LITs must learn the values that guide the community if they hope to move up to Maslow's third level of needs: love / belonging. This section will examine the key values of traveler culture and how they manifest themselves.

If one had to select an overarching value that underpins almost all of traveler culture, the likely choice would be hardship. That is to say, the narrative to which LITs are almost invariably drawn is one which features a fearless, heroic individual overcoming the many obstacles and difficulties that she encounters. The corollary to that is the antipathy they demonstrate towards counter-narratives that would cast them in a different role. Thus, we saw above in the motivation section the strong rejection of the word "escapism". Similarly, although many LITs profess to reject the judgments of their home culture, the preoccupation with the opinions expressed by people from "back home" reveal the difficulty of truly liberating oneself from the pull of ingrained values. Thus, Alan (42, New Zealand) was quick to point out that "traveling can be difficult. Sometimes it's bloody hard work," and Veronica (35, Austria), who sailed around the world for a few years, described how she always had to tell people that it was not all fun and games: "It's no vacation. I mean, it is incredibly exhausting to travel by boat, and sometimes a real challenge." Similarly, Brian (43, USA), emphasized the false impressions of his friends and family in America: "Americans always visualize this beach where you're just sitting there, and it's all one huge vacation. They don't get it that you may be sitting on a bus for 4 days."

One value that derives from this core principle is the emphasis on maintaining a low budget and avoiding any trappings of luxury. Some LITs even mentioned this mentality when describing the process before their departure. Thus, several LITs alluded to having rid themselves of the material baggage of their home lives before even setting out to travel. For Max (30, Austria), the decision to leave coincided with the realization that he needed to free himself from his former life by "shedding all those material things" because he realized that he cannot start his journey with the burden of having to pay rent to store his belongings. Max needed to burn his material bridges, because only then he could feel completely liberated to travel indefinitely:

> I have just shed all material things because I knew that I couldn't start traveling if I felt burdened by something, when I know I have to pay rent somewhere to keep all my things. This is essential for me. There can't be a reason why I have to be home on day X. This is why I gradually let go of all the things that entrenched me with [my hometown] and my apartment. Now it's all gone.

Max reduced his plethora of "stuff" to a small box of memorabilia, which he stored in his parent's house. This story rang true for me, as I took the same approach before my first

8.4 Encounters with the traveler culture

long trip: selling my car, giving up my apartment, and storing my few belongings in my mother's basement.

Once on the road, most LITs practiced what they preached. Of the LITs I interviewed, 29 were in the low range ($10-20 a day), and 12 were in the low-medium range ($ 20-40 a day). Beyond extending their travels, there is another key perceived benefit of traveling on the cheap, which Lars (28, Belgium) pointed out in his interview: "And budget travel is nice for the budget, but it's also nice for the story. It's just because you're looking for the cheapest, sometimes you're getting in difficult situations, you've got all these stories". Of course, these are the stories that are incorporated into one's internal identity narrative, but they are also important currency for negotiating one's identity and status within the traveler community (and eventually back in one's home culture). Brian (43, USA) showed his awareness of the traveler budget scale in his response to my question about his typical travel budget: "It depends on the country, but low, low, low. I'm as low as… I am probably just one notch above as cheap as you can go. I would eat street food." While direct talk about a budget is rare among travelers, when groups of travelers assemble and begin telling stories, it frequently devolves into an effort to one-up each other with tales of the cheapest food, accommodation, or mode of transport one has experienced and the misfortunes it caused.

Besides the stories that highlight low budget, there are also key visual signs used to indicate low-budget travel: clothing and equipment. Although to the outsider, typical traveler clothing and backpacks may appear shabby, within the traveler culture, they are an indicator for endurance, hardship, experience and competence (Sørensen, 2003). I met novice travelers who went to great length to make newer backpacks look well-used by deliberately making them dirty or by attaching labels of countries visited or other visual signs to suggest that they were well-traveled. Similarly, there is a certain clothing style that travelers deem acceptable. Of course, there is a range there as well, but one does not generally see travelers with Ralph Lauren polo shirts or Lacoste shoes. Rather, some travelers incorporate key items of local attire (boatman pants are a popular choice in India and Southeast Asia), and others opt for more traveler-specific garb. For example, "Beer Laos" (the local brew) shirts were popular in my time in that area of the world, and clothing featuring favorite iconic figures of the travel culture (most notably Che Guevara and Bob Marley, and sometimes a mash-up of the two) was universally prominent.

Indeed, with many travelers, these clothes take on a symbolic significance as part of their travel identity. A former travel companion of mine from Japan recently posted a picture of his favorite travel pants that he wore throughout his long-term journey through South

America on his social media website with just the caption, "I miss..." The pants had been worn down and many times patched and sewn, but he has been unable to part with them, even after years back in his home culture in Japan. I was able to write back to express my understanding, as I have a very similar pair of pants from my own travels, also more patches and thread than fabric at this point, buried in a corner of my closet, waiting patiently for the day they will be called into action again. For both of us, our pants have become icons that evoke our former identities as LITs.

For Oliver and Veronica (51 & 35, Austria), our travelers who sailed around the world for almost 5 years, they have the same connection, but with a much larger iconic object: their boat: "The boat has received a soul. [...] When you get on the boat, you love it, when you open the hatch, the smell and all that, it's just incredibly beautiful. There is this strong connection." Despite their love of the boat, they, too, are quick to point out that it is a "low-budget" boat. That is, they discussed at length how the boat is of modest size and style, even explicitly linking it to an iconic vehicle of the earlier hippie traveler movement: "And we always said our boat is a VW van from the 1960s, a hippie boat. And with such a van, people went on grand journeys". Veronica also argued that the modest scale of their boat encouraged interaction with the locals on shore: "You have to imagine, if you show up there with such an expensive boat, the locals know exactly, they are not stupid, that's a millionaire". She went on to describe how their boat was always where "the best parties" happened, and the people on expensive yachts would peer at them with envy. Oliver took the contrast with the upper-class boaters a step further when he suggested, "And these people don't understand that they can't travel as long because they need more money for their boats." Although one could question the generalization that all mega-wealthy owners of massive yachts have serious money concerns that keep them from spending time on their boats, the story serves as a prime example of a narrative carefully constructed to celebrate the values of frugality and simplicity that travelers hold dear, as well as to highlight the link between these values and the meaningful intercultural interactions that they promote.

Moving on from physical symbols of values, a corollary value to the low-budget ethos is the pride travelers take in their ability to avoid getting swindled by unscrupulous characters and to negotiate the best possible price for the goods and services they consume on the road. This might be considered a kind of "road savvy", which many travelers interpret as a sign of experience and "tenure" on the road. In some cases, the stories designed to point out one's own wisdom come at the expense of others. Thus, Aimee (26, England)

8.4 Encounters with the traveler culture

told a story of some young female travelers who got ripped off by a tour provider and then explained:

> I think that comes from experience of traveling. Because you can see that in the naivety of first-time travelers. Like those girls that we saw in Uyuni, who paid that extortionate amount for the first trip that they came across because they liked the agent and he was a good salesman. [...] So I think you can definitely tell the difference between first-time travelers and experienced ones...and we're probably somewhere in the middle.

By placing herself in the middle of a continuum, Aimee demonstrates her awareness that this is a competence that must be acquired through travel experience and also reveals her desire to achieve greater mastery in this area.

Of course, despite celebrating this type of negotiating skill, it is also a source of tension within the overall traveler ethos. First, on some level, it is clearly at odds with the usual traveler's proclaimed disdain for materialism. If one really does not care about material things, should one really be so concerned about clinging to every dollar or euro? Second, as we saw above, the ever-present awareness of the stark contrast between the travelers' own material circumstances and those of the locals in the poorer countries where most LITs travel gives rise to lingering guilt feelings in travelers. In this context, the ability to squeeze the most possible goods or services out of the poorer local culture starts to look less and less heroic. And here, it is necessary to mention again the Israeli travelers whose negotiating behavior is so often the target of criticism from their fellow travelers. In the context of bargaining, this strong antipathy certainly calls to mind a quote by Hermann Hesse (1919): "If you hate a person, you hate something in him that is a part of yourself." (p. 182).

Moving away from the theme of hardship, it is important to mention autonomy, one of the most crucial traveler values. To express the value of this concept, many travelers fall back on comparisons to their lives back in the "real world." For example, Lilly (31, England) vividly recounted the moment of transition from the stress of life in her home culture to the relief of her life on the road:

> All that stress in that mad month before I left. I mean, I was up till 2 in the morning the two nights before I left....I was on it... ...internet banking, sorting all my stuff out....emailing...setting up my Hotmail account, I mean, just....it's a huge project before you go. And then you get here, and you don't have anything to do...suddenly, other than sending emails to mom and dad. And yeah, no more work stress, no more car, no more traffic....yeah, wonderful. And I just remember thinking [deep inhale and exhale]....freedom...wow!

Time and again, travelers stressed the importance of being able to structure their days in whatever way they saw fit, with nobody else telling them what to do:

> For me travel is about absolute freedom. [...] It's waking up in the morning and being able to say, well today I'm gonna stay in and read my book or I'm going to climb a volcano, or just jump on a train or bus and go to wherever, or just hang out with those guys because... just because. (Dan, 34, England)

> I'm sitting here, drinking coffee, doing a crossword puzzle, which I would love to do on any normal day. But no, I can't because I have to go off to work. It's about the confines that other people put upon you, whereas here they're my self-constraints. You do whatever you want. It's freedom, and options. Even if you don't take them all. (Brian, 43, USA)

> ...because traveling independently gives you more freedom, which is also one of the reasons why you travel, it gives you freedom and I, I want to do what I want to do when I travel. As I said earlier, when I get somewhere and I don't like it, then I go somewhere else. If I get somewhere where I'm not supposed to stay and I really like it, then I stay. (Alice, 29, Sweden)

Some LITs were already aware of the importance of this freedom in the planning stages of their trips. Of the 41 LITs I interviewed, only three had left their home countries on a "traditional" round-the-world ticket, with pre-booked flights dividing up their travel. Others had investigated this option, but ultimately rejected it because they did not want to be limited by pre-defined flight dates or itineraries. Thus, Max (30, Austria), who did not have much previous travel experience, researched his options before leaving because he "had no clue about backpacking and all these round-the-world trips". He soon decided that such trips would be "quite limiting in that they are only valid for one year, always go in one direction and are tied to time windows in that you have to move on to the next destination within two months".

Of course, in the context of autonomy and freedom, the length of travel is another key factor. In the ideal case, according to many travelers, one not only leaves aside an itinerary but is able to travel with no fixed return date at all. As one LIT stated: "If I had a return date, then I would be already on the countdown to being home, even though I might actually have to go home at the same time, it doesn't feel like I have to" (Nick, 34, Ireland). Likewise, Ben (31, England) explained the attraction of traveling without a specified return date:

> You just feel like getting away from it all and you just head out in some random direction and see where it takes you. If you're away for a month, you are very structured, and you know exactly what you're gonna do, but if you've got plenty of time and you got freedom to do whatever you want, there's no point in having rigid plans.

Many LITs pointed out how this abundance of time had a profound impact on their mindsets and the way they react to certain situations. For example, Emilia (36, Germany) described her experience trying to take a bus from one town to another:

8.4 Encounters with the traveler culture

> In India on an island, the bus was supposed to come at 6 in the morning. AT 1 pm it still wasn't there. And then they said 'Oh, maybe not today, maybe tomorrow'. You know, and then you go home, and look for a room and what not, and try again the next day. And all that with a big smile.

Because she is not chained to a fixed schedule, this experience does not really bother Emilia in the least. Similarly, Lukas (27, Germany) described settling into the rhythm of life in a different culture: "Then you get in the rhythm where you know when stores are open, or that bus departure times are sometimes delayed [laugh] a good 5 hours, and you should be happy if they depart at all." Richards and Wilson (2004c) emphasize this important characteristic of long-term independent travel in their book *The Global Nomad: Backpacker Travel in Theory and Practice*:

> Because backpackers are time-rich individuals, they can also engage in time-intensive activities that they may not be able to indulge in at home – such as 'doing nothing'. The time-richness of the destination allows them to adjust their expectations to suit the time culture they are in. It is no problem to the backpacker to arrive a day late, particularly if this generates a usable story of travel hardship, but for the package tourist, delay is a loss of experience; for the backpacker, it is an integral part of the experience (p. 258).

Since the quote above brings up package tourists, this is an appropriate place to mention a key aspect of traveler identity—touristophobia. As with most cultures, traveler culture is prone to self-definition by contrasting with the perceived "other." Of course, the first obvious target for this type of self-definition through opposition is the group of "regular people back home" who do not engage in intercultural travel at all. However, the difference between LITs and these "non-travelers" is rather obvious, and the relationship between them tends to be one of mutual rejection (i.e. the folks back home tend to reject the travelers as well). Furthermore, by definition, this group of people is not present during travel, so there is very little interaction with this culture (at least physically, although modern communication technology has blurred this line as well). For these reasons, the rejection of "regular people" is almost taken for granted among travelers, which makes the contrast with this group less useful for LITs as a tool for defining their values and identities.

For this purpose, LITs turn instead to another group of people who, because they are engaged in an activity similar to that of the LITs, are more threatening to the LIT identity—tourists, and in particular, package tourists. As the LIT identity, as discussed above, is fundamentally grounded in the concepts of hardship and challenge, package tourists are obviously the perfect foil for demarcating their identities. Thus, as one would expect, LITs' opinions of package tourists range from simple rejection to profound disdain bordering on hatred. At the less emotionally charged end of the spectrum, LITs are quick to point out that most package travelers travel in groups, thereby forfeiting the freedom and autonomy that LITs prize. Thus, Brian (USA, 43) hated the idea of being "stuck with people you may not like", while Heather (36, Australia) argued:

> I don't want to go on a package tour to stop and then eat for 2 hours. I am traveling to experience and see something that I don't normally experience or see. I don't care if I don't eat for 12 hours. That's ok for me. Even if you get a bunch of travelers on a tour, you're gonna get people with different time schedules and habits and needs and different expectations.

Package tours also violate LITs' low-budget ethos, and many LITs were quick to point out the insulating, sanitizing effect wealth exerts on the travel experience:

> It's an issue of social contact really. You stay in expensive hotels and you never get to meet anybody. The room is always very nice, you've got your own TV and everything like that, so basically you spend the time traveling through the lobby in three minutes. (Alan, 42, New Zealand)

> You're stuck in a hotel. You don't meet people in the Intercontinental or the Marriott Hotel that you wanna spend time with, do you? You meet interesting people when you stay in backpacker places or when you just go out and stay in the middle of nowhere. Or you just meet local people and chat with them. [...] If you're inside that Marriott Hotel, you could be in London, New York, Panama City, Sao Paolo, it could be anywhere. They're all just the same the world over. I can't see any other way of [traveling] if you wanna actually see the world. (Ben, 31, England)

For most LITs, these kinds of package experiences do not even qualify as travel. Asked if he had ever experienced this kind of package vacation, Lukas (27, Germany) replied, "That happened to me once (laughs), a week in Crete. It wasn't all inclusive, but it was a hotel with breakfast. I don't know. That's a waste of time, that's not traveling."

While luxury is soundly rejected, the ultimate fault of the package traveler, from the LIT perspective, is the complete lack of initiative and self-reliance they display by choosing to engage in such travel activities. A brief sampling of LIT comments about package tours will highlight their deep antipathy for the concept of "hav[ing] somebody sort it all out for you" (Ben, 31, England):

> I could not go on a package tour again…that was the one and only time I did it and I am glad that I did it. And now I can say "I've done it and not a chance we'll ever do it again." [...] It was simultaneously the most amusing and most horrendous experience of my life. (Dan, 34, England)

> I hated it, and despised it, never want to do it again. I wish I would have never done it. (Matt, 28, USA).

> I'd fucking kill somebody. Oh my God no…I hate that stuff. I hate that. The idea of paying somebody else to organize your shit for you….it sucks. (Nick, 34, Ireland)

Max (36, Austria, 2nd) expanded on the point, calling package tourism "a highly optimized business process [that] has nothing to do with traveling" where the tourist is treated like a "piece of luggage that is being passed around like in a distribution center at the airport."

8.4 Encounters with the traveler culture

He then described the perspective of those with whom the tourists interact: "Nobody is interested in you as a human being [...] and you don't meet any real people because it's so hard to escape this setup." Thus, in line with MacCannell (1976), for LITs package tourism represents the polar opposite of their prized authenticity, which they believe gives value to travel and therefore to the people who experience it. Ryan (26, Canada) summed up the LIT condemnation of the package traveler:

> I hate them, I despise them, I just hate seeing people on package tours because it just makes me think that they can't ...they can't think for themselves. It's horrible but they're like lemmings, they follow the group and...and I don't think they get anything out of it. At all...I don't think they experience the culture.... I don't think they get the thrill of having things go wrong and having things go right, and having to figure things out for yourself (Ryan, 26, Canada).

In contrast, Max (36, Austria, 2nd) provides a definition of "real" travel: "You meet real people, you see real fascinating things, but also real gruesome things, and nothing is staged or somehow prepared for you, but it just happens, naturally, and you participate."

The participants' stories demonstrate the significance of (perceived) freedom, autonomy and independence on their intrinsic motivation to travel. As Ryan & Deci, (2000) pointed out, intrinsic motivation is closely linked with a feeling of self-determination and control over one's life. The touristophobia expressed by the overwhelming majority of LITs in this study also supports previous research on the tourist / traveler dichotomy (e.g. Cohen, 2003; Fussell, 1980; Galani-Moutafi, 2000; MacCannell, 1976; Munt, 1994; Welk, 2004).

8.4.4 Communitas – Travel relationships and community bonds

Of course, beyond drawing on the contrast between tourist and traveler to delineate their identities, LITs also rely on establishing relationships within the traveler community. Here it is important to recall Turner's (1974) idea of liminality (see section 4.1.4), which connotes a stage or place free from previous bonds where the individual is in a state of transition. Drawing on Turner's ideas, Bowie (2006, p. 149) describes individuals who pass thorough a liminal stage as "neither one thing nor another, but betwixt and between". And as we heard above, Matthews (2014) pointed out:

> It is the freedom, licentiousness, creativity, indulgence and experimentation that liminality engenders and the intensified social bonds which may emerge from such experience, which leaves ritual participants changed, renewed or transformed. (p. 161)

As LITs begin to learn the values of the community, they can start to form relationships that help bond them to the community and address the third level of Maslow's pyramid—the need for love and belonging, or as Turner (1969) called it, a sense of *communitas*.

The unstructured, spontaneous nature of long-term independent travel through a liminal space encourages a spirit of companionship and togetherness and fosters a special unity among travelers, that is a "spontaneous, immediate, and concrete relatedness typical of bonds formed between people in the middle, liminal stage of a rite of passage" (Bowie, 2006, p. 153). Turner (1969) contended that communitas "transgresses or dissolves the norms that govern structured and institutionalized relationships and is accompanied by experiences of unprecedented potency" (p. 128). One LIT I interviewed even remarked how travel could alter existing bonds of friendship. Nick, (34, Ireland) traveled with his friends from home in a van in South America. He was surprised at how the experience deepened his bonds to the "guys" whom he had already considered quite close friends:

> The guys from traveling, like I've known them for fucking years, basically, but the last six months I've certainly learned so much more about them than I ever knew about them before. Cause we're guys, so we don't talk to each other. But when we talk to each other 24/7, even though you still don't talk very much, you just figure each other out.

He explained that living in such a small space (the van) also caused some friction and "every now and again somebody's in bad form, and if it happened at home, you just leave them and see them tomorrow". But because they were forced to work through these issues on the road, their friendship became stronger.

Of course, traveling with friends is not the norm for LITs, and in fact Nick went on to travel much longer on his own after his other friends went home. For those traveling independently, Turner's comment about breaking down the norms which regulate the formation and maintenance of relationships in one's native culture is even more relevant. In traveler community, barriers and restrictions to forming relationships are broken down. Individuals are removed from their protective friend groups and forced to meet others. Furthermore, stripped of their comfortable stereotypes or preconceived ideas, travelers do not know what to expect when they encounter each other, and they are essentially forced to engage each individual with an open mind. Nadine, (23, Canada) described this process of meeting new people on the road: "It's always strangers that you're meeting, so you're always more open, willing to talk with them, and even talk about things I wouldn't want to talk about with friends at home, cause they wouldn't understand." Similarly, Nora, (49, Germany) spoke enthusiastically of how the foreign environment actually enhances the process of meeting new people:

> You meet special people when traveling, people that you just wouldn't meet at home in Germany. [...] When you travel you talk about completely different things, and that's what's so exciting. You approach people differently. When I meet someone, I am not interested in someone's job at home. It's a free space, and that's what I like.

8.4 Encounters with the traveler culture

Emilia (36, Germany) emphasized how quickly and easily new relationships are formed: "You meet on the bus and talk 2 sentences and because you want to save money you share a room and so on". And Alan (42, New Zealand) pointed out that the travel setting even altered the dynamic of interactions between genders: "Women don't just assume you're trying to hit on them just because you're talking to them about what they've done and that sort of stuff." In fact, I met Alan scuba diving in Honduras and ended up traveling with him through Nicaragua for three weeks strictly as a travel companion, which seemed perfectly normal in that context.

Brian (43, USA) spoke at length about the meaningful relationships he had formed on the road and how he felt at home in the multi-cultural traveler community:

> And of course it is possible at home to make friends that are like me, but it just doesn't happen as often or as fast of course. But the other thing is that [...] I would just call them my tribe, cause they are the people that are most like me that I meet out there. We're just roaming. We're just kinda like a homeless, aimless, shifty, kinda tribe. So we don't stay in one place. So we find each other by roaming about. And we're all out there [...] There is a certain connection that we all must have or we wouldn't be doing it. I mean, granted, we could go to easy places and meet rich tourists, and that's kind of a different thing, but us backpackers, there is an overwhelming similarity.

By contrasting travelers with both people in his native culture and the wealthier tourists he occasionally encounters in his travels, Brian evokes the traveler values discussed above and emphasizes the way in which these values bond the community together and make him feel a true sense of belonging.

For those who travel together for longer periods of time, the initial bonds are quickly intensified by shared experience. Communitas is manifested primarily through storytelling and spending time with each other. LITs cook meals together, embark on hiking trips, or travel long distances on busses or boats, using this time to exchange stories of their home cultures and previous road experience, thereby deepening relationships. Aaron (35, USA) gave an example of an experience with some travelers he met randomly on a multi-day trek: "There were effectively four of us that became a team. And as we trekked for like 17 days, and then we were together for three or four days after that. You know, we really bonded, and these were people that I really enjoyed." He also pointed out that they were a good team because they respected his desire to walk silently most of the time ("I like to trek silently. I don't like to shoot the shit while I'm walking"), but then he appreciated the camaraderie with the three other travelers at the end of the day, when they would "unwind" together and talk about their experiences. Such reflective discourse, a cornerstone in Mezirow's (1991a) TLT, is important in order to validate beliefs, values, intentions and feelings. It has also been argued that relationships play a vital role in the transformative learning process and friendship, trust and support are necessary aspects for effective rational or reflective discourse to take place (Taylor 2000, p. 306). Eric (48, Canada), explains his views on reflective discourse with other travelers:

> I learn from other travelers all the time. I keep this information in my mind, and I know that this is just one opinion. But I always think there are more ways to see one thing. Sometimes I had an exchange about spirituality or something, and those times I learn something. Or sometimes it reminds me of something that I know and that I forgot and that brings these thoughts back.

Such reflective discourse with other travelers is vital in order to help LITs understand and make sense of their experience, a critical factor to higher-order learning and transformation.

The traveler community and the relationships travelers form within it can also be a source of support in difficult times. We already saw above how more experienced travelers often help new arrivals adapt to the challenges of life on the road. As another example, Nora (49, Germany) described how she drew inspiration from fellow travelers at a time of weakness. After six months on the road, she started to feel homesick and hit a low point, which lasted for about three to four weeks: "I was sitting in Kerala and didn't know where else to go." Rather than aborting the trip and returning home sooner, she teamed up with some other travelers who were on their way to Goa: "They convinced me to come along, and I just did." This example shows the power the travel community can have on someone in difficult times. Nora had been to India several times and had always refused to go to Goa because in her mind it was a "tourist trap". During that low point in her trip, she let herself be talked into overcoming her prejudice and joining the other travelers to go to Goa: "And that was good because my Goa prejudice was gone. It was so large, so different. Everyone's got a place there. And I was reconciled and happy again in India." Not only did the formation of communitas get her out of her homesickness, it also contributed to the transformation of a meaning scheme by helping to overcome her prejudice against Goa. Had she given up and returned home during her low point of homesickness, the entire trip to India would have left a bad taste in her mouth. Instead, meeting these people turned out to be a highlight and resulted in her looking at the trip in a positive way.

8.4.5 *Exploring roles*

One other important feature of the traveler community is the opportunity it grants travelers to experiment and play with their identities, which corresponds to phase eight of Mezirow's (1991a) model for transformative learning (provisional trying of new roles). In fact, due to the relative anonymity that prevails throughout the culture, travelers benefit from a

8.4 Encounters with the traveler culture

high degree of flexibility and freedom to engage in such experimentation. In terms of the local culture, Sarah (36, Austria) described the freedom from social restraints she felt on the road:

> In Africa as a white person you're always an outsider. And nobody expects anything from you. You're completely outside of society. You don't have any obligations, not even as a white woman, you don't have to stick to any rules, except maybe clothing, cover your arms and shoulders and legs, but that's it. You can be whoever you want to be.

Lena (26, Germany) focused more on the lack of pre-conceived ideas about other people that is characteristic of the traveler community:

> I found out who is Lena, what is Lena? I don't have to prove anything to anyone. And this is the advantage of anonymity; you don't have to disguise yourself. No one knows your past or anything of your life at home. You can be completely yourself.

This is echoed by Brian (43, USA), who asserts "When you travel you can be whoever you want to be. People don't care who you are at home because that's just not important." When I first met Brian in Panama and exchanged some initial pleasantries, he told me that he was 38 years old. When I contacted him again for another interview 13 years later, I found out that he was much older than I thought. He laughed and explained that at the time he pretended to be 38 rather than 43 for many years.

Several other LITs reported deliberately temporarily "altering their identities" (a nice euphemism for lying, I suppose) from time to time. We already heard from the couple above who discovered the need to lie to survive in the host culture, but this kind of "creative embellishment" was a strategy travelers used to adapt to the traveler culture as well. Ally (33), a travel agent from Switzerland, described changing her stated profession depending on her mood or the identity of her interlocutors:

> When I speak with people who didn't go to university, I'm a travel agent. But when I speak with people who went to university or whatever, then I say that I was also a trainer or things like that, and a manager at [name of company]. Then I am telling the truth, but better...it depends. When I'm tired, then I'm a travel agent. When I like to speak a little bit, then I'm a manager.

This quote offers a prime example of narrative identity building. In the first part, it seems Ally offers the real reason for claiming to be a manager—that she wants to put herself on the same social level as people she meets who are more highly educated. However, she then seems to realize that this is not consistent with the egalitarian traveler ethos, which claims to reject the value standards of home society (e.g. education, income status). Thus, she offers a second rationalization for her deception which sounds somewhat more neutral, namely that her choice of identity is based on her interest in engaging in conversation at any particular moment. Of course, logically, this makes little sense, since it is possible to talk just as long about being a travel agent as about being a manager, particularly when the former happens to be one's actual job, thereby relieving the burden of fabrication. Thus, beyond revealing the true difficulty of truly leaving behind the values of one's native culture when entering the traveler culture, this short answer also illustrates the narrative identity building process in action during the interview.

Brian (43, USA) was more open in describing how he manipulated his identity to facilitate or inhibit communication with both the local people and fellow travelers, although his story also reveals some tension with a fellow traveler:

> I lied about my age all the time. Sometimes out of boredom. I don't get carried away, but sometimes you get tired of these conversations, so I lied to get out of them and make them shorter. And also when they ask you like "where's your family?" and all that kind of stuff. And I remember Alice [his German travel companion] gave me a hard time as I was talking to this guy and I was like, "Yeah, I was married once and then she died." And then the conversation will end. Nobody wants to talk about death. And she was like, "you shouldn't tell people lies", and I was like, "well, you're telling people that you're gonna meet your husband and all that at the train station so they leave you alone. So what's the difference?" And I don't wanna talk about it. And also, to make it easier for them, like they won't understand what a computer programmer is cause they've never seen a computer, then I'd tell them I'm a teacher. Or a taxi driver, so they can understand that, and also that you're in a lower class and you're more at eye level with them. So if you put yourself down, they feel more comfortable with you. And then you can just turn around and be someone else.

Brian was truly a virtuoso fabricator, and his examples perfectly illuminate the common motivations for this deception. First, lying about his age reveals the age bias in the traveler community, in that Brian, at 43 years old, was often quite a bit older than the travelers he met during his low-budget travels, who were usually in their low to mid-20s. Second, just as back home, Brian was confronted on the road with the social expectation that someone of his age should have a family or at least a wife, an accusation against which he had no interest in defending himself. Third, his final motivation is rather more positive, in that it was designed to stimulate conversation with local people who would either be confused or intimidated by his social background. One could argue that his assumption of the locals' ignorance is somewhat condescending, but the intention behind his deception was at least earnest. Finally, the conversation with his fellow traveler reveals the underlying discomfort some travelers have with the traveler tendency to bend the truth. Although many recognize the usefulness of the practice, it still undermines a somewhat utopian belief many travelers like to have that they are forming meaningful, honest bonds in the open-minded traveler culture.

Indeed, navigating social scenes within the traveler culture compels many LITs to alter the social personas they usually assume in similar situations back home and change their

8.4 Encounters with the traveler culture

styles of social interaction. For example, Aaron (35, USA), who considers himself a very social person when at home, discovered that he is quite happy to be by himself when traveling, a revelation that affected his behavior as well: "I'm a pretty heavy drinker at home, and I have no problem going out and getting sloshed and all that. But when traveling, I don't need to be that me." In fact, he reported that his traveling had made him a healthier person and also more at peace with himself, a change that carried over to his post-travel life. Similarly, Alan (42, New Zealand) described how he learned on the road to go to bars or restaurants alone, with no fear about meeting other people or even simply having some time to himself. Alan, too, reported taking this new attitude and behavior back to his home culture, despite the social stigma in New Zealand against people being alone in a bar:

> I have no problems at all now going to bars and restaurants by myself so just, you know that whole thing about being self-conscious, about being by yourself, just doesn't exist with me now, whereas before I would have never done that.

In fact, many LITs reported that travel helped them come out of their shells somewhat and learn how to interact more comfortably with strangers. For example, Nadine (23, Canada) said she is a much more social person when traveling: "I'm really a more solitary person at home. When I went to school I preferred to be by myself and 'leave me alone.'" She described how travel had taught her to open up to strangers. Nadine asserted that her newfound gregarious side would likely never have surfaced at home, where she was too entrenched in her habitual antisocial behavior. It was only in the new environment and cultural value system that gave her the courage to try out a new social persona.

One other area of identity exploration that came up in several interviews was experimenting with sexual mores. While the image that some people have of traveler culture as a hedonistic, sex-soaked sub-culture is exaggerated (with the possible exception of a few popular party destinations, which most LITs would not recognize as part of their culture anyway), it cannot be denied that attitudes towards sexual relations are less restrictive in traveler culture than they are in the native cultures of most LITs. Furthermore, due to the aforementioned relative anonymity of traveler culture, as well as the assumed short-term nature of relationships on the road, many LITs feel more open to intimate encounters on the road than they would at home. In particular, female travelers noted a difference. This makes sense when one considers the repressive sexual mores to which women are subjected in most of the LITs' home cultures, a double standard that is encoded in many languages (e.g. in English, sexually active women are labeled "slut", "whore", and many other negative terms, while sexually active men are "studs" who are just "sowing their wild oats").

The story of Chelsea, (25, England) is a good example of a traveler experimenting with a mode of social interaction which was essentially forbidden by the values she learned through her conservative Catholic upbringing. While it is tempting to parse this story to highlight the key aspects it reveals one at a time, here I will provide the entire story in its complete, somewhat rambling form (with only a couple paragraph breaks inserted to make it a bit more coherent), so that the reader can see the narrative identity building process in action, before I comment on some individual features of the tale. In essence, Chelsea's frequent self-critical digressions and editorial comments show not only the conflicting emotions she felt during the experiences she describes, but also the value conflict she feels in the moment of telling the story, as she seeks to construct a meaningful and "acceptable" (for herself and for me) identity narrative for a fellow (female) traveler (i.e. me, the interviewer):

> The two years I travel to Africa, this is gonna sound really freaking pretentious, but I called it, I called the second year, "The Year of Ego", and it was because I was very conscious. I was a really confident person and literally just beaming with confidence, and I could pretty much, at the time anyway... this is just sounding so pretentious, but it's true... This is how I feel about how I was. I could twist anyone around my finger. And you know let anyone do, you know, I was quite conscious of how much power I had when I went traveling. You know, you'd go and maybe there is a couple of. I was very conscious of male attention I got, and I loved it because suddenly I could be anybody I wanted to be because no one knew me. And I just walk in, and you know, you can spot, who is who, and it was great, but it was ego.
>
> It wasn't just about male attention, it was just about people liking who you are. And I really, I think I really, I don't think I abused it, but I really dissected it while I was doing it as well. So I didn't like myself very much because I could see myself literally playing a room, playing a room of travelers even, and talking, and saying the right things, and.... And I could've hated myself for it because it was just a fucking ego trip, basically. 'Cause that's what happens when you go traveling. You are a different person...You are a beaming with confidence... the kind of confidence you don't always have at home, and you can use it to your advantage, and I often did it. You can be whoever you want to be. But everyone else is on the same trip on the same ego trip, and it was really a good exploration for me. I had a lot of fun, ahm....[laughs]... jumping in out of bed with gorgeous travelers, and it was really good fun.
>
> And at the same time, I ended up coming away from those trips feeling a bit ashamed of myself because I knew it wasn't really necessary, and I hadn't really been myself. But it's just an extraordinary amount of power you're suddenly given, you know. Of, you know, there is no one to tell you what to do. It's you, you and your judgment, and you can just do whatever you like; no one's judging you. But ahm, yeah, I've still got this religious upbringing, and this Catholic guilt, if you like. But it's the same bloody stuff. I ended up giving myself a really hard time and having to dissect everything and work out why I had to do this and why it was necessary to sleep with that guy and...you know. It's just what every person does. I just happened to do it traveling, but most people do it anyway at uni or something. So that was interesting.

To point out some of the key features of this story, first, her description of the traveler cultural environment perfectly captures the openness involved ("There is no one to tell you

8.4 Encounters with the traveler culture

what to do [...] no one's judging you.") and the liberating effect it had on her ("beaming with confidence", "an extraordinary amount of power you're suddenly given", "I had a lot of fun".). Second, the story shows the inner conflict she had during the events recounted in the story ("I really dissected it while I was doing it [...] I didn't like myself very much."). On another level, her repeated return to this theme of critical self-analysis reveals the importance of this ability for her own self-perception and the image she is trying to construct through this narrative for her audience (i.e. herself and me). The conscious awareness of the narrative construction in progress is also evident in the repetition of the phrase "this is just sounding so pretentious", which is a kind of "on-the-fly" self-criticism of the pride she is projecting in her narrative, an emotion that her Catholic upbringing does not sanction, especially considering the source of that pride. Nevertheless, she feel this pride for discovering her own power. Finally, the story describes vividly the self-reflection that occurred during and after the event, as well as the interpretation she eventually arrived at in order to fit it into a larger narrative identity construct in a way that would preserve her sense of self-worth and identity coherence. That is, although her Catholic values ultimately prevailed in her own judgement of her behavior ("a fucking ego trip"), she has justified it in her head as something normal ("everyone else is on the same ego trip", "It's just what every person does [...] but most people do it anyway at uni or something.") and she didn't hurt anybody ("I don't think I abused it"). However, beyond simply being "normal", she has built a narrative in her head that makes this a necessary growing experience for her that helped her understand herself and her values better. Although she "hadn't really been [her]self" it was "a good exploration" for her, and presumably she now has a better understanding of what her "self" is, along with an enhanced self-confidence and an idea of how her sexuality fits into her own identity equation. One final feature of Chelsea's narrative bears mention, which is the outstanding title she has assigned to this period of her life. "The Year of Ego" would make a perfect chapter title, to use the book metaphor, or episode title, if one prefers the more modern metaphor of a TV series. Indeed, the assignment of a handy title to a learning experience in one's life is perhaps the quintessential indicator of the conscious, reflective narrative identity construction process in action.

Shortly after this story, Chelsea showed an awareness of the entire learning process when she summed up the value of travel as follows:

> I think this is all cliché that you go traveling to find yourself and you don't ever want to admit it, but that's what a lot of it is about. And for me traveling is all about coming closer to the truth about things – about myself and about everything that I don't know about. And I think that is the best education that you can get if you can just come closer to that truth. I mean, I don't know if there's one big truth, but the more I travel, the more I feel closer to the answer.

Chelsea ultimately concluded that this period of identity play was a valuable learning experience, and her story evokes several of the stages in Mezirow's transformative learning model (1991a), including a disorienting dilemma, critical evaluation of both herself and the cultural values behind her feelings of disturbance, and trying out new roles.

This section had focused, in particular, on the stage of trying out new roles, in order to emphasize how traveler culture provides not only a wide range of disorienting experiences, but also a wealth of opportunities to experiment with finding effective solutions for these challenges, which often lead to long-term changes in values and identities. Before proceeding, I will just mention my own experiences with trying out new roles. Although I, too, leveraged the anonymity of traveler culture to strike up relationships with locals and fellow travelers that ranged from superficial to intimate, these represent just a small portion of the many roles I was able to try out in my longest journey through Latin America. The most obvious of course, was the role of long-term independent traveler. I left with 5,000 dollars in my bank account and a vague plan for six months of travel and then ended up supporting myself for four and a half years on the road by taking on various jobs and scaling down to the basics, thereby switching my role from a middle-class individual to assuming the role of a budget traveler (Riley, 1988), yet feeling wealthier than ever before in my life. Along the way, I taught English to people ranging from children to business executives in Costa Rica; I discovered my love for diving and became a divemaster; I discovered my love for the mountains and engaged in increasingly challenging activities, culminating in tackling two peaks above 6,000 meters with sections of ice-climbing in between; and I worked as a jungle guide in Bolivia for three months, guiding small independent travelers through virgin forests, armed with a machete, among other experiences. None of the above-mentioned events took place in the first few months of my travels, but unfolded with time spent on the road, and none of those experiences, which I consider formative for my current identity, could have unfolded in the same way back home. For me, it was necessary to get off the beaten path of typical life in Austria, and this brings me to the next topic of traveler culture.

8.4.6 *Traveler status and the evolution of traveler identity*

While the previous sections focused on the ways in which LITs assimilate into traveler culture, we will now look a little deeper into the complexity of that culture itself. Despite the common bonds and values that unite many travelers into a "tribe", as one of the LITs labeled it above, it would be a mistake to conceive of traveler culture as some sort of homogenous, utopian "society" where everyone coexists happily. Quite the contrary, as with

8.4 Encounters with the traveler culture

any culture, traveler culture is a highly diverse structure filled with subcultures and perceived hierarchies. In keeping with Maslow's model, the level above belonging is the esteem level, which is at least partly dependent on feeling esteemed by others. The necessity of validation from one's fellow human beings is also evident in Erikson's (1968) emphasis on the importance of social context for individual identity development (see Section 2.1).

In this context, commonly accepted values can be quickly transformed from indicators of cultural cohesion to markers of cultural status. And indeed, anyone who has spent any time listening to a group of travelers swap stories cannot help but notice how this exchange soon takes on a subtle (and sometimes not-so-subtle) air of one-upmanship, as each individual tries to outdo the stories of the others—the longest bus ride, the lowest budget, the most run-down accommodation, the oddest food eaten, the worst sickness, etc. The stories go on and on, with each traveler trying to stake out a claim to a certain status. Many researchers have dived head-first into this fray, picking a metric and trying to use it to classify travelers, with various degrees of implied (or openly attributed) value allotted to each group. Examples include Gray's (1970) sunlust vs. wanderlust, Plog's (1974) psychocentric vs. allocentric tourists, and Cohen's (1972) institutionalized vs. non-institutionalized travelers, which he later broke down further by adding two subcategories for each of those main categories, as described in section 3.2.1 of this paper. Of course, these various systems of classification overlap and interact in complex ways.

Fortunately, categorization is not the goal of this paper. Indeed, by defining the research subjects for this study in terms of minimum length of travel (to maximize the possibility that real learning and transformation may have occurred) and style of travel (to exclude groups backed by a more defined support structure and a more stationary intercultural experience), the goal was to keep the population sample as broad as possible in order to capture the rich diversity of the traveler culture. Therefore, rather than attempting categorization, here I will focus on providing some insight into how certain overlapping value metrics function within the community and within the individuals themselves in terms of the process of establishing and reinforcing evolving values and identities.

Perhaps the one metric that best illustrates the process by which travelers establish their own position within the traveler cultural hierarchy itself is the degree of remoteness of the destinations to which individuals travel. To clarify, in this case, remoteness does not necessarily connote physical distance from human society or even from one's home society (although these factors can play a role), but rather the degree of engagement with, or, more precisely, disengagement from traveler culture itself. This concept was discussed above (section 6.2.2.5), when we looked at the different meanings travelers assign to the phrases "solo travel" or "traveling alone." To clarify this distinction further, we can consider the expression "off the beaten path", which is popular among travelers but can also mean different things to different travelers. The implicit question contained within this expression is exactly whose feet are beating the path from which one is trying to escape? To some degree, as discussed above, this beating might be done by the package tourists so widely disparaged within the independent traveler community. However, when considering the process of stratification and identity definition within this community itself, some travelers would argue that it is the independent travelers themselves whose feet have worn out certain paths. Thus, they suggest, the goal is to minimize contact not with package tourists, but rather with the independent traveler culture itself. In a culture consisting of people linked at least to some extent by an inherent rejection of their individual native cultures, it is perhaps not surprising to find this mechanism repeating itself in the form of an urge to set oneself apart from the adopted community as well.

Before proceeding, it is important to highlight two corollaries to the concept of remoteness from the traveler culture. First, apart from cases of travelers who truly seek solitary travel experiences (as discussed in section 7.2.3), this degree of disengagement with traveler culture frequently corresponds to the degree of engagement with the local culture(s), which some travelers consider more valuable or meritorious. Second, the remoteness metric also typically serves as a perceived stand-in for an individual's degree of autonomy, the important traveler value discussed above. That is to say, it is assumed that those who choose to forsake the support of the traveler community and infrastructure incur a larger burden of self-organization, or a larger freedom of self-determination, depending on one's perspective. Once again, this does not necessarily depend on physical distance. The luxury resort, upscale hostel, run-down guest house, and local person's couch may very well exist within a few kilometers or even meters of each other in some cases, but the selection among these options has a significant influence on determining where one falls on the scale of remoteness.

The importance of the concept of a beaten path is evident in the traveler vocabulary. In South America, it has even been assigned a name—the Gringo Trail. In the following passage, Lilly (31, England) expresses the perceived contrast between "real" independent travel and the more mainstream alternative in describing her travels in Peru:

> I took a cargo boat to Iquitos, all on my own, had met some amazing people, spoke shitloads of Spanish to various people and locals and whoever was sitting next to me on the bus. Very independent. [...] And then, actually, when I had to go back to the south of Peru, it was the real Gringo Trail. It was July, August. Everyone in the northern hemisphere is on holiday. They're all out for three weeks, four

8.4 Encounters with the traveler culture

weeks...paying God knows how many thousands of pounds or dollars for bloody getting picked up and transfers and all that

In the case of Southern Peru, perhaps the leading destination for tourists from North America and Europe due to its well-known Inca sites and relatively well-developed travel infrastructure, the Gringo Trail may also include the much-maligned short-term package tourists. However, throughout the rest of South America, the phrase "Gringo Trail" connotes any place where many foreign backpackers travel, and where they can find plenty of backpacker infrastructure to support them. Many travelers were keen to point out that they did everything in their power to avoid places along this trail or to only visit these places during unpopular times. For example, Lukas (39, Germany, 2nd) said of his travels in South America, "I go where there are no people, or in low season. In South America I avoided most highlights. I just did the most important ones". Aimee (26, England) captured the perceived authenticity that travelers accord to harder-to-reach destinations when she mentioned that she was "always personally impressed by people who've traveled to a lot more places [...] and come out with these real remote tales. [...] People who are looking for kind of more than just tick places off and then brag about it at home". Here, Aimee implies that a destination choice is an indicator of motivation. In other words, while people who travel to "easier" locations are motivated by vanity, traveling farther afield indicates a desire to challenge oneself and have true adventures. Her use of the word "tales" is also telling, as it implies something more than a story—an exotic adventure of some sort. Of course, the word also has connotations of an exaggerated or perhaps even fabricated story, but Aimee seemed content to overlook those.

In fact, many travelers who have already experienced different typical "regions" of travel culture (e.g. Southeast Asia, India, South America) develop their own meaning scheme that defines traveler values and identities based on their chosen travel region, similar to the way people around the world develop their images of a "typical" French person, American person, etc. As I conducted much of my field research in South America, the most common "destination-based" meaning scheme I encountered in my interviews was a belief that travelers in South America were more experienced than those in Southeast Asia. For example, Brian (43, USA) believes that there is "just a different crowd in South America. It's a little more mixed in South America, definitely more experienced travelers". However, Brian also mentioned his perception of India as an indicator of traveler identity: "I'm not traveling in superficial places. Like when you're in Europe or something, it's kind of different. In India, for example, they have a certain quality already or they wouldn't be there." Here we see Brian making the assumption that people who travel to India will automatically be less superficial than those traveling in Europe.

Of course, this fits comfortably into the definition of stereotyping, "when people expect all cultural group members to have the same characteristics and engage in the same behaviors" (Kurylo, 2013, p. 7), which can lead to prejudice and discrimination in terms of how travelers treat each other. And certainly, prejudice and discrimination are present in the massive, nebulous traveler culture. However, unlike most stereotypes, the geography-based images of travelers are usually derived from some form of meaningful interaction with the culture being defined (i.e. Indian travelers, in the present case), and thus tend to be less rigid. This is evident in the following quote from Ben (31, England), who also had the impression that travelers in South America are different:

> The backpackers I've met in South America have been a fascinating bunch of people. It's generally not the first place they've been, so they're more experienced, and they're not just out to get laid and get pissed all the time, and there's real... I mean, age is no limit. And these people have a lot more to say, more interesting things, and you learn a lot more from them, rather than the 19-year-old pisshead who's got nothing to say for themselves... really quite dull at the end of the day. Yeah, you meet people that are older, and people have reasons for traveling. Some people are just escaping, running away from shit at home, doing whatever works for them. And then they do themselves even more damage when they end up in places like Columbia, and they turn into big cokeheads. [...] You see that in India as well. You see so many smackheads there. So if you've got problems like that and you go to places like India... but they're still travelers I suppose, by definition.

As the last word indicates, this quote shows Ben actually working out his meaning scheme for the term "traveler" in the context of the interview. He begins with a stereotype that seems to accept destination choice as a marker of traveler value (i.e. how interesting they are) and then almost instantly rejects that concept by moving to a different value system. This new system classifies travelers based on their motivations, whereby he clearly expresses his personal value scheme, which obviously ranks "learning" above "sex and inebriation" as acceptable travel motivations. Next, he realizes that his geography-based stereotype is problematic when he mentions that "drug travelers" are in India as well. Finally, in an illuminating final sentence, we see how his reflection during the interview also leads to his realization that drug travelers are still somehow part of the culture to which he, too, belongs. This, in turn, seems to lead to an expansion of his empathy towards those people as well, who, within the space of two sentences, go from the negative label "smackheads" to the far more sympathetic descriptor of people "with problems like that". Such moments in interviews are truly fascinating, as one can witness the critical reflection actually occurring within the narrative process of the interview.

In addition, this passage shows the kind of cognitive flexibility that many travelers develop or refine through their travels. In this example, we can see that Ben's destination-based stereotype is actually more of a generalization, which Kurylo (2013) defines as "statements about the characteristics and behaviors that describe a percentage of the members of a cultural group" (p. 6). Of course, the word "percentage" is the key here, as it implies recognition on the part of the individual possessing the generalization that it is not a universal truth. Despite the danger of slipping into stereotype, prejudice and discrimination, Kurylo (2013) points out the potential benefits of generalizations:

> Knowing a generalization about a culture is helpful to understand where you may be similar to or differ from members. Generalizations also help you to be aware of how you might adapt to its behavior when interacting with someone from that culture. Generalizations about a culture affect how you think about and communicate with members of a culture. (p. 7)

While most people would assume travelers might develop an awareness of the subtle but important difference between stereotypes and generalizations via their interactions with local cultures, my research showed many examples similar to Ben's, where this kind of perspective change and development of cognitive flexibility stems from interactions with the traveler culture itself. In the present case, while Ben is not about to run off and start shooting up drugs with the drug users, it is reasonable to expect that he would be somewhat more tolerant and understanding of the root problems of their self-destructive behavior after having expanded his empathy by reflecting on his travel experiences—an empathy that may even carry over to his opinions about people back in his home culture with similar problems.

Ben's quote above also testifies to the diversity of traveler culture and the complex system of subcultures within it, which can be segmented via destination choice, motivation, etc. Returning to the aforementioned concept of the value of destination remoteness and the related spectrum from a complete traveler-culture focus to a complete local-culture focus, this diversity plays a role there as well. Although there is a near universal awareness among travelers of the existence of this meaning scheme, there are no universally accepted value judgements regarding the two ends of the scale. An example from "mainstream" society (i.e. in the present context, most travelers' native cultures) may help illustrate the point. Although many mainstream cultures define a university education and its related degrees and titles as signs of value, there are an abundance of people in such cultures who invert this implied value judgment by explicitly rejecting that standard and defining their identities in intentional opposition to elitists and their "ivory towers".

In the same way, travelers display different attitudes towards traveler culture and "the beaten path" which range across the spectrum. On one side, we find the travelers discussed above in the Communitas section (7.4.4), some of whom have fully embraced the beaten path and the enclaves and travelers who populate it. For example, Keith (23, Australia) describes his preference for travelers over locals:

> Most of the countries I go to, I hang out more with the backpackers than I would with the local residents because probably 95% of the local residents are.. ok, they're nice people, but they're not the kind of people I wanna be with. If they're the people I wanna be with, then they're not in the country. They're traveling somewhere else. And I probably meet them when they're somewhere else.

Here, Keith equates the local people with people back home who lack the key characteristic (courage? creativity? autonomy?) that makes LITs different. One could point out that this generalization is rather insensitive to the fact that most of the people in the communities where he travels lack the *resources* to embark on long-term travel, even if they had whatever specific characteristic it is that Keith believes sets LITs apart. However, the point here is not to criticize people's meaning schemes (although I obviously cannot resist the temptation in some cases), but rather to point out how Keith defines his own identity by emphasizing the link he shares with his fellow travelers, no matter how non-specifically that link may be defined.

Other LITs are careful to emphasize that the motivation for their travels is *not* to meet other travelers:

> I'm not traveling to meet other travelers. I'm traveling to meet people from here, so I'm always, always trying to be with local people, talking to local people, going to local places, not in tourist cafes or things like that, you know. Some people are just doing that. I don't like that. I really prefer to be with people from here. Like just the fact when I went to El Balcon in Cafayate, all the travel people were together, and I was the only one... I was always with a guy from there...always always. We were always doing things together, and that was enough for me. You know, I don't care about other people. This was a guy really nice, from Argentina. He told me a lot of things about the political or health system and things like that. It was just so interesting. (Nadine, 23, canada)

Nadine's strong statement that she does not "care about other people" (meaning other travelers, in this context) and her frequent repetition of the word "always" to describe the amount of time she spends with locals show that this is an emotionally charged issue for her. Likewise, Syd (32, Switzerland) pointed out:

> We haven't experienced a lot of encounters [*with other travelers*] because I'm more inclined to go to see local people than other travelers. So I'm a social traveler, if you want, but more with people living in a place, you know, see how they live, what they think, how they react to something. But travelers...we didn't go to places where most backpackers go to. Most of the time, especially in Central America we tried to avoid them.

Despite these statements, I met both of these travelers in relatively "traditional" backpacker settings, and although they professed to be far on the "anti-traveler-culture" end of the spectrum, they both could recount positive stories involving fellow travelers as well.

8.4 Encounters with the traveler culture

Indeed, the vast majority of LITs place themselves somewhere in the middle of the spectrum, acknowledging the benefits of interacting with both locals and fellow travelers.

In fact, the most common (although by no means universal) pattern I observed in terms of this spectrum is a gradual movement over time away from the "beaten path". This highlights the important point that traveler identities on the road are not fixed. Rather, they typically evolve over the course of a longer trip or, in some cases, over the course of successive trips. As certain tensions are resolved and lessons learned, new tensions arise that lead to a renewed disorientation that gives rise to new needs. For example, as discussed above (section 7.4.1), during initial travels it is common for new LITs to turn to the traveler community to help overcome their initial shock and learn the ins and outs of long-term independent travel. In some cases, this leads to the honeymoon posited in Oberg's (1960) culture shock model, as new LITs become intoxicated with the novel experience of meeting new people from other cultures. Lilly (31, England) described this early travel phase:

> Hostels are full of other people like me, and I said I'm gonna meet them and travel with them. And the first four months were charmed. Three weeks with somebody, six weeks with somebody, six weeks with somebody else.

During this phase, new travelers are fascinated by the "standard" discussion between travelers who have just met. Where are you from? Where have you been? How long have you been traveling? Did you go to [insert place]? No you didn't? Oh, that's one of the best places I've been to. For some, however, the constant parade of new people in and out of their lives soon becomes overwhelming, as described by Emilia (36, Germany):

> I sometimes need my freedom. I know that I sometimes meet too many people. And even non-stop. I say bye to people at a train station and 6 minutes later I'm in a bus and meet someone else. And I'm thinking, wow, that's great, but then I also need time to write, to think, to digest and so on.

With still more time, the novelty of the standard traveler discussion soon wears off and is even replaced by a feeling of annoyance. Thus, Lilly (31, England), who in the quote above was "charmed" by these conversations, soon grew weary of them:

> And I suddenly realized that I was spending two or three days with people, and then two, and then another two or three days with someone else. And I tell you I was boring myself. Yes, I've been traveling here and there and I've done this and that…and I'm just like, God, I can't have this conversation again, I'm so sorry. And it was really tiring. It was really tiring.

As their travel experiences proceed, many LITs settle into a position somewhere between the two extremes, as was the case with Aaron (35, USA) at the time of our interview. Within the space of a few minutes during the interview, Aaron first pointed out that the value of solo travel is that it allows you to get nearer to local culture ("I just had some crazy amazing experiences with locals that I just wouldn't have had if I was traveling with somebody else.") and then emphasized how solo travel helps you meet other travelers ("Part of the joy of traveling alone is meeting other travelers.").

In order to strike a balance, many travelers reported changing their "friend-making" behavior to become more selective about the people with whom they chose to travel with or even, in some cases, speak with. Eric (48, Canada) described his modus operandi that developed after some time traveling:

> Now I choose [the people I want to travel with]. I discovered that there are some good travelers and some people that are really interesting [...] I don't do it just to be nice with people or just not to be alone. I prefer to be alone than being in bad company.

Dana (39, Denmark) reported a similar evolution of her approach to fellow travelers:

> I'm into party too, but it's like the same stories you hear over and over again. I enjoy meeting some travelers, but I am very selective [...] I would definitely say I am antisocial. I am like trying to avoid other travelers. But then, every so often, there comes a person along that's different. Then I really, listen, so when there is somebody. If you [indicates the interviewer] had not been the person you are, I wouldn't have talked the way that I talk. So when somebody comes along that is interesting, that I like. Then, OMG, because I miss it. I do miss to have good conversations.

Although Dana's use of the word "anti-social" to describe herself reveals her awareness of the social standards and expectations of the traveler culture, her response makes it clear that she has come to terms with those expectations and found a method for interacting with that culture that works for her.

Dana alludes to the pressures of loneliness (also covered above in section 7.2.1), whereby one's travel experiences begin to feel less rewarding due to the lack of a sympathetic companion with whom one can share those experiences. From the perspective of narrative identity, we could say that these experiences cannot be fully processed and assimilated into one's identity scheme until one has the opportunity to articulate these experiences by sharing them in narrative form with a companion. Some travelers who find that over time they can no longer find compatible companions in the traveler culture at large eventually seek out a more meaningful, long-term travel companion. Lars (28, Belgium) offers a prime example of the evolution of a traveler identity from committed solo traveler to one who feels the need for a travel companion. In the early part of our interview, he professed his preference for solo travel:

> Definitely travel is more intense when you do it alone. And even when you're with somebody for a short time, like on a bus, you don't experience your surroundings as intense cause you're talking with the guy or girl next to you. So for that it's better to travel alone. And I also have loads of contact with the local people, really good things.

8.4 Encounters with the traveler culture

However, (as mentioned in section 6.2.2.4) at the time of our interview, Lars, who had already been traveling for 2 years, also expressed a recently found need to change his solo travel style: "I'm sick of being alone. I won't go alone anymore. I just need somebody else. I'm done traveling by myself." He had even considered how this would affect his future travel plans: "I'd like to go Africa on a motorbike, but I don't want to do it alone anymore." The importance of trusting and supportive interpersonal relationships for personal well-being has been a focus of scientific scrutiny for some time. It has been shown that not the quantity of interactions, but rather the quality of relatedness predicts well-being (e.g. Kasser & Ryan, 1999; Nezlek, 2000). This seems to apply for traveling as well.

From my own experience, I can testify to the effect of having a more long-term, emotionally connected travel companion on one's travel experiences. In my case, I believe I could have traveled indefinitely because I found someone (my future husband) to share my experiences with. I doubt I could have traveled for over four years if I had been limited to a series of short-term traveling companions. Although I consider myself a very sociable person and enjoy meeting different types of people, I, too, soon began to feel the fatigues of the same old traveler conversations; and as my own traveler identity and my perceived relationship to the larger traveler culture evolved, it was comforting to have a well-known confidant with whom I could discuss these changes. This is not to say we were always in agreement on travel-related issues (far from it), but at least I had someone who knew the experiences and background context for the identity and value changes that I was going through at any given time on the road.

On that topic, one of the key changes that I had to deal with as my trip proceeded was travel fatigue, and indeed, this topic came up often when I interviewed LITs with more travel experience. In the context of travel companions, Chelsea (25, England) described how this fatigue factor caused problems in her relationship with her travel companion at the time of the interview, who had more travel experience than she had:

> It's hard traveling with [boyfriend] in some sense, and I think,...no, it's not hard traveling with him but it's harder to wow him because he'd traveled a lot more before than I had. For example, when we met in Mozambique, we were on this amazing beach on this beautiful archipelago and he was always picking holes like "yeah, but the palm trees aren't close enough to the water, and the beaches in Mexico are much nicer." And eventually I had to tell him off and say, "You know what, you're really spoiling this for me, you just gotta shut up and look at this place, you know. It's fucking beautiful."

However, Chelsea's boyfriend's jaded outlook on travel was fairly typical among more experienced travelers, for whom the thrill of seeing new sights had worn off to some extent, as the following quotes describe:

> There's only so much your brain can take in and there's only one highest waterfall in the world and there's only one biggest this and everything else is relative. [...] I'm certainly not as excited about going through Central America as I was about going through South America. Cause I don't know, can you see so many different things all through your life or do you stop getting excited after a while? [...] So what do you do then? Do you stop doing it? (Ben, 31, England)

> What was great in South America was that I saw so many things for the first time. And in New Zealand, for example, that's a country that so many people rave about. But this wasn't the case with me. I also think it's beautiful, but it wasn't that special because I've kind of seen things like that before. You know, New Zealand.... I mean I saw the fjords in Norway, the glaciers in Patagonia, ... and I think, that's maybe the reason, once you've been in the desert, the mountains, and have seen these things, then it's .... not that it's all a copy and that you don't have to go look at them but what's so great about traveling is that "Wow effect" when something great comes along that you've never seen before. And the third and fourth desert, after a while they all look the same. (Lukas, 39, 2nd)

> It's also harder to get excited about things. Like I had this stopover in Singapore and spent the day there, and I went to this Asian market, and I was just like, you know, it's not even interesting to me anymore. I get it, it's a major market, but I've been to sooo many Asian markets where there's all this different food. And I've been to a million of those. It's really not new. So the novelty factor kind of wears off. (Brian, 43, USA)

Brian, one of the most experienced travelers I interviewed for this research, even had his own term for this change in mindset—"travel math". He described his efforts to describe his impressions of an American national park that he was visiting with friends: "It's kinda cool, it's like Ireland, and a little bit Scotland. And I do travel math. And I've been to so many places that you start comparing them in your head. You get jaded the more you travel". By devising their own terms such as "wow effect" and "travel math", travelers label a feeling or behavior they have experienced in order to cement these concepts in their meaning schemes and facilitate the explanation of these concepts to others in their traveler narratives.

Beyond the loss of the "wow-effect" or the novelty factor, many travelers also described how they lost, and truly missed, the challenge factor. Andy (30, USA) draws on a familiar metaphor from his home culture to explain this process:

> I plateaued in my job after three years. And I learned 90% of what I learned in my job in the first year. The learning curve was huge at the beginning. And even with traveling, I think, probably in the first six months, I learned more than in the 10 months after that. I know how to find guesthouses, I know how to eat...

Similarly, Lars (28, Belgium) described the process of adapting to the traveler lifestyle so thoroughly that it ceased to be interesting for him:

> And that was interesting to learn, too. After a while, everything becomes routine. First you think, "Wow, traveling's different!" And you're seeing new places all the time, new cultures, new countries, and that's true. But it's still the routine of

8.4 Encounters with the traveler culture

> travel. And that's what people at home don't understand. And at the beginning it is a challenge, just the logistics. "Oh my God, I landed in Jakarta, how am I gonna get to the hotel, how am I going to get money, food, and so on?" But having done it for 3 and a half years, then it's like, "yeah, I get this." [...] I really miss the challenge of traveling. I call it postcard tourism. One nice site to the next one, it all fits nicely on a postcard. And there's no story behind it. And now I feel like travel's become a routine for me, and I hate routine.

When travel loses the satisfying thrill, travelers have to find some way of adapting or relieving this sense of ennui. For example, Andy (30, USA) posited that a change of scenery to a different traveler location might be enough to re-engage his interest in travel: "If I went to Asia now that's a different story. Different experience, different governments, different culture. So that would be a completely different experience." For myself, this often meant pausing my travels for a time to settle into a place and take on a new challenge, (e.g. becoming a divemaster, jungle guide, English teacher). After these breaks, my travel desire was normally re-kindled, and, as a bonus, I had a bit more money in my pocket to extend my travels.

For many travelers, the experience of becoming jaded with travel led to a newfound or expanded appreciation for one final key traveler value: spontaneity and the serendipitous experiences to which it can lead. In some cases, LITs who are by nature spontaneous people and therefore detest planning already anticipated this aspect of travel before embarking on their first journey, as was the case with Lena (26, Germany):

> I didn't want to plan anything, and that's why I was so attracted to just travel with a backpack because for me this is the best, the most beautiful and the simplest form of travel. Because you're independent, there's no planned tour, no guide, you don't depend on anyone, you can plan everything on your own, plans that most often don't turn out the way you imagined anyway, but that's the beauty of it.

While Lena looked forward to this aspect even before her first long-term independent travel experience, many LITs described how they had to learn to relinquish their need for control and embrace the random nature of travel. For example, Aaron (35, USA) described his background in business trips, which were often fully planned to the last detail six months in advance, which meant for him, "the concept of showing up in a place and not having a place [to stay] was alien and weird". However, by the time of our interview, which was nine months into his trip, his travel behavior had changed completely:

> The whole beauty of this kind of travel is that you're your own boss. There's no reason that you should spoil the adventure of it by having to sit and architect things out and do work related to traveling. It shouldn't be that way... and so that's when I sort of, you know, found less and less use for the guidebook, except for getting from point a to point b and actually using their maps of the cities – the city maps...which is pretty much what I use the guidebooks for now.

It is revealing that he starts with a metaphor from his pre-travel life, being a "boss", which implies imposing order in some way, and then immediately deploys the word "architect" in an uncommon verb usage to reject the strong sense of structure implied by this word.

Aaron also touches upon a key symbol of traveler status or philosophy—the guidebook. Most often, this means the *Lonely Planet* guide to the particular destination, although one finds travelers with strong loyalties to other texts as well. Such books, often referred to as the "traveler Bible", either reverently or derisively, depending on one's attitude towards travel planning, take on a strong symbolic significance for travelers. While many start off relying on them, many LITs reported that they either reduced their dependence on these books over time (as Aaron described above) or even go out of their way to emphasize their rejection of such guides on philosophical grounds. Thus, Nora (49, Germany) was quick to point out, "I never travel with a guidebook. I know where I will arrive, and I have somewhat of an idea, but I don't plan. I can't do that. I also hardly ever research countries in advance."

To sum up the topic of spontaneity, it is perhaps appropriate to point out that one can view spontaneity, or an embrace of long-term independent travel's potential for random, uncontrollable, serendipitous experience, as an evolution beyond the coveted traveler value of autonomy. While people seeking autonomy express a fierce desire to secure control over their own decisions and experience, this new evolution involves letting go of that need for control; or perhaps discovering that the satisfaction of seeing a plan or expectation fulfilled cannot compare to the enjoyment of being surprised by something unexpected. In fact, an appreciation for the unexpected came up consistently in my interviews, particularly with those travelers who had greater amounts of experience. We already heard above from LITs who learned to understand that the "beauty" of travel is when things do not work out as planned, and perhaps the following two representative quotes will sum this up:

> I've learned that I don't need to plan everything. I also learned that I don't need to think more than a day ahead.... you know, that's the other part of planning...and you know, going into things without expectations...this is another one for me....[...] expectation reduces joy. (Aaron, 35, USA)

> What I really like about traveling is that you learn to let go, and to just drift, instead of swimming against the tide, or to take a certain direction. You just take it as it comes, and that for me was what I learned the most, to not stress about little things. Sometimes I find that we stress about tiny things, which is totally unnecessary. (Julia, 37, Germany)

Of course, in most cases, there is an important prerequisite to being able to give up control and go with the flow: individuals must first overcome the fear of the unknown and be-

8.4 Encounters with the traveler culture

lieve that they can handle whatever life may throw at them. And indeed, as already discussed briefly above (6.2.2.4), one of the most important outcomes of long-term independent travel is the increased self-efficacy travelers gain by facing and overcoming adversity. This includes a confidence in one's ability to deal with people who may not have the best of intentions, as Aimee (26, England) explained:

> We were a lot naïve 5 years ago [...] We were just like stupid, young and just generally too naïve in believing people, in wanting to see the best in everybody, whereas now we're much more careful and skeptical because you learn from your mistakes. And most of all, because you meet so many different kinds of people. You get a feel for how they are, whether they are dodgy or you can trust them, and you learn about human nature. And that only develops over time and with travel experience.

Similarly, Lukas (27, Germany) mentioned that he had learned to "improvise" when dealing with other people and added: "You definitely learn a lot by dealing with people, to handle any unexpected situation, and overall crisis management." Heather (36, Australia) broadened this theme more generally by mentioning crises and mistakes made in general:

> Things do happen on the road, and you get more and more and more confident because you deal with it. You deal with whatever life throws at you. And sometimes you deal with it well, and sometimes you deal with it very badly, but you get through it. And I think, "OK, well, all this has happened, and this has happened, and this has happened, and I am still here. I am still doing it, and I can get through it." And so I think my confidence is good that way.

In mentioning mistakes, Heather (and Aimee above) both reveal a meaning-making process that took place after such mistakes, whereby the individual builds a narrative that gives value to these experiences by recognizing the learning they triggered. This frees them to forgive themselves for these mistakes and even embrace them as part of the identity narrative they tell others, in which they cast themselves as veteran travelers and survivors. In fact, the internal dialogue she describes at the end of this quote highlights the process of telling oneself these stories as well, and based on her stated confidence, it is clear that repeated internal reflection on stories of past challenges overcome has truly changed her self-image. This newfound confidence gives travelers the courage to release their need for control and embrace spontaneity, a theme that will be explored more in detail down below.

Beyond minimizing the dependence on planning, a few other themes emerged in terms of how travelers' attitudes and behaviors evolve with experience. First, as mentioned above, many reported a gradual drift away from the traveler culture, where they no longer feel they fit in. For some, this is simply due to age and the perceived motivations of the "mainstream" backpacker culture:

> But a lot of the people I come across, are in that young gap year age, and although I'm sure a lot of them are very nice and probably highly educated, more so than myself, I would choose to avoid them, because they are more inclined to just wanna go from city to city drinking beer. (Jake, 45, England)

Brian (55, USA, 2nd) also reported feeling that he had outgrown the backpacker scene:

> ... because I'm more experienced now as a traveler, I don't really meet other backpackers anymore. Because I'm kind of past that. And I don't really want to listen to their excitement over seeing something that I've already seen. So I more bond with the locals and I more bond with the people there, cause you just kind of get past that. It's another experience level.

Brian's quote also shows one coping strategy, which is a general move towards increased engagement with the local culture.

Another area where travelers begin to drift away from one core value mentioned above as they get more experienced is the travel budget. Jake (45, England) mentioned how he got frustrated with that aspect of the culture, which he grew to perceive as stinginess: "I don't like that 'well, we only paid three dollars for that room.' I can't stand that." Julia (50, Germany, 2nd) also described how her budget had grown:

> My comfort level has clearly changed. I'm not up for cheap pigsties anymore, and I'd happily pay a few Euros more and get a room with a nicer view. This whole backpacking and the scene is just not my thing anymore, and I prefer to be off-the-beaten-track and don't need to talk to anyone. But I still like to camp with my tent, and when I was in Baja I lived out of the trunk of a car for two months. That I don't mind at all. So it's not the comfort, but more the being alone in beautiful surroundings, rather than with many people and on-the-cheap.

Here, Julia is careful to point out that she maintains the "anti-materialism" ethos of traveler culture in that she does not need luxury. Her quote also captures a second coping strategy for those who feel they have outgrown the backpacking scene. Whereas above Brian showed the typical external-focused response of engaging with the local culture, Julia describes a more common approach for those more internally focused, which is to seek more solitude and space for the contemplation they find rewarding.

In further discussions of his travel style, Brian also mentioned that he has expanded his budget, while being careful to emphasize that he is still not a luxury package tourist:

> I'm not saying I have to stay at the Ritz Carlton, but I'd rather pay 10 dollars than three dollars and get a matrass that doesn't kill your back. So I'm not anymore trying to stretch my money to go as long as possible and be all uptight about it. I never spend anything more than 10 dollars a night for a hotel room in India, and you don't need to. And I used to spend a lot less. And then a thing it's also the age thing. You realize you don't have as much time. Like for me now, I know that it's more precious. Like if I get a whole month of travel now, it's a lot more precious than a month was before. Like I know like I am really lucky. I may not get to do this next year. And I'm not gonna waste any time looking for a room to save a couple of dollars.

8.4 Encounters with the traveler culture

Brian's quote also shows the reality for many travelers as they get older: even if they have more money, life circumstances make it harder to take extended trips, so they have to be savored more.

This brings us to the next theme that came up time and again in discussions with travelers about how their travel styles evolved over time—pace of travel. In short, most travelers mentioned that they had slowed down their pace of travel, opting to spend more time in fewer places. Here is a brief sampling of those responses:

> Well, at the beginning, and that has changed a bit now with age, I would say. At the beginning I loved to travel a lot, also in the country. Now I travel a bit less. Now I like to stay longer in one place. That has changed a bit. But still new locations. (Nora, 57, Germany, 2nd)

> I travel more slowly. I'd rather have less stress, see fewer things but comfortably, maybe a bit more quiet, sometimes meet a few people. And just generally a bit more quiet than I did it back in the day. (Emilia, 49, Germany, 2 nd)

> We have calmed down a bit. At the beginning we felt like we had to sail here and there, and do this and that. And now we have realized that if we sail less and just find a nice spot, it's also really nice. (Veronica, 43, Austria, 2nd)

> So my travel style changed. After that 6 month trip I did a three month trip back to India the next year but only went to three places. I stayed 1 month in each place. And I knew everyone there. (Brian, 55, USA, 2nd)

In some sense, this slower travel pace is the logical consequence of the aforementioned traveler ennui—that is, for travelers who feel like they have seen it all, there is less a sense that they have to keep moving or they might miss something. For Emilia, this also reflects a turning inward to some extent, as she does not need to meet as many people and wants to have time to focus on herself. For Brian, on the other hand, this change in pace shows a desire to foster some sense of community and belonging, a feeling which he had already alluded to in our first interview many years earlier:

> Like you only need that hut. That's my distance. Like my little triangle is here, the marketplace, you go to the same restaurant for breakfast, for lunch, the same people. It's a routine, which you hate, but at the same time you love it because it's a different kind or routine. Cause you're seeing the same people, and they know you. They're friendly and they're chatty. I guess routine is not necessarily bad, as long as you choose to go for that routine.

Brian's response is another prime example of an individual working out his meaning schemes in the process of the interview. We can see his tension about the concept of routine, which, as a traveler, should be anathema to him. However, he devises an interpretation that places that in the context of his own personal free-will, which makes the idea of enjoying a routine acceptable.

This once again highlights how different personalities construct meaning in different ways. Before, we heard from Julia, an introspective person, articulate clearly her interpretation of the change in her travel behavior—she will spend more money if necessary for cleanliness and a nice view and to get off the beaten path, all of which are prerequisites for her desire to have an appropriate surrounding for the inner contemplation she enjoys. As she has clearly contemplated these issues before, she can easily and coherently explain the links between her needs, values and travel behaviors; whereas Brian, as a more extroverted personality, has clearly spent less time reflecting on the meanings and values behind the evolution in his travel style. This supports Taylor's (1994b, 2001) assertion that perspective transformation may also occur implicitly (i.e. in a non-reflective manner) and is not contingent on critical reflection. However, in this case, the interview is essentially forcing Brian to engage in this type of contemplation, and we witness him working out these connections on the fly.

To be clear, this is not to imply a value judgment of either individual. These are simply two different personality types which, in the context of transformative learning, can be distinguished by two key differences. First, although they presumably share the natural human goal of achieving contentment and identity coherence, the conditions they require to reach this goal are very different. One needs a lifestyle and environment that foster more social contact, while the other needs a lifestyle and environment that provide more space for alone time and contemplation. Second, their methods of learning and evolving are quite different. Where one thrives on inner contemplation and careful meaning construction, the other evolves instinctually by having different experiences and then reacting to the feelings that arise and incorporating them into their identity construct on a more emotional level. And once again, the goal here is not to prioritize one over the other, but rather to highlight the differences and emphasize that long-term independent travel has vast potential for both types as a vehicle for development and evolution.

8.5 Outcomes

As a way of drawing this section on traveler experience on the road to a close, here I will summarize some of the key outcomes of these experiences. These include new knowledge obtained, value changes, perspective changes, and changes to both identity and behavior.

8.5 Outcomes

8.5.1 Expanded horizons

At the highest level, expanded global awareness involves recognition of the planetary ecosystem in which we live and how human actions can impact it. Thus, Eric (48, Canada) stated, "It made me very sad because I discovered that there is so much environmental destruction all around the world, and it is really grave." And Chelsea (25, England) provided a graphic example from her travels that helped her grasp the connection between politics and environmental destruction:

> Going back to a piece of coast six years later and it had been shat on by bad developments. Really shit developments. And I could remember the place six years earlier, and it was like a paradise. And I remember realizing how lucky we are in the West to have protection, environmental regulations, to have planning permissions, national parks, all those things that we have, that they don't have in Brazil, and this amazing stretch of coast was just like bought up by people with the most money and had shit buildings put on them, bad planning, no environmental protection. And as soon as you go to Uruguay, it was completely different again, cause they are very careful with their planning. The architecture is nice, you know. But in Brazil that whole coast, I remember going around and just crying. This was just upsetting. This is just horrible.

Beyond the natural environment, travelers also reported gaining a new understanding of the vast diversity and difference in the world:

> The learning process was to realize that people on this planet live just like we do, but under completely different circumstances. Certain things at home are part of our life, like you have to have social security and a fixed income, or at least set meals and a roof over your head. In other countries, people don't have that, but they also turn 80. They have their own fixed rules that we don't have. It's a learning process that you recognize this clearly, but also that you understand that it is possible to live totally differently (Jakob, 34, Austria).

In some cases, traveler reported shifts in their viewpoints of specific cultures that they had experienced:

> What has definitely changed is the impression of cultures that we are skeptical of in Europe, or even hostile towards or critical of, such as Muslims or these extremely poor people in Pakistan. When I was there, it was completely different than what I expected. They are really nice people, and I was really surprised about that, and their hospitality. (Lukas, 27, Germany)

For many travelers, witnessing this wide cultural variety and seeing that some things were not how they expected them to be based on what they had learned in their own cultures also helped them understand the constructed view of their own cultural perspective, an important first step in changing or expanding that perspective:

> It makes you realize that there's a whole different world out there. That their needs, issues, their history, their background are different than yours, and you know, some of that's better, some of that's worse, but in general it's just that it's different... and that your perspective on things comes from your background, your history, your education. And so it's interesting. It's great to experience that and to understand that variety makes the world go round" (Aaron, 35, USA)

For many, this experience widened their perspectives well beyond the borders of their own native countries: "The world's problems have become much more tangible. I take an active interest in things that happen in the world, rather than just in Germany." (Tom, 46, Germany)

8.5.2 Changed views of home culture and cultural values

With this expanded awareness came many changes in the travelers' views about their own cultures as well. Heather (36, Australia) summed up the process nicely:

> I think when you meet people who are different from yourself, you actually learn more about yourself, and you learn more about your own culture than you do about theirs. And I think I've actually learned more about Australian culture and the way we are than sometimes about the culture I'm currently traveling. Because of the way I see them. Every time I see a different culture, my culture is reflected. Either it's so similar or it's so different. So, I just think you learn more about your own way of doing things.

As most LITs traveled to less developed countries, by far the most common response was a newfound appreciation and gratefulness for the higher standard of living they enjoy in their home countries. As Ryan (26, Canada) commented, "[Travel] just opens your eyes to the rest of the world. Seeing an impoverished nation for the first time is a shock, and it makes you realize how much you took for granted when you were growing up." Their travel experiences also compel most LITs to grasp the connection between the material wealth of their countries and the freedom they cherish. Many recognized that this wealth enables them to travel, calling it "a huge privilege" (Alan, 42, New Zealand), and many travelers expressed an even deeper gratitude for the life possibilities afforded by their native cultures:

> Before, I always denied being German [...] I would have never ever put a German flag on my backpack. But I am still totally happy that I grew up there, that I could take advantage of our educational system and also that I could freely decide what I want to do in my life. If I want to study, I can study. I can do whatever I want to do. (Julia, 37, Germany)

However, despite their enhanced appreciation for the living standards of their home countries, they also returned with a new awareness of some perceived faults. The most common theme, as mentioned above, was a view that despite (or perhaps because of) all the technological advances, the more developed countries had become estranged from their natural environment and from each other.

> For me, the most important thing about traveling is to get to know this totally different way of life, these other cultures, to participate in a different way of living, a different culture that doesn't exist in Germany. And what was most fascinating so far was Nepal. Because it is unique in its primitiveness. Life there is just so simple, and it also works. And that's probably what I somehow keep looking for. In Germany, in our world the way we know it, everything is perfect, highly indus-

trialized, everything is highly organized and sterile in a certain way. But I always feel that the authentic is missing, the natural way of dealing with one another, the basis, so to speak has been lost. And especially in countries that are poorer, more primitive, I get the feeling this is where we all originate from. (Eva, 26, Germany)

Furthermore, some travelers described how their experiences had taught them to be more skeptical and think more critically about the information they received from governments or media, and even to shift their political views:

And afterwards that really changed my whole political philosophy or how I digest information. I'm not into conspiracy theories or extremist, but I just don't believe everything that I read anymore[...] And I'm definitely more skeptical because you realize there's a lot more to it than you were taught in school. I'm more likely to question what you hear [...]It makes you much more skeptical of right-wing politics [...] My outlook on politics has completely shifted honestly. (Andy, 30, USA)

As mentioned above, one major effect of travel is to awaken a conscious awareness of the cultural values that individuals had often blindly accepted and incorporated into their own personal value systems as well. This prompts most travelers to examine those values more critically and decide whether or not they still wish to subscribe to those values. For example, we saw the internal dissonance aroused by seeing people living with little material wealth who were nonetheless quite content. The most common response to this, which I heard again and again, was a renewed appreciation for the importance of social relationships and the dangers of materialism:

What is important? You get down to the very, very basics, family, friends, and I think that's a good thing, that that's revealed to you by going traveling...it's what is revealed to you. In terms of what is my utopia, shit, I don't know. But we've already found out at a very young age and we don't want to aspire to a black BMW, which is alright, but a lot of people do. (Glen, 26, England)

Furthermore, a few travelers expanded their perspectives beyond their own lives to acknowledge the responsibility that comes with privilege. Chelsea (35, England) described the effect of seeing so many people in Africa, and particularly girls and women, whose prospects were so incredibly limited compared to her own: "Just realizing God if I don't do something important with my life than I've really fucked something up. Do you know what I mean? If I was given all these opportunities in all these chances." Similarly, Andy described the responsibility he felt to share his experiences and lessons learned with people back home in order to help effect positive change in his homeland and his fellow citizens. After describing the shock he felt when he learned about America's negative influence on El Salvador and realized that all this information is suppressed or conveniently omitted in the US media, Andy stated:

> Traveling opens up your eyes, no doubt. And my own ignorance. I mean, how can I not have known what happened in El Salvador? I was a bit younger then but none of the news made the US, other than when the nuns were raped and killed and thousands of people disappeared, and that's when the US finally opened their eyes. And we spent 6 billion dollars in 12 years to a war that made no sense. Talk about illogical, and I never even thought about it. I mean, in the States you just don't hear about it. You hear about things the government wants me to hear. And when I go back to the States I'll go back and tell people what I've seen cause it's just so impressive, what we miss.

In a final example of a deepened sense of communal responsibility, Nick (34, Ireland) described how experiencing the generosity of others awakened in him a desire to give back to other people, saying that he planned to

> ...try to make a commitment to being a better part of the community when you go home... when you're taken aback by how generous completely random strangers are to you here. Especially when someone gives you a mate mug, and you're wondering why is he doing this, and you're completely suspicious, and then there is no catch....and you feel like shit the next day cause you're a cynical person.

This outcome reflects Maslow's (1970) highest-level of growth, which he labeled "transcendence", that is, the need to help others in order to achieve true self-actualization. This transition from self-orientation to other-orientation was evident in other LITs who voiced the desire to give back to others in an altruistic fashion.

8.5.3 Changes in feeling, thinking and being

The previous quote from Nick highlights the powerful link between people's perceptions of their connections and responsibilities to their fellow humans and their self-esteem. As Syd (32, Switzerland) suggested: "It's questioning myself, questioning the things you do and you act and maybe who you are [...] And I've seen during my travels more differences about myself than in Switzerland," In fact, all of the LITs I interviewed spoke of how travel had fundamentally changed them. Contrary to the popular perception of long-term travel as a never-ending hedonistic party, some travelers reported that their travels had helped build their awareness of their own health and what they needed to do to improve it:

> This last trip has been cleansing for me. Now I've quit smoking, I've lost weight, I've gotten myself in shape, it's been really cleansing for me. I didn't think for a second I'd quit smoking or cut back on drinking. That just happened. (Matt, 28, USA)

This expanded self-awareness also includes a better understanding of themselves, an appreciation for their abilities, and a higher self-efficacy:

> I am more self-confident now. I found out more about who is Lena, what is Lena. (Lena, 26, Germany)

8.5 Outcomes

> I discovered all the resources I had inside, and I've just become much more resourceful overall. (Eric, 48, Canada)

Several LITs also described how this awareness of their own abilities gave them a new sense of inner peace and an increased patience when dealing with the little problems in life:

> I just felt like an inner calm. I've had a calmness that I never had before I went to, certainly to Asia. (Jake, 45, England)

> I think that sometimes we take ourselves too seriously. And that's changed a lot because now I say that tomorrow it can all be over, and take it a lot easier now. (Julia, 37, Germany)

This creates a virtuous circle, in which overcoming a challenge boosts self-confidence and inner calm, which makes it easier to meet the next challenge, which further boosts self-confidence, and so on. With enough practice and reinforcement, this leads to true self-efficacy, or a firm belief in one's ability to successful meet any challenge:

> Now I know that I can be anywhere, and I can adapt. Sometimes it can take longer; sometimes it's more easy. [....] You have to know about yourself, and when you're traveling, you're always learning about yourself. So the more you travel, the more you're able to adapt to different situations. (Nadine, 23, Canada)

> The most important thing was that I was able to face, I won't say any situation, but a lot of situations. [...] I can more appreciate what I have. And I also appreciate myself more. Cause I know that I can face a lot of situations, and I know that I can adapt myself. And this is a very important thing in my mind, because to be able to adapt yourself you can respect the others more. (Eric, 48, Canada)

The final quote from Eric also makes the connection between self-efficacy and the ability to open oneself to outside influences. In fact, many LITs felt they had become more open-minded. Brian (43, USA) described how travel had helped quell his inner doubts and given him the courage to let other people and ideas into his mind: "[Travel] trained me to become more willing to try, like not to question myself all the time. To be more open to experiences and people and also about not being open and closing other people out."

On the other hand, while travel cured the doubts of some, others had to learn a bit of humility. Dana (39, Denmark) described how she learned the hard way that she was a little too confident in her own opinions, and she could perhaps do with a little more self-questioning:

> By being confronted with my own feelings and emotions, and judgment on other people, I've learned a lot about myself, about my judgment, and I found that most of the time, I am wrong about my judgment. So I've had many people confront me. I had one girl confront me directly because she couldn't take it. It was too much for her. I was too intense for her, and she had the guts to confront me. She said that I scared her, that she got really, really uncomfortable, and be-

> cause I was pissed off. And ahm....yeah, so... about my own behavior, I do learn. I learn from other people, the way I interact, the way I judge, the way I am wrong.

In a similar vein, Keith (23, Australia) described coming to grips with his own *over-confidence* and discovering the importance of being willing to learn from others:

> And now I've realized that there's a lot to be said about looking at and listening to other people, about what they say, what they do, just to learn from their experience. I always thought that I could do everything, that I knew everything, but now I know I really, really don't, and I really, really do need people in my life to help me and to teach me. I always knew that in theory, but I never felt it. And now I feel it. That I can learn from other people more than I thought I could. I guess that's probably what traveling has taught me the most.

In fact, Eric (48, Canada) vividly described how the ongoing challenge of dealing with difference, which is inherent to long-term independent travel, offers the opportunity to develop and refine one's ability to see beyond one's own perspective and remain open to new ideas:

> You can think more rapidly to stop your first opinion and be more open. I can also practice it more traveling. It's a real good way to practice. If I see somebody that I don't want to speak to, but if I say, no, c'mon, open your mind and heart, and be more open, and this is what I do a lot.

In terms of *how* people think, the step after open-mindedness is empathy. That is to say, rather than simply opening one's mind to receive the ideas or values of others, one develops the ability to actively project oneself into the other person's mental framework in an effort to truly understand how this other person thinks or feels. And indeed, this was one area where many travelers reported perceived self-improvement:

> I also think that I am more empathetic than before, that I find it easier to put myself in someone else's shoes. This is something that I wasn't aware of before, and now I notice it all the time. (Lena, 26, Germany)

Beyond just saying that he felt more empathetic, Brian (55, USA, 2nd) even described a travel situation where his travel companion helped him to develop this ability:

> And I always remember this situation in Cuba when I was with [companion] and she said, and she's smart too. We had this weird run in with this guy for money and food. And she said to me, "You don't know that you wouldn't do the exact same thing if you were poor." And I always try to remember that thing, like you've never been that poor, and you don't know what you would do if you were that poor. You don't know what you would do if you were in that position, if you were that poor.

As a final word on empathy, I will share a story from Brian's (43, USA) original interview, in which he describes how he actually put his empathy into practice and let it guide him to a kind action with one local person he encountered on his travels:

8.5 Outcomes

I was walking the streets in India, and this guy was carving this thing and he was like, "Fuck!" cause he broke off an arm of that piece. And I was like, "I know what that's like to work on that thing and then something happens and the whole thing's ruined." So I bought it from him with the broken arm so he would feel better about it. You wanna pass on a little good karma, if you can. So I mean…that time made me feel better, and it's something I would never have done before I started traveling.

9 Post-travel Experiences and Learning Outcomes

As Geoffrey Chaucer wrote, "All good things must come to an end." In time, every LIT that I interviewed eventually went home, although some of them did not stay there for long. In some cases, they decided for themselves to end their journey:

> I was just done with it from one day to another. This didn't happen gradually, but it happened from one day to the next. I woke up, walked outside and thought: "Aha, another building, another street, another sight". And even with people I felt the same way. Another one that I should get to know now. All of a sudden I did not want to anymore, because I was just saturated, I was full. I knew that from that moment onwards I wouldn't be able to absorb anything else. Before this time it was different. Everything was clear and sharp. I was like a dry sponge that soaks up the rain. (Max 36, Austria, 2nd)

In other cases, financial limitations or commitments back home compelled their returns. Although their journeys were ending, for most, the transformational leaning experience was still very much in progress, or perhaps we should say a new transformational learning experience was just beginning. Returning with new ideas, perspectives, values, and even self-images, the challenge now was to figure out how or if these new selves could fit back into their home environments. In fact, it has also been noted, that the magnitude of reverse culture shock can be greater than the culture shock experienced when entering a new culture (e.g. Sussmann, 1986, Szkudlarek, 2010), simply because it is often unexpected (e.g. Martin, 1993; Smith, 1998; Storti, 2003; Sussmann; 2001). For this reason, before proceeding to the LITs' experiences back home, we will take a brief look at the expectations brought with them into their re-entries.

9.1 Pre-return expectations

The emotions that arise when travelers contemplate the return to their native cultures vary widely across a spectrum ranging from eager anticipation to ominous dread. These emotions are grounded in travelers' expectations, which arise as they imagine their homecoming, and can have a distinct effect on how their returns play out in reality. In fact, reentry researchers have argued that when expectations are met or even exceeded, the individual experiences well-being; whereas unfulfilled expectations lead to poor readjustment (Martin & Harrell, 2004; Rogers & Ward, 1993). In their Systems Theory of Intercultural Reentry, Martin & Harrell (2004) identified "realistic expectations" as a key factor in the successful re-adaptation to one's home environment, arguing that the larger the gap between the expectations and the reality at home, the more distressful the reentry experience. Thus, in this section, I will look at the feelings and expectations of travelers before returning home, which will help to inform subsequent discussions about the actual processes of coming home and attempting to re-integrate into their native cultures.

In rare cases, LITs expressed enthusiasm and optimism about their return home. In fact, some travelers expressed a version of the old proverb, "Absence makes the heart grow fonder." Lukas (27, Germany), who had been traveling by himself in South America for several months, compared his feelings to those he had experienced toward the end of previous, shorter trips and pointed out that this was the first time he had felt "homesick":

> I'm doing my big trip now, and I think I will be really happy when I am home again and when I see my family. And this feeling of connection to your homeland, that is, this comforting security that you have in the place that you know well, this is what I first came to understand on this trip. In any event, I have the impression that now, for the first time, I notice that I am very connected to my home, more than I ever thought I wanted to be, or maybe I always had this feeling, but I never consciously registered it.

Unlike his previous trips, he also mentioned that he was ready to "try life at home", whereas before he had usually been planning the next trip before the current one was even over. Similarly, Nadine (23, Canada) described how travel had forced her to come to grips with how dissatisfied she had been with her pre-travel life and instilled in her a belief that she would be able to make changes for the better when she went back:

> I'm always saying "That's a new thing in my life, and when I'm going back, that's gonna change." I know that when I'm going back, I could never live the life that I was living before. Everything will be different.

While Nadine had a vague expectation that things would be different and somehow better, Aaron (35, USA) was eager to point out a key lesson he had learned through travel that was helping him keep a positive, optimistic outlook: "expectation reduces joy". However, with a little more prodding, it became clear that he did have an expectation. Travel had helped him make a break with his past life and career, and he was now eager to get back and start his own company and try a new career: "As much as I love [traveling], I have things to prove to myself because part of who I am is a businessperson". Travel had helped Aaron make a break with his old career, but also taught him that a core aspect of his identity concept involved his role as a businessperson. This realization had helped him form a plan in his mind with a goal and a mission which he could look forward to.

And indeed, this goal or mission was the thing that most often seemed to instill a positive optimism in the minds of some LITs in their pre-return phase. In most cases, this was

9.1 Pre-return expectations

some kind of education program into which they had already been accepted. Dan (34, England), for example, had a girlfriend waiting for him and was looking forward to starting a new chapter in his life: "I was really, really excited about going to university. I wouldn't have kept traveling to miss out on university." And Tom (46, Germany) was looking forward to his upcoming return because of an extended further education program he was planning on pursuing, which he had postponed because of his travels. Finally, Emma (41, England) mentioned that she was simply "looking forward to going home and settling down again and being in a nice routine". In her case, however, it is important to point out that she had taken a break from an already established career where she was confident in her ability to quickly find a new job upon her return, due to the high demand for people in her profession.

On the other hand, those LITs who had no fixed plan for their post-travel life expressed more apprehension about their imminent returns, as one might expect. Chelsea (25, England), who was on her second extended trip when we did our first interview, compared her feelings at that time to how she had felt before the end of her first trip. She pointed out how she had been excited to return from her first trip because she was looking forward to starting university, but this trip was different: "This time, I think it will be different, cause I'm not sure what I'm going to go back to. I won't be going back to a really structured life." This was a common theme during the interviews. While a few LITs had rented out their apartments or houses while they were gone so they would have a place to live when they returned, many had sold all but a few of their belongings before leaving. This meant going back to staying with friends and family for some time before they found a place of their own.

In addition, the majority of them had quit their jobs to travel and were faced with the prospect of finding a new job. Thus, Ally (33, Switzerland) expressed her feelings of uncertainty about her future professional life: "I don't know what kind of work I would like to do. This is my problem. But if I want to work, I will find a job. Could be barmaid, or in an office or something like that." Similarly, Andy (30, USA) first explained how the trip had given him a different philosophy on his career path: "I don't need to start my career at 25 and slave away. I don't need to be a top executive at my company." He even thought his extended travel might "open up a whole other avenue, possibly, career-wise". However, he soon confessed that he was not feeling 100% secure about this aspect of his return:

> I'm a bit nervous, honestly, cause I'm 30 and two years out of work on a resume in the States looks terrible. I'm probably gonna go into a different field than marketing, and I have no job experience, so it's pretty risky.

While Andy and Ally were worried they would have trouble finding a job, Glen was more worried about what would happen after he found a job. After enjoying the freedom of travel for two years, he did not know if he could go back to the 9-to-5 routine: "I can't fucking stand it. I'll be miserable. It depends on what I'm doing. I know I'll have to do it, cause I'm 26. I know I'll have to work to get money." Indeed, this anxiety was present even in travelers who did not have to worry about finding a job. For example, Lena (26, Germany) had a post-travel job lined up, but she already had a feeling that her travel had either changed her or given her a better understanding of herself, which in some way would make her unable to fit back into life in Germany:

> And that's also the reason why I don't necessarily want to spend the rest of my life in Germany. And maybe someday I'll do my divemaster somewhere, and disappear for two years or something. Because my job, the one that I'll start next year, will be my last one. I'll do that for 2 or 3 years and then see how it goes. I just know that I won't spend the rest of my life wasting away in Germany. I just don't think I'm that kind of person. I'm not cut out for that.

The topic of fitting in back at home was not just related to careers, but also to how one would fit back in with circles of friends and loved ones back home. Heather (36, Australia), who maintained a blog during her seven and a half years of travel, stated that during this entire time she had made an effort to maintain contact with her close friends, either through phone or email because she "values [her] friends rather highly". She then expressed her optimism about post-travel relationships with her pre-travel friends back home:

> I wanna go home, and settle and be with my friends and see them. And I'm sure it'll almost be like I never left, but I'm sure that I've changed more than they have. I still anticipate I'll be able to walk back into their lives like I never left.

However, Heather was in the minority on this front, as many LITs already anticipated that their changed values and personalities might turn out to be incompatible with their social circles back home. In the case of Lars (28, Belgium), his concern stemmed from his knowledge that his friends' lives had proceeded in very different ways than his own since he had been gone:

> Before I left it was all like friends going out together. And now most of them are at least living together, lots of them have been married in the meantime. And a lot of them have even children or are going to have children by the time I get home. So they all kind of settled down completely, which I don't want to do. So I'm going to be, hm...lonely again when I get home.

In Aimee's case, she linked her anticipated discomfort with her old friends more to the way she felt *she* had grown through her travels, in particular with regard to her new views on materialism and consumerism:

9.1 Pre-return expectations

> I think when we go back home we're gonna find it very difficult because a lot of the people around us are just very fickle, not very deep, like.... "Ok, you bought a new BMW. Is that really important? Big deal." I mean these are people who have not experienced the things that we have and had their eyes opened in the ways that we had over the last couple of years, and they might be like "Wow, look at that BMW. It's the be-all end-all." And we're like, "Yeah, it's a car. So what?"

Like Aimee, Dana (39, Denmark) expressed the importance of her newfound minimalist ethos and her determination to put it into action upon her return. She explained how, before her trip, she

> rented like a storage place with all the things that I believe that I care about, and I still have that, and I've paid 5 years, 4, or 5 years to this storage room. Which is insane, cause it's a lot of rent. And the rent I'm paying is probably more money than what's worth in there. So I do feel confident enough now to go home and clean that room, and I didn't before. I always thought I would one day find a home where I want to have all these things, where these things would be good for me to have. And so what does that mean? That means that I can't see myself in a regular house anymore. When I do get a house, I would need extremely little.

While Dana is convinced about her new values and confident in her ability to adjust her post-travel life accordingly, other LITs expressed doubts about whether their newfound values would hold up to the pressure of their home environments. For example, Emma (41, England) stated, "I probably will go home and, you know, hopefully I won't forget it, but I'll probably just carry on with what you have to do with work and the usual mundane things that we end up doing." Similarly, Lena (26, Germany), despite feeling that she was not "cut out for" life in Germany, wondered if she would be able to preserve her minimalist lifestyle back home: "And I don't know if I really need all that stuff that I have at home. At the moment I'm living out of a backpack and I don't miss anything. I've been wondering about that a lot, if I could do with less in Germany, but maybe you'll get used to it again fast."

Eric (48, Canada) shared these concerns about all of the changes he had experienced during his travels. He worried that he would simply slip back into old habitual ways of thinking and acting. In his case, his concerns also arose from his experiences after his first long-term trip to Nepal at the age of 30:

> During the trip I was thinking, when I get back, I'll never do this kind of thing again, or I will never think like this again. But when I came back, I realized that you go back in your old track exactly like you did before, like to be anxious about things, and to be rude with people sometimes, you know, and not to appreciate what you have.

Since Eric was on a sabbatical, he was guaranteed to get his job back when he returned. Nevertheless, he was haunted by this anxiety. Asked to speculate on why this regression occurred, Eric offered the following explanation:

> I think that when we get back home, the social pressure and the life is so fast, and you cannot share your experiences with anybody. So you forget it, and you have to get back to work, and I think that's why we lose a lot of what we have learned during traveling.

Indeed, Eric mentions some key challenges that we will cover later in this chapter, and it was clear that he had spent some time reflecting on his initial travel experience and constructing a narrative that explained the perceived failure of his first travel experience as a transformational experience. However, as he continued, it was also clear that he had learned something from this perceived failure, since he had changed his approach the second time around and was hoping for better results in terms of transferring the lessons of travel back into his life in Canada. He mentioned that this time he had consciously "worked on himself", and then suggested:

> You know, it depends what you do during your trip. If you don't work on yourself during your trip, there will be no change when you get back. If you do some work on yourself during the trip, then you will bring this change home.

While this note of optimism is encouraging, the fact is that most LITs had some deep-seated concerns about their return and how they would fit in. Emilia (36, Germany) mentioned that this anxiety can start to creep in far before the actual return date: "I'm going home in 5, 6 months, and I mean, this sounds silly, but I'm slowly feeling the stress about it. It always starts around 5 to 6 months before I should go home [...] I try to block the actual return date out of my mind." For Lars (28, Belgium), who could no longer block out his return date, the overwhelming feeling was one of confusion and uncertainty:

> I just want to know what I'm supposed to do here, in this world. You know, I wanna go home, cause I don't wanna stay here, but I don't think I really want to go home. I just don't know where I want to go. And I'm going home in two weeks.

While Lars worries about what is to come, Heather, in a heartfelt blog post right before returning to Australia, looked back on her travel experience and was already anticipating how much she would miss it:

> Sitting on the bus to Santiago - my final bus journey, with my favourite music playing on my disc man... reflecting on the beautiful scenery of Chile and suddenly found myself in tears that just wouldn't stop. I just had a sense of overwhelming loss and what I came to suspect is that it is all because I am giving up something that I love very much. It is like losing a lover... even though I'm choosing this. That is exactly what this is, too - a lost lover. I have been in love with the journey and it has returned that love many times over. Even though I've had other loves along the way, this one has always won out.

> It is still daunting to also believe I have deserted this lifestyle- never to reclaim it. [...] Where else can I find such wonder, excitement, social activity, interest, positive interaction, affirmation stimulation and challenges but most of all inspiration? I don't know anywhere or anything quite as fulfilling.

If there is a consistent theme that unites all of the highly diverse passages above about pre-return expectations it is the near universal recognition by the travelers themselves that their travels have influenced them strongly and changed them in some way. While some are confident in their ability to implement the lessons of travel and re-integrate their new selves into their former cultures, many more have reservations about this process and anticipate some tough times ahead. In the following section, we will take a look at the rare cases when re-integration caused very little hardship at all, at least at the beginning.

9.2 Smooth sailing and the honeymoon phase

In total, of the 31 participants who told me about their reentry experiences, only 5 were consistently positive, while the remaining 26 reported experiencing significant difficulties upon their initial return to their native culture. Since the positive experiences were very much in the minority, I will cover the positive accounts first. This will include the 6 people who had a generally positive overall experience, as well as some people who reported a "honeymoon phase"—that is, a temporary very positive period before the challenges began to emerge.

Emma (53, England 2nd) and Jake (57, England, 2nd), who had traveled together for two years through Latin America, were both looking forward to their post-travel lives and found their reentry relatively smooth sailing. In an email to me after her travels, Emma wrote "Coming home is always a joy. To be with my parents, sister. To open our house and be with friends. I have never felt stressed about returning and starting work it's the norm for most." This was echoed by her husband Jake, who said:

> Coming home has always been easy. To see friends, family, be in my own house – hot and cold running water, small luxuries that you sometimes do not have, whilst traveling. I have never felt stressed about being home, after two or three days I'm settled with friends, family, work, and normal life.

Of course, Jake and Emma are not the typical travelers for several reasons: First, they both had flexible but dependable jobs to return to (as mentioned above for Emma); second, they had started their relationship just before embarking on their travels, so after two years one the road, they were excited to return and start a new life together; and third, they both had pretty extensive previous travel experience and knew what it was like to return home. In fact, Emma explained that reentry was pretty natural for her: "Work and a normal life have always enabled me to travel, they go hand in hand." In essence, they are lifestyle travelers, for whom re-integration is a routine procedure.

Although Lukas (27, Germany) was not as experienced as Jake and Emma, he, too, had been looking forward to going home (as explained above) because he had been feeling lonely the last few weeks of his journey. He, too, had a relatively unproblematic reentry. Although he acknowledged that it took him some time to get used to "a completely different rhythm" at home, he found that it was relatively easy. He thinks it has to do with the relatively short time he was gone (i.e. 8 months): "If I had been gone longer, like several years, and I hadn't had any family or old friends at home, then it would've been different, too." Although Lukas felt that his trip had profoundly changed him, he felt ready to get home and move on in life.

In the case of Patrick (37, Austria), who had been away for three years, his travels essentially segued back into his real life. He described how he was ready to come home by the end of three years of travel:

> I was just looking forward to home and I didn't have very high expectations. This trip had changed me anyway, traveling for three years. I liked traveling, but at the same time I also felt that it was time to go home, to visit friends. The idea of the trip was to [gather material for a book about my travels], and that's why it was clear when I get back, I'll write a book.

Patrick had accomplished what he had set out to do in his travels, and he had a pretty clear plan for what he wanted to do back home. And although he did not have any real expectations (or perhaps one could say partially *because* he had no expectations), it worked out quite well for him, as he quickly found a cheap place to stay and was able to put together a presentation about his travels, which he gave in various locations, and finish his book.

Max (36, Austria, 2nd) was a bit different. Having traveled for just under two years, he, too, felt ready to return. As described in his quote that opened this chapter, he felt like a saturated sponge that could not soak up any more experience. Nevertheless, he described how he devised a careful plan for a gradual return to Austria, flying first to Germany, where he traveled for a month and visited friends, "…and then in Vienna, I was slowly easing my way back. I was back in Europe, speaking German again, certain routines, but not really fully. I have to say, it was pretty unspectacular." He also benefited from supportive friends, who let him crash on their couches, and even a surprise bonus from the Austrian government: Upon registering as a "job seeker" with the local government, he was pleasantly surprised to find that he still qualified for three months of unemployment, as he had only collected the first three months before his trip. For Max, with his newfound minimalist lifestyle, this was easily enough money to allow him to ease his way back into society by finding a cheap apartment and, soon enough, a job.

The five people mentioned above were the only ones who reported a mostly unproblematic reentry. To one degree or another, they all benefited from some key advantages: supportive relationships, reasonable expectations, some sense of purpose, or a reasonably fixed plan for their return. The rest of the LITs lacked one or more of these key components, which led to some re-integration difficulties. However, some of them did benefit from a brief period of relative enjoyment before the problems kicked in. Aaron (35, USA, email), who was mentioned above in the pre-return expectations section as having an ambitious plans to write a book and re-start his business career, is an interesting case. He contacted me via email a couple months after the end of his 8-month journey to report that his positive momentum from the trip was still carrying over:

> Thankfully for me I have not been forced to adjust fully to the real world as of yet. I don't have a job and the looking is great but it is slow. At the same time, I am really fired up about the writing that I am doing. I need to get my fill almost every day. Need to finish my re-writes before I do actually start work.

He went on to say that he was "gainfully unemployed", an excellent phrase that shows that he had at least partially convinced himself that his unemployment was still productive and useful. However, it also reveals that he knows he is back in his home culture, which expects him to have some kind of "gainful employment". Indeed, about two years later, when he contacted me to give me an update, he described how shortly after writing the first email he had taken a bad job that put an end to his stress-free post-travel period: "I was working way too hard and it was dreadful." Although by the time of the second email, he had found a better job and was once again happy (including looking forward to his next trip), Aaron's experiences also provide support for Gullahorn & Gullahorn's (1963) W-Curve reentry hypothesis, which posits that returnees are initially euphoric about being home, but soon become frustrated and anxious when their expectations are not met. In fact, several LITs described this initial "honeymoon phase" when they just feel happy to be home again. For example, Nick (47, Ireland, 2nd) reported:

> The first few weeks were particularly easy, as there were lots of people to catch up with - friends in [hometown] and family at home. Everyone had been keeping track of our travels through the website, so everyone knew the story and wanted to talk about South America [...]. So I kicked back (as the Yanks say) and enjoyed the limelight a little. A few weeks later, and you've met everyone and talk moves on. But most people I know have travelled, so everyone understands the 'low' after the initial 'prodigal son homecoming' - so people were sympathetic. Then I moved on to the next thing, which was job-hunting. Now, those weeks were not so much fun. It was tough being back in the daily grind or looking for a

job, especially with everything from the trip so fresh in mind. It was also strange to be 'living' somewhere with no expectation of moving on anytime soon.

Brian (43, USA), who has had many reentry experiences, has even coined his own term for the honeymoon phase:

> Sometimes I really ahm, I will draw out a trip, like I try to relish it. And I always call it afterglow, and people will be like "What's with you?" And I'll be like, "Well, I'm still in my week afterglow." My theory is always, the longer the trip, the longer the afterglow. Like you go for a whole year, you get a longer afterglow. After two weeks maybe your afterglow fades. And nothing kills the afterglow faster than work.

While my data is not sufficient to confirm the precise correlation between trip length and honeymoon period Brian posits, it does show that for those lucky enough to have a honeymoon phases, the length can vary widely:

> The first three days are great cause everybody is happy to see you again. And then on Monday everybody goes to work again, and then the shitty time starts: getting used to the fast place of life, finding a job... (Lars, 28, Belgium).

> We've been back in the UK now for about six weeks and the novelty of being home is wearing thin already. (Glen, 26, England, email)

> I would say the first six months were great, it was magnificent. You have a large apartment, you have a bathtub, you have as much drinking water as you need at your disposal... family, just great. Then, after half a year, somehow it starts again. (Veronica, 35, Austria)

The "it" then Veronica mentions is everything that starts to go bad and causes stress or discomfort. The next section will examine these stressors in more detail

9.3 Facing the friends and family

Perhaps the most upsetting aspect of reentry for most LITs is the difficulty they experience in attempting to re-connect with people in their home culture, particularly those friends and family members who are most important in their lives. This frustration speaks to the immense importance of social context for identity. As we saw above, in most cases LITs' pre-return anxieties tend to focus more on the big picture—that is, the pressure to find a job and re-integrate into a society whose values they have either consciously or subconsciously begun to question during their travels. However, many assume that close personal bonds with family and friends will transcend any value changes that may have occurred in the course of their travels and preserve their most important relationships. Although the travelers described in the previous section were fortunate enough to blend

9.3 Facing the friends and family

back in relatively seamlessly, the vast majority of LITs struggle to re-connect with their friends and family upon their return.

Once the honeymoon phase is over, the disorientation sets in. In fact, many LITs skipped the euphoria phase altogether and experienced cognitive, affective and behavioral dissonance practically the moment they set foot in their homelands. On the most superficial level, even the climate can be a shock:

> And then I remember, just getting off the plane in [hometown], and it must have been September or something. Because that cool, autumn wind, just getting out of the plane and feeling that it was like…it did not go on in my mind, it was just my whole body remembered where I was. And it was the wind. I was like, my heart started pounding and I was like nooo, no no no. but it wasn't my mind, it was just my whole body that just went "Nooooooo! Don't do this!" (Dana, 51, Denmark, 2nd)

> On top of that, it was mid-March at home, which means there was not a single leaf on the trees. It was always grey and raining, and I had just come from colorful South America. And it just completely shattered me. (Lena, 41, Germany, 2nd)

Even in these reactions to the weather we can already see the magnitude of the emotions LITs experience when they return home, which should not be underestimated. When focusing on social or cultural issues, the language can get even stronger, such as "a total shock to the system" (Alan, 56, New Zealand, 2nd), "full on post-travel depression" (Brian, 55, USA, 2nd), and "it was hell" (Matt, 39, USA).

Indeed, LITs come home with their newly evolved values and identities and are sometimes shocked to find that their new identities do not fit into their home environments very well:

> My house looks the same, the city the same. I am not sure that much has changed. But I have. (Aaron, 35, USA)

> When I came back, I did not see many changes around me. It seems to me that everything is the same as when I left. Life flows normally and without much change. It's rather my state of mind that has changed. (Eric, 59, Canada, 2nd)

> I felt more out of place than I ever did when I was still traveling. I felt like an outsider. And it smacked me off my feet. I wasn't prepared for it at all. (Alan, 56, New Zealand)

In fact, as with Alan in the previous quote, many LITs report that the return home is actually far more disturbing their initial exposure to a foreign culture had been, as the culture shock during travel is often mitigated somewhat by feelings of excitement and adventure. Lena (41, Germany, 2nd) addressed this issue in her interview:

> What I find interesting with traveling is that you don't get the culture shock when you travel to another country, but you get it when your return. That really struck me a lot. When I arrived in Ecuador, for example, everything was new and excit-

ing, and then I came back and for all the people at home, family, friends, for them life just went on. Nothing significant happened, whereas my entire worldview had changed. And I came back into the same daily grind, and for all the other people, I was also the same. But I wasn't the same anymore. And that really got to me, especially in the first weeks.

Reentry research has identified a wide range of negative emotions that are associated with the return home, including frustration, anger, hostility, lethargy, helplessness, boredom, restlessness, anxiety and depression (e.g. Allison, et al., 2011: Foust, et al. 1981; Gaw, 2000; Rogers & Ward, 1993; Walling et al., 2006). Research has also suggested that the cultural distance between the host and home culture plays a role in the readjustment to the LITs' home countries (Martin & Harrell, 2004), and since most LITs travel to countries that are extremely different to their home cultures, it is not surprising that their reentry shock can be powerful. Szkudlarek (2010) has shown that the lack of preparation for reentry and the unexpectedness of the difficulties encountered at home can intensify this shock. These factors are already evident in the two examples above, and we will see below how this theme returns again and again, as those who had not anticipated the challenges suffered the greatest shock.

Lena's quote above alludes to the two leading subjects that arise consistently when LITs discuss the problems of reentry: re-establishing contact with friends and family and fitting back into the "daily grind", that is the rituals and routines of life in their native cultures. In this section, we will address the first of these topics by looking at the ways in which people react to the returning LITs, the feelings this causes in the LITs themselves, the interpretations they put on the reactions of their friends and families, and how managing the tensions in these relationships changes LITs' perspectives, identities and behaviors.

9.3.1 The lucky few

As with stories of completely smooth re-entries, the stories of supportive, understanding friends and family are rare. However, some LITs were indeed fortunate enough to receive support from friends and family throughout their re-integration process. One theme that emerged in these positive stories was that they usually involved friendships that dated back far before the LIT left to travel. Thus, Lukas (39, Germany, 2nd), who was mentioned above as having a smooth reentry, mentioned:

> My circle of friends is very close-knit. There are some who have known me for 15, 20 years. And they were there right from the start. And at the beginning they rolled their eyes a bit, but after all this time, they must have learned that that's part of who Lukas is and that's also how they introduce me in new circles. Like "yes, that's the school buddy of [name], and he's a roaming vagabond, and you should be happy that you get to meet him because normally he is in the desert

or somewhere." And then they all accepted it. Nobody's trying to improve me. (Lukas, 39, Germany, 2nd)

In one case, the support through the reentry process was even enough to make one LIT get married and decide to stay in the country: "And it was really my wife, who I had already known before the trip, but I didn't know then that she was the right one. Being in love with her made the decision for me that I ended up staying" (Philipp, 46, Austria).

While marriage is not often the outcome, many LITs expressed appreciation for those of their friends who tried to support them after their trips. Eric (48, Canada), who we will hear from below talking about his own reentry problems, nevertheless reports that some of his friends at least realize that travel is something that he needs: "My friends, they are happy for me, cause they see that it's good for me. They know that I love to do it." In some cases, LITs are lucky enough to have families that also recognize the value of travel, despite their anxieties about the perceived dangers involved: "They support it as much as they can. My parents are always worried, but they also say, 'Do it. You don't know when you'll have that opportunity again. Take it, kid, and get to know the world'" (Lena, 26, Germany). In other cases, the parents are supportive, but a little less convinced about the necessity for travel:

> They worry about me, but they think it's good cause they want me to get it out of my system. They want me to get back to the States because they miss me. My Dad's more objective. He says, "Do it to the best of your ability, but we want you back here, because we want you to think about a career path cause you're coming up to your thirties, you know. You're not spring chicken anymore, you're not coming right out of college." (Andy, 30, USA)

Although the fundamental support of his parents causes Andy to see this idea that travel is a "phase" as a harmless opinion, we will see below that some LITs are far more threatened by that assumption. In contrast, Aimee (26, Canada) reported how her parents had taken an active interest in her travels and were rather living vicariously through her, with the support of some home-based research:

> I've actually been quite impressed with my parents, cause like I said they have not traveled, and it's been a whole like educational experience for them, cause every place that we got to, they are doing their own research, cause they wanna know where their daughter is, and they're picking up an atlas and they've got maps and they know where we are, and they're really kind of interested.

Finally, in a few cases, LITs reported that their family really did not understand their travels at all, but they still offered support. For Matt (39, USA), this was enough, and he was grateful that he could rely on his family to accept him no matter what he chose to do with his life:

> I mean nobody in my family has ever really lived anywhere outside of Texas. So as far as talking about [transitions], they don't have a real strong grasp of that. But I have a good family and good people, and they all listen, and they'll laugh, and they do their best to try and understand. But I'm not really asking them to understand either. (Matt, 39, USA, 2nd)

Unfortunately, Matt's perfect combination of his own reasonable expectations and unconditional love from his family was an exception within my research, as we will see below.

One final source of support throughout the reentry process was friends who had done some traveling themselves. In Sarah's (37, Austria) case, it was her husband. Since they had traveled together, they could also go through the reentry process together: "He was the only person I could talk to. He understood what I was going through." In other cases, it was simply a friend who had traveled in the past as well. For example, Lena (41, Germany, 2nd) described how one friend helped ease the pain of reentry:

> A few days later, I met with a good friend who was also gone for half a year, and she had exactly the same problem I had. And she really understood me so well. And so we just teamed up. She was doing an internship in Cologne, and I visited her for a few days there. And afterwards, I felt much better because she was the only one who really understood me. And I didn't know how to handle myself. I wanted to break up with my boyfriend. I wanted to get away again. I didn't care about anything anymore. I just wanted to leave. (Lena, 41, Germany, 2nd)

Having lived through the reentry process herself, it was not surprising that Lena's friend could help ease the stress of reentry. This story also highlights the main problem that arises with most relationships when one returns from a long trip—communication. In a vulnerable and confusing time of their lives, when many LITs are perhaps looking for confirmation about the changed values and identities they developed during their travels, friends and family often prove unable to provide that confirmation or, in some case, even understand what they are supposed to be confirming. I witnessed this in some of my interviews as well, when it was evident that some of the LITs were very pleased and even relieved to have a sympathetic audience. For example, when I asked Max (36, Austria, 2nd) how travel had changed him, he paused for a moment, smiled and said, "Up until today, I don't think anyone has ever asked me what has changed, or how I have changed, like you asked me. Like how have you changed? Are you a different person? That just never happened." And when I asked Sarah (37, Austria) who she felt she could talk to about her travel experiences, she replied that there was basically nobody "except people like you, cause you've been abroad." She then continued, "It's hard to share these experiences with people who haven't gone abroad because they don't know what you're talking about."

9.3 Facing the friends and family

Indeed, reentry stories are often replete with examples of communication barriers or complete communication breakdowns, and in the next section, we will take a deeper look into why these breakdowns so often occur.

9.3.2 Communication breakdowns

In traveling to another culture, one expects communication barriers. However, back home, where everyone speaks the same language and has the "same" cultural background (which may be an inherently simplistic concept, but is still something implicitly accepted by many people), there is a basic assumption that one can express one's thoughts and values and be understood, especially among one's closest friends. This expectation makes the reality of feeling like an "outsider" within ones closest social circles, as Alan described it above, highly disturbing for some LITs. In the context of a narrative identity paradigm, which views communication with others as a key mechanism for constructing and projecting one's identity, the LITs' strong emotional reaction to the loss of sympathetic communication with their closest friends is even less surprising.

In this section, we will explore the root causes of this frustration. We will look not only at the reactions LITs face from their friends and family, but, perhaps more importantly, at the ways in which the LITs interpret these reactions, for these interpretations are the key component of the learning process that occurs during reentry. While the reactions of friends and family offer the disorienting experience that triggers the learning process, in the LITs interpretations we can see the process of negotiating newfound differences and trying to fit them into a meaning scheme that can preserve their own values and sense of self-esteem, and ideally LITs' relationships with their loved ones. After discussing these value negotiations, both internal and interpersonal, we will look at the meaning schemes that LITs derive from this experience and the behavioral strategies they adopt to preserve their sense of belonging to a community either by preserving their relationships or developing new ones.

9.3.2.1 Two to tango

In some cases, LITs seemed to grasp the fact that they are also partly responsible for the communication breakdown—that is, they expressed a frustration with their own inability to properly explain an experience that had been extremely meaningful for them:

> I was really impressed by this trip, and it was difficult for me because I couldn't share it with anybody. I can, for sure, I can tell them my trip was like this, like that, but I didn't feel that they can understand what it was, what my experience was. So I felt a little bit alone. (Eric, 48, Canada)

> It's so hard to explain because there's also these really amazing moments where you have these really great feelings, like "Wow, I did it. But fuck me, and it's fucking sunrise, and there's the Taj Mahal"... And you can't really put it into words, and then you explain it to someone else, but you can't really get it across how you felt then. (Brian, 43, USA)

In Brian's case, we can see how even in the context of the interview, speaking to a fellow traveler, he found it hard to explain his feelings. Nick's (47, Ireland, 2nd) response captures a similar feeling, but also begins to hint at a possible deeper root cause for the communication problem:

> I still find it frustrating to explain what it 'meant' to me to have achieved some lifelong goals - I can't really communicate what being alone in Patagonia meant to me, something I've wanted since I first read Chatwin's *In Patagonia* as an impressionable young man.

It is worth pointing out that this passage comes from a written questionnaire, and Nick placed the quotation marks around the word 'meant'. Here, the punctuation marks themselves speak volumes. They express Nick's rejection of the very idea that one could possibly put something this important into words. Of course, despite his protestations of the incommunicability of the experience, simply stating that he achieved a lifelong dream is an attempt to do precisely that. That is, for anyone who has achieved a lifelong dream, they should understand the feeling at least partially just from hearing that phrase. This reveals the other possible interpretation of the quote marks—that they are a written indicator to intensify the sarcasm of the passage, which is intended to criticize some people's inability to understand the feeling associated with accomplishing a lifelong dream. This implies some other questions. Do they lack the imagination to understand what that would feel like? Have they themselves never actually achieved (or possibly even had) a lifelong dream? In some cases, there may be some truth to these implied accusations, but perhaps the easiest answer here is that most people simply do not share the lifelong dream of being alone in a distant mountain range, and this is perhaps the fundamental value dissonance at the root of this conflict and Nick's feelings of frustration.

Julia (37, Germany) also expressed a belief that it is impossible to explain the meaning of her travels, and her answer illuminates another implied value dissonance. She begins with a complaint about a specific question she received upon her return:

> For me, the worst question was always, "So, how was it?" Am I supposed to tell you something about the last 2 years? That is tough. When you come back from a 2-week vacation, then sure, "We had a super party, it was a great island, and so forth." But after 2 years, you can't just say how it was. With long journeys it's more like you are changing every day. It's an incredible growth... A working on yourself, an accomplishment and effort. I believe it is really a process.

9.3 Facing the friends and family

The dreaded "how was it?" question was mentioned in several interviews. Here, this reaction expresses a frustration with the interlocutor's assumption that something so incredibly meaningful could be explained in a few simple words. However, in Julia's quote, we again see a LIT trying to do just that, and doing a credible job of it. In a few short phrases, she expresses the value that she places on travel, which is that it serves as a tool for self-exploration and personal growth. As this idea is neither complex nor radical, it would seem that once again, the barrier to communication is not a lack of understanding, but rather that Julia assumes people back home will either refuse to believe that travel could actually promote self-exploration and personal growth, or will reject the value Julia assigns to these endeavors. Thus, even in these cases where LITs evoke the "incommunicability" of their experience, their stories reveal that the frustration actually stems from a perceived difference between their values and those of their interlocutors. And in most cases, this is based on an underlying assumption that the other person either lacks the imagination or empathy to grasp the meaning of the travel experience or is so firmly rooted in their own conservative, "shallow" values that they would automatically deny the value of a non-mainstream activity such as long-term independent travel. As we will see below, in most places this criticism of their non-traveler friends is stated far more explicitly. However, before we look at the LITs' interpretations of their friends' responses, it is worth providing a brief list of the most common and most disturbing responses the LITs actually receive from their non-traveler friends back home.

9.3.2.2 Sentence is passed

While some LITs, as mentioned above, are fortunate enough to receive some understanding and even appreciation for what the LITs themselves deem the important accomplishment of their trips abroad, the vast majority faced a variety of criticisms, both stated and implied, from their friends back home.

The first response that LITs find so troubling is a flat-out denial of their experiences, which their friends demonstrate by refusing to show any interest in what actually transpired during the journeys. In extreme cases, people even pretend that the journey never happened. For example, after four years of traveling around the world, Oliver (59, Austria, 2nd) reported his surprise that "there were really people who never once asked us how our trip was". Similarly, when asked about his family's opinion of his travels, Eric (48, Canada) commented, "I don't really know what they think about it cause they say nothing about it." Brian (43, USA) expressed the pain caused by this response, particularly when it comes from one's own family: "I get this huge slap in the face from my family. They're not interested. And it was so hard for me to figure that out. My father, he's just genuinely not interested. So don't bring it up. He's not interested. He never asks about it." Similarly, Dan (34, England) described the following scene from his first few nights after his return:

> And then the first couple of nights, I remember being absolutely appalled at how disinterested everybody else was to hear those stories. Everybody would be like "excellent, it's great to see you", "great that you're back" and da da da. "How was it?" and that was it. And then I started actually telling them something, and they were just like, "Ah, yeah, yeah," and had absolutely no interest, and were back to talking about the same things they were talking about before I left.

Here again, we see that the extent of people's interest amounts to the dreaded "How was it?", to which they don't generally expect or want a real response. And as with Brian's "slap in the face", this is genuinely perplexing to many LITs. Thus, Eric (59, Canada) reported:

> Obviously, I experienced great frustration on my return, and no one actually came to help me get back into ordinary life. They were all too absorbed and caught up in their daily reality that they had not left. [...] I do not really understand the reaction of people around me. If someone leaves for a week's holiday in the south, everyone asks him how his trip went, and they listen at length to the person's story of a stay in an all-inclusive hotel, which, in my opinion, is totally irrelevant. On the other hand, when I come back from a year of travel, nobody asks me anything! Why?! That's what I've been wondering for a long time.

For those friends who at least show some interest, that interest usually comes with some highly disturbing (for the LITs) assumptions. In fact, Eric's quote above alludes to the first area of tension, which we have already seen in our discussion of the perceived traveler vs. tourist dichotomy. Since travelers are keen to distinguish themselves from simple vacationers, it is no surprise that they are not too pleased when their friends ask, "So how was your vacation?" For example, Alan (42, New Zealand) reports, "Another good friend of mine, he doesn't do a great deal of traveling, he's always like, 'you're always on bloody holiday.'" Similarly, Emilia (36, Germany) sums up her co-workers' view of travel, while simultaneously doing a bit of her own judging: "At work, there are some people, ahm, somewhat stupid people. When I say I go traveling for two years, then they think I'll be lying on a beach doing nothing. They equate holiday with travel." In terms of reentry shock, Glen (38, England, 2nd) described how this view of travel as holiday gives rise to unrealistic expectations from his friends: "Others, who regarded travel as an extensive vacation, almost expected me to fit back into their 'style' of living straight away, just like themselves when returning from their two-week vacation in the sun, usually [at] a Mediterranean resort!" Brian (43, USA) talked about how the conflation of travel and vacation leads to a complete lack of sympathy for the difficulties LITs face, either during reentry or just in their post-travel (or "inter-travel" in some cases) lives in general. When I asked how he was handling his reentry, he replied:

9.3 Facing the friends and family

> Full on post-travel depression. It's horrible. And it's nice that you even ask that because I say that a lot of times, and people don't understand. And I get that same bullshit, like "what are you complaining about?" […] I always hate it because I complain about work, and no one lets me because they go, "What are you complaining about? You only worked for 8 months this year. Let's see, do I have sympathy for you? No!"

In some cases, not only do non-travelers assume that travel life is simply relaxing, but they also assume that it involves luxury and that the LITs must therefore be rich. Needless to say, in light of the typical traveler low-budget ethos discussed above, this is particularly offensive for returning travelers.

> The number one question I get is, "How do you pay for all that?" They think I'm super rich. And that's what they're doing. They're projecting because they're thinking of their own travels, and they think you are super rich. "How can you afford travel like that?" (Brian, 43, USA)

Brian, who at the time of this first interview had already experienced reentry many times, had gotten to the point that he would even prefer the apathy described above to the loaded questions he gets from people back home: "The questions are not very interesting, and then I don't really feel like explaining everything in detail." Heather (36, Australia) faced similar assumptions from her friends back home:

> I think they think I'm living it up and living the life of luxury, actually. They've never done it, so they don't really know how hard work this is. They've never traveled really. They've never backpacked. They've never lived this lifestyle. Cause it's really become a lifestyle. And so they would say sometimes, "Oh, you're living the life of luxury traveling here and there and everywhere. You must be making a fortune." Which is not true.

Heather is annoyed by the assumption that her imagined riches make travel easy. This denigrates the value of the sacrifices she feels she has made, in terms of career, money and finance, and completely fails to acknowledge the whole purpose of travel from Heather's perspective—learning and personal development.

Of course, it must be pointed out that this anxiety about being perceived as a "slacker" shows the continued insecurity LITs feel in the face of their home culture's assumption that "responsible", "normal" people work for 47-50 weeks a year (depending on the particular social system). While many LITs reject this belief, they still feel a longing to be accepted (or even loved) by the people who espouse this belief. Although deep down they might be thinking, "Yes, I don't want to be a slave to the system like you," they know that such statements are unlikely to foster supportive friendships because they will trigger their friends' own insecurities. So they fall back on the strategy of making travel sound more like work, something that their friends can understand and for which the LITs will hopefully receive some "credit" from their friends. Of course, this strategy is rarely successful. First, it forces the LITs to downplay the joy they get from travel, which breeds frustration and some level of resentment towards the people forcing them to do this. Second, it rarely works, as their friends' are unlikely to believe them.

As an example, we can look at the final disturbing reaction LITs often face. While LITs desperately want people to understand how they have grown from their travels, or how travel has fundamentally altered their values and identities, many people at home insist on viewing the experience as some sort of aberration in the LITs' autobiographies. That is, traveling is just a phase to be outgrown, like the "excessive" (by social standards) sexual energy of adolescence. Here are just a few of the stories where LITs related their experience with this form of judgement:

> Most just wanted me to move on with my life I guess. I mean, I wasn't 20 anymore either. I guess most people thought that I'd finally gotten it out of my system. (Alan, 56, New Zealand)
>
> My mom keeps asking me when I'll go back to leading a "normal life", and I always answer that I am living a normal life. The others see me as a dropout. (Chris, 36, Czech Republic)
>
> Most of [my parents'] reactions and that of [my boyfriend's mom] is the same, is that we'll get it out of our system, eventually. You know, that we'll get over it. (Chelsea, 25, England)
>
> The thing I get, which I don't like, is that they're all ready for it to end. So they ask me if I ever want to stop traveling, and I don't know how to answer that. Like they are ready for me to become like them. I think that's what that question feels like to me. They want me to settle down and stop traveling. (Brian, 43, USA)
>
> And at one point it just slipped out of my brother's mouth: "Yeah, I've already talked about it with our mom, and we believe, but we've never said anything, now that you're back, and it'll take a while before you are 'normal' again, and you're acclimatized again." So this change, they did notice it subliminally, but they saw it as an anomaly, as a mistake. And then again the hook is that they are the one's affected by my mistakes and anomalies. Like I have to iron it out again, and then it'll all be ok again. (Max, 36, Austria, 2nd)

In the most generous of these judgements, travel is a pointless immature thing that people have to outgrow, while the harshest judges condemn it as some kind of psychological disorder that needs to be cured. This latter response fits in with the long history of society's attempts to pathologize long-term independent travel in order to repress a form of behavior viewed as threatening, as discussed above in section 3.1.

While friends can (and do) simply reject returning LITs and phase them out of their lives, family bonds are not so easily renounced. Some parents, in particular, go far beyond refusing to speak about their children's travels and resort to extreme measures in an attempt to "cure" their wayward offspring. For example, Max's (35, Austria, 2nd) mother de-

9.3 Facing the friends and family

ploys the classic parental guilt trip, with "bitter crying" and questions such as, "How can you do this to us that you leave us worrying for so long about whether you're going to come home ok?" Julia (37, Germany) reported that her mother actually has asthma attacks that only seem to go away when Julia is home. This did not stop Julia from traveling, but it did change the way she communicated with her mother: "I have to admit, I constantly lie to my mother just to make her life easier. I was always traveling with a non-existent travel companion." In one case, one mother even decided to give money she had promised to her LIT son to her non-traveling daughter instead to send a message of disapproval to her son. Obviously, stories about parents who are upset by their children's unwillingness to accept their values and ideas about how to live life are hardly rare. Lars (28, Belgium), the recipient of such parental disapproval, explained it himself, "My family is probably not too happy, cause it's not only me, it's my sister as well. They probably just want a nice family and grandkids and all that stuff, which they don't have." Ultimately, the case of LITs and their parents simply proves the lesson that parents have been failing to learn for centuries: condemnation and persecution, either emotional or financial, is rarely successful when people have their hearts set on something.

And indeed, it is clear from my research, and from many researchers who came before me, that traveling is an essential part of most LITs' identities. Here are some sample replies I received when asking LITs how important travel was to them:

> Traveling is one of the most important things in my life. I always wanted to travel. (Nadine, 23, Canada)

> Very important. I guess it's my number 1 love. Some people like to play tennis, some people like to go swimming, and I like to travel. (Keith, 23, Australia)

> The most important thing. (Sarah, 37, Austria)

> And for me, that's my life. My life is travel. And if I'm not traveling, then I'm not living my life. It's what makes me feel alive. (Magnus, 25, Denmark)

> Traveling is definitely the number one priority in my life; well, logically, number one after my health. (Emilia, 36, Germany)

When something is so important that people only reluctantly concede first place on their priority list to their own health, it is not surprising that they feel hurt and threatened when people refuse to acknowledge its importance or even claim that it is worthless or harmful. Particularly when one considers the generally fragile emotional state that many travelers experience upon reentry, it is understandable that these attacks put many LITs on the defensive. In the following section, we will look at some of the defense strategies LITs develop to help them deal with these attacks and what these defense strategies reveal about the value struggles they are undergoing.

9.3.2.3 Negotiating difference: From confrontation to acceptance

Most returning LITs realize relatively quickly that they are dealing with a conflict of values. As they try to deal with the feelings of being rejected, many of them fall into the pattern of accepting the binary opposition implied by their friends' attacks and then essentially return the favor. That is, they denigrate their friends' values in order to privilege their own. The battle usually revolves around the traveler value of autonomy and willingness to take risk discussed in previous sections. On one side of the conflict, many non-travelers devalue travel by making comments about travel being a vacation or even an escape, thereby implying that LITs are not tough enough to handle "reality". On the other side, during the interviews the travelers often seek to turn the tables by inserting their own comments about how comfortable and automatic "prescribed" mainstream life is, thereby portraying their non-traveler friends as weak sheeple (i.e. people who blindly follow the herd mentality) and themselves as the heroic adventurers who escape the oppression (or boredom) of society. While the charge of lacking courage is at the root of most LIT criticisms of non-travelers, there are a two recurring auxiliary themes that LITs employ to lend rhetorical force to their criticisms: materialism and lack of intellectual curiosity or imagination. Obviously, these are the flip sides of the prized traveler values of low-budget minimalism and desire for self-exploration and development. Thus, the LITs are implicitly (and sometimes more explicitly) extoling their own values, thereby helping them to re-affirm their own sense of self-worth. As these strategies tend to blend together, it is difficult to isolate examples of one or the other. Therefore, below I offer a sampling of these principles in action for the reader's enjoyment:

> And my friends, well, a few of them said they'd love to come, but somehow, I don't know. They could've joined me, theoretically, because I'm sure they have as much money as I do, but I think they were anchored in their 'normal lives' too much. Nobody wants to let go of their job, at least none of them. They got their first jobs right after uni and just didn't want to do that. One of them also told me that he doesn't have the courage, despite being interested, but he'll stick to watching documentaries on TV. (Lukas, 27, Germany).

> Indeed, when we return from a long journey, the people around us are in a different universe than ours. For my part, I am full of my whole trip and experiences that I have experienced but the people around are caught up in their daily lives that they have not left. They have little interest in everything I've experienced on a trip, and they do not really want to hear about it. (Eric, 59, Canada, 2nd)

> But it is difficult to go back home in the sense that no one… you know… you think that why am I wasting my breath telling people about it and they don't understand?

9.3 Facing the friends and family

> They don't wanna understand it. They're just in this safe little life that they've gotten into and it's difficult. (Aimee, 26, England)

> I remember being absolutely... I think it was the first night in the pub, [...] It was the same pub that we'd always gone to and they were still talking about the same things. I just remember being appalled that they hadn't moved on. (Dan, 34, England)

> Last time we got back home we talked to our friends about traveling for like half an hour and then it'll be like ah...such and such just got a new car, and.. you know...they are not on the same wavelength as you, and that's hard. We found that hard last time. (Aimee, 26, England)

> People at home haven't changed. When you come back and ask, 'What have you done in the last two years?' You get, 'We bought a new TV, and last year we were on Corsica on holiday', and yes, that's what happens in two years. And of 20 friends, 10 split up, with or without kids. And that's what I can say about my friends and what's changed. (Emilia, 36, Germany)

> The friends... that's a difficult one. I don't know, I guess they all kind of, some part of them wants to [travel] as well, but they just want to stay home and live a regular life, a serious life. And some of them are jealous because they see what we are doing. They are saying, "Wow! They are doing all this stuff, and we are just sitting at home." That's what I miss in my friends back home: they all take the easy way. I look at my friends back home differently. It's easier to take the easy way. I don't know why. (Lars, 28, Belgium)

> And I always put that down to one being my family, you know, they love me but they're not curious about that stuff, they're quite homebodies [...] and my brother might have bought a new van, and one of them might have been on holiday somewhere, but I don't know, they're just not that curious. And also with my friends from [hometown] who just don't leave [hometown] very much, and they're not looking beyond the horizon a great deal, and they kind of don't want to. I don't know. I never really understood it. (Chelsea, 37, England, 2nd)

> They all kind of jokingly said, "We're jealous. We're envious. bla bla bla... I wish I was doing that." And you know, it's true, cause most of them are sort of married with children at this point and living pretty dull lives. (Aaron, 35, USA)

The final quote from Aaron highlights one further rhetorical strategy popular with LITs—argue that those attacking you are envious or jealous.[2] Indeed, many of their friends will openly state their envy. However, LITs are prone to seizing upon this concept and amplifying it, or perhaps even finding it where it does not truly exist, all for rhetorical effect. Perhaps the most direct example of this came from Sarah (37, Austria):

> We came back and we put a mirror in front of their faces. We told them, "Yes, you can do it." But when we told them stories or showed them the pictures, they didn't really want it because it was like... We showed them their own weaknesses, to not be able to live up to your dreams. [...] All of them envied us for what we did. Most of them wanted to travel, but they were all stuck in their lives

---

[2] For the sake of this discussion, we have to accept that these two terms are synonyms in modern English usage for a meaning that used to be reserved for "envy" alone: "painful or resentful awareness of an advantage enjoyed by another joined with a desire to possess the same advantage" (Merriam Dictionary, 2017).

> somehow. [...] So our friends in a way they don't understand that we've become stronger and more courageous.

To be clear, my point here is not to argue that Sarah's arguments are completely invalid. On the contrary, common sense, as well as having lived this process myself and spoken to many people on both sides of the "debate", have convinced me that these value differences are quite real, and many non-travelers are deeply threatened by LITs. My point here is simply to highlight the fact that the reentry is truly a shocking experience and draw attention to some of the mental strategies LITs deploy in attempting to resolve this inner conflict, particularly as they play out in the storytelling context of the interviews.

However, one of the desired learning outcomes of long-term independent travel would presumably be a more refined self-awareness and a deeper insight into the mental processes that go into value formation and construction, as well as how cultural influences operate, which in turn might lead to more tolerance and acceptance of difference. In this context, it is difficult not to point out the irony in the following response to the question, "Have you ever experienced culture shock?": "More when I came home. I am a person who can adjust well to foreign settings and is open to new things. At home, everything had all just remained the same" (Philipp, 46, Austria). Here we see a LIT lauding his own skills for being able to adapt to difference, and then describing his difficulty in adjusting to a culture where the values had not evolved to his liking. It is an interesting quote, as it also highlights the inherent power discrepancy involved in most long-term independent travel. That is to say, as many LITs themselves pointed out, they mostly travel in less developed countries, where their relative wealth, mobile lifestyle, and the traveler infrastructure culture largely shields them from the burden of having to adjust to the "foreign setting". Alan (42, New Zealand) showed his awareness of this irony when he described his own efforts to re-integrate:

> I obsessively searched for a job, hoping that getting back to routine would get me out of my blues. My first instinct was to get out again as fast as possible. But that would've been a cop out. I was proud of being able to adapt to all kinds of different cultures, and would have felt pathetic to not be able to adapt to normal life.

As we will see below, Alan's efforts to fit into "normal" life ultimately proved futile, as he ended up moving abroad. Nevertheless, this quote shows Alan's awareness of the difficulty of maintaining the open, accepting mindset many LITs claim to have developed or refined in the course of their travels when trying to re-integrate into their native cultures. And in this context, it is easy to understand how some LITs can get defensive and lash out at the values others would like to impose upon them.

9.3 Facing the friends and family

However, despite this tendency, most interviews showed that LITs were at least trying to resist the temptation of condemning others to confirm their own values. For example, even Sarah (37, Austria), who above was holding up incriminating mirrors to reveal the alleged "weaknesses" of her non-traveler friends, struck a less judgmental tone during a less emotionally charged moment of the interview:

> You just realize that you drift apart somehow. Once you meet for a beer or a party, and it's just like before, but then you drift apart. You don't have the same background anymore. So much has changed in my life.

Although the underlying emotion is the same for both of these constructed explanations (i.e. a feeling of isolation and that one does not fit in), this latter one is far less aggressive, assigning blame for the felt dissonance to a simple difference in values rather than labeling either of those values weak or inferior. A similar process is evident in the following response from Veronica (43, Austria, 2nd):

> Relationships have changed a bit. We just notice that we have grown quite a bit. Others have too, but in a different direction. And I guess that's just the way it is with children and a house and all these things.

Here, we can almost see Veronica catching herself being too judgmental and then censoring herself to acknowledge respect for those whose values and lifestyles may be different. In other cases, one can see the meaning-making process in action in the interview itself. Once again, one can see the LITs struggling to assemble a coherent answer to the sometimes challenging questions I was asking, which some of them may not have considered prior to the interview. For example, when asked about his friends' reactions to his travel, Andy (30, USA) answered:

> My one friend, he's a bit envious. He thinks I'm a bit crazy. He's married and has two kids now. And he's outdoorsy, but he can't do anything now. And I kind of envy him a bit because he's set for life. He has his career. He can find any job he likes. He's stable. But the difference, I think, I go back, and even now it seems not so easy, when I get my first job, I'm stable again. And I had this [travel] experience, whereas he can't break off and do what I'm doing.

This interview took place when Andy was one and a half years into his three-year motorcycle journey through South America, so he was still speculating on how it would be to come back, but it is still evident that he is weighing up the pros and cons of his experience as he speaks while trying to resist the easy way out of passing judgement on his friend.

Similarly, in my second interview with Alan (56, New Zealand, 2nd), which took place 10 years after he had returned to his home culture, he was able to reflect back on his experiences upon first arriving home and then explain how his perspective had evolved since then. He first explained his initial reentry shock:

> I guess for me the hardest thing I had to face when I returned was the disconnection from my friends. I guess I didn't want to see it at first, but they had all moved on with their lives. I had lived in England before I went traveling. Some had gotten married, many of them had kids, or their kids had grown older. One friend had died, others just stopped being friends and didn't return my call. When I first came home I felt that I didn't fit in at all. I was really ticked off by all the stupid conversations about changing nappies or petty complaints.

He then went on to explain how his perspective has evolved since then:

> On a more broader level, I also realized how people change over time, and I've learned to appreciate that not everyone's got the same values, and that's also what makes it interesting. I'm much more family-focused than I was before, but I understand that not everyone's into that.

With regard to managing reentry shock and tension with friends, perhaps the most insightful answer of all came from Max (36, Austria, 2nd). Based on Max's pre-travel interview and his travel blog, it is rather clear that Max is a person given to self-reflection. When I asked if he thought his friends at home understood his travel experiences, his response was:

> No, definitely not. I think that's a process that you have to experience for yourself. Of course I can talk about it, and of course they'll understand on a semantic level, because they're not idiots… but this profound understanding, that's missing. And I'm not saying that because I'm so much smarter and the others more stupid, but it's just about the fact that one has had experiences and others haven't. To give you a simple example, you can talk about the birth of your kids, and I will understand it, because I'm not an idiot, but the emotional universe, I won't be able to grasp.

In the context of narrative identity construction, Ben (31, England) somewhat accidentally hit upon perhaps the real explanation for the common traveler complaint that people back home are not interested in their travel stories:

> If you travel with your best friend, you can go back home and sit in a pub and three years down the line he'll bring up a story that you've completely forgotten about and you roll over laughing from something that you've completely forgotten about. If you're just by yourself, then nobody really wants to know back home. Nobody's interested. They might be interested for 5 minutes, but they're not really interested.

This is the thing about stories. Most people prefer stories with characters that they can somehow identify with. Ideally, as Ben mentions above, the people were actually part of the story themselves, in which case people are happy to hear the stories again. However, if they are not in the story themselves, and if the story involves events they have never experienced, or is based on values and meanings they do not share or possibly even understand, the interest is not going to be there. This is simple confirmation bias. Most people seek stories that re-affirm their own values and beliefs. As traveler stories are usually based in a profoundly different system of values and meanings, many people find them either boring or threatening, and therefore stop listening.

To sum up, trying to re-integrate into one's social circles at home almost always proves to be a significant challenge for LITs. For most of them, their friends and family are the living embodiment of the values of their home cultures, so it is not surprising that tension arises when LITs return with their altered value systems and identities. Here we have looked at how they attempt to process these emotions and create meanings with which they can live. In the following section, we will look at some of the practical behavioral approaches and attitudes they learn to adopt to resolve the dissonance they feel between themselves and those in their social circles.

9.3.3 Shock-proofing the reentry experience

Under adaptation, the first small group to cover is the hard core lifestyle travels who have extensive experience with facing reentry shock and have learned to minimize the impact. They all described how they developed a routine that eases them back into their native culture. For example, Nora (57, Germany, 2nd) stays with a friend for a week of reentry therapy:

> I stayed for one week in the countryside, and only three people knew that I was here. I was just watching TV. They recorded Lindenstraße for me. I'm such a Lindenstraßen-fan. So I just watched Lindenstraße for three hours every day in order to arrive slowly, and then I went home after this week. That was ok then. Then it was ok.

Similarly, Emilia (36, Germany), who was born in Germany but now lives in France, first makes sure she comes back at the right time of year: "I never want to come home sometime in October and then have 6 months of winter! [...] I need the first month or two of sun, otherwise I go crazy." Second, she spends some time in Germany before returning to her "real world" in France:

> I always go to Germany first. Germany is a bit like holiday. It eases me back into the system. And I'm happy to see my family again, friends. But I know in Germany I don't have to fully integrate yet... that is, digging out my clothes from garbage bags, where do you sleep? And finding insurance and a phone, and all that crap.

Brian (55, USA, 2nd), the most experienced traveler in this study, also had a routine, for which he even had a suitable metaphor:

> I kind of allow myself as much time as I need to ease back into that old person. And it's a lot like you're an actor, and you're playing a part. And you don't know, when does the actor merge with the role? And that's what it feels like. Like this is what I used to do, so I should do that, too. But I don't force it. Like if you don't want to talk to anybody, I take it as slow as possible. Also, [...] because of the experiences I've had, my expectations are so low. So I don't expect anything from other people. I no longer expect them to call, or send me emails about how my trip when and all that.

Brian's quote brings us back to the concept mentioned at the beginning of this chapter: To avoid being disappointed, it is a good idea to keep one's expectations low. As Brian's response shows, this includes expectation regarding support from other people as well as expectations for oneself regarding how quickly one can re-adjust to life back home. It is important to mention that even these (and other) experienced travelers did not claim that their reentry shock went away as they did more trips, but simply that they learned from their experience and developed a way to minimize the discomfort.

9.3.4 Re-building community connections

The descriptions in the previous section show that, if nothing else, surviving the shock of reentry is a learning experience that pays off for the next time one has to go through that experience, if there is one. However, for those who then have to remain in their home cultures, the bigger question is one of how they can find a way to overcome the disorientation of reentry and re-connect with their fellow human beings in order to establish a sense of belonging. In essence, this involves two primary options: making peace with old friends and finding new ones.

9.3.4.1 Re-connecting with pre-travel friends

Looking first at the attempt to re-connect with pre-travel friends, several patterns emerged in the interviews. For those who truly managed to re-integrate into their friend circles, the first step was usually an adjustment of their expectations. That is, LITs learn to accept the limits of their interest and understanding. Glen (England, 38, 2nd) described this process as follows:

> Only a few friends were genuinely interested in my global goings on. Other friends switched off as soon as they felt they couldn't relate to what I would be talking about. It was frustrating, and I became agitated at that. But then I always asked myself the question, "Did I go travelling purely to come back here and share my experiences with my peers?" Answer: "No, I didn't."

Here we see Glen using an internal dialog with himself to re-interpret his perceived rejection by his friends. In essence, he creates a story in which his own knowledge and appre-

9.3 Facing the friends and family

ciation of what his travels meant for him make him secure enough in himself that he does not require his friends' approval or recognition. This interpretation has the advantage of not only allowing him to forgive his friends for their indifference or ignorance, but also reaffirming his own sense of autonomy, a key value of the traveler ethos. Philipp (46, Austria) expanded on this idea even further by positioning himself not just as autonomous and secure, but also as a leader for any who would care to follow:

> I realized quite soon that it's impossible to communicate my impressions to those at home with language. You can only set an example. I can't tell them, I just do it, what's important to me. And that realization came relatively quickly.

Nadine (36, Canada, 2nd), was far less interested in leading others and more focused on her own mental state. For her, the key to re-connecting with her friends was moderating her own expectations and then focusing in on what she really needed from her friends:

> [Travel] is a personal experience, and nobody will ever understand it as yourself. But that's ok. That's not the point of traveling. I didn't really care about the understanding of people of my travel experiences. I was more worried about people understanding my sense of loss when I came back.

Like Glen, she points out that she was not traveling for external approval or recognition. Freeing herself from the compulsion to make her friends understand her travels and give her this recognition allowed her to simply turn to them for whatever comfort and understanding they could provide her during her difficult reentry time and beyond. One can easily imagine this being a successful strategy, as people are far more likely to be able to engage their empathy for a friend if their defenses have not been raised by being forced to confront different values that may stir confusion or even insecurity in themselves.

In a similar vein, Jakob (34, Austria) described his struggles with his friends' defensive instincts upon his initial return:

> At first they were curious, I talked [*about my travels*], and was shocked about the things that I noticed at home. Unfortunately I was too focused on all the negative things, but they were the things that I noticed. I sometimes said, "I don't like this" or "that's totally negative". "Why do you have to gulp down 5 beers and just sit there so boringly?" And of course people reacted defensively. In the end, I realized that there is absolutely no point in talking about my travel experiences because people who haven't had such experiences themselves won't understand.

This final point gets to the heart of the lesson that most LITs ultimately learn about dealing with their old friends—namely, that a bit of self-censorship is necessary if they want to get along with their non-traveler friends. In his first interview, Brian (43, USA), who had already done several trips at that point, mentioned that he had already come to this conclusion:

> Usually it's a lot of masked jealousy, I suppose. Maybe it's not even so masked. I think they are confused by it, and confused by the process, and so it's kind of bewildering to them, and they are confused by how much I travel. So, when I come back they are genuinely interested, but only on a minimal level, and I have learned not to thrust my travels upon them because they are not really listening. They don't really care, and that's their loss not mine.

This quote shows Brian actively engaging his empathy and trying to imagine how his friends feel and why they are not interested, and we can see the tension between the "jealousy" interpretation and the more charitable or understanding "confusion" interpretation. Thirteen years and many trips later, Brian's (55, USA, 2nd) expectations were even lower:

> I think I've learned to talk about [my travels] less and keep it to myself. Something will come up where I could add a personal story...like, "That reminds me of a time when I was in..." And then they kind of don't know what to say. Do you know what I mean? So you have this record book of stories. And I've learned to accept that no one wants to hear them. Like sometimes you slip them in, but no one's really interested 'cause they can't relate to them.

In the case of Lukas (39, Germany, 2nd), who already mentioned his innate confidence in his core group of childhood friends in his first interview, he described in his second interview how his feelings about his friends interest in his travels evolved over time:

> And the boys, well, if they ask me then I'll show them my pictures. And I gotta say, of course that makes me happy. Because that's what's important for me, and if others are interested, it's a confirmation. But I wouldn't go advertise it, and I'm also not upset if they say "not interested".

Essentially, Lukas's ability to let go of his need for confirmation from his friend helps him appreciate the occasional confirmation he actually does get.

9.3.4.2 Evolving social circles

Although most travelers find a way to re-connect with old friends at least to some extent, most report that their circles of friends change after their travels. For some, travel seems to bring them a deepened sense of independence, as they report a decreased interest in having many friends. In her first interview, Sarah (45, Austria, 2nd) mentioned her discomfort with the demands associated with having too many friends: "I always used to be a very reliable person. People could always rely on me. But now I feel that puts too much pressure on me, other people relying on me. I don't like that idea." Eight years later, she reports how this change has affected her circle of friends. Asked if her relationships with friends at home had changed, she replied:

> Not really, except that they have become fewer. After coming back from Africa, where we lived [for four years], the number of friends has drastically decreased, and we did not really bother to make new friends.

9.3 Facing the friends and family

Similarly, comparing responses from Tom's (46/59, Germany) two interviews show how he was able to resolve the tension he initially felt with some of his friends and even incorporate it into the meaning-construct that defines their friendship. The quote from the first interview shows Tom struggling to come to grips with the value difference between his friends and himself:

> In my circle of friends, I've always been the only one who did such things, who always wanted to leave. There were other people who are much more down-to-earth, and they always laughed when I started talking about how much I wanted to go away. [...] It's just this restlessness of being in the same spot, and others were like "Oh yes, look, he's packing again [...] Let's see what he wants now."

In contrast, in the second interview, Tom describes how he and his friends learned to live with their differences:

> I have fewer friends than before. Most just don't know what to do with my type of traveling. Nonetheless, these friendships are intense, and they accept me with my wanderlust. Some friends also adorn themselves with me. I've often been introduced to new circles as "the globetrotter". I often find that amusing because travel is such a normal thing for me, but for others it's probably something very special.

While some friendships clearly did not survive, other friends found a way to come to grips and appreciate Tom's travels in their own way, seemingly even going so far as to "borrow" some of his status within their own social circles.

In fact, in most cases, there was a shift in the composition of LITs' friend groups. In the first stage, many of them were lucky enough to have existing friends who had also done some travel, and they gravitated towards these friends and the understanding and support they could provide. In Nick's (47, Ireland, 2nd) case, this even included two friends who had been with him on his travels:

> Most of my friends are like-minded wanna-be travelers. Probably the most important people were the two guys I shared most of the road with. We are way closer as buddies since, shared experiences and all that.

Alan (42, New Zealand) focused on friends who had had travel experiences similar to his own, a revelation that first occurred to him during the interview:

> I never thought about it until now, but I guess I hung out with those friends who had traveled as well. There were only three who had traveled for more than the usual 2-week holiday, and I hung out with them the most. I felt they could understand a bit better of what it's like to have a fresh start and return to your home country after having been gone for so long.

In some cases, LITs leveraged the advantages of modern communications technology to remain in contact with new friends they had made during their travels:

> I have some close friends, but I always keep in touch with far-away friends who have become an important part of my life, that I have met on the road. Like I am still in touch with people I met traveling, and this is the beauty of the internet, and I re-

member traveling before the internet. And I hook up with these travel buddies, and we keep in touch. (Brian, 43, USA)

In my own case, I have traveler friends spread throughout the world, and I make an effort to stay in touch with them primarily via social networking sites and Skype. I have met up with several of them in various parts of the world, have been invited to their weddings, and had traveler friends come to my own wedding in New York and come visit me at home in Austria. Although the geographical distance makes it difficult to be fully involved in each other's lives, shared memories of our travels together have forged a unique connection between us that makes it easy to pick up even after long periods of not being in touch. I noticed this special connection with some of the LITs that I contacted again for this study, and it was not uncommon that the planned one-hour interview turned into 4 hours, with invitations to come visit thrown in for good measure.

Returning to circles of friends back home, Oliver and Veronica (59, Austria, 2nd) described how their friend circle evolved organically after their extended sailing trip based on the extent of their friends' interest in the trip:

> People that weren't in our lives so much before, all of a sudden were. I don't know. They just started to be more interested in what we were doing and our story. And that's what made it more interesting. And some were jealous, and we've just grown apart.

Here we see Oliver falling back on the "jealousy" defense, whereas Veronica is a bit more generous to the friends that have fallen by the wayside and more precise about what distinguishes those friends who are still in their lives. Describing her reaction to people who are not interested in her travel stories, she explains:

> This is where you simply say, "That is too foreign for some people." And that is ok, too. Not everybody has to feel the same way. But this is the reason why you don't see some people as often anymore, because it's always the same. And that's what I like about the new friendships because they think differently, and they're intellectually curious, and we are intellectually curious.

Here, Veronica highlights a key traveler value: intellectual curiosity. For many travelers, their intellectual curiosity is focused largely on experiencing cultural difference. Thus, they look to build themselves a community of likeminded people who share this value. For Nora (49, Germany), this played into her search for a roommate. In our first interview, she described her roommate as follows:

> She is like me, she also travels a lot, is very open-minded, and we have, and that's great, we have a very intercultural circle of friends. We always have people from other countries at home, even staying with us for short periods. We have like an 'open house'. And that's great, of course, when you live with someone who is just as open. And when one of us is gone for three months or something like that, then someone else lives there.

9.3 Facing the friends and family

In our second interview, Nora (57, Germany, 2nd) reported that her roommate had gotten married and moved out, but she had found another roommate to replace her. Although her new roommate is nearly 30 years younger than Nora, she is also a traveler and interculturally minded person, so they "get along just fine."

While the examples above show LITs fulfilling their need for inter-cultural experience by forming relationships with like-minded people with whom they can share stories of their intercultural experiences, some LITs fulfill this need by actually maintaining some form of contact with the cultures in which they had traveled and with which they had forged some sort of identity bond. In some cases, LITs are fortunate enough to have elements of the relevant foreign cultures within their own communities. For example, Nora (57, Germany, 2nd) also reported: "I organize an intercultural festival, so I have regular contact with people from all over the world. And I need that as well." Similarly, as part of his post-travel job as a university lecturer, Dan (34, England) volunteered to manage the university's international exchange student program.

Some LITs fulfil their need for intercultural contact by making a conscious effort to engage with the languages they learned in their travels. For example, Nick (36, Ireland, 2nd), who above mentioned the influence of Chatwin's writing on his younger self, described how he was dealing with his reentry shock by doing some reading that appealed to both his love of travel and his love of the Spanish language: "On a sidenote, I'm still not over [my reentry shock] - right now I am reading Chatwin's collected letters and I have a Spanish language version of 'In Patagonia' on order from the local bookshop."

For people who are not from English-speaking countries, their efforts to use language to maintain a link to their traveler lives and selves can take the form of simply seizing every opportunity to speak English, since it is the language they associate with their travels. For example, Veronica (43, Austria, 2nd) described how they hired a native New Yorker, Joe, to give their son guitar lessons each week: "And when Joe comes in, it is like vacation. And he is also so nice and chilled out." On the other hand, for Andy (42, USA, 2nd) the language of his traveler self is Spanish, and in his second interview he mentioned how he uses his Spanish skills at every opportunity to engage with Latin Americans back in his community in the States:

> Being able to speak Spanish, I mean when I see people speak Spanish I go "Hey, where're you from? Oh, I've been there." And that's just so great. I've been all throughout Central America, and you can jump on a real personal level, and for them as well because they're away from home and it's just respect for their culture. So yeah, it's opened up doors.

On a related personal note, I can relate very much to the desire to use foreign language skills and the emotions one feels when engaging with people from cultures in which one has traveled. Listening to or speaking Spanish immediately transports me back to my travels, of which I have fond memories that are deeply ingrained in my personal identity and life story. Since my travels in Latin America, I have tried to maintain my Spanish skills in many different ways. I have taken evening classes, listened to Spanish podcasts on my commute to work and taken every opportunity to speak Spanish with my Spanish-speaking friends in Austria. I am also trying to pass on my passion for languages (and especially Spanish) to my children, who already have the advantage of being raised bilingually. For example, we took a backpacking trip to Spain, and we recently sent our daughter to a Latin American-themed summer camp run by some Latin American expats in our community. She loved it, and was ready to sign up for next year's camp right away. However, I think her mother may have enjoyed the "parents' day" at the end even more, as I had the chance to talk to some Latin Americans (in Spanish!) about their home countries.

Beyond the local Spanish-speaking community, I also use modern communication technology to keep in touch with our friends from Paraguay, Bolivia, Honduras, and Costa Rica. In fact, I recently received an email from our friend in Paraguay telling us that his niece, whose *fiesta de quinceañera* I attended when I was in South America, just had her first child! Similarly, Brian (55, USA, 2nd) has a weekly Skype call with a friend in India, while Andy (42, USA, 2nd) reported the following:

> I stay in touch with one of my best friends in the world from Peru. And he came and visited me for six months. And I hadn't seen him for ten years, and he came and visited me for 6 months. And we reconnected, and then I went down and I telecommuted and I worked out of Peru for three months. That was this past January.

Of course, this final quote from Andy raises the issue of how LITs use further travels to continue to satisfy their need for intercultural experience. This topic will be covered in more detail below, when we look at LITs who have integrated themselves back into their home cultures and how they fit travel into the equation. For the moment, however, it is important to point out that all of the examples above show how people can leverage relationships with friends made during or after travels to maintain a sense of connection with the cultures they encountered, including the traveler culture itself and the values it represents for them. Essentially, LITs look to establish or maintain contact with people who share values that they think are important. From a narrative identity standpoint, this means finding people who listen to, understand and appreciate their stories, and also have their own stories to tell that are based in the same values and understandings. Participants in such exchanges derive the pleasure and comfort that come from having one's own values confirmed and reinforced. That is, a traveler storytelling circle is a ritual that functions like a prayer circle, in which the participants gather to express and re-affirm their values and beliefs.

Before proceeding to the next section, we will look at one final example of relationship building that highlights a slightly different aspect of the process of re-building one's sense of belonging after an extended journey. Chelsea (37, England, 2nd) traveled for several years—first on her own, and then with a boyfriend. In the long run, though, she decided the time had come to go home, describing her reasoning as follows:

> I think [travel has] given me a real appreciation for freedom. And a real appreciation for all the freedom we have in Western society. You know, all the stories you come across when you're traveling, and you realize that people really don't have a great deal of choice in what they do and where they end up, and we have an abundance. And that's always been a propeller for me in terms of, it's made me always want to use the opportunities I've been given and really to rinse them and to get every last drop of opportunity out of things because you realize that so many people can't.

Despite her enduring love of travel, Chelsea felt a desire to do something to give back to humanity, one might say. In fact, she cited this as a reason for her break-up with her boyfriend, who was not terribly concerned with using the advantages he had been given to do something meaningful:

> I didn't really feel like he totally understood his privilege. And was really using it to the best that he could. And I think it led to a breakdown of respect in our relationship. Though, I think that's what happened, basically. I really feel like if you're given these opportunities, you really have to take the ball and you run as far as you can with it, basically. And it's a value that I think so many people I know don't have. I don't think I would have had this value if I hadn't been traveling and met these people first hand, and spoken to them. I mean you see it on tele, but it's not the same.

Chelsea describes a classic situation in which two people's values simply grow in different directions. Although they continued to share a love of travel, their perspectives on the deeper meaning of travel and how it changed their worldviews were no longer in harmony. Returning to England, she faced a significant reentry shock, but by the time of our second interview, she was able to look back and describe the process of re-establishing her sense of community and belonging:

> And when I got back I didn't know anyone in London anymore. All my friends had moved on. [...] It took about, I would say it took about 4 years to finally feel back. During these years, even in the third year I was still finding it difficult to feel like I had a big network of friends. Even though I did, but it wasn't cohesive. It was very messy, and it didn't feel like it used to, and it took very long to build up again [...]

> And I'd lived in London before that for six or seven years so I had some strong friendships. I've made a lot of new friends. A lot of my friends now, I would say, most of the friends I have now are new friends that I met through [my job...], be-

cause it's a passion as well. And also the relationships that I have built in my thirties they are quite strong. Cause you really know who you are by the time you are thirty. You're not meeting them because you both like clubbing or because you've both worked in the same bar. You're passionate about something.

Here, Chelsea makes the important link between social relationships and one's overall lifestyle and occupation. Beyond establishing healthy interpersonal relationships with old friends or new friends, for most LITs, part of having a meaningful life and positive sense of identity involves connecting with their larger culture. Of course, friendships are one primary tool for building this sense of belonging to a culture, but they are not the only tool. That is, beyond choosing one's friends, the other way people perform their identity and live out their values is in how they choose to structure and live out their lives, including balancing commitments to their occupations, families, and themselves. Therefore, in the following section we will begin to explore some of the important lifestyle decisions LITs make and how these decisions reflect the values they may have either acquired or strengthened during their travels, as well as helping them establish a place for themselves within their culture as a whole.

9.4 Cultural value dissonance

Before looking at how LITs seek to re-connect with their cultures, it is worth examining their views of that culture itself. By now, some of the themes discussed below will be quite familiar to the reader, as I have covered them in different contexts at various points above. Nevertheless, one of the goals of making this a longitudinal study was to see how lessons learned on the road affected choices made upon reentry and, in turn, how reentry experiences impacted the lessons learned on the road (i.e. the LITs' new set of values). Overall, one could say that the second round of interviews generally showed that the experience of reentering most often confirmed or even intensified feelings and ideas from the travel stage. However, as we have already seen in the context of the above discussion about relationships, reentry is very much a case of bi-directional influence, or one could say a cyclical process. That is, values acquired through travel inform decisions, and the outcomes of the resulting experiences then alter the original values, which then influence the next set of decisions, and so forth. This process is evident in some of the following examples.

One phrase that I heard consistently throughout the interviews was "broadening my horizons", which captures people's sense of the shift in their perspectives. Setting aside the universal or spiritual perspective until the end of this section, I will start with the broadest

9.4 Cultural value dissonance

worldly perspective—the global perspective. Within this context, the widest perspective involves people's views on humanity and its relationship to the planet. We already heard above how LITs' experiences with both the beauty of nature and the destruction of nature on the road heightened their awareness of the effects of this relationship, and in the second round of interviews, many LITs mentioned how they were appalled to get back home and see how unaware some people in their native cultures were. For example, one common theme was people at home throwing out food, and many LITs reported that they were no longer willing or even able to do this:

> It's like leaving food on your plate. There's people starving. You can't do that. You gotta put it in the fridge and eat it later or something. You can't just throw it out. It's disrespectful to the universe. And traveling's made me aware of that. (Andy, 42, USA, 2nd)

Recycling was another consistent theme, as with Alan, who changed his private habits and incorporated his environmental awareness into his new business practices (56, New Zealand, 2nd):

> I hate to admit it, but when I was living in England, I hardly ever recycled. I didn't care so much about the environment or wasn't very environmentally conscious. Having seen the immense destruction and environmental pollution around the world was a big eye-opener. Of course I know I won't change the world, but now I believe that it's my duty as a good citizen to do my best to protect our environment. We have a big compost at our B&B where we recycle all of our organic waste. We even have our own chicken and goats and a small herd of sheep.

Beyond recycling, Philipp (46, Austria) also mentioned his efforts to travel by bike rather than car whenever possible and even mentioned how his newfound environmental awareness guided him when he built his own house. He reported that he used recycled bricks from old houses and generally:

> ... the least possible amount of unnatural building material. Very little expanding foam, silicon only in the bathroom, very little cement because it has a negative ecological balance and uses lots of energy. Everything brick-built with lime mortar. That that was very important for me... as close to nature as possible.

In general, Philipp said travel had taught him how to maintain "a frugal lifestyle, and how to get by and be satisfied with less... and to think twice before buying something new about whether I really need it."

Beyond the environmental aspect, many LITs also mentioned their expanded awareness of international politics:

> Travel, getting to know the world has changed me. I perceive the world more globally, not only since globalization. Other continents seem closer now, and when reading/watching the news I am interested in global changes. I see humanity as a whole, and national politics is less important. (Tom, 59, Germany, 2nd)

With this awareness come value judgements about the political actions of their own countries and others. For example, Nick (47, Ireland, 2nd) mentioned that he has a greater understanding of "international economics and politics" and what he called "the debilitating influence of bully countries." In some cases, these realizations involved their own countries. Perhaps not surprisingly, this theme was particularly prevalent among the Americans I interviewed, although it was by no means limited to them. Brian's (55, USA, 2nd) response is fairly representative of a typical American comment:

> Americans are taught that we're the best, and we should do whatever we want, and like, you know, God bless America. You don't hear God bless Argentina. Most Americans don't travel, and so they don't realize there are other ways of doing things and that we're not necessarily the best. Like socialized medicine is much better than what we have. But Americans are always taught that we're doing things the right way, and we're not. And so you get exposed to different ways when you're traveling, whereas the rest of the country doesn't. And most Americans just don't travel. So travel has made me less patriotic.

However, it is important to mention that, overall, the criticisms of their own cultures were far outnumbered by the expressions of newfound appreciation for the advantages of their first-world home countries. This theme was already mentioned above in terms of experiencing poverty on the road and other contexts, but it must be stressed that this feeling of gratitude was widespread, even among those who had the harshest criticism for their countries. For example, Julia (37, Germany), who is rarely in Germany and has some definite issues with her homeland, reported:

> I appreciate Germany far more. It's not that I am necessarily happier when I am there... totally not. But everything that we have... it's crazy... from insurance to going to the doctor. We just had a new reform whereby we have to pay €10 when we go to the doctor. And everyone is all bothered about it. But I think, "Ten Euros? I am so happy that we have all this... When we're pregnant, everything is paid for."

In fact, Julia's quote highlights another very common theme that came up when LITs discussed coming home—annoyance with their fellow citizens' lack of gratitude for their many advantages:

> When people start whinging, I can't stand that. Then I say, for example, my [university education] did not cost me anything. I was appalled when I was there and people just don't get it that they only have to pay 16 Euros per semester as a study fee, and they get everything! All the seminars and lectures [...] Everything for free! (Veronica, 43, Austria, 2nd)

Aimee (26, England) even suggested the remedy for this problem: "It just makes you ashamed to be British. Especially when you get people whining about how difficult it is in England. You know... you wanna buy a plane ticket and tell them to go to some other country...anywhere outside of Europe!"

9.4 Cultural value dissonance

Of course, this general appreciation for their home countries does not equate to uncritical acceptance. Far from it. To varying degrees, all of them had criticisms for their countries. At the root of almost all of these criticisms is a fundamental antipathy for the materialist ethos that underpins modern capitalist, or perhaps more accurately consumerist, societies. Max (36, Austria, 2nd) summed up the thought process of his fellow citizens thusly: "I have to buy it because I have to do something with my money or else I am not me... or this is the newest crap and I am not cool if I don't have it." Here again, I could fill 20 pages with interview quotes about this topic. However, as I have already covered this issue above, I will only add one succinct statement and one tragically amusing story that relate specifically to reentry into one's home society:

> What I find hard about it is to see the shops full of food, telling you that you need it, must have it... the ipod, the latest telephone... it's a must-have society that we live in...horrible. (Emma, 53, England, 2nd)

> And then my mom asked me to go shopping and buy some cheese. And in Asia there is no cheese, and I went to a supermarket and had to choose from a hundred cheeses. I was totally shocked and left the supermarket and only bought a pack of gum. And I said, "I'm not going shopping in the next month in such a stupid supermarket. No way, too much." It's just, there's too much everywhere. (Emilia, 36, Germany)

Of course, being back home, the LITs also recognize even more powerfully the effects of this consumerism on their fellow citizens. As Julia (37, Germany) mentioned, "I am not necessarily happier [in Germany]. Not at all, because I see how we destroy ourselves and stress ourselves out with many stupid things." Similarly, Max (36, Austria, 2nd) argues that this materialism brings "general dissatisfaction... it is spiritually sick. It's simply spiritually sick. We can't laugh, we can't live. We can't live at all." And of course, for the LITs, this translates to a highly disturbing fundamental lack of freedom.

> Most people have so many appointments and responsibilities and don't even realize that they no longer have any freedom to decide for themselves because everything's predetermined anyway. Like you have to arrange it half a year in advance if you want to go skiing with someone. And something like that would be a prison for me. (Lukas, 39, Germany, 2nd)

This lack of freedom resonates particularly strongly when they are faced with friends back home who complain that they can't afford to travel:

> It's always funny when people keep asking how to fund such travels, while at the same time they have two cars, a large apartment and I don't know how many other possessions that I don't have. I just have to sell a car and then I can also travel wherever I want to. (Patrick, 37, Austria)

And from there, it is obviously just a short step to the view of one's fellow citizens as automatons, or as Lars (28, Belgium) described them: "from my perspective they're just mindlessly marching along." This LIT viewpoint was already covered above, so here it is just important to mention that most LITs have a strong desire not to fall back into this lifestyle (if they were even in it to begin with) and are keenly aware of the risk of this happening. As Veronica (43, Austria, 2nd) stated: "And when you are back again, you really have to resist it, so you don't get sucked back in."

Armed with an awareness of this danger, at some point all LITs must nevertheless re-enter the "real word". That is, if we return to Maslow's pyramid, there are certain basic needs that need to be met, and for most people that involves some form of labor. Needless to say, the responsibilities and routine involved with a job are at odds with the strong values most LITs place on independence, freedom, and autonomy. Indeed, because of this love of autonomy, contemplating an occupation is a serious challenge for LITs, as they have a heightened awareness of the need for what is commonly called a proper "work-life balance."

In devising solutions that strike this balance, LITs are forced to navigate between two fundamentally opposed viewpoints about the relationship between occupation and identity that one finds in most cultures. The first viewpoint places a high emphasis on one's job as a key source of meaning and contentment in one's life. This is the perspective behind the popular aphorism (often misattributed to Confucious) "Choose a job you love, and you will never have to work a day in your life." This philosophy places a strong emphasis on finding a job one loves, as it must bring meaning, joy and a sense of purpose to one's life. The other view on the role of work was captured nicely in the following lecture by the fictional Red Forman to his son, Eric, on the popular TV series *That 70s Show* (Schiff & Trainer, 2000):

> Work is work, Eric. You don't show up late, you don't make excuses, and you don't not work. If it wasn't "work," they wouldn't call it work. They'd call it "super-wonderful, crazy-fun time!" Or "Skippedydoo!"

In other words, work is more or less something that you have to do to support your life and not something that is supposed to be fun or spiritually fulfilling. Of course, one could argue that the prior view of work is a luxury only afforded to people in the developed world or perhaps only to people in certain socio-economic classes, but a proper discussion about this topic is beyond the scope of this thesis. For the present purposes, it is simply important to point out that the latter view of work is one that most LITs oppose. As we have seen above, in some cases, they instinctively rejected this view before their travels and then had this rejection confirmed by their travels. In other cases, it was experiencing the freedom of travel or the wider perspectives they received from this travel that caused them to reject this view of enslavement to work. And for most, the truth lies somewhere between those possibilities. In any event, one way or another, most LITs emerge from their travels with a strong resistance to the idea of devoting a significant amount of their time to something they do no find fulfilling.

9.5 From theory into practice

Naturally, LITs are not alone in this feeling, as evidenced by the widespread phenomenon of mid-life crises. However, a heightened awareness of the tension between freedom and responsibility is unquestionably a dominant theme in LIT research, and the question is how LITs resolve this tension by finding a way to incorporate their "traveler" values (e.g. autonomy, freedom, intercultural experience, mobility) into a lifestyle with which they can support themselves and, in some case, their families. There is a complex equation at play in solving this problem, which features many variables. I would propose viewing this question as a kind of complex balance sheet. In the world of corporate sustainability, many companies have adopted a triple bottom line strategy, which seeks to balance the financial, social and environmental costs and benefits of their operations. Here, we could speak of a double bottom line, which links the costs (i.e. the energy one invests in an activity) and benefits in terms of both finances and fulfillment. For example, a high-paying 80-hour-a-week job that one does not particularly find meaningful would obviously bring large financial benefits, but would pay no fulfillment dividends. On the other hand, if one had the same job but found true fulfillment in doing it, one would reap the same financial benefits but also receive a fulfillment dividend to go along with it. Of course, all of this depends on the individual. An accountant and an actor might both love their jobs, but ask them to switch for a day and the fulfillment dividends would likely plunge for both parties.

Similarly, although we can presume that the goal of this budgeting exercise is to achieve maximum fulfillment, each individual has a different definition of fulfillment as well. Many pages have been written about the difference between terms such as joy, happiness, fulfillment, and satisfaction in fields ranging from psychology to philosophy to behavioral economics. For the present purposes, I would remind the reader of Erikson's concept of "identity synthesis" (section 2.1), which involves a sense of coherence between values, beliefs and social roles. However, here again it is important to point out that this desired result is highly person-specific, as values will differ widely from one person to the next. Even within the LIT population, one LIT might seek a lifestyle that provides constant novel experience, while another may seek time for solitary contemplation, and another may seek physical challenges.

Although the possible variations to this equation are endless, the final point to be made before proceeding to the LIT solutions to this problem is that, in the world we live in, one of the factors is, indeed, financial. Although most LITs might protest the implied concept of money buying happiness, most of them are keenly aware from their travels that their relative level of affluence (when considered on the global scale) was a key enabler for the freedom they enjoyed on their travels. At the very least, the physical needs of the body must be met, and most people feel other needs for safety and security as well, as shown in the second level of Maslow's pyramid. Balancing all these needs with one's limited resources of time and energy is the question at stake, and we will now look at the approaches taken by LITs to answer this question. In the big picture, we can identify two key strategies: minimizing one's needs, and maximizing the fulfillment return on investment for the activities in which one engages. Since the former is far less complicated, the next section will tackle this issue first.

9.5.1 KISS: Keep It Simple, Stupid

I have already written at length above about the complicated relationship between LITs and their budgets. Despite their professed lack of concern with money, LITs cannot escape the power of money as a signifier in their value system, as shown above. Just as budget figures and the symbolic values assigned to them can differ widely between LITs on the road and even over the travel career of individual LITs, there is one extremely prevalent (bordering on universal) value that LITs take home with them after their journeys, and that is a sense that less can be more. Again, the definition of "less" in this case, in terms of what material circumstances one truly "needs", varies widely, but almost all LITs come to appreciate more deeply the relationship between their material needs and their level of autonomy and freedom. And in this area, every single LIT that I interviewed at one point or another raised the issue of simplifying one's life to maximize one's freedom. In fact, I could fill several pages with LIT stories of how they have accomplished this. The stories range from the standard refusal to own a television (a possession that has particular symbolic relevance due to its link to the media/entertainment complex that helps keep their fellow citizens in line) to extremely frugal living situations, such as Chelsea's (37, England) decision to live on a house boat ("And then I moved to the boat I certainly won't get more stuff because you can't put it anywhere. So everything has to have a function. And I like it.") or Dana's (51, Denmark) camper van ("It was pretty tough, without a car, you need to carry the big heavy gas thing, but I did that too."). In fact, the eagerness

9.5 From theory into practice

with which LITs tell these stories testifies to the importance of frugality in their own identity constructs. Here is a brief sampling of some "wealth-defying" stories:

> I don't see the need for so many materialistic things in life. It's not that important to have the latest car, stereo. It's nice if you can have them but it's not that important. (Jake, 57, England)

> Another thing that I noticed, and I think it's all related of course, but I am much more careful with my money. I don't spend it as easily. Like I most of the furniture I bought for the B&B is used... refurbished but still old. And it looks great! (Alan, 56, New Zealand)

> We don't have a TV, no dishwasher... we drive a used car that needs very little gas and is very cheap, but we like that. We reduce. And this is difficult for many people to understand. (Veronica, 43, Austria, 2nd)

> I would decorate an apartment totally different than before. Before, I had many things in my apartment. Today, I live very, very simply, as simply as possible, so that you have space to live. (Julia, 50 Germany, 2nd)

> I have little desire for useless materialistic things and really avoid any and all advertising as much as I can as well. I do invest in toys, if you will, such as backcountry ski gear, bikes, climbing gear, active adventure toys if you will. I am also proudly 100% debt free and have been for 8 years now, so I also learned to live on a budget and within my means while travelling [...] This is the truest statement of all. "Do more things, own less stuff." My wife and I are all about experiences and investing our time, energy and money into living our lives. My wife drove her 1999 VW Jetta off the lot brand new and is still driving it. (Ryan, Canada, 40, 2nd)

The final quote from Ryan makes the important link between fewer material possessions and more resources (both financial and temporal) to fuel adventures or any other activity that brings true fulfillment, as alluded to above in our concept of the double bottom line. Thus, having covered the relatively simple factor of minimizing expenses, we can move to the more complicated factor of maximizing fulfillment in the context of work-life balance.

9.5.2 The courage to change

Before moving on to look at the specific ways that LITs alter their lives to maximize their fulfillment, I must once again mention a vital theme that runs throughout all these stories of change: self-confidence. Indeed, while the LITs were eager to discuss the creative ways in which they simplified their lives, they were even keener to emphasize the risks they have taken and the initiative they have shown in changing their lives to make them more fulfilling. As self-confidence and its relative, courage, are key components in the LITs' self-images, allusions to these qualities will appear frequently in their own accounts of the lifestyle changes they have made. However, before proceeding to these accounts, I will offer some key quotes from the later round of interviews in which the LITs, having had time to test their self-confidence by mastering the challenge of reentry, express their firm convictions that travel did indeed play a key role in building this key characteristic:

> Traveling really made me brave. You know, to follow your dreams just makes you stronger. (Sarah, 45, Austria, 2nd)

> And you have that feeling, if you really want something, when I really want it and I have to know if I really want it, then I can do it. And that was different before. Before you just functioned, you had your rhythm,...and it's kind of like stepping out of that rhythm. Your personal limits shift. And I always rise to this challenge because it keeps you alive. (Nora, 57, Germany, 2nd)

> I just got a certain self-confidence and sense of self-worth [...] I didn't let other people deter me, from those who said it won't work out, because I knew I walked the Inca trail, and that person's just babbling nonsense and has no clue, has different experiences. And people have always confronted me with their own fears and because of [my travels], I let them influence me less and less. (Patrick, 37, Austria)

> It has given me an ability to feel like I can do anything I set my mind to. If I set my mind to something I can do it, I can do it well, I might not be the most organized one, I might not be the best at it, but I can do my best at it and make it happen. (Matt, 39, USA, 2nd)

> I believe travel set me up to realize that I could accomplish big goals by simply committing to making it happen. Not listening to the naysayers and blocking out everything that doesn't matter. You only need to do that a few times to realize that you can dream bigger and pursue larger goals. Sometimes you come up short, but it takes confidence accrued over years to point to something that others say is impossible or not worth the time and effort and to be like, nope, I'm gonna make it happen. I've done it before with smaller goals that were insurmountable at the time. (Ryan, 40, Canada, 2nd)

> The year in the Americas was the single standout 'achievement' for me. It colours so much of what I do, in a positive way. It makes me feel that any half-assed plan sketched on the back of a beermat can be accomplished. (Nick, 47, Ireland, 2nd)

Having heard from the LITs about the travel origins of their self-confidence, we turn now to an examination of the ways they put this self-confidence to use to build new, more fulfilling lives.

9.6 Striking a proper work-life balance

Drawing again on the concept of the double bottom line, several LITs reported that their travel experiences had given them the courage to change to a career they believed would be more fulfilling. Shortly after his return from his trip, Glen (27, England, email) reported:

> I have begun a training course in a completely different path to the one I was on before travelling. My 18 mth trip and the experiences I lived through have definitely given me the strength to make decisions for myself, to do what I want to do and not worry about what other people think – the current example being returning to full-time education at 27yrs old, with no cash or definite job at the end. Family mem-

9.6 Striking a proper work-life balance

bers and some friends frowned upon my decision – I feel nothing but sympathy when I listen to their work-related grumblings!

Ten years later, Glen has a successful career in the business world that brings him more fulfillment and supports his travels with his wife and two children.

Upon reentry, Patrick (37, Austria), who had worked in banking, first put together a presentation about his travels and toured around the German-speaking world to share his travel experiences with others. He is now self-employed and makes a living doing motivational speeches, where he draws on his experiences. He described how his time alone in the Andes helped him realize how he wanted to live his life:

> Being alone for months high up in the Andes has also [...] helped create a certain spiritual foundation on which I can now build. And that's also changed. I still cannot imagine taking a path that is not my path. To sit in an office, even though this is not for me, I cannot imagine that.

He then describes how his work/life balance evolved in the wake of this realization:

> I am really so happy that I am so free [...] that I don't have to ask any boss permission to go somewhere [...] I no longer distinguish between work and living. [My work] is living. It is a part of my life [...] it brings me joy.

The combination of a simplified living style and a highly rewarding job has resulted in a very fulfilling life for Patrick.

In Ryan's (40, Canada, 2nd) case, after his extended cycling journey and other travel experiences in Latin America, he decided to pursue a career as a professional expedition adventure racer, where he has become quite successful. I already quoted Ryan above on how he learned to balance his finances and focus on the activities that he loves. He also had the following to say about how he has incorporated his love of travel into his life:

> Travel is one of the most important things to me and my family [...], though travel can also mean exploring our own backyard here in BC, Canada. [...] I did not get back out on the road for another extended trip, but rather found the balance of living and adventuring from a home base here in Canada."

Ryan's career contributes doubly to his fulfillment dividend by satisfying his need for travel and his need for physical challenge.

In Ryan's case, his relative youth at the time of his first trip made his job choices less of a career change and more of a career choice, as he did not have an established career before his trip. However, other travelers were older at the time of their travels but nevertheless ended up making significant changes in already established careers. For example, Alan (56, New Zealand, 2nd) actually tried to return to his job in banking after his first long journey, but soon found that the equations on his fulfillment balance sheet no longer added up at his old job:

> I can say with 100% certainty that the Latin America trip has marked me for life. [...] I realized that I was fooling myself, thinking I could go back my old job, the whole banking industry, which I never really liked to begin with, but just got into because it was lucrative and paid for nice vacations.

And when he thought about what to do with his life, the answer, opening an ecologically friendly B&B, came from his travels:

> And the idea didn't even sound so crazy...I'd been toying with that idea all this time in Latin America. I remember staying in these amazing places with compost toilets, all built with sustainable materials and all that. I went back to New Zealand, sold the house and everything I owned and moved to Israel where I bought a small farm that I turned into a B&B.

Other examples of people changing their occupation to something that they found more fulfilling include: Philipp (46, Austria), who went from his job as an engineer in the construction industry to doing social work; Chelsea (37, England, 2nd), who left her marketing career behind to start a career in a creative industry; and Lilly (43, England), who gave up her corporate career to become a yoga instructor.

Many of the careers on which LITs embarked offered a greater fulfillment dividend due to the fact that they somehow incorporated one of the key traveler values. For example, Sarah (45, Austria) left her job as a teacher and first became a travel writer and then opened her own adventure travel company that organizes customized, sustainable adventure trips in Africa. Not only does she find this job rewarding, but it also allows her to spend several months per years traveling to do "research" for future tours that she would like to offer. Similarly, Julia (50, Germany) took on a job as an adventure travel tour guide, for which she accompanies German tourists on extended journeys primarily through less developed countries. Here again, this job pays triple fulfillment dividends for Julia because it gives her the opportunity to travel for her job, it gives her schedule flexibility to do her own travels (e.g. 6-months tour guiding, 6 months independent travel or whatever else she might choose to do), and it feeds her curiosity about different cultures, since she is required to research new destinations for her job: "And in my job, because often I don't know the countries, I have to read very much and study, and at least pretend that I know something." One final example of a creative way to bring an intercultural element into one's job is Eric (59, Canada), who organized a program at the high school where he works whereby he takes a group of students abroad (e.g. Holland, Belgium, Mexico) each year.

Another key strategy deployed by some LITs is to improve their work-life balance by simply working less, which enables them to engage in activities that pay high fulfillment dividends (quite often independent travel, of course). Eric (59, Canada, 2nd) is a good example of this strategy as well, as he has an arrangement with his school that allows him to

9.6 Striking a proper work-life balance

take a one-year sabbatical every fourth year, which he uses to go on extended journeys. Tom (59, Germany, 2nd), who works as a social worker in Germany, has made the same arrangement with his employer. Similar to Eric, he finds his job fulfilling, but he nevertheless needs the extra fulfillment that comes from his extended journeys: "Travel has definitely affected my career. I could never imagine having a job that prevented me from traveling." In a similar vein, Max (36, Austria, 2nd) persuaded his employer to give him a half-time job, while Oliver (59, Austria, 2nd) gave up his own company and took a half-time position to free up time for more fulfilling endeavors, including playing in a band. Perhaps the extreme version of this strategy is Lukas (39, Germany, 2nd), who has greatly minimized his material needs to the extent that he can survive with only three days a week working in an outdoor equipment shop. The job brings minimal financial rewards, but also some fulfillment because he is able to advise people on mountaineering gear, an area of particular interest for him. However, the main fulfillment in his life comes from the free-time his lifestyle affords him to do all of the outdoor activities that he truly enjoys the most:

> And it's kind of luxury to be able to have the freedom to do whatever I want three days a week, to think about whether I want to go biking or do something else [...] All these short trips, micro-adventures as I call them, that's already traveling for many people. And this kind of traveling I definitely need. I have designed my entire life so I can travel half the time during the week. Just working with 30 vacation days a year would be too little for me, I wouldn't accept that.

Whereas Lukas gets his fulfillment dividends from frequent local trips, Brian (55, USA, 2nd) has built a lifestyle that allows him to spend several months per year in foreign countries. Brian's work-life balance is similar to Julia's (the international travel guide mentioned above) in that he, too, can work for several months each year and then have several months to himself. On the positive side, Brian mentioned how travel had prepared him well to meet the challenges of being a freelance worker:

> [Travel] has given me more openness and more ability to fit in and adapt. It's trained me to become more willing to try... like not to question myself all the time. To be more open to experiences and people [...] But I mean, it's kinda weird because my job as well feels like traveling cause, I move from different places.

However, Brian went on to describe how over time his jobs, while remaining financially lucrative, began to pay lower and lower fulfillment dividends, as they became less challenging and interesting:

> Like I can work on a project, and after 8 days, I've had enough. Alright then, let's move on, somewhere else. And you can't. You gotta keep at it. I mean, I worked one job five months this year, and I was like sick of it. I mean, that part becomes more painful because I know that life doesn't have to be that monotonous.

Brian's story can also help us bring another factor into the fulfillment equation: interpersonal bonds. Although this section has focused on the lifestyle aspects of occupation and work-life balance in examining people's efforts to maximize their fulfillment balance, the interpersonal relationships covered in the earlier section are obviously part of this equation as well. In Brian's case, he spoke of how his travels had also reduced his sense of belonging to his community in America. Speaking of his co-workers on a recent project, he reported:

> So you do your best to kind of partake and pretend and all that kind of stuff, but I think in the end [travel] does make me feel more alienated. Like this year, my whole focus [at work] was like, this is all interesting and everything, but I want the money so I can leave. That's what I'm here for. I don't wanna get involved in all this work stuff. In other ways [travel] also makes me feel more a part of [society] because I live in a big city and I am more involved in like, I found a real good Indian market where I can get Indian food and movies to rent. I know where the best Laotian restaurant in [hometown] is. So I know where I can pull those kind of things out cause they are remnants of trips to kind of keep that whole thing alive. So that kind of connects me more. But on a personal level, you know, it probably makes me more detached.

Here, we can see Brian trying to compensate for the lower sense of fulfillment he gets from work and interpersonal relationships by tapping into local resources that stimulate his sense of belonging to the intercultural travel community and some of the local communities he has visited, a strategy mentioned above.

Fast forward 13 years to my second interview with Brian, and we see that his sense of cultural dislocation had increased. His job situation had not become any more fulfilling, and his feeling of connection to American culture had deteriorated even further:

> I don't really feel American, necessarily. Like, for example [...] They're really uptight now. You have to put your hand on your heart when you hear the national anthem. And that's bullshit. I'm not doing that anymore. And there were times when it's really awkward to say that around other people. But I mean, yeah, I don't love America, I don't ...maybe I'm like 30% American, not 100%.

However, Brian has devised some coping strategies to compensate for the lack of fulfillment resulting from his decreased job satisfaction and increased sense of cultural dislocation. The first involved a change to his travel style. He now returns to India each year, where he has developed a circle of Indian friends, many of whom he sees each year. In a sense, he now goes to India to replace the feelings of community and belonging that he no longer gets in America. To get through his times back in America, he has also become deeply involved with the Indian community in his home city:

> I am active in the Indian community here. You would think I am Indian at this point! I am involved with the Indian film festival here every year [...] I still have a group of friends from the Indian community. Like we get together and we watch Indian movies. [...] And part of it is, for me, that white people are kind of boring.

The net effect is that Brian has truly developed a transcultural identity. In fact, Brian has coined his own term for this phenomenon:

> I have this joke and I'm telling everybody that I'm transracial and I'm transitioning to become an Indian person. Like I'll dye my hair. Like sometimes I see an Indian person, and I just wanna go "Oh, come be my friend. I wanna talk to you." I have had to learn to tone it back because I get too eager sometimes when I see them. And they might get scared. I feel like "oh my god you're Indian, let's talk, let's be friends". I get that a lot.

In essence, Brian's identity has truly shifted, to the point where a change of locations may be necessary to fully restore his sense of well-being. And indeed, when asked about his future plans, Brian mentioned that he could see himself going to India to open "a yoga place in India, or a guesthouse [...] where people stay long-term. [...] You're working and getting the traveling thing without having to travel." In essence, Brian's plan is to shift from the "work to pay for your true passions" to the "make your passion your work" mentality, but it would require a change of location.

And this brings me to a final theme regarding traveler re-integration—namely, travelers who find themselves unable to re-integrate in the local culture where they lived before their travels. The mildest form of this outcome pertains to those who move to another region of their home country where they believe they will fit in better. To provide a few examples, Judy (57, Germany, 2nd) figured out very early in her travels that she needed to live in a more intercultural environment, which led her to move to a big German city: "I don't think I could ever live in a small city again. In [hometown] I am in contact with people from all over the world on a regular basis." Similarly, Ryan (40, Canada, 2nd) described how he moved from eastern to western Canada because not only is it "one of the most beautiful places on the planet", but the people there are also far more outdoors-oriented, and there is an active extreme sports scene there as well. Finally, Matt (39, USA, 2nd) described why he chose to move to a new city:

> [Hometown] has great nature here, real nature and green, and when I do find a place I'm really only looking for places that have giant natural areas. And I think that will be one thing that'll help a lot. That being closer to nature.

Beyond these examples, of the 31 LITs I interviewed or have long-term information on, 8 of them ended up settling down in countries other than those in which they were born. In the case of LITs settling abroad, the motivations are also quite complex. As such, a detailed examination of the expat experience is beyond the scope of this thesis, so here I will just mention a few examples to highlight the connection between long-term travel and the ultimate decision to leave one's native culture. In most cases, there is some feeling of dissonance with the values of the native culture. In Lena's case, she did her first trip to South America after university and before starting her first job. When she returned and started that job, she was soon close to a burnout. In other words, her job was actively sapping her sense of fulfilment. Furthermore, she mentioned how everything from the weather to the mindset had diminished her sense of contact with her own culture: "On the one hand, it's the weather. Too grey, too cold, too much rain, too wet. [...] And also, sometimes Germans are too much 'glass-is-half-empty people', and I don't need that anymore". She traveled back to Central America, where she fell in love with a local. Checking her fulfilment balance, it was not that hard to leave for a new culture with a better climate and values about work-life balance that she felt were closer to her own: "People are so honest [...] life is simpler and priorities are a bit better aligned, you know?" If any hesitation remained, she was quick to fall back on a familiar traveler refrain to describe how she finally took the plunge:

> I think without all the traveling I wouldn't be so eager to take risks. I would have been more hesitant. Because without the long-term travel experience, I would say that your horizon's not that wide, then you take fewer risks. You're less adventurous or prepared to take risks [...]

A similar calculus led to Nick's decision to leave Ireland and settle down in Spain. Upon first returning from his extended South America trip, he suggested that his travels had given him the ability to filter out the negative things about home:

> I didn't have any of those classic returned-travellers realisations that the west is materialistic, that we have it great at home, that the working/commuting/urban rat race is a pile of poo, etc. I already knew all that; possibly because I'm older than the typical backpacker, possibly because I'm a cynic, possibly because I've always read travel books. All those things were reinforced for me. I suppose the biggest thing for me is that you act upon those notions - I've noticed that people who travel adjust well to being back home but with a sense of distance from the rat race (we're not bothered about getting into it - we work, etc., but none of us are going to stress about what we now see as trivia). (Nick, Ireland, 35, email)

However, 5 years in Ireland was enough to break Nick's filter, and he was soon off to Spain:

> In 2005 everyone in Ireland thought they were about to hit the big time - the economy was great, everyone was buying property, drinking expensive stupid coffees. It was really dull to hear about four years of conversations about mortgages. Nobody seemed to have any spark about them except to hitch a ride on the gravy train. I think having been fairly broke but happy on the road meant that I wanted to talk about other things but everyone was too busy trying to make money. [...] Also there's a dreadful negativity in Ireland that we never saw in even the shittiest places in the Americas. I didn't realise how zealously the status quo is maintained in Ireland until I came back from this trip on which we had been able and emboldened to undertake any mad idea we came up with. Self-supported kayak trip in the world's deepest canyon? Sure, good luck. In Ireland, you would be told about the danger and that you're a fool. (Nick, 47, Ireland, 2nd)

Although Nick does not mention his job, one could say that his job is not a source of major personal fulfillment for him. In fact, he expressed skepticism about the entire concept of finding fulfillment in his job in his first interview:

9.6 Striking a proper work-life balance

> I don't think anyone finds full fulfillment and total happiness just from their job, maybe very few people. [...] I just know so many people who really don't like their jobs at all, but yeah, they do it. But the bottom line is, practically speaking you're gonna spend a good portion of your waking life doing this job so it better be something that at least....you get something out of, you know, some feeling of fulfillment other than the paycheck. (Nick, 34, Ireland)

In the final analysis, as with Ryan, Nick moved to a locale where he had better access to the outdoor adventure activity that brings him great fulfillment (kayaking, in his case). In addition, although his job continues to be not much more than a minor source of fulfillment, it has the distinct advantage of being highly flexible and location-independent, or as Nick calls it, "country-independent", a feature that automatically ups the overall fulfillment value of a job by providing more of a resource that they treasure—freedom.

However, in Nick's case, the fulfillment balance sheet would not be complete without mentioning the fact that he is now the proud father of three children, a role that brings in a whole other calculation of energy investment vs. fulfillment dividends. And indeed, this section would not be complete without at least offering a few observations about how family responsibilities influence LITs' traveler "careers", as this is often the first objection people raise to the traveler lifestyle. In short, there can be no doubt that children change the equation when it comes to travel. None of the true lifestyle travelers in this study have children, as it seems this kind of completely peripatetic lifestyle is simply not conducive to raising children. Nevertheless, almost all of the LITs in this study who have children reported that they may have adjusted their trip duration, but they remain committed to traveling. For example, Ryan (40, Canada, 2nd) brings his infant son with him on all his trips to his extreme sport events: "We lead a very adventurous life and I always have. Travel is one of the most important things to me and my family. My son isn't two years old, but he's already been on something like 12 airplanes." And Alan (56, New Zealand, 2nd) reported how he has kept his traveler ethos, despite having a child:

> I still travel with my wife and our son, who's now 8. He's in school, and because of the B&B, we mostly go on short vacations in Europe. But we still travel the same way (backpack, low-cost Airbnb or farm stays or something like that). I'd actually love to go on a longer trip with the family, but that won't happen for a while, I guess.

For my part, as the mother of two small children (5 and 7 at the time of writing), I also have some experience with this issue. The truth is that the last few years have been an adjustment for me as far as balancing my roles as a university lecturer (my first real career), wife and mother, and in that time, I have definitely had to scale back my traveling activities. Nevertheless, like Alan, my husband and I have made a concerted effort to maintain our connection to the traveler lifestyle by transforming ourselves into short-term, independent travelers (SITs?) and doing shorter excursions around Europe, America and even Africa with the kids, for we both believe strongly in the travel as a tool of learning and development for kids and adults of all ages.

10 Final Learning Outcomes

In this section, I will summarize the lessons travelers learn throughout the *entire* travel process. Some of these outcomes relate directly to the reentry process discussed in the last chapter and therefore could have been placed in a conclusion section for that chapter. However, ultimately, one of the key findings of my research has been that for long-term independent travel, it is often nearly impossible to identify the precise experience that triggers a learning process or the precise moment when that process yields an outcome. In fact, in most cases, it is a combination of various events, feelings, reflective moments, and realizations, with an infinite number of possible sequences and permutations among these various factors. In this paper, I have endeavored to bring some order into this complexity by dividing the experiences travelers have into three phases (i.e. pre-travel, on the road, reentry) and then, in some cases, further subdividing into types of experiences within these phases (e.g. experiences with local cultures vs. the experiences with the traveler culture). However, ultimately, it is important to understand that the borders between all of these constructed categories are fluid at best, and in most cases, there is some overlap between them. For this reason, I have chosen to create this section to highlight once more some of the key lessons LITs have learned about the meaning-making and identity-shaping process and its related challenges, their own sense of purpose, and the more effective ways of communicating with their fellow human beings that they believe they have developed. Here again, I will try to use quotes from the interviews to let the LITs speak for themselves.

10.1 Cultural and personal meaning-making

In her interview, Dana (51, Denmark, 2nd) described the effect of experiencing and understanding different value systems: "I hope that I have a broader, wider perspective. And again, things that are just normal here are not normal somewhere else. And so it just makes me question more what is real and what is not, and what is good and what is bad, and what is things to do and what is not."

One object that many LITs come to understand better and then criticize is the way that people form meanings and opinions. For example, Chelsea (37, England, 2nd) perfectly describes ethnocentrism:

> Especially in London, you get really London-centric, and you stop to think, and I think it's everywhere you go, you just get really that's your world, and it's actually

© Springer Fachmedien Wiesbaden GmbH, part of Springer Nature 2019
B. Phillips, *Learning by Going: Transformative Learning through Long-term Independent Travel*, https://doi.org/10.1007/978-3-658-25773-6_10

very small. And as soon as you start going somewhere else, you realize there are different ways of thinking and that sounds really obvious, but there are other ways of looking at life and other ways of living and other paces which are very slow or faster, but they're just different.

Although on some level she had identified the problem of ethnocentrism during her travels, it took on more concrete meaning for her when she returned home and witnessed this same behavior played out on a more local level by her fellow Londoners, and almost by herself as well. In other words, due to her previous exposure to this cognitive bias, she was able to recognize ethnocentrism in action and then resist the temptation to fall back into this tendency herself. This is a prime example of how the occurrence of similar disorienting experiences at different points in the long-term travel process (i.e. pre-travel, on the road, re-integration) can reinforce important lessons learned.

To some degree, ethnocentrism implies an active process. That is, in attempting to interpret information, one allows one's ingrained cultural biases to alter the process. Other LITs took this a step further to argue that some people seem to have ceased even attempting to exercise their powers of rational thinking, instead becoming passive consumers of misleading information fed to them by the media. As Max (36, Austria, 2nd) explained:

> People who consume such media just believe things, they confuse them. These are not things that they see; they are images of things that they see. And I find it profoundly shocking when people, and this is another example of what we don't learn in school even though it is so important to learn, that people mix things up with stories about those things. And they think it's all the same, and that's a catastrophe. And I think it's gotten worse.

Max went on to describe how people grow completely dependent on these socially prescribed meaning schemes:

> It was amusing, with many people I just thought they just wanted to impose their picture [of me], without really putting themselves in my shoes and thinking about how I was, and how I am now, and what has really changed. And this is something that I realized when traveling, and also afterwards, people have this tremendous fear of change. It's unbelievable (Max, 36, Austria, 2nd).

Max was the victim of stereotyping, both on the road, when people made assumptions about him based on his skin color or nationality, and back home, when people made assumptions about him based on the decision he had made to quit his job and go traveling. As Max went on to explain, his experience with stereotyping at home was even more enlightening:

> People are so scared, that they wake up and are a bit different than they were the day before, and that's why they carve out their picture and the picture of others, and they like to carve it in stone, so that it doesn't change. This frantic clutching, conserving, everything has to be clear and regulated. I think I noticed it so strongly

10.1 Cultural and personal meaning-making

> because before traveling, I was like that. It was one of my main urges: Everything had to be the same; nothing can be shifting.

When confronted with his own former behaviors, he was able to recognize them and identify the source of his need for clear compartmentalizing—fear of change.

Although philosophers and psychologists have long pointed out that fear is at the root of most (if not all) negative emotions and behaviors, it would be a mistake to assume that most people have been exposed to or understood this valuable concept. Thus, it is worth pointing out that several LITs mentioned gaining an awareness or better understanding of the function of fear through their travels. Beyond the effect it has on interpersonal communication, Patrick (37, Austria) described how he now understands the way fear is exploited in the socio-political arena:

> That's what it it's about, that most people are scared of freedom. Fear is the greatest driver for the industry, for politics, they are all playing with our fear. And this is the reason why we have a world the way it is today. Because the elites, those in power have realized how to instill this fear in people.

Of course, recognizing how fear is used to manipulate is the first step towards learning to resist this manipulation and re-claim one's own independence. And here again, this is not just in the larger political arena, but how one treats one's fellow human beings. For example, Matt (39, USA, 2nd) reported how traveling had helped him free himself from the destructive influence of his own homophobia:

> I've become more liberal person over the years. I've become more comfortable with gays and that whole other LGBT movement. I've had friends but good acquaintances who were gays. And that was good for me to get over my homophobia. And that's helped in that way.

Similarly, Keith (23, Australia) described how he learned to resist the temptation to judge an individual based on their nationality:

> One thing I have also learned about Australia is that I feel we are too closely connected to the United States, especially after the last Iraqi war. But my opinion on the United States has been twofold. It's reinforced the fact that I think that the United States does a lot of bad things, and I really don't like the political system. But I've also met a bunch of really cool people from the United States. You know. Ahm...a lot of people bag off, Yankees, or gringos. But I've met some really great, great people from the United States, so it balances itself out, in my opinion.

When LITs' previously automatic or subconscious values are challenged, they are forced to engage their critical thinking capacity, and the more often this happens, the more likely they are to shake off their comfortable pre-programmed thinking practices and become true critical thinkers. Chelsea (37, England, 2nd) cited this cognitive training as the most important lesson she learned from travel:

> I think the biggest thing about traveling for me is that it just changed the way I thought about things. It changed the structure of how I deconstructed things, and that's been invaluable, and that's been incredible, and I think that's the value of traveling, how it trains you to think in certain ways, how it trains you to think about things from a different perspective.

Similarly, Dana (39, Denmark) described how her travel experience had instilled in her a healthy skepticism about traditional sources of information:

> I don't believe what's written in history books anymore. My personal perspective is that it's selective, isn't it? That you, ahm. History is very political, very cultural, and so it's through the eyes that either tell you or write the book.

And Julia (50, Germany, 2nd) described how she also learned to take the opinions of her friends and other people with a grain of salt and rather to seek out her own information, preferably through first-hand experience:

> And I also notice that the mainstream media has created a hatred of Muslims. Right now, I'm in a Muslim country, and I'd like to see it for myself, before letting the media influence me. I'd like to have my own experiences and get an even greater distance from what the news and the media preaches. I'd like to be in the country and get my own impression. This way I have a greater distance and I am very careful with first opinions. Earlier, when a friend told me this and that and this person did that, I believed it. But now, I always get a second opinion because I have seen everywhere around the world that there are two sides to a story. I think this is something that I think about the most when I am traveling. [...] I just realized there's something off in the relation to reality, and that's why I've always found travel very educational. What you are being taught and what you see for yourself, or learn for yourself.

Peter (59, Austria, 2nd) offered a story of applying his critical thinking to a particular problem in society that he had not considered before. Spending some time with some very wealthy New Yorkers who nevertheless seemed to be generally miserable in their lives prompted him to reflect on society's values:

> But what I notice is that today I question certain things. And that's even increased in the last 8 years [since the 1st interview]. For example, earlier I talked about "wealth". Simply asking the question, "What does wealth even mean?" Most people have no clue what it means [...] And it would be important for our society. And that we think about the fact that our society needs new structures.

This power to detect, analyze and resist the values thrust upon one by society is the cognitive or intellectual equivalent of the prized autonomy that LITs so often mention. Since I have covered the idea of autonomy in various contexts above, it is not necessary to discuss that again here. However, in the present context, it is simply important to point out that when LITs speak of "freedom", they are usually speaking primarily of the ability to decide what actions they will take. However, many LITs ultimately come to the conclusion that the freedom to control what you think is even more important.

10.2 Who am I?

At the end of chapter 8, we looked at some of the strategies LITs used to re-integrate in their societies and construct a life that gave them some sense of fulfillment. Since the current section is focused more on cognitive processes and examined values, here I will offer a few statements from LITs who have exercised the critical thinking described above and drawn some conclusions about how they themselves fit into the big picture.

Glen (38, England, 2nd), reflecting on his travels 10 years later, mentioned how travel taught him to think about his place in the universe:

> It's damn hard to explain yet here goes - the most important thing I learnt and continue to learn from independent travelling is that 'I', 'you', 'we', 'them', 'they' are all relatively insignificant concepts when you grasp the 'big' thing or feeling or vibe or whatever you wanna call it. And for me personally (it's impossible to answer question without using the 'I' perspective.....not trying being hypocritical!) travelling helps you appreciate your own (actually tiny) position within that big thing wholeheartedly. I respect the people who don't have to travel to live with that 'feeling'.

It is worth noting that Glen acknowledges that not everyone needs to travel to come to this realization. However, the respect he accords to people who do not need to travel is indicative of the values he himself places on his own travels and the wisdom they gave him.

Andy (42, USA, 2nd) focuses less on his perception of his role in life, which he is still figuring out, but rather on how travel trained his mind to be able to guide him on the path towards that goal and avoid the pitfalls of modern society:

> I mean, a lot of what we were talking about before, like being able to take a step back and you know, when you're caught up in the daily cycle of life, ahm. You know and the States is pretty fast-paced, and D.C. is career-driven, and like I described earlier, when I walked away and came back, I was like "holy shit, these people, they've lost perspective. They're all caught up in this rat race. And they don't even see it." And I have this view. And even if I'm caught up in it, I can see it, and I have this third, like independent party perspective of it, which helps me look at myself, and helps me realize that I am caught up in it now. And if I didn't travel and had never made that revelation, I would not be able to view myself like that. And if I'm in it, I'm aware of it. Self-awareness.

Eric (59, Canada, 2nd) recognizes the lure of his old bad habits, but nevertheless reports that his travels have given him memories that keep him grounded and help him maintain a global perspective, even if he no longer fits in completely in his home country:

> I am more relaxed, lighter, less stressed. But I take back pretty soon my old 'patterns'. Nevertheless, I keep in memory a lot of images and realities different from ours. This means that I can no longer close my eyes to the world situation. I have very different ways of seeing life on this planet. To understand how everything works between rich and poor. To see how the planet is being destroyed everywhere, everywhere, everywhere. To what extent humans lack consciousness everywhere on this Earth. Let's say that it discourages me often of the human race ... I

remain always interested in the world and global news. I think I see a bit more than what people see when they listen to international news. I have different benchmarks in the face of global news, at least for the countries I visited. It also makes me feel like an extra-terrestrial in my environment. When I talk to other people in my country, I certainly do not see things in the same way.

Lukas (39, Germany, 2nd) emphasizes how travel taught him the importance of learning your own values and priorities and then taking responsibility for your own happiness:

But I think that you learn to do those things that are important to you. And even if you do something, that in retrospect wasn't that great, and you let it be, then it's still a learning experience. You have to live with the consequences. And you can't just complain anywhere. And if you travel on a package tour where everything is pre-chewed, or even on the job, then people complain. But if you are your own boss, then you automatically criticize yourself and you have to own it. You have to motivate yourself, but it's also your own fault if nothing comes of it. You have to season your soup, but you also have to eat it when it is over-salted. There is no one you can blame. And on the one hand that's great, but it's also exhausting. But when you get the hang of it, then it's beautiful. Otherwise people just accept pre-fabricated solutions.

Some LITs expressed specific life goals that travel had helped them identify. For example Chelsea's (37, England, 2nd) goal is to start a family and continue building her career:

Yeah, I want to be a mummy. Yeah, sure. I wanna be a mummy, ahm. It doesn't necessarily have to be mine, but I do want to be a mummy. I want to ... they're very simple things really. I want to continue working in [my creative career], but like really getting, like really making stuff that I feel really belongs to me, that should be made, that needs to be made, that has some value. And that takes a long time to get into the position where you can do that, so that's a work in progress.

While her family goal reflects her travel-derived lesson that there are enough children in the world, many of whom need parents, her career goal also shows that she now knows that she will only be happy if she is doing something both creative and meaningful for society. It is also important to emphasize that she recognizes the process that leads to the goal, and understands the value of the journey as well as that of the destination.

On the other hand, Patrick (37, Austria) has largely let go of definitive goals, but he clearly articulated the guiding life principles he learned from his travels:

I don't know what I want or don't want, but I don't think about it too much anymore. There is a certain foundation which doesn't change, and that is a sustainable lifestyle, a spiritual lifestyle. It is to live my life in the moment as much as possible, not in any past or in the future. These three components, maybe more, they are like a guiding principle within which I move. (Patrick, 37, Austria).

Similarly, Lena (41, Germany, 2nd), who now has a rewarding job and a family, mentions that she travels less, but the lessons of travel remain with her and have given her a different outlook and approach to life:

In the last few years when I didn't get to travel that much, I still believe that the travel experiences that I had have given me a different perspective on life, and the ability to appreciate the little things in life, to not complain about little things. Because I got to learn about the life circumstances of so many other people and through getting to know other cultures and mentalities, I have developed an openness towards others.

As Lena's quote mentions the importance of being open to others, it serves as a good bridge to the next section, which will cover the altered modes of interacting with others that emerged from LITs travels.

10.3 Communication Skills

We have already seen the importance of interpersonal relationships for establishing a fulfilling life, and in chapter 8 we looked at the difficulties LITs faced when returning home and seeking to re-integrate with their circles of friends and family. However, in the long run, most LITs reported that the communication skills they had acquired or refined on the road helped them to overcome these difficulties. Although many were surprised to encounter difficulties communicating with people with whom communication had previously been relatively effortless, once they realized and accepted that they were facing the challenge of communicating with people who have a different values system, they were able to begin applying the skills they had learned on the road for managing such situations.

As a foundation for effective interpersonal communication, we can mention five key aspects already covered above. First, the broader perspective that LITs often mention can be viewed as a wider, more diverse set of possible meaning schemes from which they can draw on when trying to communicate with another person. Second, as mentioned earlier in this chapter, through their experience in interacting with people with different values and meanings schemes, they have gained the enhanced cognitive ability to deal with conflicting meaning schemes by taking in different views and then mixing and matching them to find a functional solution. Third, as mentioned above, many LITs develop a more secure self-image that allows them to overcome or at least confront some of the fears and insecurities that function as barriers to communication. To draw on a popular expression, they become more "comfortable in their own skins". This gives them the enhanced self-confidence they so often cite, which allows them to adopt the fourth important pre-requisite for effective communication—openness to new ideas. That is, their personal sense of security allows them to confront conflicting opinions without feeling threatened or automatically becoming defensive. Finally, while the previous characteristics focus more on the signal reception aspect of communication, they also need to encode and send their own messages, and here they can draw on a refined storytelling ability acquired from their broad experience in attempting to communicate their meanings to relative strangers. In short, the travel experience, and here I include the vital component of reentry, is like a real-life crash course in effective communication. Or, in the words of Alice (29, Sweden):

> You have to be open minded. You have to be wanting to learn, and I think you learn about yourself, and you... you know... you learn about how you react to things, how you react and respond to things in different situations, and also how other people react and respond, and you learn about other ways of life, how to...what's important, what you can really do without, what's luxury and what's necessary, what's ...yeah.. You learn so much, I don't even find words for everything. You learn so much about everything.

Of course, this paints a rather idealistic picture of LITs, and I certainly do not mean to imply that all travelers become some sort of super-hero communicators. As with any other form of education, outcomes vary widely, as we have seen time and again above. And indeed, even those who consciously acknowledge their increased communication skills often simultaneously demonstrate a humble awareness of their own limitations and the constant challenge that communication represents:

> There were so many things that I just could not let alone, so many things that I absolutely had to have the way I wanted them. I made some many things difficult for myself. I was quick to judge other people. I always saw things only from my own point of view. Of course, this doesn't mean that I am some kind of saint who understands all people perfectly. But at least I learned that there are always other perspectives. (Max, 36, Austria, 2nd)

In a similar vein, Nick (34, Ireland) downplays the very lessons that he nevertheless found so important: "I guess it's all that cliché crap about, you know, broadening your horizons, and seeing how other people live and all that....kind of hippie shit. [laughs] But it's true. It sounds corny when you talk about it, but you know what I mean." Indeed, while some may chuckle condescendingly at such insights, if people really look around, I think they will see that the world could do with a bit more of this kind of openness and tolerance, and perhaps this is a lesson well worth learning. Nick colorfully summed up the real outcome as follows:

> I've learned that people are fucking great, and everyone has something interesting to relate. I think I'm more engaged with people now - more aware that some random person has stories to tell, and I like to think I make more of an effort to talk to them. I'm definitely more confident in myself since.

As Nick implies, more storytelling rounds might make for happier people and a happier planet.

The claims I have made above about travel's ability to enhance interpersonal skills may seem steep. Once again, it is important to emphasize that not all LITs attain the same degree of effectiveness in this area. However, the overwhelming majority of LITs in this

10.3 Communication Skills

study emphasized interpersonal skills as one of the most important outcomes, if not the most important outcome of their travels. It is a competence of which they are rightfully proud, as most of them endured some painful struggles to acquire it. To conclude this section, I will let the LITs speak for themselves and describe the lessons learned, how they learned them, and, in particular, how these skills helped them re-integrate with their native cultures upon their returns.

For example, Chelsea (37, England, 2nd) described how she had to overcome what she sees as an unfortunate characteristic of her own culture to become a better communicator:

> I was definitely more aware of my British culture when I was traveling. I am normally the most open and direct of my friends and most of my friends say I am not very British, but I really noticed my British reserve traveling. Like when we were making friendships sometimes, I realized how British I was, and I really noticed it. Like I was suspicious sometimes.. when sometimes people really wanted to be my friend, and I was like, "oh no, I am not sure about this". And it's that Britishness. It wasn't like, "yeah, just open the doors to everybody". And I noticed it more when I was staying in places

While Chelsea had to learn the courage to open up and both give and receive more when communicating, Dana (39, Denmark) had to learn to suppress her own snap judgements and remain open to people and viewpoints that may at first have put her on the defensive:

> The people that I placed judgment on have taught me lessons in generosity. Or maybe in ...because then, you know, I've been rude to them, and they might be generous to me the next second, and I'm like, whoa, that doesn't fit in my description of you. And yes, definitely in conversations with other people, where I was like, this person has nothing whatsoever that I would find interesting, and then later on in the night, yes, there was a story that I wouldn't have wanted to miss for the life of it. And I've had quite a few experiences like that while traveling, and I can definitely say that it's made me more accepting, more critical of myself and more accepting of others. Now I don't think anymore that my opinion is the right one.

Where Dana had developed an awareness of how the background cognitive processes (i.e. judgement) can inhibit communication, Brian (43, USA) mentioned his increased awareness of a barrier in the spoken communication process itself:

> [Travel] made me way more conscious of including other people in conversations, and I try to do that when I know there are people who don't speak the language because I know what that's like when someone's not a part of it, and they're not getting something.

Brian's quote calls to mind a skill that many travelers, and particularly English native speakers, develop almost instinctually. I often find myself in groups of people consisting of native English speakers and non-native English speakers. And with the native English speakers, you can always tell the ones who have limited experience in intercultural interactions. They speak quickly and use too many higher-level words or idiomatic expressions, and I sometimes find myself interpreting for the non-native speakers in the group. It is encouraging to see that, after I do this enough times, most native speakers start to get the point and alter their speaking style accordingly, which shows that people really can learn from experience.

While Brian acquired his sensitivity through his experience handling a language barrier (both as a sender and receiver of signals), it is important to mention that this sensitivity can also cross over into any form of interpersonal communication, even if there is no language barrier present. Essentially, Brian is describing an enhanced empathy that gives him a greater awareness of the needs and perspectives of others in a conversation, a competence that Max (36, Austria, 2nd) described exercising in his communications with his fellow native German speakers. Describing his interactions with his fellow Austrians shortly after his return, he reported:

> I said to myself, "OK, I am not important now, and I don't want to push myself in the foreground." I didn't even have the desire to talk about [my travels] specifically, because I knew there was no point in it. When people asked me, of course I was happy to talk about it, but I knew that it was going to be simply impossible to give them an understanding of my experiences. I also noticed back then that people had problems, and generally speaking, they were talking about themselves a lot. And I said to myself, "OK, that's fine. I'm just trying to put myself in their shoes in a selfless manner."

Max was fortunate, as he had intuited the difficulty of communicating the meaning of his travel experience before he even returned home. This, combined with the self-confidence he had acquired through his travels, allowed him to put aside his own needs in an interpersonal setting and focus on the needs of others. Others had to learn the hard way about the difficulty of communicating one's new post-travel values and meanings to an often non-receptive audience back home:

> I love my background, my childhood. But [travel] also opened my eyes. I also had trouble with my family. The first time I went away, I came back and I was like, "Hey, wake up! There's so much going on in this world, and you live in this shelter." And I was very aggressive because traveling changed my life. And then I pushed a lot of people. And of course, people didn't want to hear that. And I had that attitude, everything that's good for me is good for you. And now I feel like I am wiser, I don't do that anymore. (Magnus, 25, Denmark)

Magnus touches on a theme mentioned above—the need for a certain degree of self-editing when dealing with people who have conflicting views. However, this does not necessarily involve completely relinquishing one's own views and values, but rather finding more effective ways to incorporate them into a conversation with people with different values. For example, Chelsea (37, England, 2nd) mentioned an adjustment she made to her conversation practices in order to bring traveler values that she considers more authentic into the conversation:

> Like in Spain I had friends that just didn't know what I do for a year, and I had no clue how they made their money, and it's not what we talked about. And try getting away with that here [in the UK]. Like within 5 minutes, you know what someone does. And when I left, when I returned, that's one thing I did bring from traveling, like I try not to ask people what they do. I ask people what they dedicate themselves to, when we have to have that conversation. What do they dedicate themselves to? Cause it's not always their job.

Rather than challenging their values (e.g. "Why are all English people so obsessed with work and money? Can't you see that there are more important things in the world?"), Chelsea has devised a subtle, non-confrontational means of steering her interlocutor towards a different value set. Perhaps this conversation may even slightly alter her interlocutor's own value system or at least provide her with some level of conscious or unconscious awareness of another possible value system that could serve as a foundation for human interaction.

And this brings me to Patrick (37, Austria), who is worth quoting at length, as the following passage does a fine job of tying together the many steps by which LITs learn through their travels and ultimately come to an outcome that affects both their self-image and the way they live their lives:

> On the one hand my worldview has changed in that new perspectives were added. I have seen new ways of living and have seen that there are other ways of living one's life and have integrated that in my own life. I have confidence now and self-esteem and have realized that I can go my own way, and I noticed how beautiful life can be when I go my own way. How beautiful life is when I go my own way and that I can do it even if some people say it can't be done. It has also heightened my awareness about how we deal with the world as humans, and that we are confronted with a huge challenge if we want to continue to be a guest on this planet. Whether we can do it or not, I have no idea. I can only try to take a step myself. And whether or not I can inspire others or not, I don't know, but I think the challenge is anyway to start with oneself. My guiding principle on my three-year tour was Mahatma Ghandi's sentence "Be the change that you want to see in others". And this is what I contemplated the whole time, and this sentence inspired me the entire time.

No doubt countless people have seen this phrase. In fact, a quick Google search turns up hundreds of images of bumper stickers and inspirational posters with this quote, as well as a healthy collection of images of people who have tattooed it on their skin. [Note: It also reveals that Ghandi did not actually say this, but I will leave it to the reader to do the requisite Googling if they are interested in the full story.] And perhaps for some people, reading these words would be enough to motivate them to change their lives. However, for Patrick, 3 years of travel firmly implanted this idea in his value system and gave him the courage to live by these words when he returned home.

To be clear, Patrick's interpretation of "Ghandi's" words has not led him to a life of solitary contemplation or withdrawal from the world. Like Ghandi, albeit on a smaller scale, Patrick is doing what he can to make a difference in the world. As mentioned above, Patrick has made a career as a motivational speaker giving presentations that draw on his travel experiences to receptive audiences to try to raise their awareness, expand their horizons and motivate them to become part of the solution, both for their own good and for that of the planet.

10.4 On stories and storytellers

Thus, Patrick's story brings us back to the final outcome of the travel experience: stories and storytelling competence. This may be the one thing that unites all travelers—they all emerge from their experiences with a wealth of stories and a strong desire to share these stories. Throughout this paper, we have seen the vital role of narrative in the transformative learning process. Going back to the motivations section, on some level all disorienting experiences can be viewed as conflicting narratives. For example, future LITs hear a story from a traveler that somehow does not match up with the stories they are being told in school and by the media surrounding them. Once on the road, LITs learn by listening to the stories of locals, a new way of learning that connects powerfully for many LITs:

> You ask a local about their country, and you get to see how passionate they are about the idiot who was running the country 30 years before, for example, and that's the best way to find out about it. [....] With a history book, you have to use your imagination, but when talking to a person, you're hearing the story first hand. It's a personal experience.

They also hear stories from fellow travelers, which open their minds to new horizons and soon gives rise to a desire to create their own stories. Brian (55, USA, 2nd) explained this process:

> I wanted to backpack through Europe and see the sights, like the Eiffel Tower and those things [...] And that was all about European history, cause that's really the Classic Grand Tour. And on my first trip, I was like 27 or 28. And then it became a different thing when I was doing it. Like meeting the other backpackers, and hearing their stories. And that's when it really became a drug. Like, "Oh my God, you're talking about Turkey. What's that like?" So it became this like drug that fed ...maybe that trip was like a big gateway drug to other trips.

Here, Brian shows off his own improvisational narrative flair with an amusing but effective drug-related metaphor produced on the spot. And indeed, most travelers soon become avid storytellers. On the road, they share their stories with others to explore new meanings, reinforce shared values and establish their status within the community. In time, they come to prize these stories, and the awareness of their value as tools of communication and identity building even begins to affect their behavior and their ability to handle situa-

10.4 On stories and storytellers

tions. Risks are taken in the interest of not only testing oneself, but possibly gaining a good story. And when things go wrong, they get through it by imagining the story that will come out of it:

> And I think that being a "Yes man" gets me in trouble a lot when I'm overseas. And makes me regret some of the situations that I get myself into. But they also make for good stories sometimes, - the situations I get myself into. You know, there's an upside to it. [...] These stories are important for me. I enjoy having good stories to tell. And when something happens that I can really remember, I usually try to write it down so that I can remember it later, but usually they are not hard to remember. And yeah, they are important to me. (Matt, 39, USA, 2nd)

Indeed, these stories become vehicles for transmitting meaning and expressing their own identities, which also accounts for part of the shock they experience upon coming home. Almost unanimously, the LITs describe their reentry experience in terms of who is and is not interested in listening to their stories. There's the honeymoon period: "The first few weeks back were great, because everyone was eager to hear your stories, and you're catching up with everyone, telling them all your tall tales" (Nick, 47, Ireland, 2nd). But sooner or later (and sometimes right from the beginning), their attention fades, as Ryan (40, Canada, 2nd) explained when describing one of his early trips:

> This was my second trip. After my first year-long trip [...], I did feel frustration after returning to my then hometown [...] Many people didn't even realize I'd been gone a year. They thought we just hadn't crossed paths in a while. I think this experience allowed me to understand better that travel was for me and that most people really aren't that interested in other people's tales. That's what led to the website.

And indeed, even on the road, travelers learn to develop outlets for their storytelling, from conversations with fellow travelers and locals, to personal journals, to websites and emails to folks back home. For Ryan, it was his website:

> I wrote about my travels on the road and published to a website. [...] This was a great outlet for me, and allowed me to tell my story as I went. [...] Having this platform allowed me to connect with people while I was away and left me feeling less of a need to express my story to people beyond that. Those who cared, followed along. I was okay knowing that most people could never truly understand how long-term travel can change a person.

And when they return home (for those who do return home), a key component of the reentry process is finding people to listen to their stories, to help themselves process the meaning of these stories, to re-affirm their own values, and hopefully to somehow establish a feeling of belonging. Thus, they read travel books, they re-connect with old friends, they make new friends, they stay in touch with their traveler buddies, and, if they get lucky, a friendly and inquisitive researcher might even come along with a strong desire to listen to all of their stories. And if they have trouble finding a receptive audience, many of them look forward to producing their own audience, who they can force to listen to their stories:

> When I came back I felt like I had a lot of really great experiences, and I feel like my horizon's just widened. That's just... I wouldn't do it differently at all now. Not whatsoever. I don't regret my travels at all, cause one day, when I have kids and maybe even grandkids, I'll be the coolest storyteller. (Chelsea, 37, England, 2nd)

10.5 Summary of LITs' (transformative) learning outcomes

- **Expanded environmental awareness** (i.e. of planetary ecosystem and the impact humans have on it)
- **Expanded global awareness** (i.e. of socio-economic inequality and injustice)
- **Changed views on one's own culture and its values** (e.g. enhanced appreciation for living standard; new awareness of perceived faults, weakening communal and familial bonds, consumerism, etc.)
- **Deepened sense of social responsibility** (e.g. giving back to society, raising awareness of social injustice and environmental issues)
- **Increased understanding of cultural difference and diversity** (reduced ethnocentrism)
- **Increased tolerance, acceptance and even curiosity** (i.e. the ability to see beyond stereotypes and biases and handle difference)
- **New or refined interpersonal communication skills** (enhanced cognitive ability to deal with different values and conflicting meaning schemes without feeling threatened or becoming defensive; confronting or overcoming fears & insecurities that function as a barrier to communication)
- **Expanded self-awareness and self-esteem** (e.g. better understanding of oneself & appreciation for one's abilities)
- **Increased self-efficacy** (i.e. ability to deal with difficult situations and adapt to novel situations; ability to identify life goals and take responsibility for one's own happiness)
- **Increased competence in critical thinking** (e.g. freedom to control one's thinking; shifted political views, ability to detect, analyze and resist socially prescribed values such as materialism)
- **Increased competence in narrative meaning-making** (e.g. ability to explore new meanings, communicate values and identity to others and self)
- **Increased open-mindedness** (e.g. willingness to learn from others; ability to see beyond one's own perspective)
- **Enhanced empathy** (ability to project oneself into the other person's mental framework and increased awareness of the needs and perspectives of others)

11 Conclusion

In this final chapter, I will begin by providing some summary answers to the research questions. I will then move on to discuss how the results reflect or refute certain key points from various theoretical fields, before finally offering some reflections on the limitations of this study and a future outlook for both research and practical applications of the present results.

11.1 Answering research questions

The overarching research question was: *How does long-term independent travel transform the values and identities of travelers?* The "how" at the beginning of this question embraces both the processes by which transformative learning takes place and the outcomes to which these processes lead. In order to address both of these issues in a coherent and logical fashion, I will simply address the three research sub-questions, which will help to structure the information.

1: What are the critical motivating factors for extended travel?

The most important outcome with regards to motivations is to understand that the factors that spur an individual to embark on a long-term independent journey are legion, and the combination of factors will vary from one individual to the next. To help bring some conceptual coherence, I proposed the concept of a tipping point, whereby each individual has a certain threshold that she must reach before deciding to head out on the road. A variety of disorienting factors will usually contribute to reaching this point, and here I further proposed a division of these experiences into three types: seed experiences, which first plant the idea to travel in a future LIT's consciousness; lifestyle dissonance, which develops over time due to a sense that one's values and roles somehow come out of alignment with those prescribed by the culture and environment; and trigger experiences, which represent the final event that causes a LIT to make the conscious decision to leave behind her established life and embark on a journey. I also explored the final obstacles they faced in making this plan come to fruition and identified four common overarching themes LITs mentioned when discussing what they expected to gain via their travels: autonomy, novelty, challenge, and personal growth. Here again, I pointed out that most LITs went into their travel experience expecting to gain with some blend of these four factors, with autonomy being perhaps the most dominant anticipated benefit.

© Springer Fachmedien Wiesbaden GmbH, part of Springer Nature 2019
B. Phillips, *Learning by Going: Transformative Learning through Long-term Independent Travel*, https://doi.org/10.1007/978-3-658-25773-6_11

2: What different forms do (transformative) learning experiences take?

Here again, the research revealed a wide variety of possible paths towards learning outcomes. However, I have suggested some key points shared by these learning processes, which parallel some of the important steps in Mezirow's transformative learning model (1991a). The most important is Mezirow's disorienting experience, and the results have shown that long-term independent travel offers a wealth of disorienting experiences. As we saw in answering question 1 above, for most LITs, the disorienting experiences start well before the journey itself. Once underway, the disorienting experiences come fast and furious, as LITs soon come into contact with "foreign" practices, meanings and values within the local cultures, the diverse traveler culture itself, and even within themselves, as their own actions and values begin to change. Finally, the return home brings a whole new set of disorienting experiences when the travelers' altered meaning schemes and perspectives come back into contact with their pre-travel values, as expressed through personal acquaintances and other environmental factors.

In addressing these disorienting experiences, the data showed that LITs try out a wide variety of roles, relationships and actions (see section 10.2 below for a more detailed discussion of how this relates to the stages of Mezirow's model) to resolve the tension that arises from these disorienting experiences. On the road, this often involves leveraging the autonomy and, to some degree, the anonymity of traveler culture to experiment with new values and roles. In chapter 7, I explored how the resolution of this tension typically involves positioning oneself in relation to both the local community and the traveler community, as the travelers are exposed to values and behaviors from both of these communities, and seek to incorporate these elements into their own sense of identity. However, the data also showed clearly that these provisional travel identities also tend to change over the course of an individual trip or, for some LITs, a series of trips, with a particular focus in this area being on one's perceived relationship to the "mainstream" traveler community.

Dealing with the disorientation caused by reentry into one's own culture involves similar strategies of exploring new meanings, roles and actions. In chapter 8, I pointed out two key areas in this process: the interpersonal realm of re-establishing old social circles or building new ones, and the work-life balance realm, where LITs attempt to structure their lives in such a way that the energy they invest in their different roles and responsibilities yields the highest possible sense of fulfillment. Here, I also pointed out that the two realms obviously overlap, as energy must also be allotted to maintaining or expanding interpersonal relationships, which many find to be one of the most fulfilling aspects of their lives.

11.1 Answering research questions

Across all of these transformative processes, I have sought to emphasize the importance of narrative in meaning-making and identity construction. While I personally agree with McAdams's (2011) assertion that "narrative identity is an especially compelling construction – a psychosocial first among equals" (p. 103-4) for human beings in general, my research has shown that this model is particularly well-suited for analyzing LITs' identities. With the possible exception of the rare LITs who are focused nearly exclusively on solitary travels through nature, one would be hard-pressed to name an activity that demands more interpersonal interaction with people from diverse cultural backgrounds and value systems than long-term independent travel. And, as we saw in section 9.4, storytelling is the theme that runs throughout all these interactions. From the experienced traveler whose travel tale places the seed of an idea in some future LITs' consciousness, to the first local or fellow traveler one meets on the road, to the last friend one sees after returning home, storytelling are the main forms of communication. The narrative model applies even for the intentionally solitary travelers or those who turn to more solitary travel styles over time, as here they simply create and inner audience for their stories, sometimes even recounting competing stories in their heads to test possible meanings or values internally. In the final analysis, stories are indeed the lifeblood of the LIT experience.

3. How do long-term independent travel experiences influence travelers' values, lifestyles or life choices over the long term?

With this final question, we pivot from learning processes to learning outcomes. Here again, the data shows a wide variety of possible outcomes, but some clear themes emerge. The first is an expanded appreciation for the magnificence of the natural environment and the alarming threat to this environment posed by humanity. Indeed, a highly developed environmental awareness is nearly universal among the LITs I interviewed, and they all have behavioral outcomes to match—from more conscientious recycling, to veganism, to social activism designed to raise awareness of environmental issues. Furthermore, most LITs develop a heightened awareness of the complex interactions between the economic activities of different countries and regions of the world, including a better understanding of the power discrepancies that exist in those relationships and the effects these cause.

On the national level, most LITs in this study developed a heightened appreciation for the basic material provisions (e.g. education, healthcare) and living standards of their home countries. However, this is typically balanced by a heightened criticism of the materialist values of many of the LITs' home countries and what they perceive as the resulting loss of individual liberty due to their fellow citizens' devotion to consumerism. Related social criticisms include the perceived breakdown of community solidarity and functional social and familial relationships. These value dissonances in turn lead to feelings of partial or total alienation from their social circles and the community as a whole, as well as frustrations with the loss of freedom and autonomy involved with most occupations.

As for specific lifestyle and behavioral outcomes, these, too, differ widely. Perhaps the unifying theme is the desire to simplify one's life and reduce unnecessary consumption, which includes choice of living spaces, means of transportation, the electronic devices that have come to dominate modern culture, and so forth. Beyond that, I emphasized the two key criteria applied when choosing an occupation: degree of fulfillment offered by the job itself and loss of autonomy and free time due to the job. Within these parameters, LITs develop a wide range of approaches, from taking on a job that they gives them maximum fulfilment to accepting a job that may provide very little satisfaction itself but provides sufficient free time to pursue more spiritually rewarding activities, which often means further traveling.

One other important learning outcome is that when making these decisions, most LITs display an enhanced understanding of their own values and the cost-benefit ratios for the various activities in their lives in terms of the amount of time and energy that needs to be invested vs. the amount of fulfillment one gains from the activity. Beyond this self-awareness, perhaps the most important outcome of all, cited by nearly all LITs, is an enhanced self-efficacy that gives them the confidence to take risks and experiment with possible roles in an effort to maximize their satisfaction with their lives. More concretely, this can take the form of re-locating to another country or region, making a career change, or simply choosing to adjust one's work-life balance by working less.

Finally, on the level of interpersonal relationships and identity building, the data indicates that the repeated process of negotiating difference and creating meaning out of disorienting experiences seems to lead to an enhanced cognitive flexibility that allows LITs to be more open to different perspectives, more successful in their efforts to understand these perspectives (i.e. more empathetic) and more adept at devising strategies that can serve their own purposes and, in many cases, also those of the others with whom they are engaged. Here again, the narrative identity paradigm offers a useful way to look at this issue. For communication with others, one could say that the LITs can use their empathy to perceive the meaning structures of their interlocutors and then adjust their narratives appropriately to increase the odds of successful communication. In terms of identity building, LITs can draw from a rich reserve of meaningful experiences, including a wealth of experiences both positive and negative, and then use their deeper self-awareness and cognitive skills to weave these events into an autobiographical narrative that features both causal and thematic coherence.

It is important to mention that, particularly with regards to the cognitive and emotional competences mentioned in the paragraph above, I am not claiming that all LITs achieve this level of identity coherence or intercultural and interpersonal competence. Some of them struggle to establish post-travel lifestyles that meet their increased desire for autonomy and meaningful human interaction. However, even the majority of those still struggling to find this balance seem to have emerged with the tools they need to meet this challenge in time—an awareness of the relationship between their own values and those of their culture, the openness and even curiosity required to obtain new ideas and impulses, and the self-confidence to pursue new opportunities.

11.2 Theoretical implications

In this section, I will highlight some connections between my findings and some of the relevant theories and previous research. To begin with motivations, my research showed that with the LIT population, the more deeply one explores the complex range of motivations, the more they resist categorization into push-pull (Dann 1977) or escape-seeking (Iso-Ahola 1982) frameworks. Rather, almost every LIT expressed a mix of various motives (Hsu & Songshan, 2008; Kim & Lee, 2002; Swarbrooke & Horner, 2007). In addition, the data shows that motivations change over time both within a single extended trip and over the course of multiple trips, which supports Pearce's (2005) travel career pattern model. However, the data did not support any particular relationship between experience and motivation, as Pearce proposed. That is, my cohort included first-time travelers focused on engagement with the local community and experienced travelers who still viewed their trips as an opportunity to seek self-actualization.

Related to the culture shock theory mentioned above (section 4.2.1), my data was consistent with Kim's (2012) criticism of the U-curve model. It seems that the U-curve model is perhaps more applicable to more structured forms of intercultural experience, such as working or studying abroad, where one is more likely to be able to identify a somewhat consistent pattern. In contrast, the high variability and lack of structure that are characteristic of long-term independent travel make it nearly impossible to propose a common pattern in terms of how and when individuals experience and manage shock.

Nevertheless, it is possible to identify one area where the LIT experience tends to differ starkly from the U-curve model: the initial phase. That is, very few first-time LITs experience a real honeymoon phase, and most report significant feelings ranging from confusion to true shock, with most falling closer to the latter end of that scale. This is logical considering that most of the LITs in this study traveled to cultures that are far different to their own. Furthermore, whereas other forms of intercultural experience offer some sort of structure for the individuals, long-term independent travel in most cases lacks this completely. On occasion, travelers will arrange their first night of accommodation, but many do not even do this. Considering the pressure imposed by complete autonomy in an extremely foreign environment, it is not surprising that many LITs experience a strong shock on arriving at their first destination, with many even experiencing doubts about whether they have made a mistake in deciding to travel.

From there, in order to capture the diversity of possible subsequent paths towards acclimatization, any model or process diagram would have to include so many possible branches and permutations as to make it relatively meaningless. This is particularly true when one considers one of the main points which I have emphasized in the travel section of this paper, which is that most travelers to one degree or another are attempting to integrate into *two* different cultures—local culture and traveler culture. In fact, those who travel at a faster pace or in regions that feature smaller countries (e.g. Southeast Asia, Central America) can be confronted with even more different cultures, which complicates the question of acclimatization even further. Furthermore, any model seeking to explain the LIT acclimatization process would have to capture the dynamic discussed above by which LITs gradually shift the focus of their efforts to acclimatize between the traveler community and the local community. However, as was evident in the discussion above, this shift of focus between local and traveler communities is itself highly variable. Thus, the only meaningful generalization one could make about the LIT acclimatization process would be that it generally does *not* follow a smooth line—that is, it usually consists of a variety of ups and downs, as LIT are confronted with a series of disorienting challenges and forced to find methods of overcoming them.

This leads to the most important theoretical model addressed in this paper, which is transformative learning as a form of lifelong learning. Here, I can begin by mentioning some previous works which were strongly confirmed by my research. First, my research on LITs obviously supports Cranton's (2006) observation that learning occurs when "an individual encounters an alternative perspective and prior habits of mind are called into question" (p. 23). However, Cranton also speculated that learning can be a "gradual cumulative process" or a dramatic event (Cranton, 2006, p. 23). As was evident from the discussion above about the acclimatization process, for LITs, the experience clearly tends towards

11.2 Theoretical implications

the "cumulative process". That is, the LIT experience proceeds in most cases at a very fast pace, with several disorienting experiences occurring in sequence and the LITs forced to adapt quickly. Although flashes of profound insight (i.e. epiphanies) may occur along the way, it normally takes time for these insights to combine into a true transformation. To use Mezirow's terminology, we might say that many individual meaning schemes are often transformed at a dizzying pace, but it takes some time for these changes to coalesce into a true perspective transformation.

On a related note, delving deeper into the complicated nature of LIT motivations provided strong support for Tisdell's (2012) argument that, although it can take a long time, seemingly small events that create cognitive dissonance can eventually result in transformative learning that significantly alters an individual's perspectives. Here again, it is useful to bring in the narrative meaning-making paradigm, for my research certainly supports Desforges's (2000) assertion that storytelling and interpreting our experiences is part of the meaning-making process in the construction of identity and "touristic stories are used to present new self-identities" (p. 927). When one listens to LIT stories, they often tie together the smallest seed events from their pre-travel lives with disorienting events on the road (including peaks and valleys), and then in turn link these with significant reentry shocks they experienced upon returning home. Indeed, to draw on Habermas' & Bluck's (2000) terminology, by linking these events together into a narrative, they first establish causal coherence and, eventually, thematic coherence.

In essence, this creates a positive feedback loop in the narrative process. As various causal links are established, an overarching thematic link begins to emerge. This thematic link, in turn, informs further narrative construction efforts, as LITs begin to alter the meanings created by causal links established in previous narrative efforts as well as bringing in new events and causal links to strengthen the overall tapestry of meaning and support the overarching thematic coherence. As a simple example, by adopting the typical traveler thematic principle that values curiosity, learning and growth, every mistake made on the road or hardship endured can be re-interpreted as a valuable learning experience or suffering endured to enhance one's overall resilience. Continuous re-tellings of these reconstructed stories then further enhance the sense of thematic coherence—that is, the traveler's image of herself as a bold adventurer on a quest for knowledge and wisdom. As an extra bonus, these stories help build this image in the minds of the people listening to these stories. This, in turn, can result in positive reinforcement for the travelers themselves, such as every time a friend introduces them to someone new as "the globetrotter" or "the crazy kayaker", etc.

This final point highlights another key argument that my research strongly supports; namely, Lyon's (2001) assertion that there should be more focus on the importance of relationships in transformative learning. In this case, they serve as audiences for the LITs' stories; however, as Lyon pointed out, on a higher level, other people can be both a source of disorienting dilemmas and a means for resolving such dilemmas. In the local communities, the "relationships" range from fending off dangerous attackers to families who welcome travelers with previously unimaginable generosity, while in the traveler community, such relationships range from supportive mentors and traveling companions to travelers with different traveler values and styles who may be subtly or even openly hostile. While there is certainly a place for solitary reflection in the LIT experience, which I will discuss below, in the overwhelming majority of cases, the transformation involved in long-term independent travel is a highly social process involving extensive interaction with different individuals.

In keeping with the importance of relationships for transformational learning, my research also strongly supports Taylor & Cranton's (2013) argument that more focus should be placed on the role of empathy in TLT, as it is empathy that

> …provides the learner with the ability to identify with the perspectives of others; lessens the likelihood of prejudgment; increases the opportunity for identifying shared understanding; and facilitates critical reflection through the emotive valence of assumptions. (pp. 37-38)

Indeed, my data is replete with both statements in which LITs cite increased empathy as one of the main learning outcomes of long-term independent travel and, perhaps more importantly, stories that show how their empathy was both developed and deployed.

In terms of the reintegration process, there are also two specific concepts related to reentry where my research has shed some light. The first is Sussman's (1986) argument that reentry becomes easier and less stressful the more often it is experienced because the individual has already learned and can now refine adaptation skills and strategies (p. 242). On the one hand, my research supports this assertion, in that several LITs talked about how they devised strategies for reentry (e.g. a transition period spent in a "similar" culture to one's own home culture) and, perhaps more importantly, learned to adjust their expectations (e.g. not expecting people to be interested in their traveler stories). On the other hand, there were counter-examples that showed that reentry does not always become easier, as other factors often complicate this equation. For example, one LIT reported that his first reentry was easier because he had gone straight into a further education program to which he had been accepted before the trip, whereas on return from the second trip, he had no fixed plans waiting for him. In addition, some of the most experi-

11.2 Theoretical implications

enced LITs (i.e. the real lifestyle travelers) reported that, despite their adjusted expectations and modified reentry techniques, the reentry process eventually became more difficult. In the long run, the more time they spent outside their own culture, the more their values shifted away from those of their home societies, which left them less able to readjust upon their return, or perhaps even less interested in re-adjusting. This process even leads some of them to eventually decide to leave their home culture and settle abroad somewhere.

The second reentry-related assertion upon which my research can shed some light is the concept that transformative learning cannot be reversed or undone (e.g. Mezirow, 2000, 2012; O'Sullivan, 1999, 2012). While there are many LITs who firmly endorse this concept by emphasizing how deeply travel affected them and how confident they are that they could never go back to the way they were, some LITs also mentioned the need to fight against the tendency to "slide back into one's old ways" upon reentry into their native cultures. For example, they mentioned that it was easy to get sucked back into the consumerism of their home countries, or that it was difficult to follow resolutions made on the road to be more patient and empathetic when dealing with one's fellow human beings. Although one could argue that this shows that no true transformation took place, I would suggest that it is more helpful to view this as a reminder of the fluidity of values and identities. In addition, this supports the common perception that mental habits and behaviors are like muscles, in that they require constant exercise to keep them strong. If one resolves to be more empathetic, but then returns to a highly competitive atmosphere where one receives little empathy oneself and has limited opportunities to exercise one's own empathy, that vital mental competence will soon begin to atrophy.

This bring us to one of the most significant questions, which has long loomed over the debate surrounding transformative learning—the balance between the roles of conscious critical reflection and non-rational adaptation, or what Mezirow (2000), in his initial begrudging admission of the role of this mode of transformation, called "mindless assimilation." My research lands fully in the camp of those who suggest that the rational and extra-rational dimensions of transformative learning are complimentary rather than contradictory (Dirkx, Mezirow & Cranton, 2006). In fact, while Clark and Wilson (1991) criticized Mezirow for allegedly neglecting the historical, cultural and social context, for me the one key aspect of context that seems to be lacking in many discussions about transformative learning is the personality context. That is, while some individuals are inclined towards introspection and reflection to make meaning, others are more outward directed and therefore may undergo transformations in their values and even behaviors without consciously contemplating or even acknowledging these changes.

This distinction has received more attention recently with an increased focus on the introvert-extrovert personality spectrum. For example, popular books such as Marti Olsen Laney's (2002) *The Introvert Advantage: How Quiet People Can Thrive in an Extrovert World* or Susan Cain's (2012) *Quiet: The Power of Introverts in a World That Can't Stop Talking* have drawn attention to the common bias in "Western" society towards extroverts. However, while these books read as introvert manifestos, in the context of academia, it is perhaps not surprising to find the opposite bias at play. That is, there is a tendency to favor rational self-reflection over more instinctual ways of learning and making meaning. This bias is evident in a term such as "mindless assimilation". Although the more neutral term "extra-rational learning" is somewhat less loaded, it still implies the primacy of the rational, whereas all other emotional or intuitive forms of meaning-making are relegated to the status of outside or beyond the normal. In light of the importance and prevalence of these other forms of learning, it would seem that a more neutral term such as "intuitive transformation" might be more appropriate.

Indeed, the semi-structured life-world interviews are a very effective means of exploring this distinction. As we saw above, some LITs had nicely constructed narratives with which they could express their values and meanings. One could almost see the conscious reflection and careful narrative construction behind the stories. However, in other cases, some of which I highlighted above, I could see that the LITs were forming the meaning on the spot. LIT responses to my questions would often even begin with phrases such as "Well, I never thought about that" or "Hmm. Nobody ever asked me that", and then I could watch them constructing links to create causal coherence and, in some cases, arriving at a larger thematic coherence as the interview proceeded. Occasionally, this involved some leading questions from me, in which case one could say with Pritchard, Morgan & Ateljevic (2011) that we became "co-participative storytellers". However, in other cases, responses began with a phrase such as "It's difficult to explain," and then the LIT would go on to provide a wonderfully coherent explanation of the principle they wanted to express, which in some cases seemed to surprise even them. In these cases, this indicates that on some level, the meaning-making had already occurred; it simply had not been consciously examined. This calls to mind a passage from Peg Tittle's (2011) fine text book *Critical Thinking: An Appeal to Reason*, which I use in some of my critical thinking courses. Tittle explains the logical fallacy of an appeal to intuition, which is considered an invalid form of argument in logic:

> Perhaps what some people call intuition is unconscious reasoning: maybe they have reasons for thinking as they do, but they just haven't done the work required to acknowledge and articulate those reasons, to themselves or to others. In that case, appeals to intuition, gut feeling, a sixth sense—they're all just ways to avoid the hard work of using one's intellect. At the very least, intuition might be simply our apprehension of our physiological responses to emotion; we "sense" we're uncomfortable with something because we've unconsciously felt a slight increase in our heart rate or a slight sweat, so we say our intuition is telling us it's wrong. Such apprehension (increased heart rate, sweat, and so on) may be useful as a signal that something is significant enough to warrant our rational deliberation, but as such, it should be our starting point—that's where our work should begin, not end. Take the time to figure out why you're uncomfortable; maybe what's causing a slight sweat is actually a very good thing, it's just something you've never done before. (pp. 29-30)

Tittle provides a very useful way of looking at intuition. In the context of communication or trying to convince others, Tittle's obvious bias towards rational thinking is appropriate, since "it feels right to me" is not a very persuasive argument. Furthermore, she points out the dangers of intuition, which is that intuition and emotions can lead one astray. On the other hand, science has documented a wide range of psychological biases (e.g. confirmation bias, availability heuristic) and cognitive distortions (e.g. illusory correlations, overgeneralizing) that routinely sabotage our allegedly rational thinking, so is it really justified to privilege rational thinking over intuition in the case of transformative learning?

In a formal education setting, the temptation to do so is strong, as one can imagine an ideal world where all human beings would be trained to recognize and avoid such fallacies. However, ample evidence from the real world shows us that a) this is far from the world we live in, and b) some people are simply not wired to think and learn that way. This is not to say that we should give up on teaching people critical thinking skills, but rather to suggest that we should consider giving equal value to positive transformations arrived at by more intuitive processes. If a traveler has developed a greater human empathy as a result of her experiences with poverty and suffering in poorer countries without spending quiet moments reflecting on this value and rationalizing it, does that decrease the value of this enhanced empathy for herself or her fellow human beings? Furthermore, perhaps it would be better to embrace different modes of meaning-making and start thinking about how we can help address the different learning needs related to those modes. We will return to this in the discussion of lifelong learning below.

However, for now, I will offer a few observations from my research about the relationship between the LIT experience and Mezirow's stages of transformative learning. The first observation is simply to agree wholeheartedly with Taylor's (1994b, 1997) assertion that these phases are in no way to imply a fixed sequence or suggest that all learners pass through all stages. The second, and more specific observation is that the LIT experience, particularly at the beginning of travel, moves fast, and LITs rarely have the time to go through some of the stages in Mezirow's process. That is, a disorienting dilemma may occur (phase 1), and LITs may have to skip straight to "provisional trying of new roles" (phase 8), without the luxury of phases 2-7, which involve analyzing feelings, contemplating options, making a plan, and acquiring the necessary information to execute that plan. In other words, for most LITs, there is a significant amount of trial and error involved in their learning. That is, they may be confronted with the same disorienting dilemma or a series of similar dilemmas over and over again, each time trying out a new solution to find one that works. As an example, many LITs speak of making snap judgements about people they meet, only to be proven wrong time and again, which eventually leads to a new perspective (i.e. I am not as smart as I think) and resulting behavior (i.e. I should reserve judgement and approach each person with a more open-minded and empathetic attitude).

Another observation related to Mezirow's stage model is that the aforementioned trial and error process, which is an inherent characteristic of most LIT experiences, is perhaps what leads to one the most important learning outcomes mentioned by travelers: an increased self-confidence and self-efficacy. That is, the process of experiencing so many "failures" (i.e. hastily devised solutions that do not work out), both cognitive and behavioral, on the way to an eventual success eventually gives rise to an increased confidence that, no matter what situation may arise, I will survive, and I will eventually figure it out. Anticipating the following section on lifelong learning, I cannot help but point out here the difference between this mode of learning and what occurs in traditional educational settings, where failure is often accompanied by strong negative messages of inadequacy, and students are granted very little freedom to devise their own learning solutions and even less encouragement to do so.

As I have mentioned one of the key traveler outcomes (self-efficacy), I will now mention one final outcome that is key to the transformative learning process of long-term independent travel. Here I will cite Young Yun Kim's (2008) concept of intercultural personhood, which she defines as "a way of relating to oneself and others that is built on a dynamic, adaptive, and transformative identity conception—one that conjoins and integrates, rather than separates and divides." In addition, she mentions that human beings are in a constant state of change, which should be guided by "an outlook on humanity that is not locked in a provincial interest of one's ascribed group membership, but one in which the individual sees himself or herself to be a part of a larger whole that includes other groups, as well."

The reader will recognize in this definition some of the elements discussed earlier in this paper, including the cognitive ability to flexibly adapt one's identity concept by building

11.2 Theoretical implications

inclusive meaning schemes and perspectives rather than binary oppositions or exclusionary definitions. Although I feel confident in stating that long-term independent travel has the potential to move participants towards this vision, I must insert two caveats. First, and perhaps most obviously, is simply that this is in no way a claim that this is a certain outcome of the long-term independent travel experience. While my research shows that nearly all LITs take meaningful steps towards this goal, few of the participants would probably qualify for a certificate of intercultural personhood, if there were such a thing. I discussed above the in-group/out-group dynamics that exist within the traveler community itself, in terms of individuals and groups staking claims of superiority based on factors including budget, level of risk taken, engagement with the local population, etc. In addition, even in the post-travel phase, many LITs exhibit a tendency to divide the world into "travelers" and "non-travelers", with significant merit assumptions applied to the two groups. As an example, I would offer this quote from Chelsea (37, England, 2nd) about what she is looking for in a life companion:

> And I could only be with someone who has a thirst to travel. [...] I'd be suspicious about why they hadn't done it ... c'mon there's something wrong. Because it's a curiosity thing. ... It's for me a very necessary requirement that someone must have. Why would someone not want to go traveling? I'd be extremely suspicious if I was with somebody who'd never been outside of Europe. What have you been doing with your life?

I do not believe Kim's model would deny Chelsea the right to choose a companion with similar interests, but I do believe that her claim a lack of desire to travel proves an inherent lack of curiosity might cost her some points on the "intercultural personhood" scorecard in the "does not separate and divide" category, if there were such a thing.

The other slight objection I would raise regarding Kim's definition is that, like Mezirow's model, it seems to privilege individuals who have not only had extensive intercultural experience but who also possess the rational, self-reflective capacity and inclination to process their experience in a way that leads to the mode of being Kim prescribes. Thus, her supporting examples are a Japanese professor of intercultural communications who has lived in America and Japan (Muneo Jay Yoshikawa), a world-renowned classical musician with a multi-cultural background who has also lived and worked in various parts of the world (Yo-Yo Ma), and the 2006 winner of the Nobel Prize in Literature, who has spent his life contemplating and writing about the interactions between the East and the West (Orhan Pamuk). Offering insightful explanations from the personal writings or interviews of these individuals, she then concludes:

> Their individuated and universalized identity orientations defy the simplistic and conventional categorizations of people and reveal a way of being in the world. Instead, their intercultural orientations can help to hold together, integrate, and ele-

vate diverse cultures, to help fellow citizens see their collective "blind spots," and to discourage excessive claims for cultural identity.

It is a wonderful vision, and I do not wish to contradict her argument that it is a worthy goal for the individual, or argue against her claim that these three individuals are appropriate role models. However, in accordance with the discussion above about intuition, I would simply point out that many people arrive at a similar mode of being with far less critical reflection and even far less intercultural experience. Here I am thinking not only of the travelers who may not be psychologically inclined to engage with these concepts on a rational, reflective basis, but also of the many individuals I heard about in my interviews (and experienced in my own travels) in different parts of the world who have welcomed these travelers into their hearts and homes without question, despite the fact that they had never been outside their own communities, and these travelers were complete strangers hailing from radically different cultures. I mention this simply to point out the fact that the open-minded, adaptive identity concept she describes is not the exclusive province of people with extensive multi-cultural experience.

11.3 Critical evaluation and future research directions

When I set out to conduct this research many years ago, my plan was to travel for six months and gather data via both participatory observation and interviews with fellow travelers, and then return home to analyze and write up my results. It did not quite turn out that way. I ended up traveling for four and a half years and coming back with an American husband (my best travel souvenir, as he likes to say). Back home, life circumstances (i.e. building a career, starting a family) soon came between me and my research, which was put on a back burner. When the time came to return to my research, I decided to conduct a second round of interviews. In hindsight (and using a bit of reflective narrative construction), I now view the hiatus from my research as a fortunate turn of events, as it allowed me to bring a more longitudinal aspect to the paper, which I feel was immensely valuable. In short, after conducting this research, it is clear to me that the reentry process is one of the richest arenas for transformational learning. Or perhaps it would be more accurate to say that the lessons learned on the road are not truly outcomes until they have been tested by the challenge of reentry and then integrated into some form of post-travel existence. I believe that the insight this paper offers into that process is perhaps its most valuable characteristic.

11.3 Critical evaluation and future research directions

On the other hand, the manner in which the study came together also introduced some noise into the data in terms of the question about the role of reflection in the transformative learning process. For example, some of my interview subjects were already experienced travelers when I first interviewed them and had therefore already had time to reflect on topics such as their original travel motivations for their first trip or their early reentry experiences. Thus, it is conceivable that, in their earlier efforts to establish causal and thematic coherence through the narrative process, some of the original feelings or provisional meanings they experienced may have been consciously or subconsciously altered or obscured over time. In theory, a longitudinal study featuring a group of first-time LITs who could be interviewed at several times throughout the travel experience (e.g. before departure, shortly after arrival in the foreign culture, shortly before return home, shortly after return home, 5 years later) would be of interest. However, such an approach would be quite difficult to arrange in practice, and it would also be highly likely to suffer from the well-known Hawthorne effect (aka Observer effect), in which objects of observation modify their behavior due to their awareness that they are being observed. In this case, the need to do periodic interviews would likely encourage people to engage in critical reflection either before or during the interview, which they might not have done under normal circumstances. Nevertheless, this would be worth exploring, particularly in the context of any type of more structured program that could be designed to encourage this form of travel (see section 10.4).

Beyond this, the main limitation of this study is the diversity of my cohort. On the one hand, it is quite diverse, as it includes people from different countries, age groups, and travel histories (i.e. amount of travel, specific destinations visited). On the other hand, all of my subjects were white people from economically developed countries, and the majority had at least some tertiary education and came from middle class or upper middle class backgrounds. The fact is that this reflects the traveler population that I experienced. Although I did have the opportunity to interview two travelers from Central America and one from Taiwan, once I broadened the scope of this study to encompass the entire travel experience (i.e. pre-travel, on the road, re-integration), I was forced to exclude these interviews. The truth is that their experiences were so radically different that I felt it would have required special treatment for each of the many aspects examined in this paper to do them justice, which would have made this (already long) paper even longer. However, these travelers are out there, and they would make for a fascinating topic for further research. In fact, I have read some such studies, including one interesting paper on female Latin American travelers traveling to other counties within their region (Hernando Terán, 2014). As another example, I had a conversation with an Asian-American woman about her travels in Southeast Asia, and she described how the local people treated her differently than her fellow (white) travelers.

In short, the goal of this study was to capture the rich diversity of the long-term independent travel experience and identify some wider themes and patterns in terms of the motivations, mechanisms and outcomes of the related transformational learning process, particularly with regard to the narrative dimension. This effort has also revealed a wealth of potential areas for more targeted research. Beyond the groups of underrepresented travelers mentioned above (including different ethnicities, socio-economic backgrounds, etc.), other influencing factors worthy of investigation include: the effect of disposition or personality aspects (e.g. degree of extroversion, openness, risk-aversion, etc.) on the transformative learning process and outcomes, the importance of technological developments (e.g. smart phones, social media) for the narrative construction process, and the specific influence of trip duration. Of course, there is another entire side of the LIT experience that this paper has excluded—an examination of how this form of travel affects the environments, economies, cultures and individuals in the locations where LITs travel.

In terms of methodology, future research into this topic may apply different research approaches, as research into narrative identity formation can take many shapes. For example, biographical case reconstruction (e.g. Rosenthal, 2004), which is also aligned with the social interpretive research paradigm, might be a fruitful research avenue for exploring human meaning-making. In contrast to the semi-structured life-world interviews and thematic data analysis employed in this study, a biographical, case-reconstructive approach uses narrative interviews (e.g. Schütze, 1983), which are initiated by an initial question that allows the interviewee to freely reconstruct their life story, with the researcher offering only empathetic paralanguage. In this context, the researcher is particularly interested in what is not mentioned or said (i.e. that which is hidden behind the curtain of self-representation). Such an approach is often coupled with grounded theory (Glaser & Strauss, 1967) and deploys abductive reasoning and complex hypothesis building in order to reconstruct an overall biography. The interviewee's self-representation is analyzed by differentiating between the experienced life history and the narrated life story.

Although this approach offers certain benefits, it was not well suited to my own research for two main reasons. First, the biographical research approach normally entails multiple successive interviews with the same participant in a controlled environment. As my goal with many of the initial interviews was to capture the LITs' feelings and experiences during an actual journey, this kind of deliberate, controlled approach was not feasible. Many of the initial interviews were conducted rather spontaneously in odd locations around the world within the real LIT environment (e.g. hostels, restaurants, trains), and the follow-up interviews were often conducted using digital technologies (e.g. Skype) or even in the form of digital questionnaires. Second, and perhaps more important, in order to do justice to the complex interview analysis required by biographical case reconstruction (e.g. attending to such factors as intertextual hermeneutics, structural language patterns, semantics, non-verbal communication etc.), it would have been necessary to drastically limit the number of participants in the study. Although in-depth explorations of individual experiences may be useful for examining certain niches of the LIT population (e.g. young, gap-year British travelers), my goal was to provide a broader picture of the highly diverse LIT population, while attempting to identify some common themes and patterns that characterized the transformative learning process. Thus, it was necessary to deploy a method that would enable me to dive into the lived experiences of a greater number of LITs.

Finally, more quantitative approaches could be suitable for targeted investigation of specific aspects of the complex learning processes involved in long-term independent travel. The challenge here would be to find a sufficiently large sample size to support such a study. Here again, the existence of some form of structured program to encourage this form of travel would also pay dividends in terms of generating a population for further study, which leads us to the next section—practical implications.

11.4 Practical implications

In this final section, I will return to the lifelong learning debate first presented in section 2.5. In terms of outcomes, I will mention again the four key areas outlined in the European Commission paper on lifelong learning with the order slightly re-arranged: personal fulfilment, social inclusion, employability/adaptability, and active citizenship.

For the first area, I have shown how long-term independent travel can provide travelers with the self-esteem and self-efficacy they need to forge meaningful, fulfilling lives. In terms of social inclusion, we have seen how this form of travel can broaden travelers' perspectives and help them to accept and even embrace difference, as well as imparting more inclusive ways of interacting with all different kinds of people. For the employability/adaptability area, I would first suggest that the dual name of this category is proof of the high relevance of this form of travel for the modern labor market. That is to say that the labor experts themselves have acknowledged that key competence in the rapidly evolving modern globalized workplace is the ability to adapt to new environments and new employment demands. Since, as many of the LITs pointed out, this form of travel is akin to a crash course in adaptability, it would seem like the perfect training ground for the workers of the future. In fact, the learning outcomes mentioned by the LITs read like the critical soft skills section of a modern job advertisement: interpersonal communication skills, problem-solving skills, ability to work creatively, autonomously and effectively.

The final category, active citizenship, is a bit more complicated. My research shows that long-term independent travel usually heightens people's understanding of politics and their desire to pay attention to such matters and even get involved. On the European level, this enthusiasm, combined with the aforementioned intercultural, inclusive perspective, could definitely pay dividends in building (or restoring) faith in a vision of a united Europe. To borrow a line from one of my LITs: "I don't know how anyone can be prejudiced or racist if you've seen the world, cause the two just don't go together" (Ben, 31, England). However, policy makers whose main focus is on preserving Europe's perceived "competitive advantage" over the developing world may be disappointed. That is to say, if their worldview is built upon the assumption that the only way for the wealthy countries of the world to prosper is to continue exploiting the poorer countries of the world, they may have trouble finding recruits among the ranks of long-term independent travelers. On the other hand, if active citizenship involves autonomous critical thinking and the ability and willingness to ask difficult questions about a global system that allows 8 men to own more wealth than half of the world's population (Oxfam, 2017) while 15,000 children die each day due to poverty (UNICEF, 2015), then former long-term independent travelers should fit the bill nicely.

This brings us to the other question regarding lifelong learning; namely, how to answer those who are skeptical about informal learning in general. Before I cite a hundred different experts on the values of experiential learning, I will take this one final opportunity to let the LITs speak for themselves. First, for those who are convinced of the sanctity of formal education, I will let Andy (42, USA, 2nd) describe the university experience for many students:

> College is a joke. I mean, you could be a complete moron and drink five nights a week, and if you study for a few hours at the end of the semester, you're gonna at least get a C and pass and get a college degree.

Even for those who do not spend their university career at the local bar, Aimee (26, England) describes the formal education experience even for some diligent students:

> Education at school is about passing exams, and you just learn what you need to learn to pass the exam, whether you're interested in it or not. For me, the way I was in school, I would learn to pass an exam, to get an A, to get a B, but then I don't remember anything like a year later because I wasn't really interested in it. [...] Whereas, when you're traveling, you're interested in it. You're in control of what's

11.4 Practical implications

actually going into your brain. You put it in, cause you wanna put it in. And you remember it.

While Aimee emphasizes the importance of empowering students to learn what they want to learn, Dana (39, Denmark) reminds us that different people have different ways of learning:

> I am so much better at remembering or learning by experiencing, by feeling and seeing and tasting and smelling it or whatever, than by reading it in a book. I was a lousy student in a way that I would fall asleep in class, and just be somewhere else. And now, it's totally different. I can just soak up new information and I love it. I feel like I am learning every day, and it's so much fun, and I really enjoy it.

Finally, to support Dana's point, here is just a sampling of the other LITs thoughts on the benefits of experiential learning:

> Traveling is all about experiential learning, going out into the world, get a feel for things and all that. Everybody goes for something else. For me the greatest thing is the people, to get a feel for who they are. Cause I mean, that's what the country is. A country is it's people. I mean, it's other things too, but more than anything, it's people. And if you get to know who the people are, then you can understand the country. (Matt, 28, USA)

> I think that you learn a lot of things going to university, but you really learn a lot more traveling...because, it just sticks with you... you're gonna remember all your life, all your experiences. [...]...when you're going to university, you have all this amount of information but you're just keeping a little amount of it. and when you're traveling.... after that you just realize everything that you have learned and everything that has changed in you and all your perspective and your perception of the world has just changed on the way...and after that you realize, oh my God..." (Nadine, 23, Canada)

> In school, you're learning things in a very structured way [...] You're learning things in modules that you then end up having to know all about in an exam and then forget right afterwards. And here you're learning things very informally, and it's so much richer because the experience is real, and you are there. It's like watching a film and being there...there's no comparison between the two types of information. (Chelsea, 25, England)

> I studied environmental sciences and now I see it hands on. [...] it's more real than if you learn about it at university. [...] And when you see the jungle, you have more feeling, you can feel regret that it is being destroyed. When you hear 80,000 acres are being destroyed and you've never seen it, it's different than 80,000 acres of something that you've seen and loved and experienced and you learn to appreciate it a lot more. And all of a sudden it becomes more important. And you can talk to the people about who is responsible, how the government plays a role [...] It's a bit more real and you get more insights." (Andy, 30, USA)

The final issue regarding long-term independent travel as a form of lifelong learning is how one can devise policy to incorporate this concept. However, the possibilities here are endless. The simplest version would be a travel grant that gave people a limited budget for a limited time. A suitable application process would need to be devised, which could consist of the typical statements of motivation, interviews, etc. usually used for study abroad or subsidized volunteer programs. People would inevitably express concerns about the unstructured nature of the experience, no doubt drawing on their pre-conceived views about travel and tourism to conclude that this would amount to a subsidized vacation on a beach somewhere. To answer such criticisms, we could tap into the traveler storytelling compulsion and require the participants to give a presentation about their travels at the end of their trip, which I suspect they would actually be more than happy to do. This would have benefits for both the travelers (post-travel reflection and processing meaning) and the potential audiences for these presentations. However, if this is too unstructured for some policy makers, there would be numerous opportunities to pair such a "travel grant" with existing exchange or volunteer programs. For example, I know from my own experience as an exchange student (as well as countless conversations with other former exchange students) that the majority of the benefit derived from that experience is not from the time spent in classrooms. Furthermore, as alluded to in the previous section, the further benefit of any such structured programs would be to provide a suitable population for further research into the processes and outcomes of such experiences, which could in turn be used to further refine the programs themselves.

Finally, in the spirit of lifelong learning, it is important to mention that this is not an activity only suitable for young people. Many governments have re-training programs for people who grow dissatisfied with their current careers, in which this form of travel could also play a role. Similarly, any person passing through a life transition or experiencing feelings of a lack of fulfillment in their lives (e.g. people looking to return to the workforce after an extended period out of the job market, people suffering from empty-nest syndrome, etc.) could benefit from some form of independent travel experience to restore or enhance their self-efficacy and motivate them to take on new, meaningful challenges in their lives. Beyond the advantages for the individual, society could benefit from having citizens with a wider perspective that would help them think outside their society's own cultural box, as well as the energy and motivation to act as agents for essential change to keep society vibrant and growing. Finally, the global perspective, increased empathy, and ability to tolerate and even embrace difference could move the world towards the vision of an inclusive harmonious world order articulated by Kofi Annan in his 2001 Nobel Peace Prize Lecture:

> *People of different religions and cultures live side by side in almost every part of the world, and most of us have overlapping identities which unite us with very different groups. We can love what we are, without hating what – and who – we are not. We can thrive in our own tradition, even as we learn from others, and come to respect their teachings.*

References

Adler, P. (1975). The transitional experience: An alternative view of culture shock. *Journal of Humanistic Psychology*, 15, 13-23.

Adler, P. (1982). Beyond cultural identity: Reflections on cultural and multicultural man. In L. Samovar & P. Porter (Eds.), *Intercultural communication: A reader* (3rd edn., pp. 389-408). Belmont, CA: Wadsworth.

Adler, P. (1987). Culture shock and the cross-cultural learning experience. In L. Luce & E. Smith (Eds.), *Toward Internationalism* (pp. 24-35). Cambridge, MA: Newbury.

Adler, N. J. (1985). Youth on the Road: Reflections on the History of Tramping. *Annals of Tourism Research* 12(3), 335-54.

Adler, N.J. (1981). Re-entry: Managing Cross Cultural Transitions. *Group and Organization Management.* 1981(6), 341-356.

Allison, P., Davis-Berman, J., & Berman, D. (2011). Changes in latitude, changes in attitude: Analysis of the effects of reverse culture shock – A study of students returning from youth expeditions. *Leisure Studies*, 30 (4), 1–17.

Anderson, J.R.L. (1970). *The Ulysses Factor. The Exploring Instinct In Man.* New York, NY: Harcourt Brace Jovanovich.

Anderson, L. E. (1994). A new look at an old construct: cross-cultural adaptation. *International Journal of Intercultural Relations*, 18(3), 293–328.

Anderson, D., & Anderson, L. A. (2001). *Beyond change management.* San Francisco, CA: Jossey-Bass.

Anderskov, C. (2002). Backpacker Culture: Meaning and Identity Making Processes in the Backpacker Culture among Backpackers in Central America. Retrieved from http://www.anthrobase.com/Txt/A/Anderskov_C_01.htm.

Arnett, J.J. (2000a). The psychology of globalization. *American Psychologist*, 55, 469-480.

Arnett, J.J. (2000b). Emerging adulthood: A theory of development from the late teens through the twenties. *American Psychologist, 55*(5), 469-480.

Arnett, J.J. (2004). *Emerging adulthood: The winding road from the late teens through the twenties.* New York, NY: Oxford University Press.

Arnett, J.J., & Hughes, M. (2012). *Adolescence and emerging adulthood: A Cultural Approach.* Harlow, England: Pearson Education Ltd.

Arthur & Bennett (1997). A comparative test of alternate models of international assignee job performance. In H. Kepir, S. Deniz & D.S. Ones (Eds.), *New Approaches to Employee Management* (pp. 141-172). Greenwich, CT: JAI Press Ltd.

Ashmore, R.D., & Jussim, L. (1997). Towards a second century of the scientific analysis of self and identity. In R.D. Ashmore & L. Jussim (Eds.), *Self and identity: Fundamental issues* (pp. 3-19). New York, NY: Oxford University Press.

Ateljevic, I., & Doorne, S. (2000a). Tourism as an Escape: Long-Term Travelers in New Zealand, *Tourism Analysis*, 5, 131-136.

Ateljevic I., & Doorne S. (2000b). 'Staying within the fence': lifestyle entrepreneurship in tourism. *Journal of Sustainable Tourism* 8(5), 378–392.

© Springer Fachmedien Wiesbaden GmbH, part of Springer Nature 2019
B. Phillips, *Learning by Going: Transformative Learning through Long-term Independent Travel*, https://doi.org/10.1007/978-3-658-25773-6

Ateljevic, I. & Doorne, S. (2004). Theoretical Encounters: A Review of Backpacker Literature. In G. Richards & J. Wilson *The Global Nomad: Backpacker Travel in Theory and Practice* (pp.60-76), Clevedon, England: Channel View.

Ateljevic, I. & Doorne, S. (2005). Dialectics of Authentication: Performing 'Exotic Otherness' in Backpacker Enclave of Dali, China. *Journal of Tourism and Cultural Change*, 3(1), 1-17.

Ateljevic, I., & Hannam, K. (2008). Conclusion: Towards a Critical Agenda for Backpacker Tourism. In K. Hannam & I. Ateljevic *Backpacker Tourism: Concepts and Profiles* (pp. 247-256), Clevedon, England: Channel View.

Ateljevic, I., Sheldon, P., & Tomljenovic, R. (2016). The new paradigm of the 21st century: silent revolution of cultural creatives and transformative travel of and for the future (pp. 12- 20). World Tourism Organization (2016), *Global Report on the Transformative Power of Tourism: a paradigm shift towards a more responsible traveller*, UNWTO, Madrid.

Baudrillard, J. (1994). *Simulacra and simulation*. Ann Arbor, MI: University of Michigan Press.

Beach, L.R. (2010). *The Psychology of Narrative Thought. How the Stories We Tell Ourselves Shape Our Lives*. Bloomington, In: Xlibris.

Beckendorff, P., Moscardo, G., & Pendergast, D. (Eds.) (2010). *Tourism and Generation Y*. Wallingford, England: CABI.

Belhassen, Y, Santos, C., & Uriely, N. (2007). Cannabis usage in tourism: a sociological perspective. *Leisure Studies*, 26(3), 303-319.

Belenky, M. & Stanton, A. (2000). Inequality, development and connected knowing. In J. Mezirow, & Associates (Eds.), *Learning as Transformation: Critical Perspectives on a Theory in Progress* (pp. 71-102). San Francisco, CA: Jossey-Bass.

Bell, C. (2002). The big 'OE': Young New Zealand travellers as secular pilgrims. *Tourist Studies*, 2(2), 143-158.

Bennett, J. (1977). Transition shock: Putting culture shock in perspective. *International and Intercultural Communication Annual*, 4, 45-52.

Bennett, J. (1993). Towards ethnorelativism: A developmental model of intercultural sensitivity. In R.M. Paige (Ed.), *Education for the intercultural experience*. Yarmouth, ME: Intercultural Press.

Berry, J.W. (1980). *Psychology of acculturation: Understanding individuals moving between cultures*. In R. Brislin (Ed.), Applied Cross-Cultural Psychology (pp 232-253). Newbury Park, CA: Sage.

Berry, J.W. (2008). Globalization and acculturation. *International Journal of International Relations*, 32, 328-336.

Berry, K.S. (2006). Research as Bricolage. Embracing Relationality, Multiplicity and Complexity. In K.G. Tobin, & J. Kincheloe (Eds.), *Doing Educational Research. A Handbook* (pp. 87-115). Rotterdam, The Netherlands: Sense Publishers.

Beyers, W., & Seiffge-Krenke, I. (2010). Does identity precede intimacy? Testing Erikson's theory on romantic development in emerging adulthood of the 21st century. *Journal of Adolescent Research*, 25(3), 387-415.

Bhaba, H. (2001). Border Lives: The Art of the Present. In S.L. Roberson *Defining Travel: Diverse Visions* (pp. 157-166). Mississippi, MS: University Press of Mississippi.

Binder, J. (2005). *Globality. Eine Ethnographie über Backpacker*. Münster, Germany: Lit. Verlag.

Boeree, C. G. (1997). Erik Erikson: 1902-1994. Retrieved from http://www.socialpsychology.de/do/pt_erikson.pdf

Boeren, E. (2016). *Lifelong Learning Participation in a Changing Policy Context: An Interdisciplinary Theory*. Baskingstoke, England:Palgrave-Macmillan.

Bok, D. (2006). *Our underachieving colleges: A candid look at how much students learn and whey they should be learning more*. Princeton, NJ: Princeton University Press.

Boneva, B.S. & Frieze, I. H. (2001). Toward a concept of a migrant personality. *Journal of Social Issues,* 57, 477-492.

Boorstin, D. 1964. *The Image: A Guide to Pseudo-Events in America*. New York, NY: Harper.

Bosangit, C., Hibbert,. S., McCabe, S. (2015). "If I was going to do I should at least be having fun": Travel blogs, meaning and tourist experience. *Annals of Tourism Research* 55, 1-14.

Boshier, R. (1998). Edgar Faure after 25 years: down but not out. In J. Holford, P. Jarvis & C. Griffin (Eds.), *International Perspectives on lifelong Learning* (pp. 3-20). London, England: Kogan Page.

Bowie, F. (2006). *The anthropology of religion: An introduction* (2nd edn.). Oxford, England: Blackwell.

Boyd, R.D. (1991). *Personal Transformations in Small Groups: A Jungian Perspective*. London, England: Routledge.

Brabant, S., Palmer, E., & Gramling, R. (1990). Returning home: An empirical investigation of cross-cultural reentry. *International Journal of Intercultural Relations*. 14, 387-404.

Brinthaupt, T.M., & Lipka, R.P. (Eds.) (1992). *The Self: Definitional and Methodological Issues*. New York, NY: State University of New York Press.

Brown, L. (2009). The transformative power of the international sojourn: An ethnographic study of the international student experience. *Annals of Tourism Research*, 36(3), 502-521.

Brown, S., & Lehto, X. (2005). Travelling with a purpose: Understanding the motives and benefits of volunteer vacationers. *Current Issues in Tourism*, 8(6), 479-496.

Bruner, E.M. (1991). Transformation of self in tourism. *Annals of Tourism Research*, 18(2), 238-50.

Bruner, J. (1986). *Actual minds, possible worlds*. Cambridge, MA: Harvard University Press.

Bruner, J. (2002). *Making stories*. Cambridge, MA: Harvard University Press.

Bryson, B. (1991). *Neither here nor there: Travels in Europe*. London, UK: Transworld.

Cain, S. (2012). *Quiet: The power of introverts in a world that can't stop talking*. New York, NY: Crown Publishers.

Callahan, C. (2010). Going home: Deculturation experiences in cultural reentry. Journal of Intercultural Communication, 22, Retrieved from http://www.immi.se/jicc/

Cambridge Dictionary & Thesaurus (2017). Retrieved from http://dictionary.cambridge.org/dictionary/english/transformation

Camus, A. (1963). *Notebooks, 1935-1942*. New York, NY: Knopf.

Carr, N. (2002). The Tourism-Leisure Behavioural Continuum. *Annals of Tourism Research*. 29(4), 972-986.

Cave, J., Thyne, M., & Ryan, C. (2007). Perceptions of backpacker accommodation facilities: A comparative study of Scotland and New Zealand. In K. Hannam, & I. Ateljevic (Eds.), *Backpacker Tourism: Concepts and Profiles* (pp. 215-246). Clevedon, England: Channel View.

Chapdelaine, R., Alexitch, L. (2004). Social skills difficulty: Model of culture shock for international graduate students. *Journal of College Student Development*, 45(2), 167-184.

Chatwin B. (1996). *Anatomy of Restlessness: Selected Writings 1969-1989*. New York, NY: Penguin Books.

Chen, G., Bao, J., & Huang, S., (2014). Segmenting Chinese Backpackers by Travel Motivations. *International Journal of Tourism Research* 16, 355–367.

Chesterton, G.K. (1901-1903). *Tremendous Trifles*. (Republished 2015), Denham Springs, LA: Cavalier Classics.

Christofi, V., Thompson, C. (2007). You cannot go home again: a phenomenological investigation of returning to the sojourn country after studying abroad. *Journal of Counseling and Development*, 85(1), 53-64.

Clandinin, D. J., & Connelly, F. M. (2000). *Narrative inquiry: Experience and story in qualitative research*. San Francisco, CA: Jossey-Bass.

Clark, C., & Rossiter, M. (2008). Narrative Learning in Adulthood. *New Directions for Adult and Continuing Education*, 119, 61-70.

Clark, C., & Wilson, A.L. (1991). Context and rationality in Mezirow's theory of transformational learning. *Adult Education Quarterly*, 41(2), 75-91.

Cloninger, C.R. (1987). A systematic method for clinical description and classification of personality disorders: A proposal. *Archives of General Psychiatry*, 44, 573-588.

Cloninger, C.R. (1994) Temperament and personality. *Current Opinion in Neurobiology*, 4, 266–273.

Cochrane, J. (2005). The backpacker plus: overlooked and underrated. Conference Paper *ATLAS SIG Meeting – Backpacker Research Group 2005: The Global Nomad – an expert meeting on backpacker tourism*. Kasetsart University, Bangkok, Thailand. 1-3 September 2005

Cohen, E. (1972). Toward a Sociology of International Tourism. *Social Research* 39, 164-182.

Cohen, E. (1973). Nomads From Affluence: Notes on the Phenomenon of Drifter-Tourism. *International Journal of Comparative Sociology* 14, 89-103.

Cohen, E. (1979). A Phenomenology of Tourist Experiences. *Sociology*, 13, 179-201.

Cohen, E. (1988). Authenticity and Commoditization in Tourism. *Annals of Tourism Research*, 15, 371-386.

Cohen, E. (2003). Backpacking: Diversity and Change. *Journal of Tourism and Cultural Change*. 1(2), 95-110.

Cohen, E. (2004). Toward a sociology of international tourism. In E. Cohen (Ed.), *Contemporary tourism: Diversity and change* (pp. 37-47). Oxford, England: Elsevier.

Cohen, E. (2005). Pai - a backpacker enclave in transition. Proceedings from The global nomad: second expert meeting on backpacker tourism Bangkok, Thailand: Kasetsart University.

Cohen, J.H. (2000). Problems in the Field: Participant Observation and the Assumption of Neutrality. *Field Methods*, 12(4), 316-333.

Cohen, S.A. (2011). Lifestyle travelers: Backpacking as a way of life. *Annals of Tourism Research*, 38(4), 1535-1555.

Côté, J. E., & Levine, C. G. (2002). *Identity formation, agency, and culture: A social psychological synthesis.* Mahwah, NJ: Lawrence Erlbaum.

Coward, R. (2002). Bali, bombs, and backpackers. *The Ecologist*, p.24.

Cranton, P. (1994). *Understanding and promoting transformative learning: A guide for educators of adults.* San Francisco, CA: Jossey-Bass.

Cranton, P. (2006). *Understanding and promoting transformative learning: A guide for educators of adults* (2nd edn.) San Francisco, CA: Jossey-Bass.

Cranton, P. & King, K. P. (2003). Transformative learning as a professional development goal. *New Perspectives on Designing and Implementing Professional Development of Teachers of Adults*, 98, 31-37.

Cranton, P., Stuckey, H. & Taylor, E. W. (2012). *Assessing transformative learning outcomes and processes: A quantitative survey.* Proceedings from the 10th International Conference on Transformative Learning, San Francisco.

Creswell, T. (2000). Mobility, Syphilis, and Democracy: pathologizing the mobile body. In R. Wrigley, & G. Revill (Eds.), *Pathologies of Travel* (pp. 261-267). Amsterdam, The Netherlands:Rodopi.

Creswell, J. (2003). *Research Design: Qualitative, Quantitative, and Mixed Methods Approaches*, Thousand Oaks, CA: Sage.

Crompton, J.L. (1979). Motivations for pleasure vacation. *Annals of Tourism Research* 6(1), 408-424.

Csikszenthmihalyi, M. (1993). *The evolving self.* New York, NY: Harper Collins.

Csikszenthmihalyi, M. (1996). *Creativity: Flow and the psychology of discovery and invention.* New York, NY: Harper Collins.

Csikszenthmihalyi, M. (1997). *Finding Flow: The Psychology of Engagement with Everyday Life.* New York, NY: Harper Collins.

D'Agostino, F. (2017). Contemporary Approaches to the Social Contract. [accessed on 03.06.2017] https://plato.stanford.edu/entries/contractarianism-contemporary/

D'Andrea, A. (2010). The Decline of Electronic Dance Scenes: The Case of Psytrance in Goa. *The local scenes and global culture of psytrance*. In G. St John *The Local Scenes and Global Culture of Psytrance* (pp. 40-54). New York, NY: Routledge.

Dann, G. (1977). Anomie, Ego-enhancement and tourism. *Annals of Tourism Research*, 5(4), 184-194.

Dann, G. (1981). Tourist Motivation: An Appraisal. *Annals of Tourism Research,* 8(2),187-219.

Dann, G. (1999). Writing out the tourist in space and time. *Annals of Tourism Research*, 26(1), 159-187.

Dann, G., & Cohen E. (1991). Sociology and Tourism. *Annals of Tourism Research*, 18, 155–169.

DeBotton, A. (2002). *The art of travel*. New York, NY: Vintage Books.

Denzin, N. (1991): *Images of Postmodern Society: Social Theory and Contemporary Cinema*. London, England: Sage.

Denzin, N.K. (1994). The art and politics of interpretation. In N.K. Denzin & Y.S. Lincoln, (Eds.), *A handbook of qualitative research* (pp. 500-515). Thousand Oaks, CA: Sage.

Denzin, N.K., & Lincoln, Y.S. (2005). *Handbook of qualitative research* (3rd edn.). Thousand Oaks, CA: Sage.

Denzin, N. K., & Lincoln, Y. S. (Eds.). (2008). *Strategies of Qualitative Inquiry* (3rd edn.). Thousand Oaks, CA: Sage.

Denzin N. K, Lincoln Y. S. (2011). Introduction: Disciplining the practice of qualitative research. In Denzin N. K, Lincoln Y. S. (Eds.), *The SAGE handbook of qualitative research* (pp. 1-6). 4th edn. Thousand Oaks, CA: Sage.

Desforges, L. (1998). Checking out the planet: global representations/local identities and youth travel. In T. Skelton and G. Valentine (Eds.), *Cool Places: Geographies of Youth Culture* (pp.175-192). New York, NY: Routledge.

Desforges, L. (2000). Traveling the world: Identity and travel biography. *Annals of Tourism Research*. 27(4), 926-945.

Deville, A., & Wearing, S. (2013). WWOOFing tourism: Beaten tracks and transformational paths. In Y. Reisinger (Ed.), *Transformational tourism: tourist perspectives* (pp. 151-168). Wallingford, England: CABI.

Dirkx, J.M. (2001). The power of feelings: Emotion, imagination, and the construction of meaning in adult learning. *New Directions for Adult and Continuing Education*, 89, 63-72.

Dirkx, J.M. (2006). Authenticity and imagination. In P. Cranton (Ed.),*New directions for adult and continuing education; Authenticity in teaching* (Vol. 111, Fall, pp. 27–39) San Francisco, CA: Jossey-Bass.

Dirkx, J.M. (2008). The meaning and role of emotions in adult learning. *New Directions for Adult and Continuing Education*, 120, 7-18.

Dirkx, J.M., Mezirow, J., & Cranton, P. (2006). Musings and reflections on the meaning, context and process of transformative learning: A dialogue between John M. Dirkx and Jack Mezirow. *Journal of Transformative Education*, 4(2), 123-139.

Durell, L. (1957). *Bitter Lemons*. New York, NY: E.P. Dutton.

Elliott, J. (2005). *Using Narrative in Social Research. Qualitative and Quantitative Approaches*. London, England, Sage.

Ellis, C., & Bochner, A. (2000). Autoethnography, personal narrative, reflexivity: Researcher as subject. In N.K. Denzin & Y.S. Lincoln (Eds.), *Handbook of qualitative research* (2nd edn.) (pp. 733-768). Thousand Oaks, CA: Sage.

Elsrud, T. (1998). Time creation in travelling. *Time and Society*, 7, 309-334.

Elsrud, T. (2001). Risk Creation in Traveling – Backpacker adventure narration. *Annals of Tourism Research,* Elsevier. 28(3), 597-617.

Erikson, E. H. (1959). *Identity and the life cycle*. New York, NY: Norton.

Erikson, E. H. (1963). *Childhood and society* (2nd edn.). New York, NY: Norton.

Erikson, E. H. (1968). *Identity: Youth and crisis*. New York, NY: Norton

Erikson, E. H. (1980). *Identity and life cycle: A reissue*. New York, NY: Norton.

Erikson, E. H. (1982). *The Life Cycle Completed*. New York, NY: Norton.

European Commission (2001). Communication from the Commission: Making a European Area of Lifelong Learning a Reality. Retrieved from http://eur-lex.europa.eu/LexUriServ/LexUriServ.do?uri=COM:2001:0678:FIN:EN:PDF

Eysenck, H.J. (1967). *The biological basis of personality*. Springfield, IL: Thomas.

Featherstone, M. (1995). *Globalization, postmodernism and identity*. London, England: Sage.

Feifer, M. (1985). *Going Places*. London, England: Macmillan.

Flick, U. (2009). *An introduction to qualitative research* (4th edn.). London, England: Sage.

Foster, G. (1962). *Traditional Cultures and the Impact of Technological Change*. New York, NY: Harper & Row.

Foust, S., Fieg, J., Koester, J., Sarbaugh, L., & Wendinger, L. (1981). Dynamics of cross-cultural adjustment: From pre-arrival to re-entry. In S. Foust (Ed.), *Learning across cultures* (pp. 7-29). Washington DC: National Association for Foreign Student Affairs.

Freedman, A. (1986). A strategy for managing "cultural" transitions: Reentry from training. In C. N. Austin (Ed.), *Cross-cultural re-entry: A book of readings*. Abilene, TX: Abilene Christian University.

Freire, P. (1970). *Pedagogy of the oppressed*. New York, NY: Herter and Herter.

Freud, S. (1915). Analysis of a phobia in a five-year-old boy. In *Collected papers*, Vol. 3, (pp. 149–289). New York, NY: Basic Books.

Frenzel, F. (2016) *Slumming it: The Tourist Valorisation of Urban Poverty*, Zed Books: London.

Frieze, I.H., & Yu Li, M. (2010). Gender, aggression, and prosocial behavior. In J.C. Chrisler & D.R. McCreary (Eds.), *Handbook of gender research in psychology*, Vol. 2 (pp. 311-335). New York, NY: Springer.

Furnham, A., & Bochner, S. (1986). *Culture Shock: Psychological reactions to unfamiliar environments*. New York, NY: Methuen.

Fussell, P. (1980). *Abroad: British Literary Traveling Between the Wars*. New York, NY: Oxford University Press.

Galani-Moutafi, V. (2000). The self and the other – Traveler, ethnographer, tourist. *Annals of Tourism Research*, 27(1), 203-224.

Garcia-Marquez, G. (2003). *Living to tell the tale*. New York, NY: Knopf.

Gaw, K., F. (2000). Reverse culture shock in students returning from overseas. *International Journal of Intercultural Relations*. 24, 83-104.

Gee, C., Choy, D., & Makens, J. (1984). *The Travel Industry*. Westport, CT: AVI.

Geertz, C. (1973). Thick Description: Toward an Interpretative Theory of Culture. In C. Geertz, *The Interpretation of Cultures: Selected Essays* (pp. 3-30). New York, NY: Basic Books.

Gergen, K.J. (1991). *The saturated self: Dilemmas of identity in contemporary life*. New York: NY: Basic Books.

Gibson, H., & Yiannakis, A. (2002). Tourist Roles. Needs and the Lifecourse. *Annals of Tourism Research.* 29(2), 358-383.

Giddens, A. (1991) *Modernity and Self-Identity: Self and Society in the Late Modern Age.* Cambridge, MA: Polity Press.

Gladwell, Malcolm (2000). *The Tipping Point: How Little Things Can Make a Big Difference.* Boston, MA: Little, Brown.

Goeldner, C.R., & Ritchie, J.R.B. (2006). *Tourism: Principles, practices, philosophies* (10th edn.). New York, NY: Wiley.

Goethe, J. W. (1816/1817). *Italian Journey (1786-1788).* Transl. by W.H. Auden and Elizabeth Mayer 1962. London, England: Penguin Books.

Goossens, C. (2000). Tourism information and pleasure motivation. *Annals of Tourism Research,* 27(2), 301-321.

Gosch, S., Stearns, P. (2008). *Premodern Travel in World History.* New York, NY: Routledge.

Graburn, N. (1983). The Anthropology of Tourism. *Annals of Tourism Research,* (10)1, 9-33.

Graburn, N. (1995). The Past and the Present in Japan. Nostalgia and Neo-Traditionalism in Contemporary Japanese Domestic Tourism. In R. Butler & P. Pearce (Eds.), *Change in Tourism. People, Places, Processes* (pp. 47-70). London, England: Routledge.

Graburn, N., & Barthel-Bouchier, D. (2001). Relocating the Tourist. *International Sociology,* 16, 147-158.

Gray, H.P. (1970). *International travel: International trade.* Lexington, M: Health.

Guba, E., & Lincoln, Y.S. (1994). Competing paradigms in qualitative research. In N.K. Denzin & Y.S. Lincoln (Eds.), *The Sage handbook of qualitative research* (pp. 105-117). Thousand Oaks, CA: Sage.

Gubrium, J. Holstein J. (2000). Analyzing Interpretive Practice. In N.K. Denzin, & Y. S. Lincoln (Eds) *Handbook of qualitative research* (4th edn.) (pp. 487–508). Thousand Oaks, CA: Sage

Gudykunst, W. B., & Hammer, M. R. (1988). Strangers and hosts: An uncertainty reduction based theory of intercultural adaptation. In Y. Y. Kim & W. B. Gudykunst (Eds.), *Cross-cultural adaptation. Current Approaches* (pp. 106-139). Newbury Park, CA: Sage.

Gullahorn, J. T., & Gullahorn, J.E. (1963). An extension of the U-Curve Hypothesis. *Journal of Social Issues,* 14, 33-47.

Gullahorn, J. T., & Gullahorn, J. E. (1963). An extension of the U-curve hypothesis. *Journal of Social Issues,* 19(1), pp. 33-47.

Habermas, J. (1971). *Knowledge of human interest.* Boston, MA: Beacon.

Habermas, J. (1984). *The theory of communicative action: Vol. 1, Reason and rationalization in society* (T. McCarthy, Trans.) Boston, MA: Beacon Press.

Habermas, T. & Bluck, S. (2000). Getting a life: The emergence of the life story in adolescence. *Psychological Bulletin,* 126, 748–769.

Hager (2011). Concepts and Definitions of Lifelong Learning. In M. London (Ed.), *The Oxford Handbook of Lifelong Learning* (pp. 12-25). New York, NY: Oxford University Press.

Hammersley, M., & Atkinson, P. (1983). *Ethnography: Principles in Practice.* London, England: Tavistock.

Hammack, P.L. (2008). Narrative and the cultural psychology of identity. *Personality and Social Psychology Review,* 222-247.

Hammack, P. L. (2016). Theoretical foundations of identity. In K. McLean & M. Syed (Eds.), *The Oxford Handbook of Identity Development,* (pp. 11-26), New York, NY: Oxford University Press.

Hampton, M.P. (1998). Backpacker Tourism and Economic Development. *Annals of Tourism Research.* 25(3), 639-660.

Hampton, M.P. (2010). Not such a rough or lonely planet? Backpacker tourism: An academic journey. In K. Hannam & A. Diekmann (Eds.), *Beyond Backpacker Tourism: Mobilities and Experiences* (pp. 8-20). Clevedon, England: Channel View.

Hannam, K. Ateljevic, I. (2008). Introduction: Conceptualising and Profiling Backpacker Tourism. In K. Hannam & I. Ateljevic (Eds.), *Backpacker Tourism: Concepts and Profiles* (pp. 1-6). Clevedon, England: Channel View.

Hannam, K., Diekmann, A. (2010). From Backpacking to Flashpacking: Developments in Backpacker Tourism Research. In K. Hannam, & Diekmann (Eds.), A. *Beyond Backpacker Tourism: Mobilities and Experiences* (pp. 1- 7). Clevedon, England: Channel View.

Hanson, A. (1996). The search for a separate theory of adult learning: Does anyone really need andragogy? In R. Edwards, A. Hanson, & P. Raggatt (Eds.), *Boundaries of adult learning* (pp. 99-108). New York, NY:Routledge.

Hecht, J. & Martin, D. (2006). Backpacking and hostel-picking: an analysis from Canada, *International Journal of Contemporary Hospitality Management,* 18(1), 69-77.

Hepner, R. (2015). The erosion of critical thinking development in post-secondary education: The need to return to liberal education. In S. Wisdom & L. Leavitt (Eds.), *Handbook of Research on Advancing Critical Thinking in Higher Education* (pp. 68-97). Hershey, PA: IGI-Global.

Hesse, H. (1919). *Demian* (first published under the pseudonym "Emil Sinclair"). London, England: Granada.

Hirschorn, S., & Hefferon, K. (2013). Leaving it all behind to travel venturing uncertainty as a means to personal growth and authenticity. *Journal of Humanistic Psychology,* 53(3), 283–306.

Hofstede, G. (2001). *Culture's consequences.* Thousand Oaks, CA: Sage.

Holliday, Adrian (2002). *Doing and writing qualitative research.* London, England: Sage.

Hopkins, D., & Putnam, R. (2012). *Personal growth through adventure* (1st edn. 1993). London, England: David Fulton.

Hottola, P. (2004). Culture Confusion: Intercultural Adaptation in Tourism. *Annals of Tourism Research.* 31(2), 447-466.

Hottola, P. (2005). The metaspatialities of control management in tourism: Backpacking in India. *Tourism Geographies* 7 (1), 1–22.

Hottola, P. (2008). Farewell, countercultural wanderer? Backpacker dress and styles in south Asia. *Tourism, Culture and Communication,* 8(1), 45-52.

Houle, C. (1980). *Continuing Learning in the Professions,* San Francisco, CA: Jossey-Bass.

Howard, R.W. (2005). Khaosan road: An evolving backpacker tourist enclave being partially reclaimed by locals. *International Journal of Tourism Research*, 7, 357–74.

Howard, R.W. (2007). Five backpacker tourist enclaves. *International Journal of Tourism Research*, 9, 73–86.

Hsu, C.H. & Lam, T. (2003). Mainland Chinese travelers' motivations and barriers of visiting Hong Kong, *Journal of Academy of Business and Economics* 2(1), 60-67.

Hsu, C., & Songshan, H. (2008). Travel Motivation: a Critical Review of the Concept's Development. In A.G. Woodside & D. Martin *Tourism Management: Analysis, Behaviour and Strategy* (pp. 14-27). Wallingford, England: CABI.

Huitt, W. (2004). Maslow's hierarchy of needs. Educational Psychology Interactive. Valdosta, GA: Valdosta State University. Retrieved from http://chiron.valdosta.edu/whuitt/col/regsys/maslow.html.

Hurn, B. J. (1999). Repatriation - the toughest assignment of all. *Industrial and Commercial Training* 31(6), 224-228.

Huxley, A. (1956). *Heaven and Hell*. New York, NY: Harper.

Huxley, L. (2005). 'Western Backpackers and the Global Experience: An Exploration of Young People's Interaction with Local People', *Tourism, Culture and Communication* 5(1), 37–44.

Hyde, K. F., & Lawson, R. (2003). The Nature of Independent Travel. *Journal of Travel Research*, 42(1), 13-23.

Imhoff, R. & Erb, H.-P. (2009). What motivates nonconformity? Uniqueness seeking blocks majority influence. *Personality and Social Psychology Bulletin*, 35, 309-320.

Ingram, J. (2011). Volunteer tourism. How do we know it is 'making a difference'?. In A.M. Benson (Ed.), *Volunteer Tourism: Theoretical Frameworks and Practical Applications* (pp. 211-222). London, England: Routledge.

Iso-Ahola, S.E. (1982). Towards a social psychological theory of tourism motivation: A rejoinder. *Annals of Tourism Research* 9(2), 256-262.

Ivanovic, M. (2008). *Cultural Tourism*. Cape Town, South Africa: Juta & Company Ltd.

Jackson, M. (1989). *Paths toward a clearing: Radical empiricism and ethnographic inquiry*. Bloomington, IN: Indiana University Press.

Jacobsen, J.K.S. (2000). Anti-Tourist Attitudes. Mediterranean Charter Tourism. *Annals of Tourism Research*, 27(2), 284-300.

James, W. (1890). *The principles of psychology*. New York, NY: Holt.

Jarvis, J., Peel, V. (2010). Flashpacking in Fiji: Reframing the 'Global Nomad' in a Developing Destination. In K. Hannam, & A. Diekmann, A. *Beyond Backpacker Tourism. Mobilities and Experiences* (pp. 21 – 39). Clevedon, England: Channel View.

Jarvis, P. (2006). *Towards a comprehensive theory of human learning*. London, England: Routledge.

Jarvis, P. (2009). Lifelong learning. A social ambiguity. In P. Jarvis (Ed.), *The Routledge International Handbook of Lifelong Learning* (pp. 9-18). New York, NY: Routledge.

Jenkins, S. (2013). Counselling and Storytelling How Did We Get Here? *Psychotherapy and Politics International*, 11, 140–151.

Kant, I. (1781). Critique of Pure Reason. Edited by P. Guyer and A. W. Wood, in: H. Allison R. Brandt, P. Guyer, R. Meerbote, C.D. Parsons, H. Robinson, J.B. Schneewind and A. W. Wood (Eds.), *The Cambridge Edition of the Works of Immanuel Kant in Translation*, Cambridge, MA: Cambridge University Press, 1999.

Kartoshkina, Y. (2015). Bitter-sweet reentry after studying abroad. International Journal of Intercultural Relations, 44, 35-45.

Kasser T., Ryan R.M. (1996). Further examining the American dream: differential correlates of intrinsic and extrinsic goals. *Personality and Social Psychology Bulletin*, 22, 280–287.

Kegan, R. (1994). *In over our heads: The mental demands of modern life*. Cambridge, MA: Harvard University Press.

Kehl, K., & Morris, J. (2008). Differences in global-mindedness between short-term and semester-long study abroad participants at selected private universities. *Frontiers: The Interdisciplinary Journal of Study Abroad*,15, 67–79.

Kennedy, B. (1900). *A man adrift: being leaves from a nomad's portfolio*. Chicago, IL: H.S. Stone.

Kim, Y.Y. (2001). *Becoming intercultural: An integrative theory of communication and cross-cultural adaptation*. Thousand Oaks, CA: Sage.

Kim, Y.Y. (2008). Intercultural personhood: Globalization and a way of being. *International Journal of Intercultural Relations*. 32, 359-368.

Kim, Y.Y. (2009). The Identity Factor in Intercultural Competence. In D. K. Deardorff (Ed.), *The SAGE Handbook of Intercultural Competence* (pp. 53-65). Thousand Oaks, CA: Sage.

Kim. Y. (2012). Beyond cultural categories. Communication, adaptation and transformation. In, J.Jackson, *The Routledge Handbook of Language and Intercultural Communication*. New York, NY: Routledge.

Kim, H., & Jamal, T. (2007). Touristic Quest for Existential Authenticity. *Annals of Tourism Research*, 34(1), 181-201.

Kim, S., & Lee, C. (2002). Push and pull relationships. *Annals of Tourism Research* 29(1), 257-260.

Kinvall, C. (2004). Globalization and Religious Nationalism: Self, Identity, and the Search for Ontological Security. *Political Psychology*, 25(5), 741-767.

Kitchenham, A. (2008). The Evolution of John Mezirow's Transformative Learning Theory. *Journal of Transformative Education*, 6(2), 104-123.

Kleiber, D.A., Walker, G.J., & Mannell, R.C. (2011). *A social psychology of leisure*. State College: Venture Publishing.

Klenosky, D.B. (2002). The "Pull" of tourism destinations: A means-end investigation. *Journal of Travel Research* 40(4), 385-395.

Annan, K. (2001). Kofi Annan – Nobel Lecture. Retrieved from http://www.nobelprize.org/nobel_prizes/peace/laureates/2001/annan-lecture.html

Kohut, H., & Wolf, E.S. (1978): The disorders of the self and their treatment: An outline. *International Journal of Psychoanalysis*, 59, 413-425.

Kontogeorgopoulos, N. (2003). Keeping up with the Joneses: Tourists, Travellers, and the Quest for Cultural Authenticity in Southern Thailand. *Tourist Studies*. 3, 171-203.

Kottler, J. A. (1997): *Travel That Can Change Your Life: how to create a transformative experience*. San Francisco, CA: Jossey-Bass.

Kottler, J.A. (1998). Transformative Travel. *The Futurist*, 4, 24-28.

Kottler, J.A. (2014). *Change: What Really Leads to Lasting Personal Transformation.* New York, NY: Oxford University Press.

Kovan, J., & Dirkx, J. (2003). Being called awake: The roles of transformative learning in the lives of environmental activists. *Adult Education Quarterly*, 5, 99-120.

Krippendorf, J. (1987). *The Holidaymakers. Understanding the Impact of Leisure and Travel.* London, England: Heinemann.

Kroger, J. (2007). *Identity development: Adolescence through adulthood.* Thousand Oaks, CA: Sage.

Kurylo, A. (Ed.) (2013). Culture and Communication. In A. Kurylo (Ed.), *Inter/Cultural Communication. Representation and Construction of Culture* (pp. 3-24). Thousand Oaks, CA: Sage.

Kvale, S., Brinkmann, S. (2009). *InterViews. Learning the craft of qualitative research interviewing.* (2nd edn.). Los Angeles, CA: Sage.

Laing, J. & Frost, W. (2012). *Books and Travel: Inspiration, Quests and Transformation.* Clevedon, England: Channel View.

Lamnek, S. (2005). *Qualitative Sozialforschung.* Weinheim, Germany:Beltz.

Laney, M.O. (2002). *The introvert advantage: How to thrive in an extrovert world.* New York, NY: Workman.

Layard, R. (2005). *Happiness: Lessons From a New Science*, New York, NY: Penguin Books.

Lean, G.L. (2009). Transformative travel: Inspiring sustainability. In R. Bushel & P. Sheldon (Eds.), *Wellness and Tourism: Mind, Body, Spirit, Place* (pp. 191-205). New York, NY: Cognizant Communication.

Lean, G.L., Staiff, R., & Waterton, E. (2014). Reimagining travel and imagination. In G.L. Lean, R. Staiff, & E. Waterton (Eds.), *Travel and Imagination* (pp. 9-22). Aldershot, England: Ashgate.

Leary, M.R., & Tangney, J. P. (Eds.) (2012). *Handbook of self and identity.* New York, NY: Guilford Press.

Lee, T.-H., & Crompton, J. (1992). Measuring novelty seeking in tourism. *Annals of Tourism Research*, 19, 732-751.

Lee, U-I. & Pearce, P.L. (2002). Travel motivation and travel career patterns. In *Proceedings of First Asia Pacific Forum for Graduate Students Research in Tourism*, 22 May, Macao (pp. 17-35). Hong Kong: The Hong Kong Polytechnic University.

Lee, U-I. & Pearce, P.L. (2003). Travel career patterns: Further conceptual adjustment of Travel Career Ladder. In J. Jun (Ed.), *Second Asia Pacific Forum for Graduate Students Research in Tourism*, 2-4 October, Busan, Korea (pp. 65-78): The Korea Academic Society of Tourism and Leisure.

Leed, E.J. (1991). *The Mind of the Traveller: From Gilgamesh to Global Tourism.* New York, NY: Basic Books.

Leed, E.J. (2001). The Ancients and the Moderns: From Suffering to Freedom. In S.L. Roberson (Ed.), *Defining Travel: Diverse Visions* (pp. 5-12). Mississippi, MS: University Press of Mississippi.

Lepp, A., Gibson, H. (2003). Tourist Roles, Perceived Risk and International Tourism. *Annals of Tourism Research.* 30(3), 606-624.

References

Levy, A. & Mary, U. (1986). *Organizational Transformation.* New York, NY: Praeger.

Levi-Strauss, C. (1966): *The savage mind.* Chicago, IL: University of Chicago.

Lincoln, Y, & Guba, E. (2013). *The Constructivist Credo.* London, England: Routledge.

Lifton, R.J. (1993): *The protean self: Human resilience in the age of fragmentation.* New York, NY: Basic Books.

Lloyd, K. (2003). Contesting control in transitional Vietnam: the development and regulation of traveller cafes in Hanoi and Ho Chi Minh City. *Tourism Geographies,* 5 (3), 350 - 366.

Lockwood, P. (2000). Could it happen to you? Predicting the impact of downward comparisons on the self. *Journal of Personality and Social Psychology,* 82, 343 –358.

Lockwood, P., Jordan, C., & Kunda, Z. (2002). Motivation by positive or negative role models: Regulatory Focus determines who will best inspire us. *Journal of Personality and Social Psychology,* 83 (4), 854-864.

Loevinger, J. (1976). *Ego Development.* San Francisco, CA: Jossey-Bass

Loker-Murphy, L., Pearce, P. (1995). Young budget travelers: Backpackers in Australia. *Annals of Tourism Research,* 22, 819-843.

Luyckx, K., Goossens, L., Soenens, B., Beyers, W., & Vansteenkiste, M. (2005). Identity statuses based on 4 rather than 2 identity dimensions: Extending and refining Marcia's paradigm. *Journal of Youth and Adolescence, 34*(6), 605-618.

Lyon, C. R. (2001). Hear our stories: Relationships and transformations of women educators who go overseas to work. *Studies in the Education of Adults,* 33(2), 118 -126.

Lynn, M., & Snyder, C. R. (2002). Uniqueness seeking. In C. R. Snyder & S. J. Lopez (Eds.), *Handbook of positive psychology* (pp. 395-419). New York, NY: Oxford University Press.

Lysgaard, S. (1955). Adjustment in a foreign society. Norwegian Fulbright grantees visiting the United States. *International Social Science Bulletin,* 7, 45-51.

MacCannell, D. (1973). Staged Authenticity: Arrangements of Social Settings. *American Journal of Sociology,* 79(3), 589-603.

MacCannell, D. (1976). *The tourist: A new theory of the leisure class.* New York, NY: Schocken Books Inc.

MacLean, R. (2006). *Magic Bus: On the Hippie Trail from Istanbul to India.* London, England: Viking.

Mannell, R.C., & Iso-Ahola, S.E. (1987). Psychological nature of leisure and tourism experience. *Annals of Tourism Research* 14, 314-331.

Maoz, D. (2006). The Mutual Gaze. *Annals of Tourism Research.* 33(1), 221-239.

Maoz, D. (2007). Backpackers' Motivations: The Role of Culture and Nationality. *Annals of Tourism Research.* 34(1), 122-140.

Maoz, D. (2008). The backpacking journey of Israeli women in mid-life. In K. Hannam and I. Ateljevic *Backpacker Tourism: Concepts and Profiles* (pp.188-198). Clevedon, England: Channel View.

Marcia, J. E. (1966). Development and validation of ego identity status. *Journal of Personality and Social Psychology,* 5, 551-558.

Marcia, J. E. (1980). Identity in adolescence. In J. Adelson (Ed.), *Handbook of adolescent psychology* (pp. 159–187). New York, NY: Wiley.

Martin, J. N. (1993). The intercultural reentry of student sojourners: Recent contributions to theory, research and training. In R. M. Paige (Ed.), *Education for the intercultural experience* (pp. 301-328). Yarmouth, ME: Intercultural Press, Inc.

Martin, J. (1984). The intercultural reentry: Conceptualization and directions for future research. *International Journal of Intercultural Relations*, 8, 115-134.

Martin, J., Harrell, T. (2004). Intercultural reentry of students and professionals: theory and practice. In S. Landis, J. Bennett & M. Bennett (Eds.), *Handbook of Intercultural Training*, (3rd edn.). (pp. 309-336).Thousand Oaks, CA: Sage.

Maslow, A. H. (1954). *Motivation and personality*. New York, NY: Harper & Row.

Maslow, A. H. (1970). *Motivation and personality* (2nd ed). New York, NY: Harper & Row.

Maslow, A. H. (1971). *The Farther Reaches of Human Nature*. Middlesex, England: Penguin Books.

Maslow, A., & Lowery, R. (Ed.). (1998).*Toward a psychology of being* (3rd edn.). New York, NY: Wiley & Sons.

Matthews, A. (2008). Negotiated selves: Exploring the impact of local-global interactions on young volunteer travelers, in K.D. Lyons, and S. Wearing (Eds). *Journeys of Discovery in Volunteer Tourism: International Case Study Perspectives* (pp. 101-117). Wallingford, England: CABI.

Matthews, A. (2014). Young Backpackers and the Rite of Passage of Travel: Examining the Transformative Effects of Liminality. In G.Lean, R. Staiff, & E. Waterton *Travel and Transformation* (2nd edn.) (pp.157-171). London, England: Routledge

Mayo, E.J. & Jarvis, L. P. (1981). *The psychology of leisure travel*. Boston, MA: CBI Publishing.

McAdams, D.P. (1985). *Power and intimacy*. New York, NY: Guilford Press.

McAdams, D.P. (1988). *Power, intimacy and the life story: Personological inquiries into identity*. New York, NY: Guilford.

McAdams, D.P. (1997). The case for unity in the (post)modern self: A modest proposal. In R. Ashmore & L. Jussim (Eds.), *Self and identity: Fundamental issues* (pp. 46-78). New York, NY: Oxford University.

McAdams, D.P. (2006a). The Problem of Narrative Coherence. *Journal of Constructivist Psychology*, 19, 109-125.

McAdams, D.P. (2006b). *The redemptive self: Stories Americans live by*. New York, NY: Oxford University Press.

McAdams, D.P. (2011). Narrative Identity. In S.J. Schwartz, K. Luyckx, & V. L. Vignoles (Eds.), *Handbook of Identity Theory and Research*, (pp. 99 – 115). New York, NY: Springer.

McAdams, D.P., Josselson, R., & Lieblich, A. (Eds.) (2006). *Identity and story: Creating self in narrative*. Washington, DC: American Psychological Association.

McLean, K. C., Pasupathi, M., & Pals, J. L. (2007). Selves creating stories creating selves: A process model of self-development. *Personality and Social Psychology Review*, 11(3), 262-278.

McLean K., & Syed, M. (2016). *The Oxford handbook of identity development*. New York, NY: Oxford University Press.

McNamara, K., & Prideaux, B. (2010). A typology of solo independent women travelers. *International Journal of Tourism Research*, 12(3), 253-64.

References

Merriam Webster Dictionary (2017). Retrieved from https://www.merriam-webster.com/dictionary/escapism

Merriam, S.B. (2004). The Role of Cognitive Development in Mezirow's Transformational Learning Theory. *Adult Education Quarterly*, 55(1), 60-68.

Merriam, S. B., Caffarella, R. S., & Baumgartner, L. M. (2007). *Learning in Adulthood: A Comprehensive Guide.* San Francisco, CA: Jossey-Bass.

Merriam, S. B., & Kim, S. (2012). Studying transformative learning theory: What methodology? In E. W. Taylor & P. Cranton (Eds.), The handbook of transformative learning: Theory, research, and practice (pp. 56-72). San Francisco, CA: Jossey-Bass.0

Mezirow, J. (1978). Perspective Transformation. *Adult Education Quarterly*, 28, 100-110.

Mezirow, J. (1981). A critical theory of adult learning and education. *Adult Education, 32*, 3-24.

Mezirow, J. (1990). *Fostering critical reflection in adulthood.* San Francisco, CA: Jossey-Bass.

Mezirow, J. (1991a). *Transformative dimensions of adult learning.* San Francisco, CA: Jossey-Bass.

Mezirow, J. (1991b). Transformation Theory and Cultural Context: A Reply to Clark and Wilson. *Adult Education Quarterly*, 41 (3), 188-92.

Mezirow, J. (1994). Understanding transformation theory. *Adult Education Quarterly*, 44(4), 222-35.

Mezirow, J. (1996). Contemporary Paradigms of Learning. *Adult Education Quarterly.* 46, 158-172.

Mezirow, J. (1998). On critical reflection. *Adult Learning Quarterly*, 48(3), 185-198.

Mezirow, J. (2000). Learning to think like an adult: Core concepts of transformation theory. In J. Mezirow & Associates (Eds.), *Learning as transformation* (pp. 3-33). San Francisco, CA: Jossey-Bass.

Mezirow, J. (2003). Transformative learning as discourse. *Journal of Transformative Education*, 1(1), 58-63.

Mezirow, J. (2006). An overview of transformative learning. In P. Sutherland, & J. Crowther (Eds.), *Lifelong Learning: Concepts and Contexts* (pp. 24–38). New York, NY: Routledge.

Mezirow, J. (2012). Learning to think like an adult: Core concepts of transformation theory. In E. W. Taylor & P. Cranton (Eds.), *The handbook of transformative learning: Theory, research, and practice* (pp. 73-96). San Francisco, CA: Jossey-Bass.

Milstein, T. (2005). Transformations abroad: Sojourning and the perceived enhancement of self-efficacy. *International Journal of Intercultural Relations*, 29, 217-238.

Mitchell, P. (2006). *Revisiting Effective Re-Entry Programs for Returnees from US Academic Programs.* Washington, DC: AED Center for International Training.

McLuhan, M. (1962). *The Gutenberg galaxy.* New York, NY: New American Library.

Molz (2012). *Travel Connections: Tourism, Technology, and Togetherness in a Mobile World.* New York, NY: Routledge.

Montuori, A., & Fahim, U. (2004). Cross-Cultural Encounter as an Opportunity for Personal Growth. *Journal of Humanistic Psychology.* 44, 243-248.

Moufakkir, O., Kelly, I. (Eds.) (2010). *Tourism, Progress and Peace*. Wallingford, England: CABI

Müller, D.K. (2006). Unplanned development of literary tourism in two municipalities in rural Sweden. *Scandinavian Journal of Hospitality and Tourism*, 6(3), 214-228.

Munt, I. (1994). The 'other' postmodern tourism: Culture, travel and the new middle classes. *Theory, Culture & Society* 11(3), 101-123.

Murphy, L. (2001). Exploring Social Interactions of Backpackers. *Annals of Tourism Research*. 28, 50-67.

Mukerji, C. (1978). Bullshitting: Road Lore Among Hitchhikers. *Social Problems*, 25(3), 241-252.

Muzaini, H. (2006). Backpacking Southeast Asia: Strategies of 'Looking Local'. *Annals of Tourism Research*. 33(1), 144-161.

Nash, D. (2001). On travelers, ethnographers, and tourists. *Annals of Tourism Research*, 28(2), 493-496.

Nelson, K., & Fivush, R. (2004). The emergence of autobiographical memory: A social cultural developmental theory. *Psychological Review*, 111, 486-511.

Nezlek, J.B. (2000). The motivational and cognitive dynamics of day-to-day social life. In J.P. Forgas, K. Williams, & L. Wheeler (Eds.), *The social mind: Cognitive and motivational aspects of interpersonal behavior* (pp. 92-111). New York, NY: Cambridge University Press.

Nicolau, J. & Mas, F. (2006). The influence of distance and prices on the choice of tourist destinations: The moderating role of motivations. *Tourism Management*, 27, 982-996.

Noggle, C.A., Rylander, M., & Soltys, S. (2013). Personality Disorders. In C.A.Noggle, & R.S. Dean, R.S. (Eds.), *The Neuropsychology of Psychopathology*. New York, NY: Springer

Noy, C. (2004). This trip really changed me: Backpackers" narratives of self-change. *Annals of Tourism Research*, 31(1), 78-102.

Noy, C., & Cohen, E. (2005). Introduction: Backpacking as a rite of passage in Israel. In C. Noy & E. Cohen *Israel Backpackers and their Society: A View from Afar* (pp. 1-43). Albany, State University of New York.

Oberg, K. (1960). Culture Shock: Adjustment to new cultural environments. *Practical Anthropology*, 7, 177-182.

Oliver, P. (2014). *Hinduism and the 1960s. The Rise of a Counter-Culture*. London, England: Bloomsbury Academic.

O'Regan, M. (2010). Backpacker Hostels: Place and Performance. In K. Hannam, & A. Diekmann (Eds.), *Beyond Backpacker Tourism: Mobilities and Experiences* (pp. 85-101). Clevedon, England: Channel View.

O'Reilly, C.C., (2006). From drifter to gap year tourist: Mainstreaming backpacker travel. *Annals of Tourism Research*, 33(4), 998-1017.

O'Sullivan, E. (1999). *Transformative learning: Educational vision for the 21st century*. New York, NY: Zen Books.

OXFAM (2017). Just 8 men on same wealth as half the world. Retrieved from https://www.oxfam.org/en/pressroom/pressreleases/2017-01-16/just-8-men-own-same-wealth-half-world

Oxford Dictionary (2017). Retrieved from https://en.oxforddictionaries.com/definition/lemming

Oyserman, D., Elmore, K., Smith, G. (2012). Self, Self-Concept, and Identity. In M.R. Leary & J. P. Tangney, (Eds.), *Handbook of self and identity* (pp. 69-104). New York, NY: Guilford Press.

Paige, R.M. (1993). On the nature of intercultural experiences and intercultural education. In R.M. Paige (Ed.) *Education for the intercultural experience* (pp. 1-19). Yarmouth, ME: Intercultural Press.

Palmer, P. J. (2004). *A hidden wholeness*. San Francisco, CA: Jossey-Bass.

Parrinello, G. (1993). Motivation and anticipation in post-industrial tourism. *Annals of Tourism Research*, 20(2), 232-248.

Parkins, W., & Craig, G. (2009). Slow Living. Oxford, NY: Berg.

Patton, M. Q. (2005). *Qualitative research & evaluation methods*. (3rd edn.), Thousand Oaks, CA: Sage.

Pearce, P.L. (1982). *The social psychology of tourist behavior*. Oxford, England: Pergamon.

Pearce, P.L. (1988). *The Ulysses Factor: Evaluating Visitors in Tourist Settings*. New York, NY: Springer.

Pearce, P.L. (1990). *The Backpacker Phenomenon Preliminary Answers to Basic Questions*. Townsville, Australia: Department of Tourism, James Cook University.

Pearce, P.L. (1993). Fundamentals of Tourist Motivation. In D. Pearce, R. Butler (Eds.), *Tourism Research: Critiques and Challenges* (pp. 113-134). London, England: Routledge.

Pearce, P. (2005). *Tourist behavior. Themes and conceptual schemes*. Clevedon, England: Channel View.

Pearce, P.L. (2006). Backpacking and backpackers - A fresh look. *Tourism Recreation Research*, 31(3), 5-10.

Pearce, P.L. (2009). Motivation for Pleasure Travel. In, C.R. Goeldner & J.R. B. Ritchie (Eds.), *Tourism: Principles, Practices, Philosophies*, 11th edn (pp. 247-266). New York, NY: John Wiley and Sons.

Pearce, P., Foster, F. (2007). A "University of Travel": Backpacker learning. *Tourism Management*, 28, 1285-1298.

Pearce, P., & Lee, U. (2005). Developing the travel career approach to tourist motivation. *Journal of Travel Research*, 43, 226-237.

Pennebaker, J. W., & Chung, C. K. (2007). Expressive writing, emotional upheavals, and health. In H. Friedman & R. Silver (Eds.), *Handbook of health psychology* (pp. 263–284). New York, NY: Oxford University Press.

Phillimore, J. (2004). From ontology, epistemology and methodology to the field. In J. Phillimore & L. Goodson (Eds.), *Qualitative research in tourism: Ontologies, epistemologies and methodologies* (pp. 185-194). London, England: Routledge.

Pine, B.J., & Gilmore, J.H. (1998). Welcome to the experience economy. *Harvard Business Review*, 76(4), 97-105.

Pine, B. J., Gilmore, J.H. (2011). *The Experience Economy. Updated Edition*. Boston, MA: Harvard Business School Publishing.

Pizam, A., Neumann, Y. & Reichel , A. (1979). Tourist satisfaction uses and misuses. *Annals of Tourism Research* 6(2), 195-197.

Plog, S. (1974). Why destinations areas rise and fall in popularity. *Cornell Hotel and Restaurant Administration Quarterly*, November, 13-16.

Plog, S. (2001). Why destination areas rise and fall in popularity: an update of a Cornell quarterly classic. *Cornell Hotel and Restaurant Administration Quarterly*, 42(3), 13-24.

Poutiatine, M. (2008). What is transformation? Nine principles toward an understanding transformational process for transformational leadership. *Journal of Transformative Education* 7(3), 189–208.

Pritchard, R. (2011). Re-entry trauma: Asian re-integration after study in the west. *Journal of Studies in International Education*, 15 (1), 93-111.

Pritchard, A., Morgan, N., & Ateljevic, I. (2011). Hopeful Tourism. A New Transformative Perspective. *Annals of Tourism Research*, 38(3), 941-63.

Pritchard, A., Morgan, N., & Ateljevic, I. (Eds.) (2012). *The Critical Turn in Tourism Studies: Creating an academy of hope.* London, England: Routledge.

Quinn, R. (1996). *Deep change.* San Francisco, CA: Jossey-Bass.

Ray, H., & Anderson, S., (2000). *The Cultural Creatives: How 50 Million People Are Changing the World,* New York, NY: Harmony Books.

Reese, E., Yan, C., Jack, F., & Hayne, H. (2010). Emerging Identities: Narrative and Self from Early Childhood to Early Adolescence. In K.C. McLean, M. Pasupathi, (Eds.), *Narrative Development in Adolescence. Creating the Storied Self* (pp. 23-43). New York, NY: Springer Science.

Reichel, A., Fuchs, G., Uriely, N. (2007). Perceived Risk and the Non-Institutionalized Tourist Role: The Case of Israeli Student Ex-Backpackers. *Journal of Travel Research.* 46, 217-226.

Reisinger, Y., Mavondo, F., (2005). *Travel Anxiety and Intentions to Travel Internationally: Implications of Travel Risk Perception.* Journal of Travel Research, 43, 212-225.

Reisinger, Y. (Ed.) (2013). *Transformational Tourism: Tourist Perspectives.* Wallingford, England: CABI.

Richards, G., & Wilson, J. (2004a). Drifting towards the global nomad. In G. Richards & J. Wilson (Eds.), *The Global nomad: Backpacker travel in theory and practice* (pp. 3-13). Clevedon, England: Channel View.

Richards, G., & Wilson, J. (2004b). The Global nomad: Motivations and behavior of independent travelers worldwide. In G. Richards & J. Wilson (Eds.), *The Global nomad: Backpacker travel in theory and practice* (pp. 14-39). Clevedon, England: Channel View.

Richards, G., & Wilson, J. (2004c). Widening perspectives in backpacker research. In G. Richards & J. Wilson (Eds.), *The Global nomad: Backpacker travel in theory and practice.* Clevedon, England: Channel View.

Ricoeur, P. (1987). *Time and Narrative III.* Chicago, IL: The University of Chicago Press.

Riessman, C.K. (2002). An analysis of personal narratives. In J.F. Gubrium & J.A. Holstein (Eds.), *Handbook of interview research: Context & method* (pp. 695-710). Thousand Oaks, CA: Sage.

Riessman, C.K. (2008). *Narrative Methods for the Human Sciences*. Thousand Oaks, CA: Sage.

Ritchie, J.R.B. (2005). Longitudinal research methods. In B.W. Ritchie, P. Burns, & C. Palmer (Eds.), Tourism Research Methods (pp. 131-148). Wallingford, England: CABI.

Riley, P. (1988). Road Culture of International Long-Term Budget Travelers. *Annals of Tourism Research*, 15, 313-328.

Robertson, D.N. (2002). *School of Travel: An Exploration of The Convergence of Andragogy and Travel*. ERIC (Education Resources Information Center). Retrieved from http://www.eric.ed.gov/PDFS/ED465075.pdf.

Rogers J. & Ward, C. (1993) 'Expectation-experience discrepancies and psychological adjustment during cross-cultural reentry', *International Journal of Intercultural Relations*, 17(2), 185-196.

Rohrlich, B., & Martin, J. (1991). Host country and reentry adjustment of student sojourners. *International Journal of Intercultural Relations* 15(2), 163-182.

Rojek, C. (1993). *Ways of Escape: Modern Transformations in Leisure and Travel*. London, England: The Macmillan Press.

Rosenthal, G. (2004). Biographical Research. In: Seale, Clive / Gobo, Giampietro / Gubrium, Jaber F. / Silverman, David (eds.), *Qualitative Research Practice*. London – Thousand Oaks – New Delhi: Sage.

Ross, S. (2010). Transformative travel: An enjoyable way to foster radical change. *ReVision* 32(1), 54-61.

Rossiter, M. (1999). A narrative approach to development: Implications for adult education. *Adult Education Quarterly*, 50(1), 56-71.

Rossiter, M. (2002). Narrative and Stories in Adult Teaching and Learning. *ERIC Digest* no. 241. Retrieved from http://calpro-online.org/eric/docs/dig241.pdf

Ryan, C. (1998). The travel career ladder: an appraisal. *Annals of Tourism Research*, 25(4), 936-957.

Ryan, C. (2003). Risk Acceptance in Adventure Tourism – Paradox and Context. In J. Wilks & S. J. Page *Managing Tourist Health and Safety in the New Millennium* (pp. 55-65). Amsterdam, The Netherlands: Pergamon.

Ryan, R., & Deci, E. (2000). Self-determination theory and the facilitation of intrinsic motivation, social development and well-being. *American Psychologist*, 55, 68-78.

Samovar, L., Porter, R., & Stefani, L. (1998). *Communication between cultures* (3rd edn.) Belmont, CA: Wadsworth Publishing Company.

Sarantakos, S. (1998). *Social Research* (2nd edn.). South Yarra, VIC: Macmillan.

Savener, A. (2016). Indigenous Cultural Solidarity in Resistance to Mass Tourism. Tourism and Travel Research Association: Advancing Tourism Research Globally. Retrieved from http://scholarworks.umass.edu/cgi/viewcontent.cgi?article=1897&context=ttra

Schachter, Elli P. (2005a). Erikson Meets the Postmodern: Can Classic Identity Theory Rise to the Challenge?" in: *Identity* 5(2), 137-60.

Schachter, Elli P. (2005b). Context and identity formation: A theoretical analysis and a case study. *Journal of Adolescent Research*, 20(3), 375-95.

Scheuch, E.K. (1981). Tourismus. In F. Stoll (Ed.), *Die Psychologie des 20. Jahrhunderts* (Vol. XIII, pp. 1089-1114). Zurich, Switzerland: Kindler.

Scheyvens, R. (2002). Backpacker Tourism and Third World Development. *Annals of Tourism Research.* 29(1), 144-164.

Schiff, D. (Writer) & Trainer, D. (Director). (2000). Red fired up (Television series episode). In C. Mandabach, M. Carsey, and T. Werner (Producers), *That '70s Show.* Century City, LA: Twentieth Century Fox Home Entertainment.

Schütze , F. (1983) .Biographieforschung und narratives Interview. In: *Neue Praxis* 3, 283-294.

Schwandt, T. A. (2000). Three epistemological stances for qualitative enquiry: interpretivism, hermeneutics and social constructionism. In Denzin, N. K., & Lincoln, Y. S. (Eds.), *Handbook of qualitative research* (189-213), 2. Thousand Oaks, CA: Sage.

Schwartz, S. J. (2001). The Evolution of Eriksonian and Neo-Eriksonian Identity Theory and Research: A Review and Integration. *Identity: An International Journal of Theory and Research,* 1(1), 7-58.

Schwartz, S. J. (2007). The structure of identity consolidation: Multiple correlated constructs or one superordinate construct? *Identity: An International Journal of Theory and Research,* 7(1), 27-49.

Schwartz-Shea, P., & Yanow, D. (2011).*Interpretive Research Design: Concepts and Processes.* New York, NY: Routledge.

Scott, S. M. (1997). The grieving soul in the transformation process. *New Directions for Adult and Continuing Education,* 74, 41-50.

Seligman, M.E.P., & Csikszentmihalyi, M. (2000). Positive psychology: an introduction. *American Psychologist,* 55(1), 5–14.

Sheehy, G. (1976). *Passages: Predictable crises in adult life.* New York, NY: Bantam.

Sheehy, G. (2011). *New Passages: Mapping your life across time.* New York, NY: Random House.

Shields, R. (1990). The "System of Pleasure": Liminality and the Carnivalesque at Brighton. *Theory, Culture and Society,* 7, 39–72.

Smith, S. (1998). Identity and intercultural communication competence in reentry. In J. N. Martin, T.K. Nakayama, & L. A. Flores (Eds.*), Readings in cultural contexts* (pp. 304-314). Belmont, CA: Mayfield.

Smith, S. (2002). The cycle of cross-cultural adaptation and re-entry. In J. Martin, Nakayama T., & L. Flores (Eds.), *Readings in Intercultural Communiation: Experiences and Contexts* (2nd Ed.) (pp. 246-258). Boston, MA: McGraw Hill.

Snyder, C. R., & Fromkin, H. L. (1980). *Uniqueness: The human pursuit of difference.* New York, NY: Plenum Press.

Sørensen, A. (2003). Backpacker ethnography. *Annals of Tourism Research,* 30(4), 847-867.

Spreitzhofer, G. (1998). Backpacking tourism in South-East Asia. *Annals of Tourism Research,* 25, 979-983.

Spreitzhofer, G. (2002). The Roaring Nineties: Low-budget backpacking in South-Easta Asia as an Appropriate Alternative to Third World Mass Tourism?. *Asien, Afrika, Lateinamerika* 30(2), 115-129.

Steinbeck, J. (1962). *Travels with Charlie: In search of America.* London, England: Penguin Books.

Steiner, C. J., Reisinger, Y. (2006). Understanding existential authenticity. *Annals of Tourism Research,* 33(2), 299-318.

Storti, C. (2003). *The art of coming home.* London, England: Nicholas Brealey.

Strickland, F. (1998). *The dynamics of change: Insights into organizational transition from the natural world.* New York, NY: Routledge.

Stringer, A., & McAvoy, L. H. (1992). The need for something different: Spirituality and wilderness adventure. *Journal of Experiential Learning,* 15, 13-20.

Sussman, N. (1986). Re-entry research and training: Methods and implications. *International Journal of Intercultural Relations,* 10(2), 235-254.

Sussman, N. (2000). The Dynamic Nature of Cultural Identity Throughout Cultural Transitions: Why Home is not so sweet. *Personality and Social Psychology Review.* 4, 355-373.

Sussman, N. (2001). Repatriation transitions: psychological preparedness, cultural identity, and attributions among American managers. *International Journal of Intercultural Relations.* 25, 109-123.

Sussman, N. (2002). Testing the cultural identity model of the cultural transition cycle: sojourners return home. *International Journal of Intercultural Relations.* 26, 391-408.

Swarbrooke, J. & Horner, S. (2007). *Consumer behaviour in tourism,* (2nd Edn.), London, England: Butterworth-Heinemann.

Syed, M. (2012). The past, present, and future of Eriksonian identity research: Introduction to the special issues. *Identity: An International Journal of Theory and Research,* 12, 1-7.

Szkudlarek, B. (2010). Reentry – A review of the literature. *International Journal of Intercultural Relations,* 34(1), 1-21.

Tartakovsky, E., & Schwartz, S.H. (2001). Motivation for emigration, values, wellbeing and identification among young Russian Jews. *International Journal of Psychology,* 36(2), 88-99.

Taylor, B. (1848). *Views Afoot: Europe Seen with Knapsack and Staff.* New York, NY: Joseph Knight.

Taylor, C. (1989). *Sources of the Self.* Cambridge, MA: Cambridge University Press.

Taylor, C. (1994a). The Politics of Recognition. In A. Gutmann (Ed.), *Multiculturalism: Examining the Politics of Recognition* (pp. 25-74). Princeton, NJ: Princeton University Press.

Taylor, E.W. (1994b). Intercultural competency: a transformative learning process. *Adult Education Quarterly.* 44(3), 154-174.

Taylor, E.W. (1997). Building upon the theoretical debate: a critical review of the empirical studies of Mezirow's transformative learning theory. *Adult Education Quarterly,* 48, 32-57.

Taylor, E.W. (2000). Fostering Transformative Learning in the Adult Education Classroom. *The Canadian Journal of the Study of Adult Education,* 14, 1-28.

Taylor, E.W. (2007). An update of transformative learning theory: a critical review of the empirical research (1999-2005). *International Journal of Lifelong Education,* 26(2), 173-191.

Taylor, E., & Cranton, P. (2013). A theory in progress? Issues in transformative learning theory. *European Journal for Research on the Education and Learning of Adults*, 4(1), 33-47.

Tedeschi, R., Calhoun, L. (1998). *Posttraumatic growth: Positive changes in the aftermath of crisis.* Mahwah, NJ: Lawrence Erlbaum.

Teo, P., Leong, S. (2006). A Postcolonial Analysis of Backpacking. *Annals of Tourism Research*. 33(1), 109-131.

Theroux, P. (1975). *The Great Railway Bazaar.* Boston, MA: Houghton Mifflin Co.

Thyne, M., Davies, S., & Nash, R. (2004). A lifestyle segmentation analysis of the backpacker market in Scotland: A case study of the Scottish Youth Hostel Association. *Journal of Quality Assurance in Hospitality & Tourism*, 5(2-4), 95-119.

Tiyce, M, & Wilson, E. (2012). Wandering Australia: independent travellers and slow journeys through time and space. In S. Fullager, K. Markwell & E. Wilson (Eds), *Slow Tourism: Experiences and Mobilities* (pp. 113-127). Bristol, England: Channel View.

Tisdell, E. J. (2012). Themes and variations of transformational learning: Interdisciplinary perspectives on forms that transform. In E. W. Taylor & P. Cranton (Eds.), *The handbook of transformative learning: Theory, research, and Practice* (pp.21-36). San Francisco, CA: Jossey-Bass.

Tittle, P. (2011). *Critical Thinking. An Appeal to Reason.* New York, NY: Routledge.

Tolliver, D. E., & Tisdell, E. J. (2006). Engaging spirituality in the transformative higher education classroom. In E. W. Taylor (Ed.), *New directions for adult and continuing education. Teaching for change: Fostering transformative learning in the classroom*, (Vol. 19, Spring). San Francisco, CA: Jossey-Bass.

Towner, J. (1985). The Grand Tour – A Key Phase in the History of Tourism. *Annals of Tourism Research*, 12, 297-333.

Turnbull, D.R. & Uysal, M. (1995). An exploratory study of German visitors to the Caribbean: push and pull motivations. *Journal of Travel & Tourism Marketing* 4(2), 85-91.

Turner, L., & Ash, J. (1976). *The Golden Hordes: International Tourism and the Pleasure Periphery.* London, England: Constable.

Turner, V. (1969). *The Ritual Process.* London, England: Routledge & Kegan Paul.

Turner, V. (1973). The Centre out there: Pilgrim's Goal. *History of Religions* 12(3), 191-230.

Turner, V. (1974). 'Liminal to Liminoid in Play, Flow and Ritual', *Rice University Studies* 60, 53–92.

Turner, V. (1982). *From Ritual to Theatre: The Human Seriousness of Play.* New York, NY: PAJ Publications.

Turner, V. (1986). Dewey, Dilthey, and Drama: An Essay in the Anthropology of Experience, In: Turner, V., & Brunder E.M. (Eds.), *The Anthropology of Experience 8* (pp. 33-44).Urbana and Chicago, IL: University of Illinois Press.

Uehara, A. (1986). The nature of American student reentry adjustment and perceptions of the sojourn experience. *International Journal of Intercultural Relations*, 10(4), 415-438.

UNICEF (2015). Levels and Trends in Child Mortality. Report 2015. Retrieved from https://www.unicef.org/publications/files/Child_Mortality_Report_2015_Web_9_Sept_1 6.pdf

UNODC (2013). Global Study on Homicide. Retrieved from https://www.unodc.org/documents/gsh/pdfs/2014_GLOBAL_HOMICIDE_BOOK_web.pdf

UNWTO (2017). Sustained growth in international tourism despite challenges. Retrieved from http://www2.unwto.org/press-release/2017-01-17/sustained-growth-international-tourism-despite-challenges;

Uriely, N., Yonay, Y., Simchai, D. (2002). Backpacking Experiences: A Type and Form Analysis. *Annals of Tourism Research*. 29(2), 520-538.

Uriely, N., Belhassen, Y. (2005). Drugs and Tourists' Experiences. *Journal of Travel Research*. 43, 238-246.

Uriely, N. (2005). The Tourist Experience. Conceptual Developments. *Annals of Tourism Research*. 32(1), 199-216.

Urry, J. (1990). *The Tourist Gaze: Leisure and Travel in Contemporary Societies.* London, England: Sage.

Urry, J. (2002). *The Tourist Gaze* (2nd edn.). Thousand Oaks, CA: Sage.

Urry, J. (2007). *Mobilities.* Cambridge, NJ: Polity Press.

Urry, J., & Larsen, J. (2011). *The Tourist Gaze 3.0.* Thousand Oaks, CA: Sage.

Van Gennep, A. (1960). *The Rites of Passage* (orig. published in 1909). London, England: Routledge & Kegan Paul.

Vignoles, V., Schwartz, S., & Luyckx, K. (2011). Introduction: Toward an Integrative View of Identity. In S. Schwartz, K. Luyckx, V. Vignoles (Eds). *Handbook of Identity Theory and Research* (pp. 1-30), New York, NY: Springer Science.

Vogt, J. (1976). Wandering: Youth and Travel Behavior. *Annals of Tourism Research* 4, 25-41.

Vrasti, W., (2009). The Politics, Economics and Ethics of Independent Travel: Rewriting the Ethnography of the Travel Trope. Retrieved from http://politicsandculture.org/2010/08/10/wanda-vrasti-the-politics-economics-andethics-of-independent-travel-rewriting-the-ethnography-of-the-travel-trope-2/

Walling, S.M., Eriksson, C.B., Meese, K.J., Ciovica, A., Gorton, D., & Foy, D.W. (2006). Cultural identity and reentry in short-term student missionaries. *Journal of Psychology and Theology*, 34, 153-164.

Walvin, J. (1978). *Beside the Seaside: Social History of the Popular Seaside Holiday.* London: Allen Lane.

Wang, N. (1999). Rethinking Authenticity in Tourism Experience. *Annals of Tourism Research* 26 (2), 349-70.

Wang, V., Dennett, S. (2014). Addressing Work Ethic in the New Century. In V. Wang (Ed.), *Handbook of Research on Education and Technology in a Changing Society* (pp. 528-538). Hershey, PA: IGI-Global.

Ward, C., Bochner, S., & Furnham, A. (2001). *The psychology of culture shock.* London: England: Routledge.

Ward, C., Kennedy, A. (2001). Coping with Cross-Cultural Transition. *Journal of Cross-Cultural Psychology*. 32, 636-642.

Wearing, S., Stevenson, D., & Young, T. (2010). *Tourist Cultures: Identity, Place and the Traveller.* London, England: Sage.

Weaver, D., & Lawton, L. (2006). *Tourism Management* (3rd edn.). Melbourne, Australia: John Wiley & Sons.

Welk, P. (2004). The Beaten Track: Anti-Tourism as an Element of Backpacker Identity Construction. In G. Richards & J. Wilson (Eds.), *The Global Nomad: Backpacker Travel in Theory and Practice* (pp. 77-91). Clevedon, England: Channel View.

Westerhausen, K. (2002). *Beyond the Beach: An Ethnography of Modern Travellers in Asia.* Bangkok, Thailand: White Lotus Press.

Wahlers, R.G. & Etzel, M.J. (1985). A Consumer Response to Incongruity Between Optimal Stimulation and Life Style Satisfaction. In E.C. Hirschman & M.B. Holbrook (Eds.) *NA - Advances in Consumer Research* 12 (pp. 97-101). Provo, UT : Association for Consumer Research.

White, N. R., & White, P. (2004). Travel as transition. Identity and place. *Annals of Tourism Research.* 31(1), 200-218.

Whitelaw, C., Sears, M., & Campbell, K. (2004). Transformative learning in a faculty professional development context. *Journal of Transformative Education*, 2, 9-27.

Willis, J. W. (2007). *Foundations of qualitative research: interpretive and critical approaches.* London, England: Sage.

Wilson, J. (2006). *Unpacking the OE: An Exploration of the New Zealand 'Overseas Experience', PhD thesis.* New Zealand: Lincoln University.

Wilson, J., Fisher, D., & Moore, K. (2009). The OE goes 'home': Cultural aspects of a working holiday experience. *Tourist Studies*, 9(1), 3-21.

Wilson, J., & Richards, G. (2008). Suspending Reality: An Exploration of Enclaves and the Backpacker Experience. In K. Hannam, & I. Ateljevic (Eds.), *Backpacker Tourism: Concepts and Profiles* (pp. 187-202). Clevedon, England: Channel View.

Wittgenstein, L. (1968). *Philosophical investigations.* Oxford, England: Basil Blackwell.

World Economic Forum (2016). The Global Gender Gap Report 2016. Retrieved from http://www3.weforum.org/docs/GGGR16/WEF_Global_Gender_Gap_Report_2016.pdf

World Tourism Organization (2016), Affiliate Members Global Reports, Volume fourteen – The Transformative Power of Tourism: a paradigm shift towards a more responsible traveller, UNWTO, Madrid. Retrieved from http://cf.cdn.unwto.org/sites/all/files/pdf/global_report_transformative_power_tourism_v5.compressed_2.pdf

Wright, J., Bolton, G. (2012). *Reflective Writing in Counselling and Psychotherapy.* Thousand Oaks, CA: Sage.

Yanow, D., & Schwartz-Shea, P. (2011). Doing Social Science in a Humanistic Manner. In D. Yanow, & P. Schwarz-Shea (Eds.), *Interpretation and Method: Empirical Research Methods and the Interpretive Turn.* New York, NY: Routledge.

Yoon, Y., & Uysal, M., (2005). An examination of the effects of motivation and satisfaction on destination loyalty: A structural model. *Tourism Management,* 26(1), 45-56.

Young, G. (1973). *Tourism, Blessing or Blight?* Harmondsworth, England: Penguin.

Zahra, A., & McIntosh, A. (2007). Volunteer tourism: Evidence of cathartic tourist experiences. *Tourism Recreation Research*, 32(1), 115-119.

Zaharna, R.S. (1989). Self-shock: The double-binding challenge of identity. *International Journal of Intercultural Relations*, 13(4), 501-525.

Appendices

Interview Guide 1

PART I: BIOGRAPHICAL INFORMATION

Name / age (birth date): Date:
Nationality: Contact details:
Highest degree: Length of this trip:

- Life history (where born & raised, family, relationships)
- Education / employment history
- Travel history (when, where & how long?)
- Life situation before leaving (employed, unemployed, student, etc.)

PART II: MOTIVATION

- Motivation for first trip / this trip
- Why long-term independent travel style vs. other styles?
- Destination choice?
- Reactions from family / friends
- Trigger experience for first trip / this trip
- Planning
- Feelings right before leaving
- Expectations before leaving

PART III: EXPERIENCES ON THE ROAD

- Adjusting to new culture / travel culture
- Culture shock / adjustment difficulties / initial challenges
- Travel budget (low/medium/high)
- Travel style (alone? travel pace? benefits & drawbacks)
- Travel breaks / work
- Traveler / backpacker or tourist?
- Planning / sticking to plans
- Sources of information / Use of guidebooks
- Dealing with language barriers
- Personal highlights / peak moments
- Dangerous situations
- Dealing with poverty
- Accomplishments
- Taking risks, pushing yourself
- Experiences with traveler community
- Feeling out of place
- Memorable situations with locals / other travelers
- Keeping in touch with friends/family at home
- Journal writing / blogs

© Springer Fachmedien Wiesbaden GmbH, part of Springer Nature 2019
B. Phillips, *Learning by Going: Transformative Learning through Long-term Independent Travel*, https://doi.org/10.1007/978-3-658-25773-6

PART IV: RE-INTEGRATION AND POST-TRAVEL LIFE

- Return expectations
- Actual return experience (feelings, impressions, difficulties…)
- Observations/views about home culture
- Reactions from friends & family
- Relationships with friends & family (changed?)
- Communicating your experiences
- Coping strategies
- Support system? Who? Why?
- Future travel plans
- Importance of travel in your life

Travel and learning

- Difference to school learning
- (Changed) views of yourself / others / the world / home country
- Learning about other cultures / travelers / yourself
- Changed values

Interview Guide 2

Name / age: **Date:**

Post-travel life

- When returned?
- Return expectations
- Actual return experience (feelings, impressions, difficulties…)
- Observations/views about home culture
- Reactions from friends & family
- Relationships with friends & family (changed?)
- Communicating your experiences
- Coping strategies
- Support system? Who? Why?

Long-term changes and learning

- Life changes since 1st interview (e.g. education, work, family, relationships)
- Changes in relationships
- Changes in values
- Changes in lifestyle
- View of home country today
- Travels since 1st interview
- Importance of travel now
- Future travel intentions
- Perceived lasting changes since LIT experience
- Regrets?

Sample Questionnaire

Individualized questionnaires were sent to the LITs who participated in the second round of interviews. The topics below are sample questions:

Your return

- When did you return to [*home country*]?
- What was it like to return to [*home country*] after having been gone for so many years? What were your feelings / emotions? What helped you get through it?
- How have your relationships with friends/family changed since your return?
- Who became the closest people to you after your return? Why?
- Did you have someone you could talk to about your travels? Did you feel that people understood you? Was it easy/frustrating to communicate your experiences? Were people interested?
- How did your feelings about [*home country*] change when you returned?
- How do you feel now about living in [*home country*]?
- What features in your home country were hard for you to face when returning?
- Did you notice any changes in personal values?

Long-term changes

- In the first interview you said that travel is extremely important in your life. How has that changed? You indicated that your future travels might change once you have children, but that you will always travel. Has that come true?
- Please give a quick summary of all your **travels since** the interview in **20XX** (please write down the destination and how many weeks/months you traveled)
- Do you still travel? Your views on travel now? How important is it? Now that you have a family, do you miss it?
- Did you pursue any further (formal) education after your travels?
- In the first interview, you said that you have no need for possessions and material things and that you have a greater appreciation for the environment. Have your travels had a lasting effect on your lifestyle? (e.g. less materialistic, more environmentally conscious, more appreciative....) How has it changed over the years?
- How have your relationships changed over the years? Are you still in touch with travel friends?
- How has the travel experience impacted you as a person in the long run? How do you think you had changed because of this experience? Has it changed over the years?
- Please read through the excerpts from the first interview below and comment on whether you still agree or whether things have changed since then?

Printed in the United States
By Bookmasters